CAR MAINTENANCE
AND REPAIR

MOTOR MANUALS VOLUME FOUR

CAR MAINTENANCE AND REPAIR

Arthur W. Judge

Associate of the Royal College of Science, London; Diplomate of Imperial College of Science and Technology (Petrol Engine Research), Whitworth Scholar; Associate Member of the Institution of Mechanical Engineers; Member, Society of Automotive Engineers, U.S.A.

SIXTH EDITION

1967

ROBERT BENTLEY INC.

872 MASSACHUSETTS AVENUE

CAMBRIDGE, MASSACHUSETTS 02139

First published	1928
Second edition	1936
Reprinted, with revisions	1940
Third edition	1941
Reprinted	1943
Reprinted	1945
Reprinted	1947
Fourth edition	1952
Reprinted	1955
Reprinted	1958
Fifth edition	1960
Sixth edition	1967

© *Arthur W. Judge* 1960, 1967

Printed in Great Britain by
Cox & Wyman Limited, Fakenham, Norfolk

PREFACE TO SIXTH EDITION

This volume, the fourth of the Motor Manual Series, was published originally in 1928 and intended for the use of the mechanically-minded car owner and engineering student, desirious of undertaking his own maintenance and servicing of the motor-car.

The demand for this manual has necessitated several editions and also reprintings and the fact that it had been adopted in motor engineering schools, technical institutions and the Services has resulted in a progressive increase in the size and scope of the book, but the original intention to deal with the elementary aspects of its subjects has been adhered to.

The new edition has been brought up to date to include more recent cars, but since it is the older models which are mostly in need of attention, some of the earlier servicing and maintenance information has been retained. In the course of the revision an appreciable amount of fresh information and very many new illustrations have been used.

In view of the Ministry of Transport's compulsory tests for cars over three years old before licences or renewals will be granted, special consideration has been given in this volume to the servicing of cars so that they will pass the Official Tests for the Braking, Steering and Electrical Systems. In this connection summaries are given at the ends of the relevant chapters of the faults looked for by the Official Examiners and the required performances. Further, an Appendix is included, at the end of the book, giving the more important Regulations, procedure for submitting a car for the Tests, Certificates, Fees, etc. for the benefit of the owner. This information is based upon the Ministry of Transport's 1960 Motor Vehicles (Tests) Regulations.

In addition to the analyses of the causes of car breakdowns on the road, based upon the R.A.C.'s Annual Reports – which are brought up to date in this revised edition – some important information is given about the faults which have been found on new cars as delivered to the car purchaser. These faults have been found on the majority of makes of cars in an appreciable proportion of such cars, by the Consumers' Association. Information on the checking of a new car for evidence of the more commonly occurring delivery faults and their rectification is given in this volume.

In conclusion the author would like to take this opportunity gratefully to acknowledge the co-operation and help given by certain manufacturers in the preparation of this edition; in particular to the British Motor Corporation, Vauxhall Motors Ltd., The Rootes Group (Humber, Hillman, Sunbeam, etc.), The Ford Motor Company Ltd. and Standard-Triumph Sales Ltd.

ARTHUR W. JUDGE

Farnham, Surrey
1966

CONTENTS

7

CHAPTER 1

SOME GENERAL CONSIDERATIONS

Introductory. Although the modern automobile has established an excellent reputation for itself in regard to good service and reliability, and seldom gives trouble to the driver, there are a number of important items which require periodic attention or inspection if the car is to be maintained at its best over its useful period of life; if so maintained the owner will certainly drive with a greater feeling of immunity from breakdown, and with minimum expense of upkeep.

This leads at once to the question of the useful life of a modern car, and here it must be admitted that we cannot give any hard and fast rule. The ordinary British car, if purchased new and run by the careful type of driver who attends periodically to the various items of adjustment and overhaul, may last over exceedingly long mileages, practically trouble-free. We know of several instances of British small cars of a well-known popular make still running well after 150,000 to 250,000 miles, when properly maintained and carefully driven. These long periods of running necessitate the replacement of the engines, by reconditioned units, every 50,000 to 60,000 miles, as a rule and gearboxes every 80,000 to 120,000 miles. Again, there are many examples, to our knowledge, of more expensive cars kept in service for hundreds of thousands of miles; for example, there was one Rolls Royce, pre-war car, which had done nearly 400,000 miles, and was still running satisfactorily. On the other hand, if a car is not properly looked after, but is neglected its life is considerably shortened. Many owner-drivers of a certain type, content only to fill the petrol tank and radiator, replenish the engine sump with oil, and inject lubricant only if the mechanism 'squeaks', find they obtain only relatively short car lives; we have come across cases of light cars, badly neglected, lasting only 40,000 to 50,000 miles, the condition of the engine, mechanism, tyres and bodywork being such that the cost of their 'rejuvenation' was practically as much as the second-hand value of the car.

With proper care and attention, however, such cars could easily have run three and even four times this mileage and still have been in marketable condition, before the post-war inflated prices.

There are many production cars still in daily use which were made some 20 to 25 years ago; although inferior in performance to highly efficient but more lightly built modern cars, they still give good service. It is true that the earlier designs were more heavily constructed, and less severely stressed, but evidently the materials and design were excellent, as the results have testified.

Previously, when fewer cars were mass-produced and one could collect a new car from the manufacturers' works it was generally found that the car had been carefully checked over and any faults discovered, rectified. Then, all one usually had to do was to see that the car was driven carefully from the works below the running-in speeds on all gears. However, it was customary, as a final precaution, to check over all of the important nuts on the car with suitable-leverage spanners. In particular, the following were tested for tightness: the nuts on the spring clips, i.e. where the springs were bolted to their axles: the engine cylinder head and chassis mounting nuts; the radiator mounting nuts and the nuts on the detachable wheels; also, the various body mounting nuts.

In the case of modern cars, now mass-produced in very large numbers, the usual procedure is for the cars to be delivered to the local agents by the manufacturers' delivery drivers, who are instructed to keep within the recommended running speeds for new cars; this, unfortunately, is not always done. After delivery to the agent, a pre-delivery check-over is carried out but in many cases the time allowed for this appears to be limited, by economic reasons, so that certain faults are not spotted. That this is so is proved by the results of a large number of checks carried out by the Consumers' Association on new cars purchased from agents in various towns.

New Car Delivery Faults. The following is a brief summary of some of the more important faults found by the Consumers'

Association on new cars, before testing. The cars included no less than 86 different makes and models ranging from the smaller cars of about £600 to the larger ones in the £1,000 to £1,500 class.

In the more expensive cars only 1 in about 4 had no delivery faults, while in the lower range about 1 in 5 to 6 had no delivery faults. The number of delivery faults per car ranged from about 12 to as many as 22.

Among the most frequent of the important faults were the following: Valve stem clearances incorrect. Ignition timing wrong. Water leakages around windscreens and other windows. Carburettor settings wrong. Wheels out of balance; this fault becomes more serious when driving above about 50 m.p.h. Faulty door and boot locks. Front wheel alignment incorrect, in particular the 'toe-in', which causes excessive tyre side wear. Brakes not properly adjusted. Cylinder head nuts not tight enough. Headlamps not properly aligned according to legal requirements. Laminated suspension spring U-bolt nuts not tight enough. Sparking plug gaps incorrect. Lubricant levels in engine sump, gearbox, steering gearbox and back axle casing incorrect.

From this list of recurring faults, for new cars, the owner-mechanic should be able to make a check and rectify any of them before taking his car on the road.

Mileages and Maintenance Items. Since this volume has been written mainly for the owner-driver, the following information has been included, as a general guide to the items needing periodical maintenance attention, at the stated mileage intervals.

500 MILES

At the end of the first 500 *miles* empty the oil out of the engine sump and replenish with fresh oil. Run the car carefully and at the recommended maximum speeds, during the first 500 miles or so, and do not attempt to drive at full throttle or to race the engine in any way; upon the treatment a car receives in its first 1,000 miles, its subsequent length of useful life depends. Certain makes of car, however, are 'run in' before leaving the works and do not, therefore, require quite such careful attention.

FREE SERVICE ATTENTION. 500 MILES

The actual servicing items requiring attention will depend upon the design of the car, its transmission, braking and suspension systems, so that it is not possible, here, to give general instructions that will be applicable to all automobiles. However, the following are brief instructions applying to an ordinary mass-produced car of 35 to 65 h.p., maximum rating:

At the end of the first 500 *miles.* Drain out the engine sump, gearbox and back axle casings and refill with the recommended grades of lubricant. Check all cylinder head nuts for tightness, using the correct tightening order described on page 76. (If a torque-indicating wrench is available, set the tightening torque to about 35 to 45 lb. ft. for smaller engines up to 70 to 90 lb. ft. for larger, e.g., 2 to 3 litre engines.) Check the inlet and exhaust manifold nuts.

Note. When aluminium cylinder heads are fitted it is important *not to tighten the nuts* down when the engine is hot, as this may cause distortion and joint leakage. Therefore, always tighten the nuts with the engine cold. Oil all working joints of the car, e.g., at the carburettor, clutch, brake mechanism, etc. joints; also the fan bearing. Tighten the fan belt if necessary. Lubricate the steering system items shown on the lubrication chart; the spring shackles; the universal joints and the other lubrication nipples on the chassis. Check the overhead valve rocker shaft bearing cap nuts for tightness. Check the valve clearances to the manufacturer's 'hot' or 'cold' clearance valves. Check all unions of the fuel system, from the main tank to carburettor for signs of leakage. Check all cooling system joints and the emptying cocks, for leakages. Examine the carburettor float bowl for signs of sediment. Clean the sparking plugs and check the automatic ignition controls, resetting same if necessary. Inspect fuel filters and, finally (after valve clearances and ignition timing have been verified), run the engine until warm and check the slow-running adjustment of the carburettor. Check front wheel alignment and steering connections. Adjust if required. Check all wheel security nuts for tightness.

All holding-down or mounting nuts of the engine, radiator,

transmission, suspension system, steering system, etc., should be given a careful check for tightness. The clutch pedal free-play should be measured and adjusted if necessary; this clearance is generally between ¾ in. and 1 in. at the pedal end of the clutch lever. Check brake fluid supply reservoir and top up, if necessary. The brakes should be tested on the road or in a brake-testing machine, for any bedding-down effects. Further, the brake fluid lines should be examined for leakage. Inspect the hydraulic shock absorbers for leakage.

The electrical system should, at this stage, be checked. Thus, all switches should be operated to test whether the lights, fuel gauge, oil pressure indicator light headlight beam and ignition indicator lights, etc., function.

The battery level should be inspected and, if necessary, the battery topped up. At this point, check the battery cable union clips for tightness and grease for corrosion protection.

All doors and the boot hinges and catches should be checked for ease of opening and closing. Grease the dovetails and striking plates lightly. Finally, adjust all tyre pressures (including also the spare wheel tyre to the recommended values.

Lubrication Chart. It is important for the mechanic and owner-driver to obtain a copy of his vehicle's lubrication chart. This is usually included in the *Owner's Instruction Book*, but a larger one is obtainable from one of the leading oil companies. Paste this chart on a piece of plywood and hang in your garage. With its aid you can undertake all lubrication of the vehicle.

1,000 MILES

In the case of many new cars a second general maintenance service is offered by the manufacturers. The principal instructions usually recommended are as follows:

Examine the engine mounting nuts and those of the suspension system by applying the necessary torque with a wrench. Inspect level of oil in gearbox (or transmission unit) and back axle. Replenish if necessary. Apply the grease gun to any grease nipples. Check level of lubricant in the steering gearbox. Check brake shoes for proper operation and braking effort. The brake shoes tend to bed down during the first 500–1,000 miles and may therefore need slight adjustment. The wheels concerned should be jacked up, to ensure that after adjustment, they just spin freely. Top up the hydraulic brake (and if fitted, the clutch) cylinder supply reservoir with brake oil. Check the ignition timing at this stage; also the valve stem end clearances. Lubricate the carburettor control joints, with engine oil. Examine all unions and pipes in the hydraulic brake-system, for leakages. When rod or cable-operated brakes are fitted inspect and lubricate all the working joints. Top up the battery and radiator, if necessary. Test the tyre pressures. Check all wheel nuts for tightness. Inspect filter on air cleaner.

3,000 MILES

At the end of 3,000 miles running of a new car and at these intervals for a car that has been continuously in service:

Repeat the 1,000 mile and check maintenance procedure, but in addition, check the ignition system as follows: Remove and clean the sparking plugs, check and if necessary re-set the points. Check the automatic ignition control, making a road test to ensure that the ignition timing is correctly adjusted. Lubricate, lightly, the camshaft of distributor bearing, dynamo and motor armature shaft bearings. Lightly grease the faces of the distributor cam. Check all cable end connections. Examine lubrication level in engine, gearbox and back axle. Replenish if necessary. Check lubricant level in steering gearbox. Grease rack-and-pinion or other steering unit. It is essential to lubricate the universal shaft coupling bearings at this stage. Check and re-adjust dynamo drive belt. Remove the air cleaner, dismantle and inspect. If necessary clean the filter and if of the oil-gauze filter pattern, wash out in paraffin and replenish the oil. The fuel feed pump filter in the fuel system to carburettor ought to be cleaned at this period. Also, the carburettor fuel inlet filter.

It is important, where recommended by the manufacturer, to drain the engine and refill with fresh oil. With certain recent cars, this procedure is not necessary till about 6,000 miles. If necessary, top up the hydraulic shock absorbers. When the braking system is of the mechanical cable-applied type clean and grease the cables where they pass through or enter guide members. Finally, change the car wheels around in the manner described on page 391. Examine the tyre treads and remove any flints or stones.

5,000 TO 6,000 MILES

At the end of these periods the following procedure is applicable to the average car:

Repeat the 3,000-mile procedure, but in addition: After draining out the engine oil, replace the felt filter element with a new element and refill the sump with fresh oil. Make certain the filter unit holding nuts are quite tight and that a new filter container washer is employed. Drain the gearbox and back axle and refill with fresh lubricant of the recommended grade. Check fluid level in hydraulic shock absorbers; replenish if necessary. Check the valve stem clearances. Remove and clean the air filter. Remove the front wheel hub caps and replenish with suitable grease. Check hydraulic shock absorbers. Replenish with correct grade oil if necessary. Check and adjust brakes, including the hand brake. Clean carburettor and filters, including fuel pump filter. Check engine valve clearances. Check front wheel camber, castor and toe-in (see page 358). Drain, flush out and refill cooling system. Check leaf-spring axle clamp U-bolt nuts. Where trafficators are fitted lubricate trafficator arm bearings. Lubricate rear hub bearings. Lubricate dynamo bearings. All door hinges and door stop plates should be examined and greased, if necessary and door plates adjusted to stop any door rattles.

Decarbonizing. Some car manufacturers, e.g. of Hillman, Humber and Sunbeam cars, recommend first decarbonizing of their engines at 5,000 to 6,000 miles. This, we consider a wise procedure in maintaining the engine performance and extending the trouble-free period of the engine. The valves should be cleaned and ground in after decarbonizing the cylinders.

10,000 MILES

Repeat the 3,000-mile procedure, but if necessary decarbonize the engine and grind in the valves. Fit new sparking plugs as

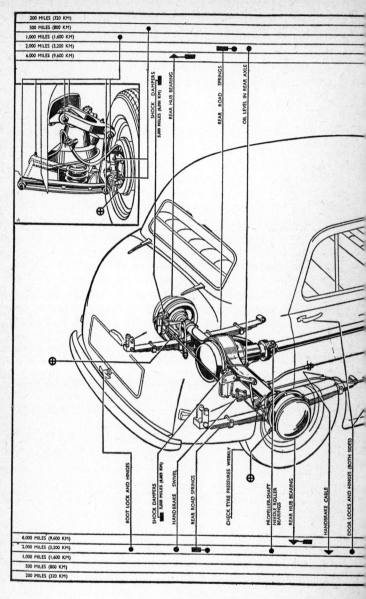

200 MILES (320 KM)
500 MILES (800 KM)
1,000 MILES (1,600 KM)
2,000 MILES (3,200 KM)
6,000 MILES (9,600 KM)

SHOCK DAMPERS
5,000 MILES (8,000 KM)

REAR HUB BEARING

REAR ROAD SPRINGS

OIL LEVEL IN REAR AXLE

BOOT LOCK AND HINGES

SHOCK DAMPERS
5,000 MILES (8,000 KM)

HANDBRAKE SWIVEL

REAR ROAD SPRINGS

CHECK TYRE PRESSURES WEEKLY

PROPELLER-SHAFT
NEEDLE ROLLER
BEARINGS

REAR HUB BEARING

HANDBRAKE CABLE

DOOR LOCKS AND HINGES (BOTH SIDES)

6,000 MILES (9,600 KM)
2,000 MILES (3,200 KM)
1,000 MILES (1,600 KM)
500 MILES (800 KM)
200 MILES (320 KM)

Fig. 1. Showing the items of maintenanc

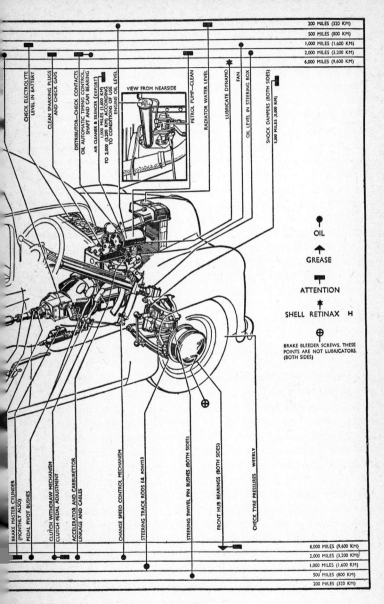

			200 MILES (320 KM)
			500 MILES (800 KM)
			1,000 MILES (1,600 KM)
			2,000 MILES (3,200 KM)
			6,000 MILES (9,600 KM)

CHECK ELECTROLYTE LEVEL IN BATTERY

CLEAN SPARKING PLUGS AND CHECK GAPS

DISTRIBUTOR—CHECK CONTACTS. OIL AUTOMATIC TIMING CONTROL, SHAFT AND CAM BEARING

AIR CLEANER & SILENCER (EXPORT) 1,000 MILES (1,600 KM) TO 2,000 KM) ACCORDING TO CONDITIONS OF USE ENGINE OIL LEVEL

VIEW FROM NEARSIDE

PETROL PUMP—CLEAN

RADIATOR WATER LEVEL

LUBRICATE DYNAMO

FAN

OIL LEVEL IN STEERING BOX

SHOCK DAMPERS (BOTH SIDES) 5,000 MILES (8,000 KM)

OIL

GREASE

ATTENTION

SHELL RETINAX H

BRAKE BLEEDER SCREWS. THESE POINTS ARE NOT LUBRICATORS. (BOTH SIDES)

BRAKE MASTER CYLINDER (MONTHLY ALSO)

PEDAL PIVOT BUSHES

CLUTCH WITHDRAW MECHANISM

CLUTCH PEDAL ADJUSTMENT

ACCELERATOR AND CARBURETTOR LINKAGE AND CABLES

CHANGE SPEED CONTROL MECHANISM

STEERING TRACK RODS (4 POINTS)

STEERING SWIVEL PIN BUSHES (BOTH SIDES)

FRONT HUB BEARINGS (BOTH SIDES)

CHECK TYRE PRESSURES WEEKLY

			6,000 MILES (9,600 KM)
			2,000 MILES (3,200 KM)
			1,000 MILES (1,600 KM)
			500 MILES (800 KM)
			200 MILES (320 KM)

tion in the case of the Hillman Minx Car.

the useful trouble-free life of ordinary plugs is 10,000–12,000 miles. Check and adjust fan and dynamo belts. Adjust clutch pedal clearance if necessary. Lubricate rack-and-pinion or other type steering members. Check the contact breaker points for erosion or 'burning' and the gap for correct opening clearance. Clean inside and out of distributor cover and check electrical leads to the ignition unit. Inspect the electrical system components, e.g., the lamps and fuses. Change any bulbs that show signs of 'blackening'. Inspect windscreen wiper arms for wear of the rubber blades. Check the arms for correct 'sweep' over the windscreen. Examine and if necessary tighten blade arm fixings to motor shaft. Examine dynamo and generator brushes for wear and commutators for clean surfaces. Replace worn brushes and clean dirty commutators. Drain and flush out the cooling system. Check the steering mechanism, including the steering gearbox members, for wear; take up any play in the worn members where means are provided for this purpose. Check alignment of front wheels. Check the front and rear suspension system for wear of working parts. At this stage a new filter should again be fitted in the engine lubrication system.

25,000 TO 35,000 MILES

The 25,000 to 35,000 miles period is probably the most important one in the existence of the car, for the cumulative effects of road usage generally begin to manifest themselves. Thus, the piston rings require replacing; the cylinders in exceptional cases of engine neglect may have to be re-ground and new pistons fitted; the clutch plates may need re-adjustment or replacement; the brakes re-lined. Spring plates are apt to fracture during or after this period. With independent front springing, the coil springs may have weakened and will require replacement; torsion bars may need re-adjustment for chassis 'trim'. Sometimes the ignition and electrical systems begin to exhibit faults, but the wise driver will see that the ignition system, the dynamo and the starting motor are cleaned and serviced at this interval. New sparking plugs should also be fitted at 20,000 miles.

As modern half-shell big-end bearings are now fitted it may be necessary to replace these at 25,000 to 35,000 miles. The crankshaft journals should be examined for wear at this stage and before bearings are replaced, since regrinding may become necessary. Renew worn gudgeon pins and bushes; renew any of the valves that are unduly worn on the stems or seatings and springs, and take up the slack in the timing gear chain drive.

Usually the front axle king-pin bearings will need renewal; the king pins, also, may have to be replaced with stock size pins. The wheel bearings will also need adjustment, to take up wear effects.

The back axle will need a careful examination at this time, for wear in the wheel bearings, loss of oil along the axle shafts (necessitating renewal of the oil seals), gear teeth mesh adjustment.

Noisy back axle operation at this stage is a sure sign that the gears need attention. The brake shoes may also need relining and any worn pins or bearings attended to.

At this period, the body should be inspected carefully for distortion, loose screws, hinges, door stops and fittings. Also the tyres, if not previously replaced, should be carefully examined for condition.

With such a thorough overhaul and inspection, no further really serious overhaul will be necessary for another 15,000 to 20,000 miles or so, but more attention will be needed every few thousand miles than in the earlier days. It should be realized, however, that with constant use the working parts of a car's mechanism must always be wearing, and that after their normal span they will require replacement. Similarly, as a car wears and, of course, becomes older, it must, necessarily, become noisier.

It is, however, a matter of some consolation to the careful owner that, thanks to the excellent system of spares supply, he can replace most of the wearing parts of a car including the engine and gearbox, and thus keep his car in commission for a very long period if he desires.

Reconditioned Engines and Components. It is now usual to supply reconditioned parts, such as complete engines, carburettors, fuel pumps, gearboxes, etc., in exchange for the worn units.

This method enables the owner of a car to keep it in service for exceptionally long periods, e.g., 100,000 to 200,000 miles.

What Troubles to Expect. After the question of maintenance, outlined briefly in the preceding paragraphs, one naturally comes to the subject of unexpected troubles, breakdowns and other causes of stoppage on the road. On the principle that 'forewarned is forearmed', it is proposed to devote some space to a consideration of the chief causes of breakdown of cars now on the roads.

The causes of such troubles may either be accidental or through neglect on the part of the owner, manufacturer or garage mechanic.

A good idea of the causes of road troubles with automobiles can be obtained from the annual Tables issued by the Royal Automobile Club in connection with their 'Get-you-home' Service, and since this volume is concerned with the maintenance of both earlier and more recent car models, the results of the R.A.C. analyses for the years 1950, 1957 and 1964 are given in the following Tables.

TABLE SHOWING CAUSES OF AUTOMOBILE BREAKDOWNS

		per cent	
		1950	1957
1.	*Power Unit*		
	(a) Ignition	23·3	31·4*
	(b) Carburation	10·2	14·5
2.	*Engine*		
	(a) Cylinders and Pistons	5·6	2·6
	(b) Valve Mechanism	1·2	1·6†
	(c) Valves	1·1	—
	(d) Lubrication	1·1	0·7
	(e) Water Circulation	3·5	3·7
	(f) Crankshaft	1·0	0·4
	(g) Not Stated	4·5	6·4
	(h) Starting	2·0	—
	(i) Bearings	0·8	2·0
3.	*Transmission and Brakes*		
	(a) Clutch	4·7	5·4
	(b) Gearbox	3·3	2·9
	(c) Couplings and Propeller Shafts	2·3	0·3
	(d) Brakes	1·0	1·5
4.	*Back Axle*		
	(a) Axle Shafts	13·8	7·0
	(b) Differential	1·3	0·2
	(c) Bevels and Worms	0·7	0·6

5. *Front Axle and Steering*	3·2	1·4
6. *Road Wheels and Suspension*	3·3	2·4
7. *Lighting Failures*	1·0	—
8. *Accidents, and Lack of petrol, etc.*	9·1	15.1‡
	100·0	100·0

Courtesy The Royal Automobile Club.
* Includes electrical failures.   † Includes Valves.
‡ Includes 8 per cent tyre failures.

ANALYSIS OF AUTOMOBILE ROAD BREAKDOWNS IN 1964

1. *Power Unit*	per cent
(*a*) Ignition System	14·3
(*b*) Fuel System (Carburettor, etc.)	15·8
2. *The Engine*	
(*a*) Cylinders and Pistons	1·6
(*b*) Valve Mechanism	0·9
(*c*) Crankshaft and Bearings	2·1
(*d*) Cooling System	8·2
(*e*) Lubrication	1·0
(*f*) Unspecified	6·6
3. *Transmission and Brakes*	
(*a*) Clutch	6·0
(*b*) Gearbox	3·8
(*c*) Couplings and Propeller Shafts	0·4
(*d*) Brakes	2·2
4. *Back Axle and Front Drives*	
(*a*) Differential Units	0·1
(*b*) Half or Drive Shafts	3·0
5. *Steering Systems*	1·1
6. *Suspension Systems* (front and rear)	1·2
7. *The Battery*	6·5
8. *Starter, Lights and Accessories*	9·7
9. *Wheels and Tyres* (including punctures)	10·1
10. *Miscellaneous: Accidents. No petrol. Lost ignition keys. Ditched. Frost and snow, etc.*	5·4
	100·0

An examination of the figures given in the tables will reveal some interesting results, some of which indicate the greater reliability of the later engines and transmissions while others show that there has been a certain increase in the failures in components of modern cars.

It is notable that the failures due to the *Power Unit* in 1950, 1957 and 1964 cars were 54·3, 50 and 50·5 per cent of all the failures, facts which show little change over the last fourteen years.

On the other hand the percentage failures due to the *Transmission System*, for the same three years were 26·1, 16·4 and 13·3, respectively. In this connection one of the more frequent causes of breakdown in the earlier cars was the back axle half-shafts. Thus, no less than 13·8 per cent of the failures in 1950 were due to this cause as against only 3·0 per cent in 1964.

The electrical system is still one of the more important causes of road breakdowns, the percentages for 1957 and 1964 being 31·4 and 30·7, respectively.

The modern car does not compare very favourably with the earlier ones in the tables, in regard to the reliability of the fuel and cooling systems. Thus, for the cars of 1950, 1957 and 1964 the percentages of failures in the *Cooling Systems* were 3·5, 3·7 and 8·2, respectively. *Fuel system* failures, which include the carburettor and fuel feed systems, for the three years mentioned accounted for 10·2, 14·5 and 15·8 per cent of the failures given in the tables. These increases are no doubt due to the more complicated carburettors used today and to the greater demands on the modern cooling systems by the higher output engines.

Official Periodic Vehicle Tests. As a result of a series of tests of road vehicles of various ages, by the Ministry of Transport, it was found that an appreciable proportion of these vehicles were in an unsatisfactory condition in regard to braking, steering and lighting equipment. Thus a sample test of vehicles submitted voluntarily at an official testing station showed that 34 per cent of the vehicles 10 years old or more and 17 per cent of newer cars had *serious defects* in the *braking or steering mechanism*; and 43 and 20 per cent, respectively, had *lighting defects* likely to cause accidents.

Provision was therefore made in the Road Traffic Act, 1956*

---

* *Road Traffic Act* 1956. *Periodic Vehicle Tests. Submitted to Parliament, May* 1958. H.M.S.O. (9d.)

for the introduction of compulsory tests for vehicles of 10 years old, or more and the issue of test certificates to be produced before a vehicle excise licence could be obtained or renewed.

Two later Amendments to this Act reduced the period of 10 years, first to 7 and then to 3 years, the latter period being now in force.

Further information regarding these official requirements, before a car licence can be granted, is given at the ends of Chapters 9, 11 and 13, while particulars of the Ministry of Transport Compulsory Vehicle Tests, based upon the Motor Vehicles (Tests) Regulations, 1960, are given in an Appendix at the end of this book (p. 450).

Nature of Tests

The vehicle owner will be required to submit his vehicle for *tests of the braking, steering systems and lighting equipment* at an officially-approved testing station, but after receiving the official report, should this indicate any faults or defects in the vehicle, the owner can either remedy these himself or have them put right at any garage of his selection.

In the majority of cases these faults can be remedied by the owner-mechanic and, in this connection the information given in this volume should prove sufficient for most of the common faults pointed out by the examiner.

Brakes. The vehicle will be examined and tested for (1) the condition and security of the braking mechanism and the means of operation, (2) the effectiveness of the brakes in bringing the vehicle to rest and holding it on an incline. The tester will examine the system for such faults as brake rods and cables that are chafed, or do not work freely; unduly worn bolts and clevis pins and their holes; leaky hydraulic brake systems; excessive wear in handbrake pawls and ratchets; oil leakage from the axles into the brake-drums; free movement and reserve travel of brake pedals.

Steering. The steering system will be examined for evidence of worn track rod, steering arm and drag-link joints; excessive wear in the king pins and bushes; too much clearance in the wheel axle bearings; looseness of attachment of the steering gearbox and excessive play in the gears; no excessive effort or amount of free movement when the steering wheel is operated when the vehicle is travelling on the road.

Lighting Equipment and Reflectors. The various lamps in the lighting system must conform to the requirements of the Road Traffic Acts. The lamps should be adjusted in accordance with official requirements. Thus headlamps or spotlamps (fog lamps) must be permanently directed downwards so that, with the vehicle on level ground an observer whose eye level is 3 ft. 6 in. from the ground, 25 ft. or more from the lamp would not be dazzled. When the reflector has a beam-dipping mechanism this must operate properly and when dipped must not dazzle an observer. The side and rear lights must operate satisfactorily.

Finally, if in the course of examination other faults are observed (for example, a *cracked chassis frame, broken spring blade or mudguard* or a *badly worn tyre*) which might affect the braking or steering, then the test certificate would not be granted.

The reader wishing for fuller information should consult the official publications mentioned on pages 22 and 440.

What the Driver can Undertake. As this Manual is written chiefly for the owner-driver and driver-mechanic of private cars, the present considerations refer principally to adjustments, repairs, overhauls and the general items of periodic attention within his scope, leaving the more serious work for the garage or service station.

The minimum outfit of tools for the ordinary maintenance of the car should be supplied in the manufacturer's tool kit, when the car is new, a typical set being those of a Hillman Minx car, shown in Fig. 2.

It will be convenient to consider the subject under two particular headings, namely: (1) Work within the scope of the driver himself, using ordinary tools, and (2) Work which the owner or driver can undertake with the aid of a well-equipped garage-workshop.

Evidently, in the former case, the work which can be done is confined to superficial repairs and adjustments necessitating the use of the normal kit of tools. Thus the person who has purchased a new or second-hand car provided with a special tool-kit and a few domestic workshop tools, can only attend, satisfactorily, to such items as the following: Adjustment of the Valve Rockers, Carburettor, Ignition Contacts, Brakes, Clutch Spring Pressure, Front Wheel Alignment, Steering Gear and Electrical

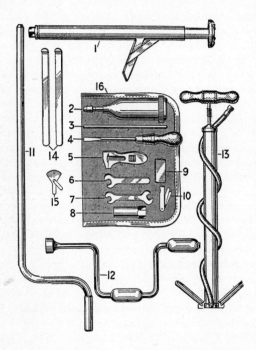

Fig. 2. Maintenance car tool kit (Hillman Minx)

1. Lifting jack.
2. Lubrication gun.
3. Tommy bar (for sparking plug spanner).
4. Screwdriver.
5. Adjustable spanner.
6. Spanner – tappet screw.
7. Spanner – tappet lock nut.
8. Spanner – sparking plug.
9. Tappet lock plate.
10. Tappet and sparking plug gauge.
11. Starting handle.
12. Wheel brace.
13. Tyre pump.
14. Tyre levers.
15. Distributor key and contact gauge.
16. Tool roll.

Equipment. In addition he can, of course, look after the Lubrication of the Engine and Chassis Members, the Cleaning of Oil and Petrol Filters, Carburettor Float Chamber, Maintenance of the Battery and Electrical System, Sparking Plugs, Radiator and Bodywork. Under favourable conditions he can undertake the Decarbonizing of the Cylinder Heads and Re-grinding of the Valves; the manufacturers usually provide special tools for lifting the cylinder head and removing the valve springs, to facilitate this procedure. In the case of most makes of modern cars, the keen driver of mechanical ability can maintain his car in good running condition for the first 15,000 to 17,000 miles or so of its life without having recourse to the garage service station.

What the Driver-Mechanic can Undertake. If the owner, or driver, of a car has a certain amount of mechanical knowledge and skill, he can do practically everything necessary to keep his car in excellent condition for at least 20,000 miles of running. It is, of course, necessary for him to have a suitably equipped garage-workshop, a garage pit and some convenient means of lifting heavy parts out of the car. Now that the supply of spare parts from the manufacturers is so general, it is not even necessary to make new parts, for when any items, e.g. Valves, Piston Rings, Springs, Bearings, Steering Pins, Gears, Clutch and Brake Linings, etc. When these become seriously worn, they can be renewed with new parts of identical design.

The more serious jobs that the mechanic cannot undertake satisfactorily are Cylinder Re-grinding, Crankshaft Turning, Re-metalling of earlier engine Big-end and Main Bearings, Welding Repairs, important Radiator Repairs, Re-setting Leaf Springs, Straightening Chassis Members and making New Gears, Universal Joints, etc.

Although we have come across instances where skilled driver-mechanics, in their own garage-workshops, have actually rehoned engine cylinders, fitted oversize pistons, and re-metalled bearings, it is generally better to leave this work to the well equipped garage rather than risk an unsatisfactory result.

A word of warning before concluding these remarks, for the benefit of those who are considering equipping a workshop with a view to undertaking the kind of work previously mentioned. Unless you have had some good mechanical experience in the use of tools and measuring instruments, are skilful in the art of obtaining the proper fits and have a knowledge of the limits and tolerances required in automobile work, it is best to confine your activities to those items mentioned in the preceding section.

The Garage Workshop and Its Equipment. The keen owner-driver, even if he does not intend to undertake any serious overhaul or repair work, will be well advised to consider the furnishing of his garage with a few items which will greatly facilitate the ordinary adjustments and cleaning of parts; what is more important is the carrying out of emergency repairs and the making of temporary devices to overcome unexpected difficulties.

The barest needs in this respect include a small bench, vice, hand grinding wheel and a few engineer's tools. Briefly, the latter include a 2 lb. and lighter-type hammer, one or two cold chisels, hack-saw, hand drilling machine with a set of drills from $\frac{1}{16}$ to $\frac{1}{4}$ inch, pin and centre punches, a set of flat, half-round, square, round and three-square (or triangular) files, file-cleaning card, large and small screwdrivers, bradawls, pliers, metal snips, 12 inch rule, feeler gauge (1 to 25 thousandths of an inch), soldering iron, and set of reamers ($\frac{1}{8}$ to $\frac{1}{2}$ inch).

Selection of Spanners, etc.

Much care should be taken in the selection of suitable spanners, as a good deal of time and trouble is saved by employing the correct spanners. Those recommended are the usual double-ended set spanners – preferably of chrome-alloy hardened steel, a set of cranked ring spanners, from $\frac{1}{8}$th to $\frac{5}{8}$th Whitworth, B.S.F. or Unified Screw Threads, in recent cars, and socket wrench set. The ring or bihexagon spanners (Fig. 3) are particularly handy for cylinder nuts and others in awkward positions, as they enable small successive angles of rotation of nuts to be obtained. The socket wrench set is also most useful for car jobs and if a ratchet unit is included this will extend the scope. Bihexagon ring spanners are made in the straight and offset double-ended types, or with a plain shank and hammering pad, for stubborn nuts.

Those who require a more complete equipment will be well advised to add the following items: Set of Whitworth, B.S.F.

and B.A. taps and dies (up to $\frac{5}{16}$ inch size in the former and from No. 0 to 6 in the latter), tap wrench, wire nippers, set of tyre levers (including forked lever for tube insertion), a small vulcanizing equipment (Harvey Frost make an inexpensive one), box spanners, hide-faced hammer, cone pliers, set of scrapers, punches for leather or fibre sheet, and one or two woodworker's tools.

Fig. 4 illustrates in plan view a well-designed garage-workshop, not too ambitious in character, intended for the motor owner wishing to carry out the type of work mentioned in the preceding

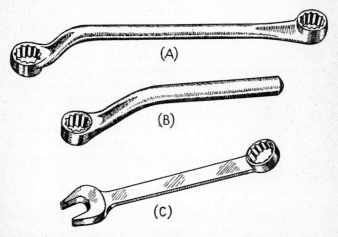

Fig. 3. Some useful spanners. (A) Bihexagon ring. (B) Single ring with hammering shank. (C) Combination ring and set spanner.

section. The lighting of the bench is an important item; in the illustration it will be observed this has received due consideration.

Regarding the bench itself, a convenient size for this is 4 feet long, 2 feet to 2 feet 6 inches wide, and about 2 feet 8 inches high (from ground level). As the height of a bench is important from the point of view of quality of work and general convenience, it is best to test for the correct height by the elbow test method shown in Fig. 5. The bench should be made of planks 2 inches thick, and the vertical supports should be at least 3 inches square, in section; it is advisable to cement the feet into the ground. Such a bench will withstand rough handling, hammering and heavy weight effects.

Workshop for the Small Garage. An ingenious solution of the small garage workshop problem, described in a motoring journal, consisted in building a platform between the longer walls of the garage and at a height above the ground that left about 2 ft. above the car's bonnet. On this platform which was over the car's bonnet a work bench, tool cabinet and other essential items for the owner-mechanic were located. A short series of steps afforded access to this raised platform.

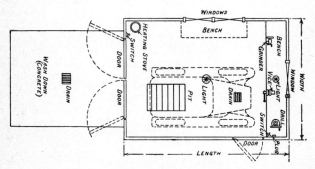

Fig. 4. Layout of a suitable garage-workshop for the owner-driver.

Regarding the equipment of the motor mechanic's workshop, it is advisable to have a $3\frac{1}{2}$ inch lathe, and if possible a sensitive drilling machine of the bench type. If electric power is available, a compact countershaft drive to the lathe, drill and grinder can readily be fitted up. The portable electric drill, grinder and saw unit now obtainable are excellent additions to the workshop. In addition, a small battery-charging equipment of 1 to 3 ampere rate for car and wireless batteries can usually be found room for.

A small grinder is necessary for the garage workshop. It can either be a power-driven 6-in. wheel model or a treadle-operated vertical pillar 6-in. wheel type, made for use where space is limited.

The garage pit is almost essential if one is going to undertake transmission and brake inspection and adjustments, more especially with the modern less accessible designs of cars; moreover, it is useful when draining lubricant from the engine sump, gearbox and rear axle casing. Suitable dimensions for a pit which can be used for the average light and medium cars are as follows: length, 6 feet; width, 3 feet; depth, from 4 feet to 4 feet 6 inches.

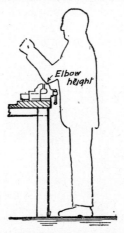

Fig. 5. Showing how to test for the most suitable height of the workshop bench.

Fig. 6 illustrates a well-designed pit in concrete, with recesses on either side to take movable boards 9 inches by 2 inches thick, in deal. There are two recesses in the walls to take movable boards, about 18 inches from the bottom; these facilitate inspection of items high up on the chassis. A sloping base with drain and soak-away pit filled with clinker overcomes the usual difficulty of water collecting in the pit. In order to descend and ascend, loops in $\frac{3}{4}$ inch round iron bar are formed at 1 foot intervals in one corner of the pit walls. The inspection pit also forms a safe means of petrol can storage if away from the house.

Garage Lighting and Ventilation. Apart from the window-lights, which should be liberal in size and well disposed, it is advisable to have a good artificial light (electric for preference) over the car's bonnet position, the bench and lathe. When electric light is not available, the incandescent mantle type of lamp with glass cylindrical globe of the Pifco type will be found most convenient; this gives about 200 c.p., uses paraffin, and is perfectly safe. One or two power plugs should be arranged at convenient

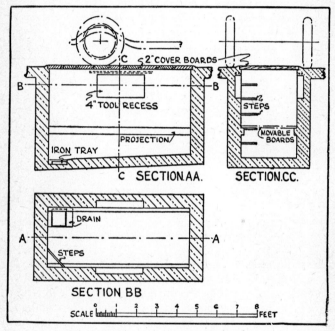

Fig. 6. A well-designed garage pit in concrete.

parts of the garage, for portable electric lamps, tools and for the battery charger or cold weather car engine heater.

It is important to arrange for permanent ventilation of the garage to prevent moisture deposition with temperature changes – more especially during the winter months – by fitting permanently open louvres or gratings high up on one or two of the walls.

In this respect condensation in the garage is the cause of rust, corrosion and mildew, so that the need for proper ventilation is an important one.

Raising the Car off Ground. In the absence of the inspection pit mentioned earlier some kind of elevating ramp is essential for the owner who wishes to do his own servicing and light repairs. Ramps for this purpose are of two kinds, namely, the home-made and the commercial models now available.

Home-made Ramps. Perhaps the simplest, if somewhat laborious method of raising a car above the ground is to jack up the chassis at the four corners and then block up the corners with stout timber supports before lowering the jack clear. In this way the car can be raised progressively up to 1 to 2 ft. This method,

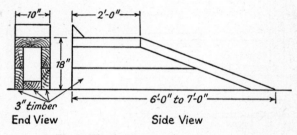

End View   Side View

Fig. 7. Wooden construction car ramp.

however, involves a risk to the person working underneath the car since cases have occurred in which rocking of the car from below has caused the supports to slip and collapse, with serious injury to the person beneath. A better method and one that can be made permanent is to make a pair of ramps either in moulded concrete on the concreted garage floor, or in stout timber, e.g. old railway sleepers, to the approximate dimensions indicated in Fig. 7. For safety reasons the two wooden ramps ought to have cross-connecting metal rod or timber ties, to ensure that they are always located at a distance equal to the car's track, apart.

It is also advisable to have end 'chocks' (Fig. 7) permanently fixed to the ramp and also, side plates of metal or timber to ensure the wheels being central on the ramps.

With this type of ramp either the front, or rear of a car can be raised above the ground; the car must, of course, be reversed on to the ramp for rear end elevation.

Proprietary Car Ramps. There are several proprietary makes of car ramps, of metal construction, available for car elevation. In the simpler model shown by the ramp illustrated in Fig. 8 (A) only one end of the car is raised but in the case of the more complete car ramp the upper longitudinal tracks are made sufficiently long to enable the front and rear wheels to be raised at the same time (Fig. 9). The ramp shown is suitable for cars up to 2 tons.

Other Car Raising Methods. An interesting method that has been used to raise a car in such a way that it could readily be

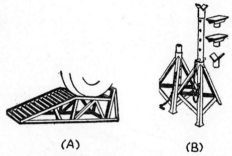

(A)   (B)

Fig. 8. (A) The Star Metal Car Ramp. (B) Typical axle stands and pads.

inspected at either end is that based on the see-saw principle. It consisted of two long channel members, for the car wheels to run along, suitably located at the correct distance apart. The car was driven up the sloping channel tracks until its centre of gravity was just over the centre of the axle member, and the wheels then carefully chocked in position by fixed stops. A worm-and-wheel handle-operated gearing was employed to tilt the channel tracks to the horizontal position; the car was then about 3 to 4 ft. above the ground. A simpler method of raising each end of the car at one time is to jack up each corner of the chassis (frame) and then lower it on to a properly-designed wheel

Fig. 9. The Westwood Portable All-metal Car Ramp.

Fig. 10. A commercial method of raising the car by
means of two wheel stands.

stand, as shown in Fig. 10. This is quite a safe method and it has
the further advantage of allowing the car end to be raised to
greater heights than with the usual run-on ramps.

CHAPTER 2

THE LUBRICATION OF THE CAR

UNDOUBTEDLY one of the most important factors in the maintenance of the car is that of lubrication, for if this is neglected in any way the mechanism wears more rapidly and troubles are apt to occur. On the other hand, liberal lubrication means long life and efficient running, with general freedom from trouble. It is always a good plan to err on the plentiful side than otherwise when lubricating a car. Nowadays the manufacturers issue excellent instruction books with their cars. These include a lubrication chart showing the chassis in plan view and indicating, by arrows and guidance lines, the various items requiring lubrication attention; the intervals at which these attentions are due and the nature of the lubricant to be used. It is a good plan to paste this chart on to a stiff card or piece of plywood, varnish it with a transparent lacquer and hang it up in the garage. Before dealing with a typical lubrication chart it is proposed to describe the method used for lubrication of chassis bearings.

Lubrication Nipples. In the past the various bearings in the suspension and steering systems were provided with lubrication holes into which were screwed oil or grease nipples, of the types shown in Fig 11.

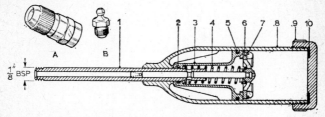

Fig. 11. A typical chassis lubrication grease gun.
1 high-pressure cylinder assembly. 2 'O' ring. 3 piston sleeve. 4 spring.
5 'O' ring. 6 piston cap assembly. 7 circlip. 8 barrel. 9 cap. 10 sealing washer. *A* nozzle or connector. *B* nipple.

Up until about 1960 there were quite a number of such nipples, which had to be lubricated through, every 1,000 to 2,000 miles or so. Thus, in a typical mass-produced car there were about 20 such nipples.

When the bearings were of the slow but heavily loaded kind, e.g. the spring shackles ones, a suitable grease was used – and indeed is still employed in a few cases today. A special grease gun of the type shown in Fig. 11 was used to inject grease at a pressure of 4,000 to 5,000 lb. per sq. in. into the bearings. The pressure was applied either by means of a screw-type handle or a push-plunger. In other instances, as with the B.M.C. cars, pressure oil was injected through the majority of the nipples.

Modern cars show a strong tendency to eliminate as many of the separate lubrication points as possible, so that (as a recent analysis of various cars has shown) the number of such nipples ranged from 1 to about 10 in the smaller to medium mass-produced cars but in a few luxury type cars in the £1,300 to £1,500 class more grease nipples, e.g. between 10 and 27 were found.

The reduction or elimination of such nipples greatly reduces maintenance attention, so that more cars are now being fitted with pin-type and ball-and-socket-type bearings, as shown in

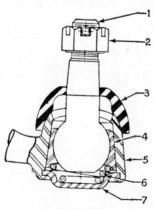

Fig. 12. Typical sealed (30,000 mile) steering bearing.
1 steel ball member. 2 nut. 3 rubber boot. 4 nylon bearing. 5 steel socket.
6 compression wear-adjusting spring. 7 steel sealing cap.

Fig. 12 which have nylon bearings and steel pins or ball members. The whole bearing is enclosed in a specially-designed rubber cover or 'boot' which prevents escape of the special long-life lubricant or ingress of water or dirt. Such bearing members do not require lubrication or adjustment attention under about 30,000 miles of service. It should be pointed out that there is always a spring inside the unit to keep the two bearing members together and thus to take up any wear.

At present in British cars the maintenance periods for lubrication of the steering, suspension, propeller shaft joints, etc. are from 3,000 to 6,000 miles, but in the case of the Triumph Herald car the period is about 12,000 miles. As mentioned later, the engine oil must be changed more frequently. It should here be mentioned that practically all American cars are now lubricated for 30,000 miles for all working members except the engine and automatic transmission unit.

Notes on Using Grease Guns. First make sure that you use the right grade of grease. Then fill the grease gun and eject any air by pressing the nozzle end on a surface while applying pressure on the handle. Wipe the end of the nipple and apply the grease gun nozzle, giving a number of strokes, until grease is seen to exude from the bearing. If the nipple is choked, unscrew it and clean with a fine wire.

Garage Power Lubrication. In the routine lubrication of motor cars compressed air is employed to force the grease from its container, which is mounted on a trolley, through a flexible pressure hose to the grease gun. The supply pressure is usually about 80 to 150 lb. per sq. inch but at the grease gun nozzle the pressure is increased from 4,000 to as much as 10,000 lb. per sq. inch. Either 'single' or 'multiple' injections or 'shots' can be applied to the grease nipples. A series of containers each with a different lubricant is available and the equipment can readily be transferred from one to another container.

Types of Lubricant to Use. The kind of lubricant used for any bearing depends upon the duty of that bearing. Thus, if the speed of rotation or rocking is high – as in the case of the cylinder and pistons, the connecting-rod and main crankshaft bearings, a special thin grade of oil is used. In the case of heavily-loaded bearings with limited or slow movements a medium body grease of the non-corrosive, temperature-resistant type is used. The extreme pressure (E.P.) and graphite greases are used for these bearings, e.g. cross-shaft, king-pins, steering link, spring pins, etc. Alternatively, oils can be used if the bearings are designed for same. Usually, special heavier grades of oils are used for chassis bearings, transmission-oils for the gearbox, and another grade viz., Hypoid or E.P. oil for the back axle.

Light machine oils are recommended for the ignition, dynamo and motor, some items, e.g. the camshaft bearings and governor advance mechanism, in the former case.

In the case of some dynamos and cooling water-pumps a high melting point grease is generally employed. For brake bearings a zinc-oxide grease may be used. The blades of leafsprings, when they become rusty or noisy are sprayed with a thin penetrating plain or graphited oil, which finds its way between the blades. In general the car manufacturers usually supply a list of recommended lubricants in connection with the lubrication chart and, since there are several motor oil supply companies, the equivalent brands of each are usually tabulated.

Typical Car Lubrication and Maintenance Chart. An example of a typical lubrication and maintenance chart for a modern car is given in Fig. 1 on pages 16 and 17. This perspective diagram shows the chassis of the Hillman Minx car, the body being also outlined. The oblique and vertical indication lines from the various chassis parts are also annotated with the names of these parts which require attention at the stated running intervals.

In the case of chassis members needing maintenance attention solid black rectangles are used at the other ends of the indication lines. Their positions in the horizontal bands or columns show – at the ends of the columns – the mileage intervals at the end of which this attention should be given. Thus, as an example, the sparking plugs need attention at 2,000 miles intervals; the shock absorbers (dampers) need replenishing every 5,000 miles and the radiator level checking every 200 miles.

The solid black discs or dots refer to items requiring lubricating with oil at the stated intervals. Thus, the rear axle oil will need replenishing or checking every 2,000 miles; the propeller shaft coupling needle bearings each 2,000 miles, and so on.

The solid black triangles show those parts needing lubrication with grease. Thus, the handbrake cable will need greasing each 2,000 miles, whilst the front and rear wheel hub bearings should be greased and, if necessary, adjusted each 6,000 miles.

The independent front wheel springing and its steering system has many moving members, the bearings of which need lubricating as indicated.

The rear leaf springs have rubber bushes at their ends and these require no lubrication, but the leaves of the springs require cleaning with a wire brush and spraying with thin oil every 2,000 miles or so, as the chart shows.

It will be noted that this chart also shows certain body items, namely, the door locks and hinges and the boot lock and hinges that need oiling at 2,000 miles intervals.

The dynamo on this car has a wick type lubricator at the commutator end bearing and this is lubricated with Shell Retinax H oil, every 6,000 miles.

The Austin and Morris Mini-car Lubrication Chart. Differing in many respects from the conventional designs, in having transverse engines with integral gearboxes and front wheel half-shaft drives, these cars, and also the Riley Elf and Wolseley Hornet cars, have quite different chassis lubrication methods.

Fig 13 shows the Lubrication Chart for all of these mini-cars, from which it will be seen that practically all of the lubrication points are at the front end of the car, leaving only the rear wheel suspension arm bearings and wheel hubs for lubrication attention.

The B.M.C. 1100 front wheel hydro-elastic suspension *cars* have a similar lubrication chart and instructions, but the fluid in the suspension circuits should be checked at about 12,000 miles for any loss of fluid and also pressure: this should be done by an agent. The following is a key to the Lubrication Chart shown in Fig. 13.

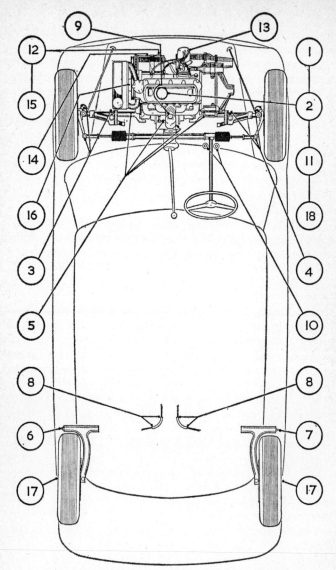

Fig. 13. Lubrication chart for the B.M.C. mini-cars.

Daily
(1) ENGINE. Inspect the oil level by the dipstick, and replenish if necessary with oil.

After the first 500 miles (800 km.)
(2) ENGINE. Drain off the old oil and refill with fresh oil.

Every 1,000 miles (1600 km.)
(3) STEERING JOINT NIPPLES.

(4) STEERING JOINT NIPPLES.

(5) DRIVE SHAFT AND GEAR

(6) REAR SUSPENSION RADIUS ARM.

(7) REAR SUSPENSION RADIUS ARM.

Give three or four strokes of the grease gun filled with grease.

(8) HAND BRAKE CABLE GUIDE CHANNELS. Slacken off the cable and lubricate with grease.

(9) CARBURETTOR. Remove the cap from the top of the suction chamber and add a teaspoonful of oil.

(10) HYDRAULIC MASTER CYLINDERS. Inspect the fluid level in the brake and clutch supply chamber, and replenish if necessary with Lockheed Genuine Brake Fluid.

Every 3,000 miles (4800 km.)
(11) ENGINE. Drain off the old oil and refill with fresh oil.

(12) OIL FILTER. Wash the element and bowl in fuel, dry, and replace.

(13) DISTRIBUTOR. Withdraw the rotor arm and add a few drops of oil to the cam bearing and to the advance mechanism through the gap around the cam spindle. Smear the distributor cam spindle and contact breaker pivot with grease.

(14) DYNAMO. Add a few drops of oil through the oil hole in the commutator end bearing.

(14A) BODY. Lubricate door hinges, bonnet lock, and operating mechanism.

Every 6,000 miles (9600 km.)
(15) OIL FILTER. Wash the bowl in fuel and fit a new element.

(16) WATER PUMP. Remove the oiling plug from the water pump body and lubricate the pump sparingly with S.A.E. 140 oil.

(17) REAR HUB. Remove each rear wheel hub disc, prise off the grease-retaining cap, refill the cap with grease, and replace securely.

Every 12,000 miles (19200 km.)
(18) ENGINE. Drain off old oil, cleanse with flushing oil, and refill with fresh oil.

The two gear change lubricating nipples shown on indicator 5, require attention at major overhaul periods only.

The Vauxhall Victor Lubrication Chart (shown in Fig. 14.)

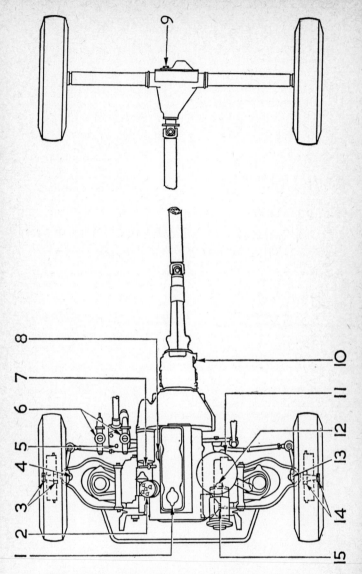

Fig. 14. Lubrication chart for the Vauxhall Victor cars.

There are now only four grease nipples on this car, namely two on each side of the car, for the front suspension arm ball joints and these only need lubricating with a special grease once every 30,000 miles; at the same time the rubber boots should be carefully inspected for defects, deterioration or correct positions. It is usually advisable to replace these boots at this distance as a safety precaution.

Vauxhall Victor Lubrication Instructions

Every 500 miles (750 km.) or weekly (whichever occurs first)

Check Oil Level in Engine Sump. Use dipstick (7). Replenish through filler (1).

Every 3,000 miles (5000 km.) or 3 months (whichever occurs first)

Change Engine Oil. Replenish with 6 pints (3·4 litres) of new oil through filler (1).

Every 6,000 miles (10000 km.) or 6 months (whichever occurs first)

Check Level of Fluid in Clutch and Brake Reservoirs (6). Level should be ¼ in. (6 mm.) below the filler plug holes. Top up only with Lockheed Brake Fluid, Super Heavy Duty S.A.E. Spec. 70 R3.
Renew AC Oil Filter Element (15).
Clean Element in Paper Element Type Air Cleaner (11).

Every 12,000 miles (20000 km.) or 12 months (whichever occurs first)

Lubricate Generator (12).
Lubricate Ignition Distributor (2).
Check Oil Level in Steering Box (5).
Check Oil Level in Gearbox (10).
Check Oil Level in Rear Axle (9).
Renew Element in Paper Element Type Air Cleaner. Wash and Re-oil Wire Wool Type Cleaner (11).
Clean Crankcase Ventilation Air Cleaner (8).

Every 30,000 miles (50000 km.) or 30 months (whichever occurs first)

Lubricate Front Suspension Arm Ball Joints (4, 13) – 4 nipples – with lubricant gun filled with the special lubricant.
Lubricate Front Wheel Bearings (3, 14).

Note. The two universal couplings at the ends of the propellor shaft are lubricated for life in this and other recent cars.

The Engine Lubrication System. The most common lubrication system utilizes a gear-wheel pump submerged in the crankcase sump so that it is always 'primed'. The pump is usually driven by a skew-gear from the camshaft by means of a vertical or inclined shaft. The suction side of the pump has an oil filter to prevent dirt from entering the pump. (Fig. 15.)

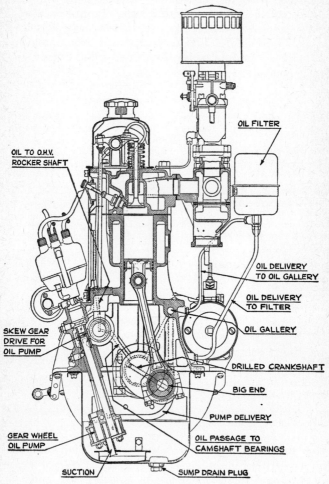

OIL FILTER

OIL TO O.H.V.
ROCKER SHAFT

OIL DELIVERY
TO OIL GALLERY

OIL DELIVERY
TO FILTER

OIL GALLERY

SKEW GEAR
DRIVE FOR
OIL PUMP

DRILLED CRANKSHAFT

BIG END

PUMP DELIVERY

GEAR WHEEL
OIL PUMP

OIL PASSAGE TO
CAMSHAFT BEARINGS

SUCTION

SUMP DRAIN PLUG

Fig. 15. Lubrication system of overhead valve type engine.

The used oil gravitates back to the sump, having, usually, to pass a large tray or filter covering most of the top area of the pump. From the pump oil is delivered to a main oil filter and thence to a horizontal pipe or passage, known as the 'oil gallery', whence it is fed to the crankshaft main bearings through pipes or passages cast in the crankcase. The crankshaft is made hollow so that oil under pressure passes from the main bearings through drilled holes in the crankshaft to the crankpins and big-end bearings.

The camshaft bearings are usually fed from the oil gallery through pipes or cast passages in the crankcase. The timing gear is generally lubricated from the end of the crankshaft, by means of an oilway cut in the latter.

Overhead valve gear is generally lubricated as follows: Oil is supplied from the front or rear camshaft supply pipe, or passage, to a pipe, or passage, leading to the top of the cylinder block and thence to one of the overhead rocker- or camshaft bearings. The rocker- or camshaft is made hollow so that oil passes along it and out of holes placed opposite the other bearings. As many as 12 to 16 rocker bearings can be lubricated satisfactorily in this way. The rockers themselves are often drilled so that oil is ejected from their tips, thus lubricating the ball-ends and the cups at the upper ends of the push-rods. After lubricating the rocker-shaft the oil is returned by gravity to the sump via the push rod or another passage.

The pistons and cylinder walls usually depend for their lubrication upon the oil splashed up from the connecting rods and crank journals, but in some cases the piston skirt end is arranged to dip into an oil trough of circular form when the piston reaches the bottom of its stroke. In other cases a hole is drilled through the top half of the connecting rod big-ends at an angle to the vertical centre line of the rod, so as to produce a jet of oil from the hollow crankpin once every revolution. In some instances each connecting rod is drilled from the big-end to the small-end for lubrication of the gudgeon pin bearing; some of this oil passes through the hollow gudgeon pin to the cylinder walls.

Fig. 16 illustrates the lubrication system of a six-cylinder overhead camshaft engine, in which the camshaft is driven by a vertical shaft from the engine by means of helical gears at each end. The

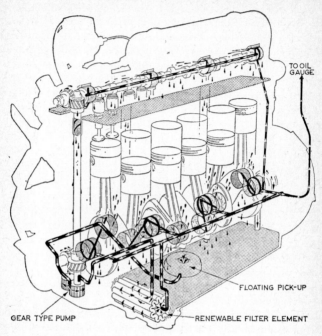

TO OIL GAUGE

FLOATING PICK-UP

GEAR TYPE PUMP

RENEWABLE FILTER ELEMENT

Fig. 16. Typical six-cylinder engine lubrication system
(overhead camshaft-operated valves). B.M.C.

lower end of the shaft is extended so as to drive the gear-wheel
type of oil pressure pump. The pump draws oil from the oil sump
at the bottom of the crankcase through a floating-type gauze filter,
and delivers the pressure oil through a drilled passage to the main
gallery, as shown by the white arrows, which lead first to an oil
filter and then upwards and horizontally to the oil gallery. Thus
only filtered oil is passed through the gallery and thence to each
of the crankshaft main bearings, of which there are four. The
crankshaft has drilled holes which lead the oil from the main to
the big-end bearings, when it escapes and splashes on to the
cylinder walls. The overhead camshaft is lubricated by oil taken
up the vertical passage, on the right, and after flowing through the

hollow camshaft, whence it lubricates each bearing, it returns to the oil sump by gravity, as indicated by the oil drops. The same method is used for the more common overhead *push-rod and rocker-arm valve system.*

Oil Pressure Failure Light. Most mass-produced car engines have a device for showing when the oil pressure is too low. It consists of a *green light* on the instrument panel which is actuated by a switch of the diaphragm type. When the oil pressure is too low – as when idling – the light is switched on, but as pressure builds up, the diaphragm is deflected so as to open the switch. Should the light show under normal operating conditions, the *engine should at once be stopped* and the cause of failure investigated (see page 52).

The Oil Gauge. This is fitted to the more expensive cars and is connected to the delivery side of the oil system, and its pipe is usually taken from the oil gallery or camshaft rear bearing supply (Fig. 16). It shows the oil pressure in the system at this place.

When an engine is started from cold the oil is more viscous, so that a higher pressure exists in the system before the oil warms up and circulates. When the engine is warm, but idling, a much lower value of the pressure will be registered. Thus in typical examples the initial, or cold oil pressures may range from 45 to 65 lb. per sq. inch, eventually falling to 30 to 40 lb. per sq. inch. Here it may be mentioned that the working oil pressures used in modern car engines range from about 45 to 65 lb. per sq. inch, according to the design.

When an engine is first started it should be run at a moderate to fast idling speed, in order to allow the oil to warm up and commence to circulate. It should not, however, be run too slowly or the oil will not be circulated and for this and another reason, cylinder corrosion or wear will occur. This early circulation of the oil is considered, by the writer, of greater importance than the possible initial risk of wear due to lack of oil on the cylinder walls.

The Oil Pressure Relief Valve. This is a spring-loaded ball valve on the oil pump delivery side – usually close to the pump – and is fitted to avoid excessive pressure being generated

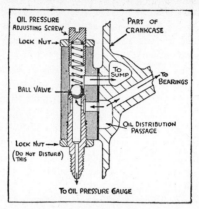

Fig. 17. Oil pressure release valve.

by the oil pump, as when running with thick, cold oils or by obstructions in the oil passages at high engine speeds.

The valve is arranged to lift at some predetermined pressure, when the surplus oil passing through the valve is returned to the sump without passing through the lubricating system.

The mechanic should always make a point of locating the oil relief valve. The manufacturer's handbook will usually indicate its position. In some cases it forms part of the oil pump unit; in other cases it is near to the oil filter on the pump delivery side. The valve spring in some designs can be varied in tension by means of a screw device so that in this manner *the oil pressure in the system can be regulated*. (Fig. 17.) If the spring is screwed down the oil pressure will be raised; if unscrewed it will be lowered. In all cases the pressure should be adjusted to the normal warm engine value recommended by the makers of the engine.

After long periods of running it is advisable to clean the relief valve by removing it from the engine and flushing it through with petrol or by reducing the spring tension and accelerating the engine for a few seconds in order to send a big flow of oil through the discharge outlet. The valve and its seating should be examined for wear. If found a new ball and reground seating are needed.

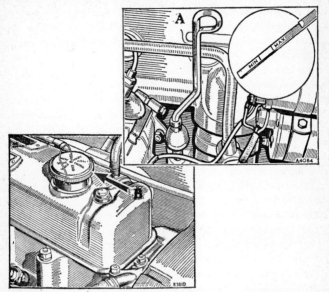

Fig. 18. Engine lubrication maintenance items (B.M.C.).

Engine Lubrication Items. Fig. 18 shows the engine lubrication items that require regular attention as previously explained.

The oil level in the sump is indicated by the dipstick shown at (*A*) and marked with lines as indicated in the upper right circle. The oil level should never be above the 'Max' or below the 'Min' marks. Before taking a reading make sure that the car is standing on level ground: any inclination to the horizontal can give a false reading. The engine should not have been running for above 15 minutes before taking a reading. Then remove the dipstick, wipe it and replace in the sump as far as it will go. Upon removal it will give the proper level reading.

The oil filler cap (*B*) on the overhead valve gear cover must be turned anti-clockwise to remove it: having a quick release action it is only turned a short amount.

It may be mentioned that with the 1,500 and 1,622 c.c. engines the amount of oil to raise the level from 'Min' to 'Max' is one pint.

Maintenance Notes. Since the life and efficiency of the engine depend upon the correct maintenance of the oiling system special attention should be given to the necessary items of regular attention.

The grade of oil used should be that recommended by the makers. The oil sump must always be maintained at the marked level by suitable replenishment. The capacity of the sump and oil filter is usually about 5 to 7 pints for a 1,000 c.c. engine; 7 to 9 pints for a 1,500 to 2,000 c.c. engine and 15 to 18 pints for a 3,500 to 4,000 c.c. engine. It is good advice to replenish with small amounts frequently, since the fresh oil has better lubrication properties than used oil.

At the end of the first 500 miles, when the car is new, drain out the oil whilst the engine is hot and replenish with fresh oil. Every 3,000 miles or so the oil in the crankcase should be changed.

If the compression is poor, there will be more dilution of the oil by the petrol vapour from the combustion chamber so that more frequent oil changing will be necessary.

Never attempt to wash out the sump with paraffin but only with flushing oil, unless the sump is removed from the engine for this purpose.

The oil strainer can be removed and cleaned with paraffin or petrol before replacing; this should be done each time the oil in the crankcase is changed.

The Oil Filter. In most modern car engines external oil-cleaning filters are fitted. These are of two patterns, namely, (1) That in which all of the engine oil is passed through the filter, as shown in Fig. 20, continuously; this is known as the *Full-flow filter*. (2) That, in which part of the oil is by-passed from the main supply to the oil gallery and is circulated through the oil filter; the latter is known as a *By-pass filter*; this type of filter has now been replaced by the full-flow one, since the latter gives a more thorough cleaning action.

The filtering elements include fabric, fabric and felt, felt, edge-type metal and impregnated paper; of these only the felt and paper element types are now used.

The filter shown in Fig. 19 has a felt element which gives very good cleaning action. Previously, multiple felt elements with fabric covers were employed and they could be cleaned every 2,000 to 3,000 miles; they had a useful full life of about 10,000 miles.

Modern felt filters are not intended to be cleaned, as they have a useful life of about 6,000 miles after which they should be removed and thrown away. Fig. 19 shows the type used on B.M.C. engines, in which the oil from the pump is delivered at the union (*A*), the filtered oil going direct from the filter bowl, internally to the oil gallery.

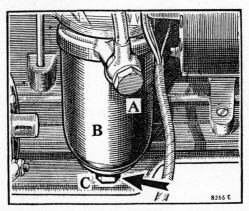

Fig. 19. The full-flow filter. *A* oil inlet. *B* filter casing. *C* cap nut. (Austin).

The filter is bolted on to the crankcase and has a casing, or bowl, *B* which can be removed by undoing the cap nut (*C*). Before a new felt element is fitted the bowl should be cleaned thoroughly and when replacing the bowl the cork or Neoprene rubber gasket should first be inspected and if faulty, replaced by a new one.

It may be mentioned that the fitting of a new element should only be done when the engine oil is changed at the same period. When draining out the old oil, with the engine 'hot', give the starting handle a few turns to help the draining action.

Paper Element Filters. These modern filters use a pleated paper element, the paper being of a novel kind impregnated

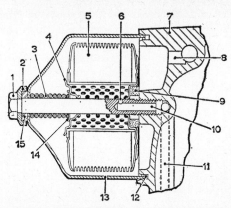

Fig. 20. The AC-Delco paper-element oil filter.
1 bowl securing bolt. 2 seal retaining collar. 3 filter element spring.
4 element retainer. 5 pleated paper element. 6 oil metering hole. 7 crankcase. 8 oil inlet from gallery. 9 element seal. 10 oil outlet. 11 oil return
passage. 12 sealing ring. 13 bowl. 14 spring seating washer. 15 sealing
washer.

with a special plastic material, which will stop dirt particles as
small as 0·0001 in. but allow a full flow of oil through the paper.
It does not, however, remove any detergents in the oil, or any
running compounds, such as colloidal graphite or molybdenum
disulphide.

Fig. 20 shows the AC-Delco paper element filter as used on
Vauxhall cars. It is attached directly to a machined face on the
crankcase and is secured to the latter by means of the central
bolt (1). It has a detachable casing sealed by two rubber washers
at (2) and (12). The filter elements cannot satisfactorily be cleaned
and so should be removed and scrapped every 6,000 miles.

Possible Causes of Lubrication Troubles. The following
are the principal possible causes of trouble in the oiling system,
with their suggested remedies:

1. *No oil pressure indicated on gauge when engine is running –*
   (*a*) No oil in engine sump.
   (*b*) Oil gauge pipe restricted or broken.
   (*c*) Oil regulator plunger or valve stuck.

(d) Weak or broken oil pressure regulator spring.

(e) Faulty indicator gauge.

(f) Oil pump not working.

2. *Low oil pressure indicated –*

  (a) Oil pressure regulator not operating correctly.

  (b) Leakage from pressure system. (This may be internal or external.)

  (c) Slack main or big-end bearings.

  (d) Oil relief valve spring pressure too weak.

3. *No oil passing to valve rockers –*

  (a) Restriction tube in crankcase to oil filter pipe choked.

Some indication of the working of the oil system can be obtained by examining the exhaust shortly after starting up the engine. If a thin smoke is observed this indicates that the engine is getting sufficient oil; after a time this smoke will disappear as the cylinders warm up.

Excessive Oil Consumption. The principal causes of excessive oil consumption are usually those associated with appreciable wear of the bearing surfaces of the engine, e.g. the cylinder walls, pistons and piston rings. In addition, oil leakage past the crankshaft end bearings – owing to worn felt washers or choked oil return passages – and the oil sump and other crankcase joints will result in higher oil consumption.

In cases of excessive oil consumption which are not traceable to the pistons and cylinders, the source of oil leakage can usually be ascertained by external visual inspection. Otherwise, it can often be found by placing a sheet of brown paper on the floor under the engine after it has been driven into the garage for the night – the engine being warm. An examination of the paper in the morning will reveal the location of any oil leakage.

One possible source of oil leakage is past the main crankshaft bearing into the clutch casing. This occurs when the felt oil retainer is worn, or the return pipe to the oil sump from the oil-thrower ring cavity is choked. Another occasional cause is a leaky main filter cover joint, due usually to a faulty washer.

The principal causes of heavy oil consumption and excessive wear in the case of the piston and cylinder unit are illustrated in Fig. 21, in which the effects of wear have been shown to an exaggerated scale. In addition to the causes thus illustrated mention should be made of the effect of oil leakage past the piston and to the backs of the piston rings where, owing to the high piston temperature the oil carbonizes and prevents the rings from contracting. If compound rings are used in such circumstances the gumming-up tendency is more serious than for plain rings, owing to the increased number of joints into which the oil can find its way.

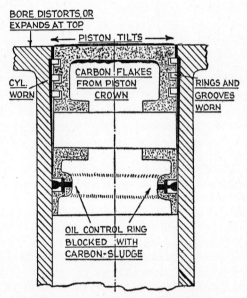

Fig. 21. Causes of excessive oil consumption.

Running-in New Engines. In the case of most makes of mass-produced engines it is left to the motorist to run the engines in during the first few hundred miles of the car's road service. Since the ultimate efficiency and life of an engine depend largely upon the manner in which it has been run-in, special precautions should be taken to ensure that the latter procedure is correctly executed.

Apart from maintaining the maximum engine revolutions below the value corresponding to a top-gear road speed of 35 to 45 m.p.h., it is a good expedient to employ a cylinder lubricating oil mixed with the petrol supply; usually about an egg-cupfull of a good mineral oil per gallon of petrol will suffice to lubricate the upper part of the cylinder barrels and the valve stems.

A well recommended procedure is to use *a colloidal graphite*, such as Acheson's, in the main lubricating oil supply. In this case the graphite is so fine that it readily diffuses in the lubricating oil. Tests have shown that such a lubricant reduces the coefficient of friction by about 15 per cent and produces on the various bearing surfaces a kind of graphoid surface, such that even should the oil film be broken, owing to bad treatment of the engine, the bearing will continue to run without undue overheating until the oil-film is once again restored.

After a new engine has done about 500 miles, as previously stated, the oil sump should be drained and new lubricant added. The maximum designed speed of the engine should gradually be worked up to, after an engine has done 1,500 to 2,000 miles.

The usual proportions for graphited oil are one pint of colloidal graphite solution to each gallon of lubricating oil in the sump. At the conclusion of the running-in period about half a pint per gallon may be used whenever the sump is drained and re-filled.

For upper cylinder lubrication half an ounce of colloidal graphite per two gallons of petrol should be used.

Molybdenum disulphide is a more recent low friction running-in additive to the engine oil, giving excellent lubricating properties. It consists of particles so fine that each is less than 1/1000 mm. When added to engine oil the compound adheres to the bearing and sliding surfaces, giving a fine polished surface. It does not have any corrosive action and has been shown to reduce or prevent carbon deposits on the piston crown.

The Clutch. Modern clutches are of the dry plate type requiring no lubrication except for the withdrawal thrust washer, if of the ball race type, the graphite type of thrust washer now used requires no lubrication.

In the case of earlier lubricated type clutch plates it is arranged for the necessary oil supply to be obtained automatically from the crank chamber.

The only other item of clutch mechanism lubrication is that of the clutch pedal shaft bearings which should be oiled or greased – according to the type – once every 2,000 miles or so.

An oil or grease nipple will usually be found on the clutch pedal boss; a few shots with the lubrication gun should be given to this and also the foot brake pedal bearing nipple. Further, all pivotal points, i.e. where there are pins and their bearings, should be lubricated with a few drops of engine or graphited oil.

Hydraulically-operated Clutch. Many recent cars dispense with the usual mechanism for operating the clutch, using instead an hydraulic method, the principle of which is shown in Fig. 22. In this case, foot pressure on the brake pedal operates a piston causing hydraulic pressure to be transmitted through an hydraulic hose to another cylinder having a piston which actuates one end of the clutch-operating lever. This method, while avoiding mechanical levers, pins, bearings, etc. enables a powerful pressure to be exerted on the clutch lever. It is also advantageous for the modern flexibly-mounted engine.

The only items of regular maintenance are (1) to maintain the hydraulic fluid reservoir at the correct fluid level, by occasional topping up of the liquid and, (2) to adjust the clutch clearance as on page 200. (3) lubricate the bearings of the levers.

The Gearbox. Modern gearboxes are lubricated with either engine oil or a heavier grade known as transmission oil. Thus, in some cases, if the double summer grade of oil is used in the engine the triple grade would be used in the gearbox. In every case, however, the manufacturer's recommended oil should be used.

The usual gearbox capacity is from about $1\frac{3}{4}$ to $4\frac{1}{2}$ pints, according to the size of gearbox.

As in the case of the engine, the lubricant should be drained out after about the first 500 miles of running, and washed out with flushing oil, and thereafter every 6,000 miles. The draining should be done after a run when the lubricant is warm; for the thicker lubricants used in older gearboxes it may be necessary to warm judiciously the bottom with an oil or blow lamp.

It is important to maintain the correct level of lubricant, for if this is too low, noise and increased wear result; if too high, unnecessary churning occurs, and power is thereby lost – as tests have shown very conclusively. Further, if engine oil is used, an excess is apt to leak out of the main shaft bearings and into the clutch or along the propeller shaft.

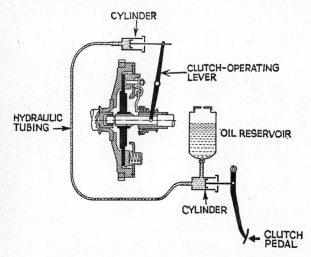

Fig. 22. Hydraulic-operation clutch system.

There is always a plug, or dipper-rod in the side of the gearbox to indicate the proper level. In the former case the plug is un-screwed, and lubricant (warmed, if it is thick), is poured into the filling cavity until it just flows out of the plug hole; the level is then correct.

In a typical instance, the Morris Minor, the filler plug and dipstick are located beneath a cover plate, as shown in Fig. 23; this plate is located by a hexagon nut under the front of the gearbox rubber cover.

The drain plug (Fig. 24) is accessible from below and before it is replaced, after draining out the lubricant, its hollow centre should be cleaned of any sediment.

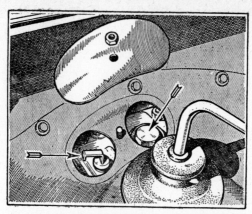

Fig. 23. Morris Minor gearbox lubrication
dipstick and filler plug.

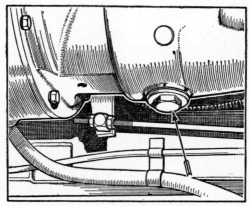

Fig. 24. The gearbox drain plug.

It is recommended that the gearbox should be drained after the first 500 miles and, thereafter, at 6,000 mile intervals. The capacity of the gearbox is $1\frac{1}{2}$ pints. The lubricant level should be checked at regular intervals, namely 500 miles intervals, to the 'Full' mark on the dipstick.

If a Morris gearbox is filled above the recommended level the surplus oil may get into the clutch casing and *cause clutch slip*.

The Universal Joints. In the popular designs of car the propeller shaft has two metal universal joints with enclosed plain or needle bearings. The front end of the shaft is splined and slides within a splined hole in the front coupling. The bearing

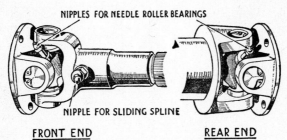

NIPPLES FOR NEEDLE ROLLER BEARINGS

NIPPLE FOR SLIDING SPLINE

FRONT END   REAR END

Fig. 25. Propeller shaft and universal joints (Sunbeam).

and splines are lubricated with an oil or grease gun through nipples, of which there are three, namely, two for the universal joint bearings and one for the splines (Fig. 25). These bearings should be lubricated every 1,000 to 2,000 miles in the case of needle bearings. Some car manufacturers recommend lubrication attention every 500 miles for plain bearings.

The nipples should be wiped clean before applying the oil or grease gun. Unless these usually 'hidden' nipples are lubricated at the stated intervals, wear will occur in the bearings and splines, with the result of backlash and noisy operation, accompanied by vibration effects.

As mentioned earlier, there are now new types of universal joints which are lubricated with special greases and will operate for 30,000 miles without any further attention.

The Back Axle. The final drive and differential gears operate in a casing which is filled to a given level, that is indicated by a *level plug* (Fig. 26) or *dipstick*, with a special transmission oil, recommended by the manufacturers. The oil should be re-plenished every 2,000 to 3,000 miles, taking care not to 'overfill',

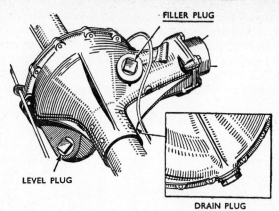

Fig. 26. Lubrication of the back axle. The oil is poured
in to the level of the 'level plug'.

otherwise the excess oil may leak out along the axles past the oil
seals and into the brake drums. Every 6,000 miles the rear axle
casing should be drained, whilst the oil is warm, and refilled.
When hypoid final drives are employed a special 'Hypoid' grade
of oil is recommended. The axle casing capacity is usually from
$1\frac{1}{2}$ to $2\frac{1}{2}$ pints.

The Steering Gear. The principal items of lubrication are
the steering column head bearing, steering gearbox, drop arm and
connecting rod bearings and wheel pivot pins.

In most cases, grease-gun lubrication is employed for all of
these parts, except the steering column, where oil is used. The
earlier type and some modern steering gearboxes are filled to the
level of the filler plug hole A (Fig. 27) with lubricant – usually
engine oil, or a heavier grade recommended by the car manufacturers. It was necessary to lubricate the steering pivot pin
bearings every 1,000 miles or so, and the steering gearbox about
twice every season of running, or every 5,000 miles or so.

In modern steering systems employed with independent front
springing there are more lubrication points than in the rigid front
axle systems. In this connection a central second fixture, known
as the 'Steering Transfer Box' (Fig. 28) is often employed.
This is provided with a grease nipple, as shown by the arrow, in

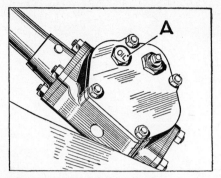

Fig. 27. Oil filler plug on steering gearbox.

Fig. 28; it should be lubricated every 1,000 miles with a soft plain or graphite grease.

The various grease nipples on the offside half of the Wolseley car steering system are shown in Fig. 29. The steering transfer

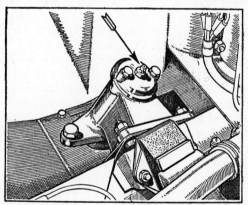

Fig. 28. The steering transfer box.

box is shown above. The grease nipples at the upper and lower ends of the steering swivel (or king) pin of the same car require grease gun lubrication every 1,000 miles.

The independent front wheel suspension system of the Armstrong-Siddeley Sapphire car which carried the steering swivel

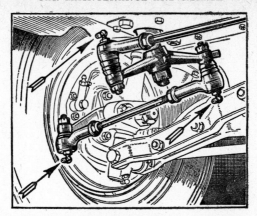

Fig. 29. Location of grease nipples on tie and
track rod ball joints.

pins is partly shown in Fig. 30. Oil nipples, shown at *A* require
oil gun application at intervals of about 1,000–1,500 miles. Fig.
30 shows also the air bleed valve *B* for the front hydraulic brake
system; this valve is referred to again, in Chapter 9.

In the earlier independent front suspension systems, every
working bearing had to be provided with a grease nipple; a
typical system, i.e. the Austin early design, had no less than 14
nipples. Modern systems, by the use of rubber-metal bushes,
nylon and steel cup-and-socket joints, either eliminate all such
nipples or reduce these to about 2 to 4, for the whole front
suspension. The manufacturers' lubrication charts should now
always be consulted; also, the owners' manuals.

The Springs. There were two types of leaf spring in common
use, namely, the open and the enclosed ones. In the former case,
the leaf blades are unprotected, whilst in the latter instance there
was a leather, or a metal casing around the springs. Expose
type springs should be lubricated every season, by jacking the car
up, placing the jack under the frame, *not the axle*, so as to let the
wheels hang and the springs relax their compression. The individual blades should be forced open with a screwdriver or special
tool such as the Terry spring opener (Fig. 31) supplied for the

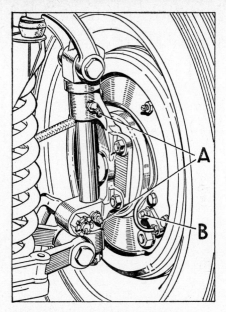

Fig. 30. Steering swivel pin lubrication nipples. (*A*) and hydraulic brake air bleed. (*B*).

purpose, and thick graphite grease forced in. In the case of enclosed springs frequent application of the grease-gun will keep the blades well lubricated.

In the case of cars that have been in service for several seasons, it is a good thing to remove the springs bodily and to clean the leaves separately before greasing and re-assembling; alternatively, 'penetrating oil' should be sprayed between the spring leaves.

The spring shackles and spring ends should be examined in order to ascertain whether the bearings are of the rubber bush or metal bush type; the former type requires no lubrication but, if the latter, grease nipples will be found. A medium-body graphite grease is used for metal bearings, the grease gun being used at intervals of about 1,000 miles.

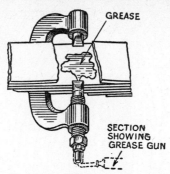

Fig. 31. Leaf spring opening and
lubricating tool.

The Brakes. In regard to the lubrication of the brakes, it should be mentioned that the working joints of the brake mechanism require occasional cleaning and oiling. The dirt should be brushed off, the bearing surfaces cleaned with paraffin, and a heavy grade of oil – or a grease – applied. Once a season in the case of internal-type brakes, take the road wheels off and examine and lubricate the fulcrum bearings of the brake shoes, the brake operating cams and other bearings. Do not allow any lubricant to get on the brake linings during this operation, or the brakes will lose their efficiency.

When brake cables are used it is important to grease the cables where they work in the outer casings; this reduces the braking effort and at the same time keeps out moisture.

Miscellaneous Items of Lubrication. There are several working parts of more or less minor importance which should occasionally be lubricated. For example, the starting motor teeth and flywheel rim teeth. Use a medium consistency grease, and take care not to get any on the Bendix pinion worm; the latter will fail to operate if there is any grease on its worm and nut. The distributor shaft bearings of the coil-ignition system, dynamo and starting motor bearings require a drop or two of machine oil every 1,000 miles or so. The front wheel hub bearings should be kept filled with grease; this operation is necessary about once every season, or every 3,000–5,000 miles.

The carburettor and ignition control lever joints should be given a spot of oil occasionally to assist their easy working.

The car's door hinges should be oiled periodically and the door wedge stops given a light smear with grease. The door lock and bonnet catches should also be oiled so as to work freely. The rear boot cover hinges also should not be overlooked.

In general, all working joints or sliding parts of the body and chassis should be lubricated to ensure smooth operation and minimize wear and noise.

Lubrication Charts. Car manufacturers supply clear lubrication charts with instructions printed thereon of the items requiring periodical lubrication attention, and the kind of lubricant recommended for each part. The mileage intervals at which lubrication attention should be given are also stated on the chart.

An example of such a chart, which also shows the chief items of maintenance attention, is given in Fig. 1. Other examples are given in Figs. 13 and 14.

CHAPTER 3

THE ENGINE*

APART from the matter of regular lubrication, the engine of a car requires periodic examination and adjustment. After it has been in service for some appreciable time, it will undoubtedly require a thorough overhaul. If the motor owner is a good mechanic, he can sometimes carry this out himself without recourse to the local garage or service station.

We shall deal first with the adjustments and general items of attention which can readily be undertaken by the skilled owner-driver, and shall then proceed with the more difficult repairs. Before, however, dealing with the subject of adjustments and repairs, it may be as well to indicate when these items become necessary.

When Does the Engine Require Attention? The recent-comer to motoring is frequently perplexed in the matter of when to attend to certain engine adjustments; ignorance of the essential facts may occasion undue wear and tear and general loss of power. Assuming that the car is purchased new, and that its lubrication has been correctly maintained in the manner outlined in the preceding chapter, it can be taken as general practice to decarbonize the engine after 5,000 to 10,000 miles. In the case of some new cars it is recommended that their engines should be decarbonized after the first 1,000 to 1,500 miles; thereafter at 5,000 miles intervals. Some engines, with well-fitting pistons and efficient oiling systems, may not require decarbonizing until 10,000 miles; others with 'oily' cylinders may require attention every 5,000 miles or sometimes less. Even with two cars of the same make there is often a marked divergence in this respect depending on how they are operated.

Recent Car Engine Decarbonizing Periods. Due to improved design and materials, e.g., alloy-iron cylinders, chrome-

* See also Chapter 15, 'Diagnosing Engine Troubles Easily'.

plated piston rings, etc. and to better cylinder lubrication control, modern engines will operate efficiently over longer intervals before decarbonizing becomes necessary. A further reason for these extended intervals is that modern engine oils contain detergents which prevent carbon formation, by the addition of chemical additives. The modern higher octane fuels also include carbon-preventing additives. For these reasons, engines will run satisfactorily without decarbonizing for periods in excess of 15,000 miles, but the extremely long periods claimed by some car users are not recommended, since periodic inspection of the valves, valve guides and seatings is not then carried out.

It is not difficult to ascertain when the engine requires de-carbonizing, for a badly carbonized engine will labour and 'pink' when the power is applied suddenly or when climbing a hill in top gear. It will 'knock' much earlier than when clean, and tend to be sluggish and to overheat.

After several decarbonizings, and valve grindings, it will usually be necessary to attend to the small- and big-end bearings, main bearings and piston rings; these operations are seldom necessary under 30,000 to 35,000 miles with modern engines. After 35,000 to 45,000 miles one begins to consider the advisability of having the cylinders rebored, new pistons and valves fitted, the crankshaft reground, big-end and main bearings replaced and new small-end bushes and gudgeon pins.

When a car engine *starts* to lose power, knocks more frequently on hills and requires earlier gear change it is usually a sign that it requires the carbon removed from the cylinder and piston heads and the valves re-grinding and adjusting.

A reliable indication of a worn engine is that of *loss of compression*. This can readily be tested by means of the starting handle when the engine is warm. A low compression or failure to hold compression are signs of worn pistons, rings or cylinders, if the valves and their seatings are in good order.

Noisier operation of the engine, assuming the tappet clearances are correct, is another symptom of wear. If, after coasting downhill, with the transmission turning the engine, i.e. the car in gear, the engine is accelerated, much blue smoke is emitted from the exhaust, this shows that the cylinders and pistons are worn, thus allowing oil to get past into the combustion chamber.

Excessive oil consumption is another indication of cylinder and piston wear.

Typical Engine Example. The principal items of occasional or routine attention are illustrated in Fig. 32 which shows the

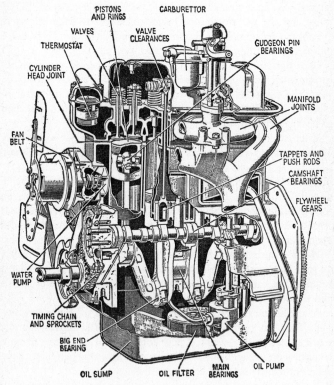

Fig. 32. The Austin A40 engine.

Austin A40 engine in part section. In addition to the components shown, the ignition system engine connected units, namely, the distributor camshaft and the sparking plugs – not given in Fig. 32

– will require routine attention. The various joints with their gaskets and tightening nuts must also be included in engine maintenance items.

Detecting Worn Bearings. If one has learned to recognize the 'knock' due to excessive carbon in the cylinder heads, it will not be difficult to test for bearing knocks.

To distinguish between bearing and ignition knocks, retard the ignition, on the distributor adjustment, when the latter noise will cease.

Loose Big-end Bearings. The effect of loose connecting rod big-end bearings is that of a metallic rattle which is usually noticeable at top gear speeds of 25 to 35 m.p.h. To confirm this fault put the gear lever into neutral and speed up the engine to about one-half of its maximum road speed revolutions per minute when the noise will increase.

Loose Small-end Bearings. These usually cause a hollow metallic knocking sound which is more noticeable at low than high speeds and is not entirely eliminated when the sparking plug of the suspected cylinder is short-circuited.

To find in which cylinder a loose or worn bearing is located, switch off each cylinder ignition in turn by shorting its sparking plug and listen with a rod held against the cylinder wall, or with a proper stethoscope sold for the purpose (Fig. 33). Any bearing play can at once be recognized by the heavy knock then heard, and located in this manner.

Minor Items of Attention. These include *Adjusting Valve Stem Clearance, Sparking Plug Points,* and *Contact Breaker Contacts Clearances, Cleaning Petrol and Oil Filters, Carburettor Float Chamber,* and *Checking of Cylinder Nuts, Fuel and Oil Pipe Unions, etc.* We shall describe the more important operations in turn.

Valve Adjustment. In the case of new engines or those just decarbonized it is very important to have the exact amount of clearance, or play, between the tappet (or rocker arm – in the case of overhead type valves) and the end of the valve stem. If this distance is too great, not only will the valve operate noisily, but there will be a loss of engine power due to insufficient valve lift and incorrect timing; overheating may be caused, also. If too small a clearance is allowed the valve may not 'seat' properly and loss of compression and valve burning will occur.

Valve Clearances. In all cases the engine manufacturer's valve stem clearances should be used, but if these are not available in the case *of early models* still in service it may be stated that for side-valve engines inlet valve clearances were usually 0·003 to

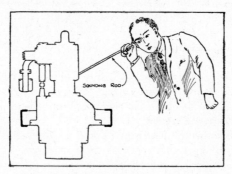

Fig. 33. Method of detecting worn bearings.

0·004 in. and exhaust clearances, 0·004 to 0·006 in. For push-rod and rocker type overhead valves inlet clearances were 0·004 to 0·005 in. and exhaust clearances, 0·005 to 0·006 in. Camshaft engines used rather smaller clearances, namely, 0·003 to 0·004 in. for both inlet and exhaust valves.

In order to avoid the necessity for frequent adjustment of the earlier type valve clearances, new designs of valve lifting cams were later adopted in practically all engines, to allow greater clearances to be used, without additional valve noise or power loss.

For modern engines of the overhead type valve clearances range from 0·010 in. to 0·018 in., the most widely used clearances being 0·013 in. to 0·015 in. With these clearances it is unnecessary to adjust the valves, except after relatively long running periods, e.g., every 5,000 miles or so. When using manufacturer's valve clearances, make certain that these refer to the engine in the hot or cold state, since there may be a difference of 0·001 to 0·003 in. between the two values.

The valve tappet clearance is tested with a thin metal strip of the correct thickness, inserted between the valve and its tappet or rocker arm. The 'feeler' gauge arranged in steel strips of multiples of one-thousandth of an inch thick, as used by engineers, is the best device for this purpose. (Fig. 34.)

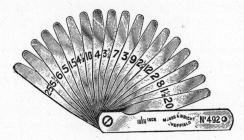

Fig. 34. Feeler gauge set, to measure in half-thousandths inch (Moore and Wright).

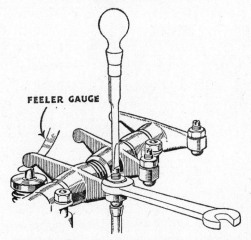

Fig. 35. Method of adjusting valve stem clearance of overhead valve engine.

Adjusting Overhead Camshaft Clearances.

The method of adjusting the valve stem clearance varies with different designs.

In some cases, where the cams operate the valves through rocker arms the same method of adjustment of the clearances as for push-rod and rocker-arm overhead valves is often used, namely, a screw with locknut (Fig. 35).

In the earlier Wolseley overhead camshaft engines the valve clearances were adjusted by means of eccentric bushes of the rocker shaft; after partial rotation, these bushes were locked by means of nuts.

The method used for the Morris Six and later Wolseley engines is illustrated in Fig. 36. In these, the inlet and exhaust valves have clearances of 0·015 in., when hot. A special tool was provided to depress the valve spring cap and turn the adjuster screw by means of a ring or 'C' spanner. The setting is automatically locked

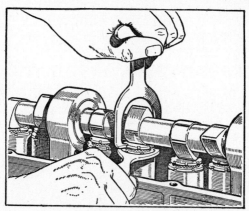

Fig. 36. Method of adjusting the Morris Six and Wolseley engine valve clearances.

on releasing the valve spring cap. If adjusted cold, an extra 0·001 in. must be allowed on the stated clearance values.

The more recent B.M.C. overhead valve engines now employ push rods and rocker arm mechanism for their overhead valves.

Adjusting Sparking Plug Points. Although the sparking plugs seldom give any trouble, it is advisable periodically to examine these. Usually after a few thousand miles it will be found that the internal insulation is coated with carbon, and the gap between the points has increased appreciably due to the burning away of the metal. The plugs should be immersed in petrol and the insulation cleaned with a thin piece of hard wood or brass until all carbon has disappeared.

The distance between the gap of a normal sparking plug was 0·016 to 0·018 in. for the earlier magneto ignition, and 0·018 to 0·025 in. for battery and coil ignition, for the average British engine. (See also page 412.)

A feeler gauge is used for checking the plug gap and in this connection the manufacturers supply a gauge of the correct thickness. The tool shown in Fig. 310 on page 412 enables the plug side wire electrode to be adjusted to give the correct gap.

Cylinder Decarbonizing. Owing to the combustion process, which involves the development of very high temperatures within the cylinder, part of the oil which gets past the piston is burnt, leaving a hard carbon deposit on all surfaces, other than the working ones in the space above the piston. When the petrol-air mixture is over-rich carbon is also formed. In addition if efficient air cleaners were not fitted, the siliceous matter drawn in with the air from the carburettor would form a deposit. If, however, the piston and its rings are a bad fit, more oil will get past and carbon will form more readily; the use of an inferior quality oil will also cause more rapid carbonizing.

The indications as to when decarbonizing an engine are necessary are given on page 67.

Since all modern engines are of the overhead-valve type there is no need to consider the solid-head units previously used with side-valve engines; these have been dealt with in earlier editions of this book.

Removing the Cylinder Head. There are two main designs of overhead-valve engines, namely the camshaft and the push-rod and rocker-arm types.

Camshaft Engines. These are the more difficult to deal with, since it is necessary to disconnect the engine drive to the camshaft. If a gear drive is used, the removal of the head will generally mean upsetting the valve timing, so that beforehand the gears should be examined for timing marks near the teeth crests and roots, as shown in Fig. 37. The dots or lines on the marked teeth should be reassembled in line, as shown. Once the engine drive has been disconnected the head can be removed. If the camshaft is chain-driven, then it is necessary to examine the chain and sprocket teeth, before taking the chain off, for bright links and tooth marks.

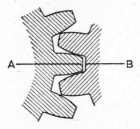

Fig. 37. Typical timing marks on gear wheels, by two lines A and B.

Push-rod and Rocker-arm Overhead Valve Engines. The heads of such engines are relatively simple to remove. To illustrate the method reference should be made to Figs. 38 and 39, in which the head is shown at H and the rocker shaft cover at S

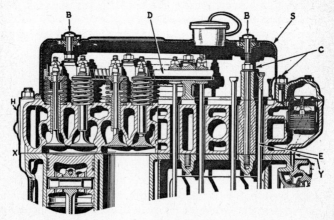

Fig. 38. Sectional view of four-cylinder engine, showing upper part of cylinder block and the complete cylinder head. The joint is shown at XY.

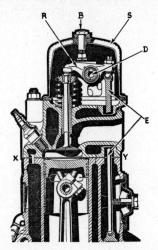

Fig. 39. Side sectional view of engine shown in Fig. 38.

First drain the cooling system by opening the tap at the bottom of the radiator and one on the cylinder jacket. Then take off the carburettor, inlet and exhaust manifolds and disconnect the sparking plug H.T. leads. The fuel pipe to the carburettor should first be disconnected and also the vacuum control pipe to the inlet manifold. When all connections from outside have been disconnected undo the screws (*B*) which hold the overhead casing (*S*) in place and take it off. This will expose the overhead valve operating parts and the rest of the cylinder head holding-down nuts, such as those shown at *C*. There is no need to remove either the rocker shaft (*D*) or the rocker arms (*R*). The push rods, (*E*), however, should be taken out. Having next removed the head holding-down nuts, unscrewing each a little at a time and in the same order as that shown in the example, on page 40, the head should be lifted. If it proves stubborn, first attempt to rock it from one end and then the other; otherwise give the sides some sharp blows with a wooden mallet or rawhide or rubber hammer. Sometimes, if the engine starting handle is turned the compression in the cylinders will help break the joint shown at *XY*.

On no account should a wedge or screwdriver blade be inserted into the joint to break it.

After Removal of the Head. Having removed the cylinder head it can be taken to a bench and the carbon scraped off with a screwdriver or special scraping tool. A stout wire brush however, is the best means, and if one can rotate this by means of a drilling

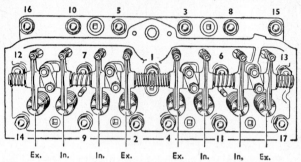

Fig. 40. Showing typical example for order of unscrewing and also tightening the cylinder head nuts on overhead valve engine.

machine spindle or electric motor (Fig. 41) the work of cleaning can be greatly facilitated. Care must be exercised when scraping off the carbon to avoid scratching or injuring the machined surface of the joint. Always plug up the water jacket holes in the cylinder top with paper or rag before decarbonizing, to keep the carbon particles out.

In a similar manner the valve-heads and piston tops can be cleaned of their carbon deposit. Each piston should be brought to its top centre position for cleaning, and as each piston, valve and cylinder top are cleaned the top of the cylinder barrel should be covered with a cloth to keep carbon particles out; a ring of grease on the piston top is another alternative.

In the case of four- and six-cylinder engines two pistons are always on top centre together and can therefore be cleaned at the same time. When decarbonizing do not forget to scrape out the carbon from inside the valve ports and on the outside of the valve guides and exhaust ports. Further, the valve guides should be cleaned with a suitable small cylindrical brush, using paraffin.

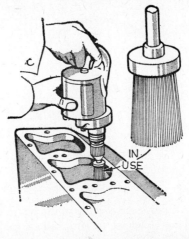

Fig. 41. Using a wire brush rotated by portable electric motor to remove carbon from cylinder head.

Piston Top Ring of Carbon. In order to prevent oil flow past the top land of the piston after decarbonizing it has been recommended by certain car manufacturers that a ring of carbon should be left on the top of the piston, i.e. about $\frac{1}{8}$ inch around the edge; the rest of the carbon should be scraped off the piston head. (Fig. 42.) A good plan is to use an old piston ring clamped or placed on the piston head as a guide, when scraping away the rest of the carbon.

Useful Hints on Dismantling an Engine.

(1) As you take off each component, e.g. the carburettor, inlet and exhaust manifolds, replace the nuts and washers on their respective studs or bolts; in the latter case put the bolts in their flanges and screw their nuts on. This will save a lot of trouble when reassembling.

(2) Keep some wooden boxes handy in which to put the different components.

(3) Always clean all the parts with paraffin or detergent solution, ease the nuts on their threads if stiff, and hang up all joints and gaskets on a convenient nail on the wall.

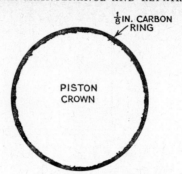

Fig. 42. Leaving a ring of carbon
on piston crown.

(4) Always mark with a chisel cut or centre punch dots the flanges
of parts bolted together to ensure their going back in the
correct position before dismantling.

(5) See that the piston crowns and valve heads are numbered
if these items have to be removed. It is essential to replace
each piston and valve in its original position.

(6) Remove any burrs from machined surfaces before replacing.

(7) Run the nuts up and down the cylinder head studs, before
replacing the head, to ensure that they are free.

(8) Protect the hands and finger-nails by smearing with yellow
soap (and filling the nails with same); certain antiseptic
preparations of a soapy nature, are excellent for this purpose.

The Valves. It is always advisable, when the cylinder head
is removed, to examine the valves. To remove a valve its spring
should be compressed, using the tool recommended by the
manufacturers or one of those illustrated in Figs. 44, 46 and 47.
Fig. 44(A) shows a powerful leverage spring compressor that
ensures parallel movement of the upper member which is located
against the valve head; the lower fork is placed under the valve
collar. The tool shown at (B) is of the screw-down type. Tools
on the principles of (A) and (B) can be used, also, for side valve
spring compression.

The Terry tool (C), is for side-valve engines, the two slotted
jaws being separated by the screw device. The same tool can be

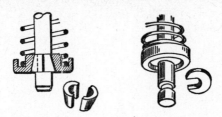

Fig. 43. Two types of valve stem securing
devices. (A) modern split cones. (B) earlier slotted cotter.

used to compress the valve spring between its jaws, for replacing
the spring when re-assembling the valve assembly. When the
spring is compressed, the valve being on its seating, the cotter
or cone can be withdrawn with a pair of pliers and the spring
released. The valve can then usually be lifted out by hand;
otherwise by rotating the engine crankshaft the valve will automatically be lifted up sufficiently to pull out; the valve spring and
spring collar can then be removed.

A typical example of a modern overhead valve method of
removal is that of the Austin engines, shown in Fig. 46. A special
cam-operated device on the spring compressor tool (T), pulls the
valve coils together thus exposing the valve stem end. The split
cone cotters (C) are located by a circlip (S) which must first be removed. Having taken out the split cotters the tension on the valve
spring is released, so that valve collar, spring and valve can then
be removed.

Typical Modern Valve Assembly. Fig. 45 shows the type
of valve used in B.M.C. engines. At the top are depicted the split
cones or collets and the retaining circlip spring which slips over
the collets when in position in the valve stem groove (3). An
interesting feature is the fitting of an oil seal to prevent oil leaking
down the valve stem into the guide and also to stop any air leaks
when the valve guides become worn.

Re-facing the Valves. It is usually necessary, when decarbonizing, to recondition the valves, for after a few thousand
miles of running the heads of the valves become carbonized, the
stems dirty – due to burnt oil and carbon – and what is perhaps

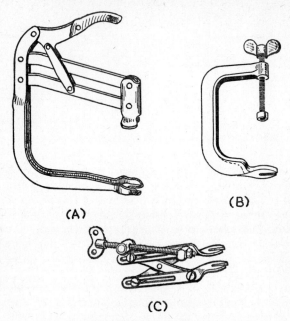

Fig. 44. Typical valve spring compressing tools.

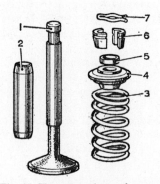

Fig. 45. Typical modern valve parts.
1 valve. 2 valve guide. 3 spring. 4 spring cap. 5 oil seal.
6 collets (split). 7 circlip.

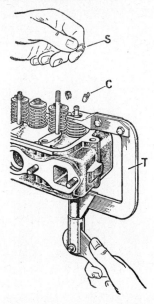

Fig. 46. Removing valve on
Austin overhead valve engine.

most important, the conical face of the valve, which makes the
gas-tight joint, may become scored or pitted. This defective
surface must be trued up, otherwise gas will leak past during the
compression and explosion strokes. The simplest method of
re-facing of valves not badly pitted is to smear the conical surface
of each valve, in turn, with a mixture of fine carborundum powder
and vaseline, or engine oil, replace the valve in position and grind
it backwards and forwards on its seating, occasionally lifting it
and re-smearing the grinding compound over the seating or face.
The valve grinding compounds sold by motor firms in coarse and
fine grades are most suitable for this operation; these mixtures
consist of carborundum powder and vaseline or petroleum jelly;
the coarse grade should be used first.

The head of the valve is usually slotted to enable a screwdriver
to be used for valve-grinding purposes. This is often a tiring job,

however, and it will greatly simplify operations if a hand-drill or brace, fitted with a bit, having a screwdriver head, be used. If a light compression spring is placed under the valve head this will

Fig. 47. A useful tool for removing overhead valve springs.

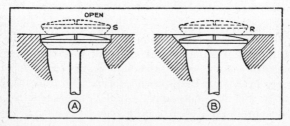

Fig. 48. Curing effect of pocketed valve *A* by removing surplus metal on seating, as shown at *B*. Dotted diagrams indicate valve lifted.

be found very useful in lifting the valve during grinding operations. Many modern engines have plain valve heads, so that a rubber-suction cup type of valve grinding tool must be used (see Figs. 56 and 57).

When grinding a valve, it is important to give the valve a reciprocating, or rocking, but not a continuous rotary movement; the latter often causes circular scratches or scores. After each one or two minutes of grinding, remove the valve, wipe off the compound with a paraffin-soaked rag, and examine the face.

Fig. 49. The Terry tool, used for holding over-head valves for grinding purposes.

When quite bright and free from black specks or pittings, wipe the remaining compound from valve seating (in cylinder), and finish off with the grinding with the finer abrasive powder or compound. In an emergency ordinary knife powder will be found to answer quite well. Finally, with paraffin or petrol, clean every trace of grinding material from the valve seat and port; also from the valve. Then replace the valve (with its spring, cotter, and collar) on its seating so that no grit can get between the surfaces. In the case of badly pitted or burnt valves, it is advisable to take a skim off the face, in a lathe, taking care to set the lathe slide rest at the correct angle; this angle is 30° in some cases and 45° in others.

Special valve-facing tools of the tool-cutter or serrated cone type are now available for those who have to deal with numbers of valves; Fig. 51 shows a typical tool.

If, on examining the stem of a valve removed after a long period of running it is found to be a slack fit in its guide, a new valve and possibly also a valve guide (Fig. 63) is indicated.

Valve Grinding Machines. The methods of grinding or refacing valves which have been described in the previous paragraphs are satisfactory where only a limited number has to be dealt with but are apt to prove too slow, and therefore expensive for motor garage purposes where a relatively large number of valves is concerned.

It is therefore the practice either to reface the valves in a lathe fitted with a swivelling-pattern grinding wheel or to use a special valve grinding machine, such as the V. L. Churchill one.

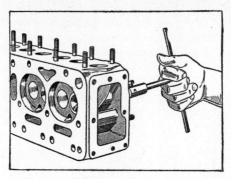

Fig. 50. Tool used for grinding overhead
valve engine.

For grinding the faces of valves in the lathe it is necessary to employ a small grinding wheel driven by an electric motor of $\frac{1}{8}$ to $\frac{1}{4}$ h.p., mounted in place of the tool box on the lathe saddle traverse unit, as shown in Fig. 52. Usually, the unit in question, which normally contains the slide rest, has a swivelling device

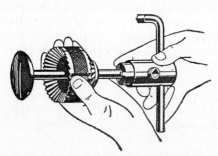

Fig. 51. A useful valve-facing tool (The J.S.).

with a scale graduated in degrees so that the grinding wheel can be set to the known valve angle; alternatively, it can be set by mounting a new valve in the lathe collet and aligning the wheel to the valve face angle.

When refacing a valve in this manner the valve should be rotated slowly in the same direction as the grinding wheel (Fig. 53).

The grinding wheel speed should be between 3,000 and 5,000

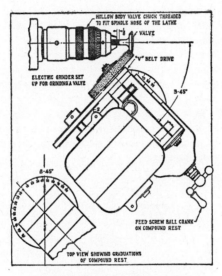

Fig. 52. Method of truing valve face with grinding wheel in the lathe.

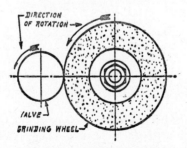

Fig. 53. Direction of rotation of valve and grinding wheel.

feet per minute so that for the mean speed of 4,000 feet per minute a 6 inch diameter wheel would revolve at 2,540 r.p.m.; a 3 inch wheel at 5,080 r.p.m., and so on. The valve it-self should rotate at a relatively low speed, namely, from 45 to 60 r.p.m.

The valve should be tested for a bent stem before placing in the collet as shown in Fig. 55. The grinding cut should be just sufficient to clean the valve face.

Fig 54 illustrates a valve grinding machine which operates on the same principle as that of the lathe previously described. The valve is held by its stem in a collet the bearings for the spindle of the latter being mounted in a member that can be rotated about a vertical axis so as to alter the relative angle between the grinding wheel and collet axis. The grinding wheel is driven from a motor below by belt and pulleys and the collet spindle from the same motor by a reduction gear.

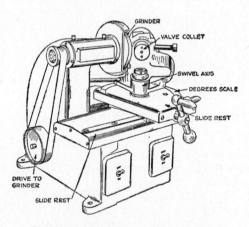

Fig. 54. Typical valve grinding machine.

Apart from its use in grinding valves of different face angles this machine can also deal with valve-seating and milling cutters of different angular patterns and for ordinary light grinding work; it will also grind the ends of valve stems.

Testing Valve Stems for Straightness. It is not an uncommon experience for valve stems to become *slightly bent* during their removal from the cylinder. All valves should therefore be tested for this possible defect by means of a pair of equal V-blocks, placed upon a face-plate. A scribing block – or better still a dial gauge reading in thousandths of an inch – should be used to test the valve stem as the latter is rotated in the V-blocks (Fig. 55).

A bent valve stem can be straightened by supporting it in V-blocks on either side of the bend and applying pressure to the bent portion with the ram or plunger of a hand press. A certain amount of skill is necessary, and unless the stem is brought to within about 0·001 to 0·0015 in. straight, it will not be satisfactory.

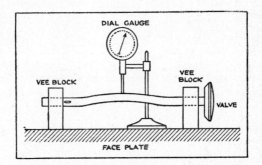

Fig. 55. Illustrating method of testing valve stems for lack of straightness. (Valve bend shown exaggerated).

Suction Cup Valve Grinder. An improvement upon the ordinary screwdriver for valve grinding is to use a wooden rod having a rubber suction cup securely attached (by glueing) to an end (Fig. 56). Any shape of valve head can be held with this device, and it has the further advantage of enabling the valve to be lifted off its seating during the grinding operation, thus obviating the necessity for a compression spring under the head. The writer has fitted one of these suction cups to a steel rod for

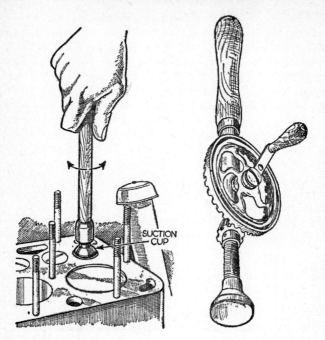

Fig. 56. Using a rubber suction cup-ended rod for valve grinding purposes (Austin).

Fig. 57. A hand drilling machine suction cup device.

use in a small hand-drilling machine (Fig. 57); the latter speeds up the valve-grinding operation with entirely satisfactory results, as the tool can be driven in each direction.

When using this tool care must be exercised to prevent any grease from getting on the rubber suction cup.

Valve Seatings. Normally speaking the valve seatings, being of very hard cast iron, do not wear so much as the steel valve faces, but after many re-grindings the seats become 'pocketed', as shown in Fig. 48 (A). The valve, being in a pocket, does not, when lifted, allow the full quantity of mixture – or gas – to pass through; a loss of power and overheating will then occur. It is necessary, therefore, to remove the metal from the top of the pocket so as to obtain a normal valve seating. Fig. 48 (B). A convenient method of doing this is to employ a special flat facing tool having a guide – either in the valve cap or valve stem guide. The cutters of this tool turn off the surplus metal above the valve seating.

If a power drilling machine is available, this operation can be expeditiously carried out by taking the cylinder block to the machine. Where special alloy-steel or Stellite valve seatings are used, ordinary tool steel cutters are useless. Special grades of conical grinding stones are now available for truing such seatings in place.

A set of valve-seat truing tools can readily be made by the motor mechanic by turning up and cutting teeth on conical cutters from high carbon steel, afterwards hardening these and tempering to a light straw colour (Fig. 58).

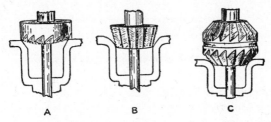

A B C

Fig. 58. Cutters for valve seat re-conditioning.

The 15° tool shown at (A) is used for removing metal from the top part of the valve seating in order to reduce the width of the latter. The 75° tool shown at (B) removes metal from the bottom of the seating for a similar purpose. The double-cutter shown at (C) consists of a coarse and fine toothed 45° cone for cutting curved seatings and truing pitted or worn ones.

Weak Valve Springs. After periods of service, namely, above about 15,000 miles, valve springs may weaken and so cause a falling off in the engine's performance. When an engine is given a complete overhaul it is advisable to test the strengths of these springs in the manner depicted in Fig. 59. In this case the spring to be checked – shown as the weak one – is placed end-on against a new spring, but with a washer between the ends. When the combination is compressed either by screw or in a vice, the weaker spring will compress, or shorten, more than the new one; if the length of the weak spring is appreciably shorter than that of the new one it should be discarded and then all of the valve springs ought to be replaced.

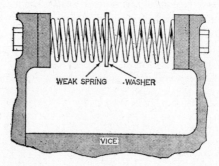

Fig. 59. Method of testing for a weak valve spring.

Replacing the Valves. The replacing of the valves and springs is likely to be a more difficult operation than their removal, and a good deal of time can be wasted in trying to compress the springs and insert the cotter if one has not the proper means available. Usually, the valve-lifting tool serves equally well for replacing. The best procedure when special tools are not available is as follows: Take the valve spring, compress it to rather less than its normal working length in a vice, and tie the coils with strong string at opposite sides of two diameters – in order to keep it square. Then, placing the valve collar at one end, push the spring into position on its valve guide, drop the valve down into its seating and insert the cotter, afterwards cutting the string. The cut pieces of the string can then be removed with a small pair of pliers; in any case if not completely removed they will do no harm.

The Terry spring compressor tool shown in Fig. 44 (C) is useful for individual valve spring compression.

Another method of compressing the springs is shown in Fig. 62. In this case a piece of metal strip notched and bent over at its ends serves to retain the spring in its compressed position, and enables it to be inserted in place on the cylinder.

A simple device for compressing *overhead-valve springs* is shown in Fig. 47. This is simply a tube having slots cut through near the lower end to allow the valve cotters to be removed. A wooden end-piece is fitted to assist in gripping the device. Valve springs can be removed or replaced very easily with this tool.

Replacing Split Cone Retainers. Unless the proper tool is is available, split cone spring retainers may prove difficult to replace.

Fig. 60. Split cone pliers.

Special tools operating on the 'scissors' principle are now available for the purpose. Each jaw end of the tool is shaped to hold one half cone, so that by inserting the open end of the tool with its jaws in either side of the valve stem – the spring having previously been compressed – the tool handles can then be compressed so as to leave the half cones in their correct positions on the valve stem recessed part. Fig. 60 illustrates a simpler form of split cone assembly tool, than some of the other available tools. It is possible to make a simple tool from a piece of metal strip, cut and bent as shown in Fig. 61. The valve spring is held by a compressor tool so that the recess or shoulder on the valve stem is clear of the spring collar. The half cone is held on the end of the tool, as shown in the lower left illustration, by using a little stiff grease. It can readily be inserted into the stem recess and held by the grease and the other half then inserted in a similar

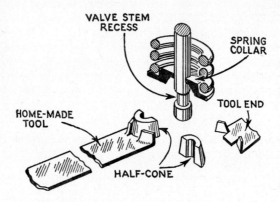

Fig. 61. A simple type of split cone replacement tool.

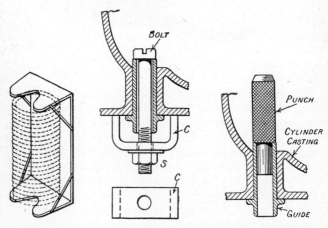

Fig. 62
A handy valve
spring compressor
device.

Fig. 63. (Left) Device for removing worn valve guides; *C* is a stirrup, and *S* the withdrawing screw. (Right) A handy punch for driving out worn valve guides.

way. A strip of wood suitably cut at one end to the outer shape of the half cone, used with stiff grease to hold the half cone in place, will act satisfactorily, as an emergency split cone replacer.

Useful Notes on Valves. After replacing a ground-in valve, the tappet clearances should be set about 1 to 2/1000 greater than the manufacturer's values; this allows for the bedding down of the surfaces under working conditions.

When the engine has run a few hundred miles, after its valves have been re-ground, check the valve clearances and re-set if necessary. Always carry a spare valve and spring in the car on long tours. If a valve breaks – although this is an uncommon occurrence – or its head becomes burnt, it can be replaced.

Removing and Adjusting the Earlier Ford Valves. Unless one is familiar with the special design of the earlier Ford valve unit some difficulty will be experienced in connection with its removal for re-grinding purposes.

This Ford valve has a mushroom extension at its lower end, the spring retaining collar fitting over this. In order to fit the valve guide over the parallel portion of the valve stem it is made in two similar parts, i.e. is split, longitudinally. The valve guide when assembled in position is held in place against its cylinder seating by means of the valve spring. Plain tappets of relatively large diameter and without provision for clearance adjustment are fitted.

To remove a Ford valve,* after having taken off the cylinder head, first compress the valve spring, with the aid of a special tool. The spring retainer can then be withdrawn and the valve spring then slipped off. Next, lift the valve as high as possible in its guide – as indicated by the dotted line position in Fig. 64 – and then with a hard wood, aluminium or copper drift knock out the valve guide, downwards; it should readily come out and the two halves can then be separated. The valve can then be withdrawn upwards. Care should be taken in regard to the replacement of the numbered valves into their respective positions. The order

---

* In the Ford Pilot V-Eight engines, the complete valve and guide unit was removed bodily by first withdrawing a special cotter in the guide slot.

of the valves, *E, I, I, E, E, I, I, E,* where *E* and *I* are the exhaust and inlet valves, respectively.

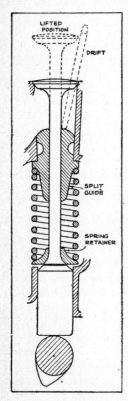

Fig. 64. Removing Ford valves.

It may be mentioned that special tools were sold for removing the split valve guides.

The correct valve clearance is 0·013 in. If the clearance *is greater* than this the face of the valve should be ground or skimmed in a lathe to reduce this clearance; in an emergency a cup liner can be inserted between the tappet and the valve stem. If the clearance *is less* the surplus metal should be ground off the stem.

Valve Seat Inserts. It is well known that the grade of iron used for cylinder castings is not the best wearing of metals, so that valve seatings become worn more readily than if harder and more durable materials are used. Apart from actual wear, the seatings are more liable to become pitted in service.

To overcome this disadvantage it is becoming the practice to use inserted valve seatings consisting of a ring of a hard corrosion and heat resisting metal or alloy. Satisfactory materials for this purpose include nickel-chrome steel, tungsten steel and chrome cast iron.

More recently alloy steel valve seat inserts have been given a hard facing of Stellite or Brightray. The former material is a synthetic compound containing cobalt, chromium, molybdenum, etc., and is also used for the cutting edges of high-speed tools. It will retain its extremely hard properties at a bright red heat and is therefore superior to any known alloy steel under these conditions. Brightray is an alloy of four parts nickel and one part chromium and it is used for facing aircraft valve seatings. These very hard materials are fused on to the base metal with an oxy-acetylene flame.

A method, obviating the heavy insertion pressures used in some cases, to fit inserted seatings is the Wellworthy one shown in Fig. 65. The ring to be fitted is provided with horizontal slots (S). The cylinder seating has a slight recess (R) turned in it. The width

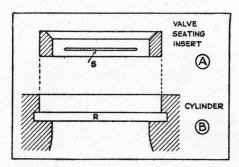

Fig. 65. The Wellworthy valve seating insert.

of this recess is such that when the insert ring is pressed into the cylinder seating the lower edge of the slot (S) springs outwards slightly and is held by the recess. A thin steel strip is inserted in these slots to prevent damage during insertion of the ring. The ring is made an interference fit in the cylinder seating; only a moderate pressure is needed for the fitting of the insert.

Replacing the Cylinder Head. After decarbonizing the cylinders, grinding and replacing the valves and cleaning the sparking plugs, the cylinder head can be replaced. It is necessary to clean carefully the machined surface of the cylinder top and detachable head, and to examine the copper-asbestos gasket for damaged places; with care this gasket can be used again, but if dented or broken the cylinder joint will leak; a new gasket is then required. When the recent type single sheet metal gaskets are employed it is essential to use a new gasket.

Checking for Head Distortion. Before the head is replaced it is advisable to check the machined face for distortion. This can be done by using blue marking on a surface plate and rubbing the machined face over it. If there is a distinct blue marked region around the edge portions this is a sign of distortion. The amount can be measured with an engineer's dial gauge. It should not exceed about 0·010 to 0·020 in. for a four- or six-cylinder (Fig. 66) engine. Distorted heads can be reground by surface grinding machines.

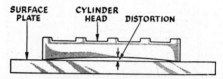

Fig. 66. Checking for cylinder head machined face distortion.

Before replacing the cylinder head, clean the cylinders with a rag damped with petrol, removing every trace of dirt, and smear each cylinder barrel lightly with engine oil. Rotate the crankshaft a few times by hand, to distribute the oil evenly over the cylinder surfaces, and then wipe off the surplus oil which is pushed over the tops of the cylinder barrels by the pistons.

Before lowering the cylinder head over its studs, smear both sides of the cleaned copper-asbestos gasket faces with a jointing compound, e.g., Osotite or with *boiled linseed oil* or *gold size* (coach varnish will do in an emergency), and then screw down the cylinder holding-down nuts. Do not use any more jointing compound than is absolutely necessary on the joint, as some of the surplus will carbonize inside the cylinder.

It is important to screw down the cylinder head nuts in a certain definite order, namely, the reverse to that indicated in Fig. 40, to distribute the pressure and avoid distorting the machined surfaces. Do not tighten each nut to its limit in one operation, but go round the sequence of nuts progressively, tightening each one a little at a time. For motor garage purposes a *torque-indicating wrench* is a necessity.

The sparking plugs should then be replaced, and the other cylinder attachments made secure.

After the engine has been run for a sufficient period to enable it to warm up thoroughly, the nuts should all be gone over, once again, with the spanner, and again after the first 100 miles of running. When aluminium cylinder heads are fitted, the cylinder nuts *should only be tightened when the engine is cold* – as mentioned earlier.

The Connecting Rod. After about 25,000 to 35,000 miles of usage it may be necessary to renew the connecting rod bearings.

With the modern detachable head-type engines, the cylinders and upper half of the crankcase are usually cast in one piece; by removing the crankcase oil sump it is possible to get at the big-end bearing caps. If these are removed the connecting rods and pistons can generally be drawn out through the tops of the cylinder barrels.

The Small-End Bearings. The small end of the connecting rod is usually bushed with bronze or gunmetal to form the bearing for the gudgeon pin. If, after cleaning both the bearing and pin, any slackness is apparent when the pin is inserted and the rod

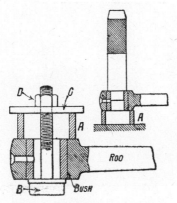

Fig. 67. Removing a worn connecting rod small-end bush. Upper illustration shows alternative method of driving bush out.

D

pressed up and down or rocked in the piston, a new bush – and possibly a new gudgeon pin – should be fitted. Remove the worn bush and replace with one of the maker's spares or a freshly turned bush taking care to get the oil hole in line with the hole in the connecting rod. Sometimes the bush can be removed by tapping gently with a drift, holding the bush over a larger hole in a piece of hard wood. If the bush is a tight fit it should be pressed out in a hand press; a drilling machine spindle can be improvised for the purpose.

A good method of removing a worn bush is illustrated in Fig. 67. In this case a bolt with a cylindrical head (*B*) slightly smaller than the outside diameter of the bush is employed. The nut (*D*) of this bolt is pulled up against a washer (*C*) bearing on a short length of tubing (*A*), having an internal diameter slightly larger than the outside diameter of the small-end bush. On tightening the nut (*D*), the bush is withdrawn into the space in tube (*A*). When turning up a new bush, make the outside diameter a *force*

Fig. 68. Testing the fit of the small-end bearing. The connecting rod should just drop under its own weight when held as shown.

fit in the small-end, and arrange for the gudgeon pin to be a shade on the loose side of a *running fit*, to allow for the closing in when the bush is forced into the connecting-rod end. Some repairers obtain an excellent 'burnish' finish and good fit by driving the gudgeon pin through the bush after forcing the latter into the small end of the connecting rod; others reamer the hole to open it out to take the gudgeon pin. A slightly worn bush can be closed in so as to become a good fit on the gudgeon pin by removing the bush, 'tinning' the outside with solder and forcing it back into the connecting rod. A bearing fit test method is shown in Fig. 68.

If the gudgeon pin floats in the piston bosses and small-end it will be necessary to reamer the holes and fit an oversize pin.

In many recent car engines the gudgeon pins are clamped to the small ends of their connecting rods, so that the exposed ends of the pins can rock in the piston boss holes that now act as bearings. No separate small end or piston boss bushes are therefore required.

Fig. 69 illustrates the complete piston and connecting rod assembly parts (shown dismantled) for the Austin engines. In this case the gudgeon pin 7 has a small central groove and is clamped symmetrically in the split small end of the connecting rod 8, by a pinch-bolt 9, which is provided with a spring washer.

The gudgeon pin should be a thumb fit in the piston boss holes, at 70° C, i.e. corresponding to a warm day. In the case of worn piston boss bearings it is usual with some makes of engines to employ a slightly oversize reamer, with a pilot extension, to true the holes in the connecting rod and piston bosses, so that an oversize gudgeon pin can be employed.

The Big-End Bearing. The big-end bearing usually wears slightly oval after about 20,000–25,000 miles of normal use.

White-metalled Bearings. In earlier engines the big-end bearings consisted of white metal run into the steel rod and cap and afterwards machined and fitted to the crank pins. The later and now current design employs replaceable half-shell bearings, which require no scraping or bedding in.

In regard to the former type of bearing the wear could be taken up – assuming the crank pins were not worn appreciably – by

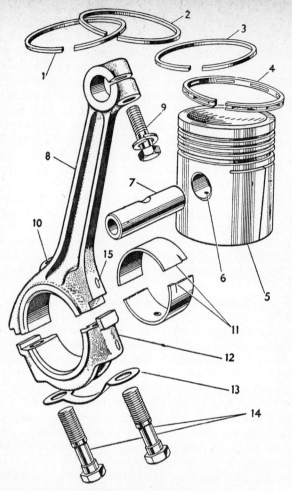

Fig. 69. Piston and connecting rod assembly. (Austin 1·5
and 1·62 litre engines).

1, 2 and 3. compression rings.
4. oil control ring.
5. piston.
6. oil hole.
7. gudgeon pin.
8. connecting rod.
9. clamping bolt.
10. oil hole.
11. bearing shells.
12. bearing cap.
13. locking plate.
14. set screws.
15. identification marking.

removing one or more of the thin metal liners known as *shims* fitted on each side between the two halves of the bearing, and replacing the cap. For the best results it was necessary to scrape in the white metal bearings after removing the shims.

Split Shell Bearings. The earlier white-metalled 'solid'

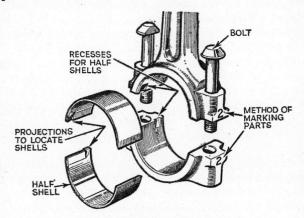

RECESSES
FOR HALF
SHELLS

BOLT

METHOD OF
MARKING
PARTS

PROJECTIONS
TO LOCATE
SHELLS

HALF
SHELL

Fig. 70. Modern shell-type big-end bearings.
(Morris Minor.)

bearings were expensive to produce and renew, so that garage servicing costs for big-end and main bearing were relatively high. To overcome these, and other minor objections to the solid bearings, a new type known as the split shell bearing was introduced. In these, the bearing consists of a pair of accurately machined half-shells, each shell being of thin steel lined with white metal or some other bearing metal of improved qualities, e.g., indium-coated whitemetal, cadmium-nickel or lead-bronze. The housings in the connecting rod big end are precision-machined to take the corresponding shell bearings, so that when the nuts or set-screws are tightened to a certain degree – as shown on a torque-wrench – the bearings are securely held, but without any distortion. Each shell is provided with a rectangular projection – as shown in Figs. 69 and 70, which engages with a corresponding recess in the rod hole, so that the shell cannot rotate in its hole.

There is one important feature concerning shell bearings, which the home mechanic should carefully note, namely, that – unlike the solid-type of bearing – it is *not possible to take up the effects of bearing wear* by the method of filing the machined faces of the bearing, or by employing shims. Once a bearing has become worn beyond the manufacturer's dimensional limit, it must be removed and scrapped.

Before fitting a new pair of shell bearings, examine the surface of the crankpin for scores or other signs of surface defects; if not completely smooth all over, the crankpin must be reground. Similarly, if smooth but – as measured at several places, the crankpin is found to be tapered or oval by more than 0·0015 to 0·002 in., the crankpin should be reground to suit the next smaller diameter (undersize) stock shell bearings. The latter are usually supplied in undersize steps of 0·005, 0·01, 0·02, 0·03, 0·04 and 0·05 in.

Before fitting new shell-type bearings carefully clean the connecting-rod housing, or bore and also the oil hole. The surfaces of the bearings themselves should be quite clean, since any solid matter on the external surface will cause distortion of the thin shell and this may cause rapid wear or seizure of the bearing. Internal dirt will result in 'grooving' of the bearing metal.

Referring back to Fig. 69 which shows a later design of connecting rod, it will be seen that, unlike the example of Fig. 70, the connecting rod big end is split at an angle, which is not a right-angle – a method that offers certain practical advantages.

Also, it will be observed that instead of using bolts and slotted nuts to clamp the big end bearing components, set screws are employed. These screw directly into the metal of the connecting rods and are provided with a tab-type lock washer.

When replacing connecting rods on to the crankshaft, it is important to ensure that each rod faces the correct way round, relatively to the crankshaft side of the engine and that each rod is fitted to its proper crankpin; the rods are marked for this purpose.

The Main Crankshaft Bearings. Shell-type bearings are used for the main crankshaft journals and, therefore, cannot be adjusted for wear. After an engine has been in service for a considerable period, namely, 30,000 miles or so, the main bearings should be removed for inspection and, if necessary, replacement. The usual procedure for removal is, as follows:

(1) Take out the sparking plug.

(2) Remove the oil sump which is bolted to the lower part of the crankcase, after having drained out the engine oil, by removing the sump plug.

(3) Remove each main bearing cap in turn, noting the position and identification marking on these. The bearing shell will readily be detached from its cap.

(4) Remove the upper bearing shell by inserting a small tool in the oil hole of the main journal. A projection on the head of this tool, of smaller height than the bearing thickness will enable the bearing to be rotated out of its upper housing when the crankshaft is turned. (Fig. 71.) In place of the tool shown in this illustration, a bent and shaped split-pin (Fig. 72) is used for Vauxhall engine main bearing removal. This device fits into the crankshaft journal oil hole.

When the bearings have been removed and cleaned they should be inspected for scores or surface cracks; bearings having such defects should be discarded. The crankshaft journal should be checked for scores. If found to be worn, by measurement of the bearings and journal, new bearings will be required. If any taper or ovality is detected on the journals, these should be reground to suit the nearest undersize stock bearing shells.

The Camshaft Bearings. The single camshaft of modern car engines runs in three or four bearings of the lined cylindrical shell type, or directly in bearings machined integral with the crankcase metal. It is seldom that the camshaft journals or their bearings wear, except over long operation periods, but if, at a major overhaul, excessive clearance is measured, new bearings should be installed, and the thrust washer renewed.

Bearing Clearances. The following are the recommended clearances between the journals or crankpins and the bearings, in the case of modern whitemetal shell-type bearings.

Main Bearings. 2·000 in. diameter. 0·0015–0·0025 in. End clearance, 0·003–0·006 in.

Big-end Bearings. 2·000 in. diameter. 0·001–0·003 in. End clearance, 0·006–0·010 in.

The majority of crankshaft main bearing diameters for engines

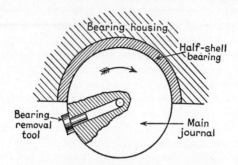

Fig. 71. Method of removing main bearing half-shell.

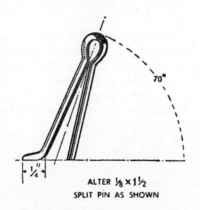

Fig. 72. Altered split-pin bearing removal tool (Vauxhall).

of 750 cc. to 2,500 cc. range from about 1·75 to 2·50 in., respectively and the bearing clearances are proportional to these diameters.

When lead-bronze lined steel shell bearings are employed – as for small Diesel engines, the clearances are appreciably greater than for whitemetal shells.

Camshaft Bearings. The camshaft runs at one-half engine speed and its bearings are not so heavily loaded as those of the crankshaft. The usual bearing clearances for a camshaft journal of 1·75 to 2·0 inch diameter are 0·002 to 0·003 inch. The end clearance, which is controlled by a thrust plate, is 0·002 to 0·004 inch, as a rule.

The end clearance of the crankshaft in its bearings, is controlled by a thrust washer or washers of certain thicknesses, at one of the main bearings. The end clearance is measured by placing a dial gauge plunger against the end of the crankshaft and then levering the latter, first, hard to the left and then to the right; the difference in the dial gauge readings gives the end clearance.

Testing for Bearing Wear. A good method of testing for wear in the small- and big-end bearings is illustrated in Fig. 73. In this method the cylinder head is removed, the piston top cleaned and a dial gauge, reading in thousandths of an inch rigged up so as to touch the crown of the piston in its top-centre position.

A rod (*R*), provided with a rubber suction cup, is used to hold the piston by the suction method. If, now the piston is alternately pulled up and pressed down, by means of the rod (*R*) any play in the bear-

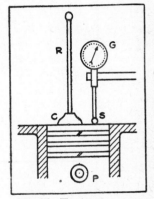

Fig. 73. Testing for connecting rod bearing wear.

ings of the connecting rod can be measured on the dial gauge, the result gives the sum of the two bearing clearances.

If, now, the sump is removed and the connecting rod is held firmly downwards by one person whilst another repeats the above procedure, only the wear or clearance in the small-end bearing will be measured. By subtracting this from the total clearance previously measured the big-end wear can be ascertained.

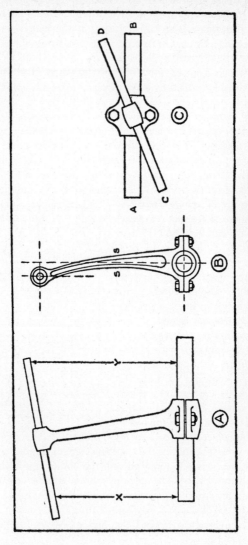

Fig. 74. Illustrating typical connecting rod faults. (Show exaggerated.)

Aligning the Connecting Rod. After dismantling an engine each of the connecting rods should be tested for bending or twisting effects. This is important, since a slightly bent or twisted rod may give rise to a knock and cause undue wear both on the cylinder walls and in its own bearings; it is a common experience for knocks to occur, even after an engine has been overhauled. They are due to the connecting rod having a slight sideways bend and were caused when fitting the cylinders down over the piston, or when removing or replacing them. The connecting rod may be bent in one of two possible directions (shown exaggerated in Diagrams A and B, Fig. 74) or it may be twisted, as in Diagram C.

The alignment may be tested by inserting rods or tubes in the big- and small-end bearings. If the connecting rod is bent side-ways (Diagram A) the two rods will not be parallel, as checked by measuring the distances X and Y; these distances should, of course, be equal.

Bending in the plane of the connecting rod (Diagram B) is not so easy to detect, for the two rods placed through the bearings will remain parallel in this case. This type of bend if not pronounced is not important, relatively.

Examination and testing of the two sides S of the rod will usually reveal any bending of this type; a straight-edge placed on the sides S will show any lack of straightness. If another connecting rod

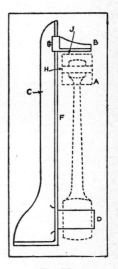

Fig. 75.
Jig for testing connecting rods.

known to be quite straight is aligned under the suspected rod, it can readily be ascertained whether the latter is bent.

A twisted rod can be detected by sighting from one end upon two rods placed through the big- and small-end bearings, as shown in Diagram C; here AB and CD represents parallel cylinder rods fitting the big- and small-end rods, respectively.

If a connecting rod is found to be bent it can be re-straightened in a suitable press, afterwards checking for straightness by each of the three methods outlined.

Special jigs are now available for checking connecting rods for bend or twist (Fig. 75). The usual pattern consists of a vertical bracket *C* having a machined face *F*, up and down which can slide a member *B* having its lower face machined so as to be at right angles to the face *F*.

At the lower end of the vertical bracket is a cylindrical boss

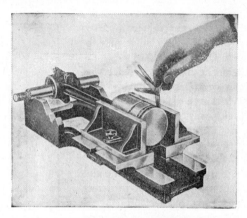

Fig. 76. The B. and T. connecting rod jig.

made in such a way that it can readily be increased or decreased in diameter by adding or removing sleeves. The big end of the rod to be tested is lightly clamped over this boss. The piston should be on the connecting rod and its alignment with the machined faces *H* and *J* checked by feeler gauge, or by sighting through. If the piston be removed and a rod be fitted in the small-end in place of the gudgeon pin, any twisting of the rod can at once be detected.

A convenient commercial form of connecting rod and piston jig is the Boneham and Turner one shown in Fig. 76. It comprises a pair of vee-blocks in which a mandrel holding the connecting rod big-ends rests. The other end of the jig set has a pair of angle plates presenting a pair of accurately parallel faces which are employed in a similar manner to the cylinder barrel for checking the piston for ovality and taper, by means of feeler gauges.

In order to test the connecting rod for twist, the piston is removed and a longer pin than the gudgeon pin is inserted through the small-end bush, which it must fit satisfactorily. The ends of this pin are then arranged to rest upon the two parallel tops of the angle plates. The smallest amount of twist will at once be evident by one side of the pin not touching the top of its angle plate; if the connecting rod bearings are parallel the two ends of the pin will rest upon the tops of the angle plates.

Straightening Connecting Rods. When a connecting rod has been shown to be twisted or bent it can be straightened in a press, using metal blocks for bent rods and torque-bar tool for twisted ones.

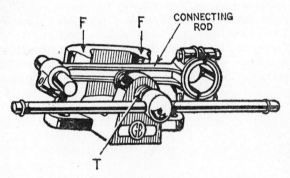

Fig. 77. Connecting rod straightening tool (G.E.).

A simple tool for straightening bent rods, known as the G.E. tool is shown in Fig. 77. The connecting rod is located, on either side of the bent region by two fulcra (*FF*) and pressure is applied to the opposite convex side of the rod by a tee-headed screw member (*T*). A soft metal pad is placed between the screw end and the rod, to avoid local damage to the latter.

Twist in a rod can be removed by holding the big-end of the rod in a vice, fitted with lead vice clamps, and applying torque to the H-section part of the rod, at the appropriate section, by means of a large adjustable spanner. The rod should be checked carefully, after each torque effort, for remaining twist, by the method previously described. It may be mentioned that in repair garages special connecting rod testing machines, such as the Buma and Newton, are provided with fitments for correcting both bending and twist.

The Crankshaft. It is usually beyond the capacity of the ordinary amateur motor owner – unless he has some mechanical experience – to undertake any of the more serious operations connected with the crankshaft. We shall, therefore, deal only superficially with the subject, considering the more simple operations and merely outlining the difficult ones.

After much usage, or if the engine oil has contained any solid matter, or the oil has not been changed at regular intervals, the crankpin journals, as previously mentioned, will often be found to have worn slightly oval – the usual differences in diameter amounting to 0·0015 to 0·002 in. Evidently it will not be possible to obtain a good bearing fit for the connecting rod big-ends under these circumstances for if the bearing is adjusted so as to be correct in one position of the crankshaft, on turning the latter it will either tighten or loosen.

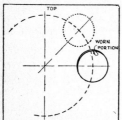

Fig. 78.
Illustrating how the crankpin wears oval.

The greatest pressure on the crankpin is during the first half of the down stroke (firing operation), and the crankpin wears in the manner shown – to exaggerated scale – in Fig. 78. There is also uneven wear due to inertia effects.

In order to true this worn pin to circularity it is necessary to remove the surplus material by suitable means, e.g. honing, turning or grinding.

Machining Methods. The most accurate method of crankpin truing is undoubtedly that of grinding in the lathe (Fig. 79) or grinding machine, using a special eccentric holder for the crankshaft.

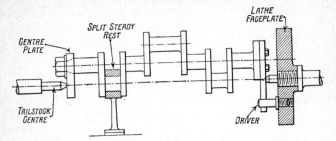

Fig. 79. Method of truing four-cylinder crankshaft in lathe.

The next best plan for the motor garage is to use a hand-operated cutter-type tool of the types shown in Figs. 80 and 81.

A number of different designs of crankshaft tools of this type are in use and it is claimed that they will true any crankshaft journal to within $\frac{1}{4}$-thousandth of an inch of round and remove any taper with $\frac{1}{2}$-thousandth, in an average time of 20 minutes.

The tool shown in Fig. 80 is the Ammco. This has only one cutter and two hardened guide planes arranged at right angles. The edge of the cutter is arranged diametrically in relation to the journal that is to be trued. A knurled screw enables the position of the tool to be varied to suit shafts of different diameters and also to adjust the cut; it is possible to take light feather cuts in this way without chatter.

In use one operator turns the crankshaft with the starting handle and another holds the tool in position. It is necessary to remove the crankshaft from the engine with the tool illustrated.

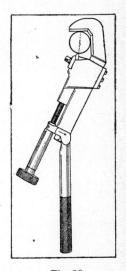

Fig. 80
The Ammco crankshaft truing tool.

The more recent B.T.S. crankshaft tool, shown in Fig. 81 has two adjustable steadies and one automatic steady, to hold the tool accurately over the crankpin. The cutter, which is screw-adjusted is located between the two steadies nearer to the handle. When the handle is rotated round the crankpin the automatic steady is tightened against the crankpin. The tool will correct both ovality and taper effects and give a good surface finish.

Another truing tool, known as the Delapena, uses a pair of honing stones mounted opposite a pair of steadies arranged as a kind of vee-block. This tool gives an excellent finish and has an

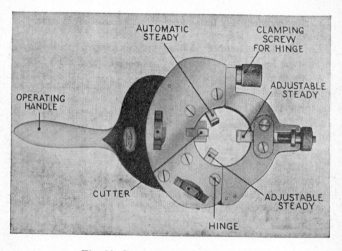

Fig. 81. Crankpin truing tool (B.T.S.).

accuracy within 0·0005 inch. Both coarse and fine hones can be used for roughing and finishing cuts, respectively.

Both of the tools described are hinged to allow them to be placed around the crankpin to be trued.

Measuring Crankshaft Wear. The crankshaft journals can be checked for ovality and taper, by measuring the diameters both around the journal at several places and along it, for taper effect. For this purpose an external micrometer may be borrowed. It should have a diameter range up to about 3·5 in. and a gap between the jaws of rather more than this. The journal must be quite clean before measuring it. With the usual micrometer it is possible to measure to 1/1000 inch and to estimate, between the divisions to about one-third to one quarter of 1/1000 inch.

If the amount of out-of-round exceeds 0·015 in. or the taper between the two ends, the same amount, this is a sign that the journals should be re-ground before fitting new shell bearings.

Undersize replacement bearings are usually available in steps of 0·010 in. so that the journals should be ground to suit, i.e. allowing for the proper running clearances, mentioned earlier.

Testing the Crankshaft. Before a crankshaft is reconditioned in respect to its journals it should be tested for truth, either in the lathe or on a pair of equal vee-blocks (Fig. 82); in the latter case the crankshaft is placed on metal vee-blocks, one at either end, and its accuracy checked by means of a dial gauge, the plunger of which is placed on top of the centre main journal bearing.

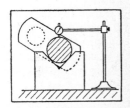

Fig. 82.
Testing the crankshaft.

Broken Crankshafts. In the event of a crankshaft fracturing it is possible to obtain a satisfactory repair at much less than the cost of a new shaft by having the crankshaft parts welded by the electric arc process. Many cases of repair of this nature give entirely satisfactory service when carried out by a specialist firm.

The Piston Rings. The careful owner usually examines his piston rings after every 20,000 miles or so of running, for these rings have a heavy duty to perform under the severe high-speed pressure and temperature conditions existing in the cylinder. When new, the piston ring is circular in outside shape in the cylinder and with only a small gap between its split ends. After much usage the ring wears in such a manner that although in the latter case the ring has preserved its external circular shape, the two ends have worn thinner and the gap has opened. The result of this opening is to cause a leakage of the compressed and exploding gases past the piston, a loss of suction on the inlet stroke and a leakage of engine oil into the combustion chamber there to form excessive carbon deposit.

To test for a worn ring, remove it from the piston and, after cleaning, insert it in the working part of the cylinder bore, keeping it quite square all round. Any opening of the gap can then at once be observed and measured. Loss of flexibility, or spring, can be checked by securing a new ring in the vice – or even in the hand – and pressing the new and old rings together; if the gap of the latter ring closes right up before the new ring alters appreciably, discard the old ring and fit a new one.

Fit of the ring in the piston groove is tested as shown in Fig. 83.

Piston rings are now stocked in a very wide variety of sizes, and as these are made by specialist firms with the latest grinding equipment and from the best material, it does not pay to attempt to make one's own rings. Special sizes or patterns can, however, be made from the *piston ring castings* sold by piston ring manufacturing firms.

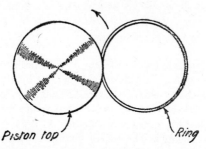

Fig. 83. Testing piston ring for wear in the piston grooves.

Removing Piston Rings. Since it is possible for the amateur to break piston rings when attempting to remove them, a few remarks on the correct procedure may not be out of place here. The simplest plan, without the aid of special piston ring tools, is to cut three strips of stout tin, each about 2 inches long, by $\frac{1}{4}$ inch wide by 20 s.w.g. Working from the gap portion of the ring, insert these strips in turn, until finally they are arranged as shown in Fig. 84 B; the ring can then be worked off without jamming in any of the other piston ring grooves. Another method, shown in Fig. 84 A, is to insert a narrow knife blade or similar tool between the ring to be removed and the piston, slipping the knife-blade around the piston and at the same time lifting the ring out and up with the hand.

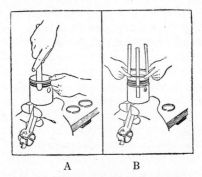

A   B

Fig. 84. Showing method of removing piston rings.

Tools for Piston Ring Removal and Replacement. Special tools, now available, enable a good deal of time and trouble to be saved, whilst avoiding risk of ring breakage.

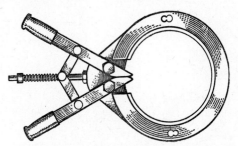

Fig. 85. The Britool piston ring tool.

Fig. 85 illustrates the Britool ring expander used in the servicing of Vauxhall engines. It has two projections at the ends of hand-operated levers for engagement with the ends of the ring i.e. in the slot portion. By the compression of the handles, the ring is expanded to the circular shape of the guide member thus avoiding any local distortion in shape. The same tool can be used to replace the rings.

Another particularly useful piston ring removing- and replacing-tool is the Wellworthy, which is of the spring-control type in which the free ends of the ring are first gripped by the tool and then, when the tool handles are depressed, the ring is expanded, but to its correct shape, so as to just clear the piston lands.

Fitting New Piston Rings. When ordering new piston rings it is best to specify oversize ones, stating the make of engine and mileage done. Since more recent engine pistons are often fitted with taper-section and chromium-plated upper rings care should be exercised when ordering replacement rings to ensure that these are of the correct types. The recommended piston ring clearances in the slots and in the cylinder are given later. Usually these rings may be found to be a tight fit both in the trued piston grooves and in the cylinder. It will then be necessary to reduce the axial widths of the rings. A method is to glue a piece of emery cloth to a board, or fasten over a surface plate, and, holding the ring as shown in Fig. 86 A, grind the surface down until the

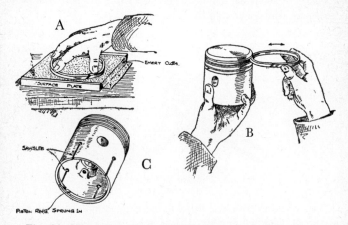

Fig. 86. Illustration of the various piston and piston ring operations described. A, Reducing width of ring by grinding; B, Testing fit of new ring; C, Curing piston slap.

ring, in all positions, just fits in its groove (Fig. 86 B). It is better, if possible, to surface grind the ring sides for the most accurate type of fit in the piston grooves. Next, test the ring for correct

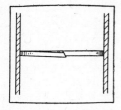

Fig. 87. Testing the fit of a piston ring in its cylinder.

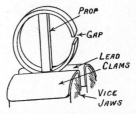

Fig. 88. Showing how to hold a piston ring when filing the slot.

diameter by inserting it in the cylinder barrel – at the working section – and examine the gap. If the two ends meet tightly or overlap at the gap (Fig. 87), this shows that the diameter is too great. To reduce this it is necessary to file away the metal at one of the gaps. The rings should be held in a vice, with a piece of wood inserted, as shown in Fig. 89, so as to hold the gap open about $\frac{3}{8}$ inch, and the surface filed down with a flat file of the 'ward' type. Every few strokes of the file release the strut and close the filed surface against the untouched surface of the gap to check for parallelism.

Special devices for filing the slot of a piston ring are now available from garage supply firms.

Piston Ring Filing Tool. The filing of slots in piston rings can be readily done with the aid of the device shown in Fig. 89. It consists of a parallel-sided metal block which is provided with a series of parallel slots of different widths. The ring to be cut or filed is inserted into the appropriate slot and, for a 45° slot the 45° groove is employed, as shown in the illustration. A fine-cut ward type of file is used. For step-cut rings there is a slot at right angles to the grooves, in another version of this tool. Both ends or sides of the ring slot can be filed at the same time with these tools.

A good test for piston ring spring is to measure with a spring

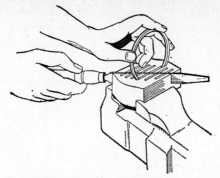

Fig. 89. The Churchill piston ring filing tool.

balance the force required to close the two sides of the gap; this should be from about 8 to 10 lb. for a $\frac{3}{16}$ inch width ring (3 in. diameter).

In the case of step-cut piston rings a useful device for holding the ring open in order to file the ends of the ring is that shown in Fig. 90. It consists of a pair of hardwood pieces, (2), bolted or

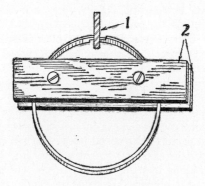

Fig. 90. Filing step-cut ring.

screwed together so as to hold the piston ring in the expanded position to enable the flat file, shown at (1), to be used. The unit in question can be held in the vice.

When fitting piston rings in the manner described it is essential
to leave the correct amount of clearance, or gap, between the ends
of the ring. The actual value of this, as explained later, depends
upon the diameter of the ring, and it is checked by inserting a

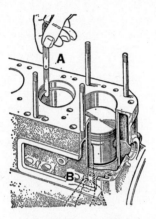

Fig. 91. Showing at (A) method of measuring piston ring gap,
and (B) piston skirt clearance in cylinder bore.

narrow feeler gauge, made for this purpose, between the ends of
the ring, as illustrated in Fig. 91; to ensure that the ring lies
squarely with the cylinder axis the piston is pushed into the bore
first and the ring then moved up against it.

Oil Scraper Rings. These piston rings are fitted with the
object of reducing the oil consumption, whilst providing adequate
lubrication for the walls of the cylinder. In the case of engines
that have had a good deal of running, the cylinder walls become
worn so that the oil is apt to leak past the piston into the upper
part of the cylinder, where it is burnt, to form carbon deposit.
In such cases the fitting of an oil-scraper ring of special design
will usually effect a temporary cure until such time as the cylinder
can be re-bored and new pistons fitted.

Most engine pistons have, hitherto, been fitted with three
rings, namely, two compression rings in the top grooves and an
oil-scraper ring in the lower groove, just above the gudgeon pin.

More recent pistons have four rings, to ensure better compression holding and adequate lubrication for the cylinder walls.

Fig. 92 shows the Standard Vanguard four-ring piston, having two compression and oil-scraper rings, located as shown above the gudgeon pin.

Recent B.M.C. engines have four rings on the pistons, namely, three compression rings, the lower two being of slightly tapered section and one oil-scraper ring.

It is important, when renewing piston rings in an engine to *make quite sure* that you use the correct types, namely, those which are supplied by the manufacturers, since there are several kinds of modern rings, of various sections, some being chrome-plated.

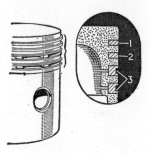

Fig. 92. The four-ring piston. (1) and (2) compression and (3) oil-scraper rings.

The action of a scraper ring is to ride over the oil with the least possible scraping action during the upstroke of the piston and to scrape the oil into the groove in the ring on the downstroke. On the next upstroke oil that is trapped in the groove is again delivered to the cylinder walls for lubrication.

When fitting scraper rings it is necessary to drill small holes (usually about $\frac{1}{16}$ in. diameter) through the bottom of the piston ring groove to the inside of the piston in order to allow any surplus oil to drain away. In some cases, as shown in Fig. 92, additional holes are drilled through the piston wall, below the scraper ring groove.

There are various forms of scraper ring available. These include the bevelled lower-edge type, the plain grooved and the slotted or 'ventilated' groove (Fig. 93). The grooved type presents two scraping edges as compared with the single one of the bevelled type (Fig. 93 A). The scraper drain ring shown in Fig. 93 D presents only one scraping edge and is suitable for very oily cylinders, as it has a larger oil scraping capacity than the other types mentioned; this ring has a series of slots (S) around its periphery.

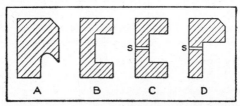

Fig. 93. Sections of typical oil-scraper rings.

Piston Ring Clearances. The piston ring should be a good fit in the piston groove, neither too tight nor too loose. Before fitting new rings see that the piston grooves are not 'stepped' or tapered through wear (Fig. 94); if so, the unworn portions at the sides near the bottoms of the grooves should be turned away so as to give parallel-sided grooves.

Fig. 94. Showing how piston ring wears groove in piston ring slot.

If the piston ring is too tight it will probably stick and eventually break. If too loose it will 'slap' and cause oil pumping past the piston.

The correct clearance between the side of the groove and the side of the ring is 0·001 in. to 0·0015 in.

The piston ring gap must also be correct and should allow for the expansion, under heat, of the ring. The following table gives the correct gap clearances between the ends of piston rings:

Cylinder Diameter in Inches	Ring-Gap, in Inches	
	Step-Cut	45° Bevel Cut
3·0	0·007	0·005
3·5	0·009	0·007
4·0	0·012	0·009
4·5	0·015	0·011
5·0	0·019	0·014

These clearances should be measured with a feeler gauge.

Replacing the Piston Rings. Owing to their comparative fragility piston rings must be handled with care, especially when

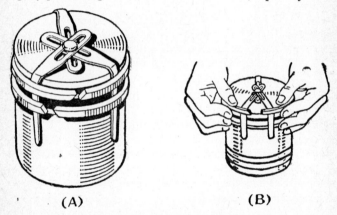

(A)   (B)

Fig. 95. The Brico ring replacer.

replacing them over the piston. The bottom ring can usually be opened and slipped over the piston skirt, if of the plain un-slotted type; otherwise it must be replaced from the top. The usual method in the absence of special piston-ring expander tools and similar devices, is to use three narrow strips of tin, each about ¼ inch wide and bent over at one end so as to rest on the top of the piston. These strips are used in a somewhat similar manner to that shown in Fig. 84 (B). A simple device for replacing the rings is the Brico one illustrated in Fig. 95 (A). It consists of three sheet-metal guides with bent-over and slotted portions for adjusting the members to suit various diameters of pistons. The method of using this device is illustrated clearly in Fig. 95 (B) where a piston ring is shown being pushed over the guides; the latter are lifted when the ring is opposite to its piston slot.

The gaps of the rings should be arranged equidistantly around the pistons, to minimize gas leakage.

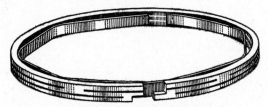

Fig. 96. The Simplex piston ring.

Rings for Worn Cylinders. Special piston rings, of which the Wellworthy Simplex, Cord and Laystall 'Perfex' are typical examples, are used to restore the compression of engines with worn cylinders, when it is not convenient to re-bore the latter.

The Wellworthy Simplex ring (Fig. 96) consists of a slotted flexible ring of a special grade of cast iron provided with a spring steel ring behind which causes the former ring to follow the shape of the worn piston so as to maintain a better compression and prevent oil leakage past the piston than the standard type of cylindrical pressure piston ring.

One of the best replacement rings for use in worn cylinders is the Duaflex type, the principle of which is shown in Fig. 97, and the complete ring in Fig. 98. Referring to Fig. 97, there are four flat section alloy steel piston rings (R), having rounded ends at the cylinder side. These rings are pressed against the sides of the piston slot, in the manner indicated by the arrows at P, by a wavy-type spring expander ring. The rings R are also, at the same time, pressed radially outwards against the cylinder wall, by another internal steel ring T similar to that used in the Simplex ring (Fig. 96) so that pressure Q is applied to all four rings, as indicated by the arrows.

This compound ring does not scrape oil from the cylinder walls and having rounded contacts at *R* it beds down at once to the shape of the worn cylinder walls

The Cords ring, now available in this country, consists of a number of thin dished spring steel rings, each of which occupies

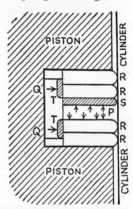

Fig. 97. Principle of the Well-worthy 'Duaflex' replacement piston ring.

exactly $\frac{1}{32}$ inch of the piston groove width. Thus, in a groove of $\frac{1}{8}$ inch width four Cords rings would be employed. For a $\frac{5}{32}$ inch groove five rings are fitted; for $\frac{3}{16}$ inch, six rings. In virtue of their radial and axial spring actions these rings give a good compression and oil seal. All the ring gaps are arranged in line with the gudgeon pin ends, alternately. The end gaps should be not less than 0·010 inch.

These, and similar replacement rings *should not be used* in the top compression ring groove.

Other types of piston rings used for new and replacement purposes are often tin-coated or, as with the British Piston Ring Company's 'Briscoseal' ring, are treated chemically to give a surface which is porous and is thus capable of absorbing oil for lubrication purposes. This surface lasts sufficiently long to enable the ring to bed itself correctly to the cylinder wall.

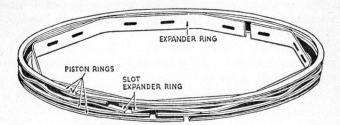

Fig. 98. The Duaflex ring for worn cylinders.

The Hepolite Dual Ring. A recent piston ring for both new and worn cylinders, and designed for long life is that shown in Fig. 99. Known as the KSS type it consists of two similar rings in the same piston slot, each having a narrow chromium-plated ridge to contact the cylinder wall. This combination is more effective than a single slotted ring, since, when tilted, it still has two ridges on the cylinder wall, instead of only one in the single ring. The oil scraped off the cylinder wall passes between the rings into a hole or holes in the piston-ring slot.

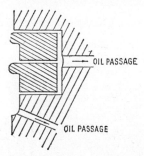

Fig. 99. The Hepolite KSS 'Long-life' piston ring unit.

The Pistons. Aluminium alloy pistons are now universally used in automobile engines. The alloys employed include die-cast and pressed Hiduminium or R.R. Alloy, Y-alloy, and aluminium copper with 5 to 11 per cent of copper. Cast-iron pistons in their early form are not used today, but high-strength alloy cast irons in relatively thin section castings have been used in certain recent American car engines. Combination steel-skirt and aluminium head pistons, such as the Flowerdew, were also used in certain engines.

Faults. Those commonly experienced with aluminium pistons which have been in service for appreciable periods may be summarized, briefly, as follows:

(1) *Scored lands*, due to carbon or siliceous particles on cylinder walls.

(2) *Scored or worn piston skirt;* the greatest wear occurs on the thrust face where the pressure effect is a maximum.

(3) *Worn piston-ring grooves.* Usually the groove wears in a stepped manner, as shown in Fig. 94; it is necessary to turn away the step before fitting a new ring.

(4) *Worn gudgeon-pin holes.* These may be reamed out to true the holes and an oversize gudgeon pin fitted; it will be necessary also to ream out the small-end connecting rod bearing.

(5) *Burnt piston crown.* This effect due to running on leaded petrols at excessive temperatures is not often experienced except in experimental engines.

Although it is seldom necessary, in order to maintain maximum

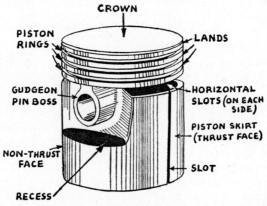

Fig. 100. Typical aluminium alloy three-ring piston, with the usual piston notation terms.

efficiency, to do anything to the pistons under 20,000 to 30,000 miles if the engine has been well cared for, it may be desirable to test the pistons for slackness of fit in the cylinders after such periods of running. Usually two or three sets of piston rings can be fitted before the piston becomes worn seriously, but, if after the last set of rings has had time to become 'bedded in' – say, after 500 to 600 miles – the engine is extravagant in oil, loses compression and generally falls off in power, these are signs that the pistons and cylinders require attention.

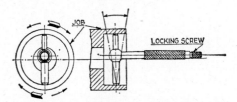

Fig. 101. A telescopic internal measurement gauge.

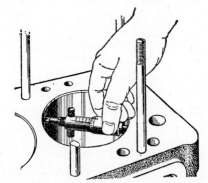

Fig. 102. Micrometer cylinder gauge, showing method of using it (Austin).

The engine should be dismantled and the parts cleaned in a paraffin, hot caustic soda bath or other degreasing solution. The caustic soda solution should *not* be used for aluminium alloy parts, since it exerts a strong chemical action on these metals.

Measuring the Cylinder Bore. After thoroughly cleaning the cylinder block and bores, the latter should each be examined for surface defects, such as longitudinal grooves or scratches and after cleaning each bore should be accurately measured at different places down and around it.

A simple internal measuring device is the Starrett telescopic gauge, shown in Fig. 101. It consists of a knurled handle and two

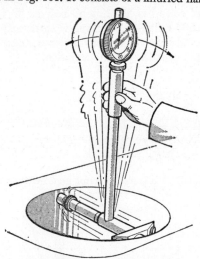

Fig. 103. The Mercer direct-reading
cylinder gauge (E. J. Baty Ltd.).

arms which telescope into each other, but with a spring to keep them outwards. To use the gauge compress the arm spring and push into the cylinder bore, at right angles to the axis of the cylinder. Then twist the small knurled top, to lock the arms, remove from the bore and measure the overall distance between the ends of the arms with a micrometer caliper.

Another method is to use an internal type, or bar micrometer (Fig. 102) which consists of a micrometer unit which with a set of standard rods will measure diameters up to 8 in.

A particularly convenient type of cylinder gauge is the 'Mercer' shown in Fig. 103. This type has an advantage over others with their reading dials close to the measuring contacts, in that its dial is at all times outside the cylinder where it can easily be read.

In use, the gauge is inserted, as shown, into the cylinder bore and the rod is rocked to and fro, when the dial needle also moves a little. The correct reading to take is the *maximum one* shown on the scale. It is possible to obtain readings accurate to within one-quarter of 1/1,000 inch with this gauge, the range of which is from 2 to 6 inch.

Typical Piston Clearances. The following are actual examples of aluminium alloy piston clearances used by a leading car engine manufacturer. It will be noticed that the lands (Fig. 100) – of which there are usually four in number – have more clearance than the skirt. The fourth land, being the hottest, has the most; next comes the first and then the second and third. In the following table the clearances represent the differences between the inside diameters of the cylinders and the outside diameters of the pistons:

Cylinder Diameter (in.)	Skirt Clearance (in.)	Piston Ring Land Clearance (in.)			
		First	Second	Third	Fourth
3·0	0·0030	0·015	0·010	0·010	0·0625
3·5	0·0035	0·017	0·012	0·012	0·0625
4·0	0·0040	0·020	0·014	0·014	0·0625
4·5	0·0045	0·023	0·016	0·016	0·0625
5·0	0·0050	0·025	0·018	0·018	0·0625

Piston Slap with Aluminium Pistons. If the clearance between the aluminium piston and the cylinder is excessive when cold, this will give rise to a knocking noise until the engine warms up. In many cases it is possible to cure this by drilling four holes through the piston skirt and slitting the latter with a hack-saw, as shown in Fig. 86 C. A small recess is turned near the base of and inside the skirt and a cast-iron split piston ring pushed into this recess; the skirt will then be sprung outwards a little and piston slap cured.

In the case of aluminium alloy pistons having a T-slot or split skirt it is sometimes possible to cure piston slap by expanding the skirt with the aid of thin wedges or a special expanding tool, such as the Fitzall. The diameter can be increased by at least 0·005

E

inch in this manner, if desired. Care is necessary to ensure even expansion of the piston skirt, and it is advisable to check the diameter at several places with a micrometer before and after the operation.

Restoring Worn Pistons. After a long period of service the pistons of automobile engines become worn and out of shape – more especially in the region of the piston skirt. It is possible not only to restore the shape but also to expand the skirt to the original new dimensions or to oversize by as much as 5-thousandths inch by a commercial process, known as the 'Koetherizer'. This method is based upon the same principle as that of hammering the insides of piston rings with a peening hammer in order to expand them, but instead of using a hammer it employs the impact effects of a controlled blast of air and lead shot – similar to a sand blast.

A vertical arm on the horizontal bracket shown in Fig. 104 holds a jig in the shape of a circle of cast iron with a centre hole of 2 inch diameter on which is placed a pad grooved out to take the piston to be restored.

The shot blast is directed through a hole in the jig and pad at an angle to the gudgeon pin boss in the interior of the piston. Whilst this is proceeding the piston is arranged to oscillate over a quarter of a circle, and the blast nozzle rises and falls in a semi-circular path in such a way that the expansion of the piston skirt (from inside it) is caused mainly on the thrust face.

An air pressure of 80 lb. per square inch is employed and the process occupies only a few seconds. The blasting action on the piston skirt produces a hard-skin and alters the shape of the skirt in the manner desired so that the final shape has the correct degree of ovality and taper.

Removing the Gudgeon Pin. In modern engines the gudgeon pin is usually a light press fit in the piston bosses and a bearing fit in the connecting rod small-end bearing. To remove the pin, if the piston has not been taken from the engine, a simple form of nut and screw device, as shown in Fig. 105, can be used. This is better than attempting to drive out the pin, since the piston may be damaged or the connecting rod bent. There are, however,

commercial tools available which will fit any size piston and screw
out the pin.

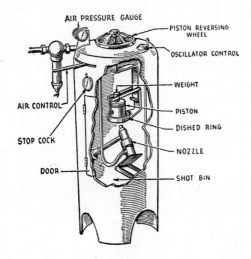

Fig. 104. Koetherizer apparatus for expanding
worn pistons.

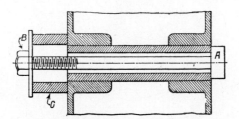

Fig. 105. Removing the gudgeon pin by means
of bolt (*A*), nut (*B*) and bush (*C*).

The method used to remove the pins of B.M.C. pistons, which
are fitted with a clamping device and setscrew, as shown in Fig.
107, is to fit a pair of soft metal or hardwood plugs at the ends

of the pin to enable the piston (removed from the engine) to be held without damage, in a vice, as depicted in Fig. 107, and then use a box spanner, or the B.M.C. tool provided for this purpose to unscrew the setscrew.

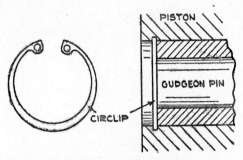

Fig. 106. Spring clip used for locating gudgeon pin.

Fig. 107. Method of holding piston to release
gudgeon pin.

In some instances the gudgeon pins are made appreciably shorter than the piston diameter and are prevented from moving endwise by means of spring slips, known as *Circlips*, an example of which is given in Fig 106. This clip fits into a circular recess turned in the piston hole.

To remove the gudgeon pin a pair of round-nosed pliers is employed to engage with the holes in the ends of the clip so that these may be drawn together, thus contracting the clip sufficiently to enable it to be removed from the piston hole.

Thermal Fit Gudgeon Pins. In many recent engines the gudgeon pins are made to fit the piston holes in such a way that when the aluminium pistons are heated to just below boiling point of water, the cold pins can be lightly tapped into place; upon cooling, the contraction of the piston metal holds the pin firmly in place. To remove the pins immerse to the level of the pin bosses in hot water and tap out.

When the gudgeon pin is clamped to the small end of its connecting rod, the correct 'rocking' fit in the piston boss holes is as described on page 98.

Re-conditioning Worn Cylinders. After an engine has run for a period of about 35,000 to 45,000 miles in the case of mass-production cars it will often be found that the cylinders have worn sufficiently to cause excessive oil consumption and loss of compression – and therefore of power. The greatest wear is invariably near the top, as indicated in Fig. 108, and the least at the bottom of the working part of the cylinder barrel. The reasons for this are that the greatest thrust occurs near the top, and the oil-film is more liable to break down there, causing increased wear; further, it is believed that the metal is exposed to the corrosive attack of the explosion products, more particularly during the warming-up period after starting from the cold.

The cylinder bore should be carefully measured at various positions along its length; in particular in the region of maximum wear indicated in Fig. 108. An inside dial-type gauge should be employed for this purpose.

Rebores and Replacements.

Pistons. When the cylinder is found to have worn appreciably out-of-round, or when the maximum clearance between the piston lands and cylinder walls exceeds about 0·015 to 0·020 in. as measured with a narrow type of feeler gauge, then the cylinder needs reboring. Before it is rebored, the dimensions of the available *oversize pistons* should be ascertained from either the engine

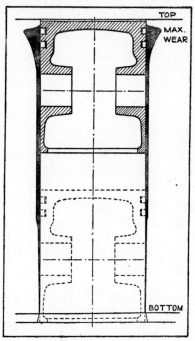

Fig. 108. Showing (exaggerated) by the blackened
areas, how the cylinder wears.

manufacturers or a firm of piston specialists. The nearest size of piston that corresponds to the minimum amount of cylinder metal removal in reboring (and finishing) should then be selected.

Here, it should be mentioned that when ordering oversize pistons from firms of piston specialists, the nominal sizes of the pistons given in the firm's list are the actual sizes of the finished rebored cylinders, as the makers allow for the correct clearances. Thus, if a cylinder is rebored to a diameter of 2·780 in., it is only necessary to order a piston of 2·780 in.; this will fit the cylinder with the proper clearances.

The maximum amount of metal that can safely be removed in one or two rebores is about $\frac{1}{16}$ inch so that if it again becomes necessary to rebore a worn cylinder it *should be fitted with a cylinder liner*. In certain instances three rebores can be made before it is necessary to fit cylinder liners.

Cylinder liners. The actual period after which excessive wear becomes apparent depends to a large extent upon the design of piston, the piston ring pressure, the lubrication of the cylinder walls and upon the quality of the metal used for the cylinder castings. The softer grades of cast iron necessary for the somewhat intricate cylinder casting wear more quickly than the harder white and alloy irons. For this reason, in the better designs of engines cylinder liners of centrifugally cast chromium (such as Chromidium iron) or nickel chromium iron are now employed. These liners when suitably heat-treated give at least twice to three times the wear of softer grades of cast iron. Another type of liner is the nitrided steel one. In this case a special grade of steel is employed and is surface-hardened by heating it to a temperature of about 500° C. and exposing it to the action of ammonia gas; the nitrogen from the latter is absorbed by the surface layer of the steel, leaving the metal glass-hard. It should be noted that a comparatively low hardening temperature is used, in comparison with that for ordinary case-hardening, viz., 900° C. so that practically no distortion can occur; moreover, no quenching is necessary.

Removing Cylinder Liner. If an hydraulic press is available this can be used to force out the liner, the block being reversed for this purpose, since most liners are inserted from the top and have a small flange at this end. By using two thick steel tubes each equal in length to the cylinder liner the latter may be removed in one operation. The tube between the press and liner end is slightly smaller in outside diameter than the outside diameter of the liner. The other tube between the other side of the cylinder block and the press table has an internal diameter about $\frac{1}{4}$ inch to $\frac{3}{8}$ inch greater than the outside diameter of the liner, so allow the latter to clear it when pressed downwards by the smaller tube. The tubes must be aligned accurately and be concentric with the liner before applying pressure.

Alternatively, the liner may be removed by means of the nut, screw and plate method illustrated in Fig. 109. The lower circular plate is conical in section to locate it centrally. The tube employed can be quite short for a wet-type cylinder liner which bears only

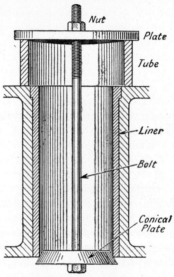

Fig. 109. Removing cylinder liner.

at the top and bottom of the cylinder block. For a dry-type liner it should have a length equal to that of the liner. The screw employed must be of ample diameter to ensure minimum thread wear. Thus, for a liner of 3 inch internal diameter a screw of $\frac{5}{8}$ inch to $\frac{3}{4}$ inch Whitworth or square thread of about six threads per inch would be used. The thread should be well-greased before putting on the nut.

Cylinder liners can be inserted with a similar ratchet screw arrangement or with a tool of the type illustrated in Fig. 110; this tool with different end fittings can also be used for removal and also insertion of cylinder liners.

Fitting Cylinder Liners. The method of fitting dry cylinder liners is to force them into the cylinder bore by mean of hydraulic or screw pressure. It is the rule to make a press fit allowance of 0·001 inch per inch of cylinder diameter, with a maximum allowance of 0·004 inch. It is usual to slightly taper the entering end.

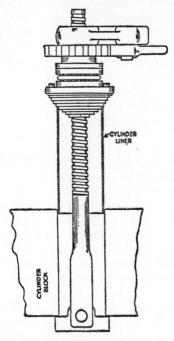

Fig. 110. The Ohio tool for inserting
(and removing) cylinder liners.

The total pressure required for a 3 inch piston is of the order, 10,000 lb. to 15,000 lb. Where a number of liners have to be inserted a quicker and simpler method is to use a liquid oxygen bath. The liners are dipped in this bath and are then rapidly transferred to the cylinder bore. The temperature of the liquid oxygen is about −180° C and the shrinkage of diameter is about 0·008 inch in the case of a 3 inch diameter liner. It should be noted that the operator must wear thickly lined gloves when handling the very cold liners; further, the liner should not touch the cylinder walls for any appreciable time during insertion.

When arranging to insert a new liner the outer surface should be coated liberally with graphite grease in the case of dry liners and soft soap for wet liners. The object of the soft soap in the latter case is to prevent the rubber rings from turning over during insertion and to avoid grease which would come into contact with the water in the jacket and possibly cause future trouble in the cooling system.

Truing Worn Cylinders. The object of this operation is to remove the minimum of cylinder metal in order to obtain a perfectly cylindrical bore having the smoothest possible surface finish. If the method used for truing the cylinder leaves the bore with tool ridges, or marks, these 'high spots' will wear down more quickly than if the surface was dead smooth, with the result that the useful life of the cylinder will be reduced appreciably. There are three principal processes in use for truing worn cylinders, as follows, namely: (1) *The Honing Method,* (2) *The Grinding Method* and (3) *The Boring Bar Method.*

In America, the reaming method was sometimes used for routine truing of worn cylinders, all of the same make and size.

The Honing Method. The honing process is a kind of grinding operation using four, five or six rectangular section stones arranged on the circumference of a circle (Fig. 111). These stones have their longer sides parallel to the axis of the cylinder. The radius of action is adjustable by means of a central control of the cone and wedge type. The honing unit is driven through one or two flexible metallic couplings from a drill-press or portable drill electric motor.

This method relies upon the unworn portions of the cylinder viz., at the top and bottom, to act as guides for the 'floating' honing stones. In practice, whilst honing gives a fine finish and a cylindrical bore, it is not always possible to ensure that the finished bore is in alignment with the original axis, i.e. the honed bore may be inclined to the original one *unless one uses the unworn part of the barrel* for location and guidance.

With the honing method, the stones may be used either dry or wet; in the latter more popular method a cutting lubricator paraffin is employed. A finer surface texture is obtainable by the wet process.

When using a honing machine it is advisable to take a light cut in order to ascertain the condition of the bore. A rougher grade of stone can be used for the initial truing part of the operation, followed by a finer grade of 'wet' stone for finishing.

It is usual to allow from 2 to 5/1000 in. for cleaning and truing the bore before using the finishing stone.

The hone should be driven at a speed of about 200 to 350 r.p.m. according to the grade of stone and cylinder bore. It is used with an up and down 'stroking' movement whilst the stones are rotating.

In some cases the hone is employed as a finishing process after using a single or multiple cutter boring tool, in order to remove the tool marks left by the latter and thus to obtain a much better surface finish.

The Grinding Method. In the grinding method a small cylindrical stone of the artificial abrasive type is rotated at a fairly high speed and is used on a bar, or head, in the same manner as a boring tool. It is usual to fix the cylinder block on to a rigid angle fixture bolted on the bed of the machine and to give the

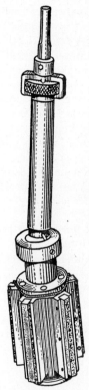

Fig. 111.
The Ammco Cylinder Hone. This has five stones equally spaced, adjustable in grinding diameter. A graduated dial is fitted. Universal joints are provided to facilitate the alignment of the stones when honing.

axis of the grinding wheel a concentric movement by means of planetary wheels, in order to grind all of the bore.

Grinding is undoubtedly the most accurate process of machining or truing cylinders; it is the method used in the original machining of the cylinder block; moreover, it gives a good surface finish. It is now possible to obtain a still finer finish by using a special 'glazing head' following the grinding operation. The glazing head is a kind of hone which removes only the 'nap' of the ground metal, representing the removal of about 0·0002 in.

It is possible to re-grind a worn cylinder in about 10 minutes, the glazing head operation taking a further 2 minutes. The grinding speeds for artificial abrasive wheels vary from 4,000 to 5,000 feet per minute.

The use of the grinding method necessitates removing the cylinder block from the chassis, taking it to the machine and setting it up. As compared with the portable types of honing and boring machines this involves an extra amount of time; on the other hand, it gives an accurate, properly aligned bore with a fine surface finish.

The Boring Bar Method. This is a portable adaptation of the well-known lathe boring bar, in which a single or multiple blade cutter is employed to turn away the high places in order to true the cylinder bore.

In order to preserve the cutting edge of the tool for very long periods the latter are now made of an extremely hard synthetic cutting alloy, belonging to the tungsten-carbide group; there are other ingredients in certain of these alloys, cobalt being one. With such alloys a large number of cylinder bores can be done before re-sharpening is necessary. The boring machine, of which the British Buma, Van Norman, Halls, K. B. Paddon, and Thomsen are typical examples, is used *in situ* on the cylinder block, it being necessary only to take off the cylinder head and remove the sump, valves, connecting rods and pistons. The boring bar is placed on the cylinder top and is centred in the bore by means of a special centring device which is always embodied in the design of the machine. The cutter is set to the desired size by means of a micrometer. The cutter is driven at a fairly low speed through gearing from the electric motor of the machine, and at

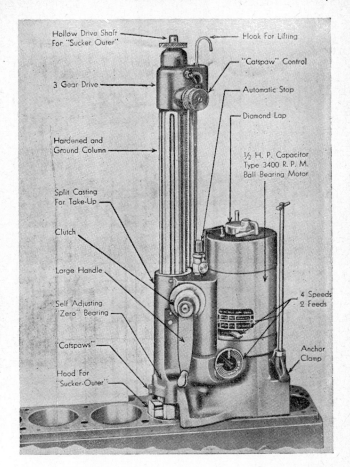

Fig. 112. The Van Norman Per-Fect-O cylinder boring machine.

the same time is fed forward by 'screw and nut' or – as in the K.B. machine – by hydraulic means.

If the setting-up has been done correctly the bore is trued in a single operation. The time taken to true a cylinder of average bore is from 8 to 12 minutes, including the setting-up time.

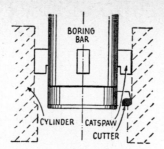

Fig. 113. The Catspaw centring device.

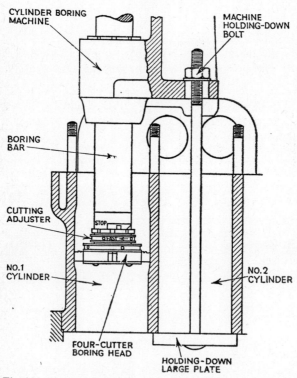

Fig. 114. Method of fixing the Van Norman boring machine using adjacent cylinder.

A Typical Machine. To illustrate the cylinder reboring machine the Van Norman Per-fect-O one is shown in Fig. 112. This uses a single tungsten-carbide cutter in a rigid boring head, the latter being centred by a device known as the 'catspaw' (Fig. 113) which has four arms that follow the bored surface made by the cutter and serve to steady and locate it. Other features of this machine are shown on Figs. 112 and 114. One special fitting is a device for sucking out the metal cuttings from the cylinder as it is bored; it is known as a 'sucker-outer' and consists of a hood near the cutter, connected to a vacuum motor through suitable passages and flexible tubing.

The machine is clamped to the cylinder block – after all the cylinder head studs have been removed – by means of a special anchor clamp device, which utilizes the adjacent cylinder to that being rebored (Fig. 114).

There is an automatic safety clutch which slips if the cutter is overloaded or if it hits an obstacle.

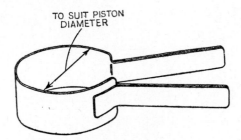

TO SUIT PISTON DIAMETER

Fig. 115. A simple but effective piston ring compressor.

The machine has four different boring speeds ranging from about 75 to 375 r.p.m. and two rates of feed. The cutter is reground when it has been in use for some time on the diamond dust lap shown in Fig. 112. Its cutting radius is set by a micrometer device to an accuracy of 0·0005 to 0·001 inch. All sizes of motor vehicle cylinders (including those with Diesel engines) are covered by these machines.

Notes on Boring Bars. The boring bar gives accurate results with a good surface. If the latter is examined microscopically it will be found to consist of numerous minute ridges and pits, but of very small magnitude. If the cylinder is afterwards polished with a cylinder honing tool using a (wet) hone of fine texture an excellent surface is obtainable.

The ordinary types of boring machine are fitted with electric motors of $\frac{1}{4}$ h.p., the boring bar being driven at speeds of 100 to 350 r.p.m. The usual rate of feed is from 1 to 2 inches, axially, per minute. Cuts of 0·010 to 0·050 inch can be taken with most machines, for roughing purposes, in order to clean up the cylinder worn barrels. Finishing cuts of 0·002 to 0·004 inch, using a fine feed are used. It is usual, however, to leave about 0·001 to 0·003 inch for finish honing or polishing, after reboring as this operation removes the tool feed marks and results in longer cylinder life. In most cases a diamond-impregnated sharpening disc is included in the machine for touching up the tungsten-carbide cutters. The machines are adjustable for bores of $2\frac{1}{8}$ to $4\frac{5}{8}$ inches and are arranged for maximum cutting depths of 10 to 13 inches.

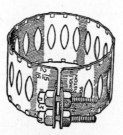

Fig. 116. Wellworthy
piston ring clamp.

Replacing the Pistons. When replacing the pistons, with their rings, into the cylinder barrels some difficulty may be experienced in entering the rings; unless special care is taken one or more of the rings may be broken. To overcome this difficulty a piston ring clamp (Figs. 115 and 116) should be employed. These consist of cylindrical bands of metal provided with means for contracting them over the rings, so that the latter are compressed to about the same diameter as the cylinder. The inside surface of the band should be made as smooth as possible and given a smear of engine oil before placing it over the rings.

The piston is then pushed into the cylinder barrel, when the band, acting as a kind of extension of the latter, enables the rings to slide readily into the cylinder.

In an emergency each of the piston rings can be compressed in turn by means of a piece of string wrapped around it in the form of a half-hitch. As the piston is pushed into the cylinder the string is forced off the ring.

Timing the Valves. It may be necessary to set the valve cams in their correct relation to the engine crankshaft after a complete overhaul, or for experimental purposes. We do not, however, recommend any alteration of the setting of the valves from the makers' positions, for the latter are the best positions for all-round efficiency. To 'time' the valves of any engine first set one of the pistons on its top dead centre; a piece of wire or a screwdriver inserted through the sparking plug hole will show this position. In most modern engines, however, there is a line on the rim or edge of the flywheel (Fig. 117) which can be observed

Fig. 117. Showing the method of marking the flywheel rim, to facilitate timing the engine.

against a mark on the crank casing on removing an inspection door to show the top centre of No. 1 piston. The makers will always supply particulars of their valve settings, and it is an easy matter to measure angles by means of their corresponding arcs on the flywheel from the top centre position.

The B.M.C. Mini- and 1100 car engines have flywheel markings for the top dead centres; in addition, there are 5° and 10° marks, to assist in timing the ignition. (See page 409.)

The other B.M.C. engines up to 1·6 litres have a small groove on the rear flange of the crankshaft pulley and three fixed marks on the timing chain case, viz., T.D.C. and 5° and 10°, respectively.

Suppose, for example, *the inlet valve opens on top dead centre*, the crankshaft, with its drive disconnected, should be turned by hand in its normal direction of rotation until the inlet valve is just about to lift. The timing gear drive should now be connected up, and it will be found that in timing the one inlet valve correctly all of the other valves are timed correctly.

It is important, before timing the valves, to set their tappet clearances to the recommended timing value. The manufacturers supply the correct valve *clearances used for valve timing* – but usually different than those for normal engine operation. Further reference to these clearance values is made later in this Chapter.

In setting a valve look for corresponding marks on the timing gear teeth, for many makers put a pair of dots on two teeth of one wheel and a single dot on the tooth of the other wheel which comes between these two teeth.

Also, look for line marks on the flywheel rim (Fig. 117), for it is sometimes the practice to mark the angles at which the valve of, say, No. 1 cylinder commences to open, or are just closed.

Camshaft Timing with Chain Drive. The majority of modern engines now employ double- or triple-roller chain drives from the engine to the camshaft; in some cases also the dynamo is driven by the same chain.

There is, in addition, an automatic chain tensioning device which may be in the form of a spring-loaded jockey pulley or a cantilever spring unit – notably in the case of overhead camshafts.

The crankshaft and camshaft sprockets are usually marked to facilitate the re-timing of the engines after dismantling and re-assembly.

A typical instance of the method of timing is illustrated in

Fig. 118, for the earlier B.M.C. engines. In this case one tooth of each sprocket is marked with the letter 'T'. These teeth are arranged in the vertical positions shown in order to give the correct relative timing positions. The chain itself is provided with two bright links in different places along its length. In order to time the valves correctly the chain is removed and the sprockets moved to the positions shown, when the bright links of the chain are then slipped over the sprocket teeth marked 'T'.

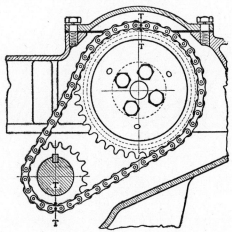

Fig. 118. The B.M.C. engine earlier timing method.

Later B.M.C. engines mark the two chain sprockets with a pair of dots which should be opposite each other and on the same line through the two sprocket wheel centres, with No. 1. piston on its T.D.C. and closest together.

A similar method is used on Hillman and Humber engines; the method for valve timing is illustrated in Fig. 119. After placing No. 1 piston on its T.D.C. the sprockets should be arranged, as shown, with their dots in line, after pushing them a short way on to their shafts. The keys of these shafts should be as indicated. The camshaft is free to turn and it should be rotated until its key is opposite the sprocket keyway. Then both sprockets should be tapped a little at a time until they are right home on their keys.

Most engines have *chain tensioners*, which are removed before valve timing and should, of course, be refitted to the correct tension afterwards.

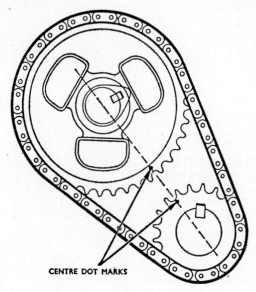

CENTRE DOT MARKS

Fig. 119. Method of timing the Hillman and Humber engine valves.

In some instances, in order to avoid the trouble of measuring the actual angle before top dead centre at which No. 1 inlet valve opens, the makers give the *additional inlet valve stem clearance*, such that when the valve is set to this clearance it will just begin to open at so many degrees before top dead centre. Thus, in Sunbeam Rapier engines for which the normal inlet valve clearance is 0·012 in., for valve timing purposes the No. 1. inlet valve clearance is set at 0·019–0·020 in. When the inlet valve just begins to open the No. 1 crank should be at 14° before T.D.C. for the Mark II engine.

The inlet closes at 52° after B.D.C., while the exhaust valve opens at 55° before B.D.C. and closes at 10° after T.D.C. The timing chain arrangement is identical with that shown in Fig. 119.

The Armstrong-Siddeley chain was of the double-roller pattern and was tensioned correctly by unslacking the dynamo flange bolts to enable the dynamo chain sprocket, seen on the extreme left in

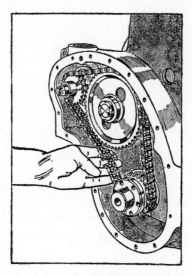

Fig. 120. Armstrong-Siddeley timing
chain adjustment.

Fig. 120, to be moved relatively to the camshaft sprocket on the right of it. When it is necessary to replace the chain the crankshaft and camshaft are rotated independently by hand until a timing indication line on the crankshaft sprocket is directly opposite a letter 'O' on the camshaft sprocket, both being closest together. The chain is then threaded over the crankshaft sprocket and around the dynamo and camshaft sprockets, taking care not to move the latter sprocket. The joint in the chain which has screw pins instead of rivets is arranged in the position indicated in Fig. 120, when the detachable link can be fitted from behind.

Before a new chain is fitted the teeth of the sprockets should be examined for wear; if excessive wear effects are observed new sprockets must be fitted. Finally, do not adjust the chain too tightly; it should have a small amount of free side play between the sprocket wheels.

Typical Valve Timings. A good average valve setting for modern car engines is as follows:

> Inlet opens at 10° to 15° before T.D.C.
> Inlet closes at 50° to 55° past B.D.C.
> Exhaust opens at 50° to 55° before B.D.C.
> Exhaust closes at 10° to 15° past T.D.C.

In high-speed engines the inlet valve is given the greatest period of opening, namely 200° to 240°, and the exhaust opens early (50° to 55° before bottom centre) and closes late (0° to 25° past top centre). This gives 240° to 260° opening.

A typical valve setting for a modern high-speed car engine is as follows:

> Inlet opens 15° to 25° before T.D.C.
> Inlet closes 53° to 58° after B.D.C.
> Exhaust opens 55° to 65° before B.D.C.
> Exhaust closes 15° to 25° after T.D.C.

Setting Angular Distances on Flywheel. Valve opening and closing periods can be converted to the equivalent flywheel distances as follows:

Let D = equivalent distance, in inches, measured from T.D.C. or B.D.C. around flywheel rim, with a flexible steel tape.

R = radius of flywheel in inches. A = timing angle in degrees.

Then $D = \dfrac{2\pi}{360} \times A \times R = 0.01745 \times AR.$

Example $A = 30°$. $R = 5$ in. $D = 0.01745 \times 30 \times 5$.
  i.e., $D = 2.62$ inches.

CHAPTER 4

THE CARBURETTOR AND FUEL SYSTEM

THE carburettor is a unit that does not usually give much trouble if not interfered with. As set by the car manufacturers it will generally be found to give the best all-round results, but since the conditions vary with the season of the year a little adjustment is sometimes necessary. As most modern carburettors are now fitted with some form of independent mixture control – as distinct from automatic mixture regulation by means of suction and similar devices – it is not difficult to 'tune' a carburettor to suit the external conditions. We shall not attempt to explain the principles or working of different carburettors, as this subject is dealt with fully in the author's *Carburettors and Fuel Systems*,* but confine our attention to the practical maintenance and overhauling of carburettors.

The Fuel System. In modern cars petrol from the main tank at the rear of the chassis and below the carburettor level, is pumped to the carburettor by means of a mechanically-driven or electric fuel pump. The earlier vacuum- and gravity-fuel-feed systems are no longer used on cars.

Fig. 121 illustrates a typical fuel system and shows the fuel tank (*A*) having a fuel level gauge unit (*B*) which indicates by electrical means the fuel level on the instrument panel. From (*A*) the fuel is drawn along the fuel pipe (*C*) by the suction effect of an engine-driven diaphragm pump (*D*), whence it is pumped under a light pressure to the float chamber of the carburettor (*E*). The cylindrical object above (*E*) is a large volume air cleaner and silencer. The fuel tank must have a breather orifice to allow air to leak in as the fuel level drops; otherwise an air lock will occur and fuel flow will become reduced or stopped altogether.

* Motor Manuals, Vol. 2. Chapman and Hall Ltd.

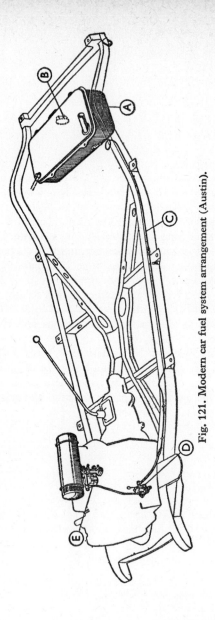

Fig. 121. Modern car fuel system arrangement (Austin).

Simple Maintenance Notes. Commencing with the carburettor as fitted to a new car and tracing the different items of attention necessary from time to time, it can be stated that, apart from small adjustments of the mixture strength to obtain the

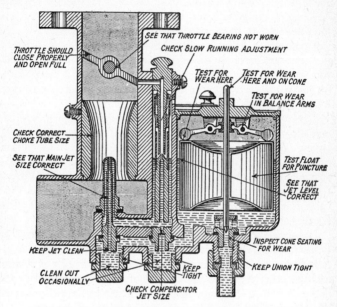

Fig. 122. Showing the principal items of attention in the case of the carburettor.

best results in both winter and summer, little attention need be given under about 3,000 to 5,000 miles. It is a good thing, however, to dismantle and clean the internal parts of the carburettor every time the engine is decarbonized and also to clean the petrol filter, say, every 2,000 miles or so.

The petrol filter usually consists of a piece of fine-mesh gauze held in a metal container unit and situated either at the petrol inlet to the float chamber or at the petrol outlet from the gravity or vacuum feed tank; in any case, it will be found in an accessible position in modern cars.

The gauze filter should be removed and cleaned with a soft bristle brush, e.g. an old toothbrush, and petrol; the interior of the filter chamber should also be scrupulously cleaned. The foreign matter found consists of solid particles from the inside of the tank and dust; water is another impurity occasionally present.

When cleaning the filter turn on the petrol tap from the tank for a moment, to wash out any impurities in the pipe.

Carburettor Adjustments. Modern carburettors as fitted to new cars are carefully adjusted in regard to the jets and choke tube by the manufacturers and since these internal components do not wear no further adjustment or exchange of parts is required during the normal life of the engine.

The only items that may need occasional attention are the adjusting screws fitted for regulating *the slow running* of the engine. With engine wear and valve clearance alterations, it may become necessary to alter these adjustments. Thus, as the valve stems and guides wear, air may leak into the cylinders and dilute the starting mixture. Again, as the pistons and cylinders wear there is a loss of compression – and suction – which will affect starting and slow-running conditions.

Practically all carburettors, on examination will be found to possess *two adjusting screws for slow-running*. One of these regulates the proportions of air and petrol for the starting jet or passage and the other regulates the amount of mixture admitted to the engine for slow-running purposes. In general a rich mixture must be supplied to enable the engine to 'fire' and this is obtained by regulating the air supply screw to the starting jet. Once the engine has started to 'operate', it is necessary to keep it running at a fairly low – but not too low – speed by adjusting a screw which regulates the stopping position of the engine throttle, i.e. it leaves the latter open by a very small amount so that enough mixture passes for slow running purposes.

The principal carburettor types in use on English cars are the Zenith, Solex, Stromberg and S.U. Whilst it is not possible here, to explain the theory and operation of these, notes will be given on their main features and adjustments.

Common Feature in Modern Carburettors. Most carburettors employ a similar engine starting and idling device principle to that shown in Fig. 123. It is well known that for starting from the cold it is necessary to shut off most of the main air supply to the carburettor and thus make the mixture richer. Also, the throttle should be opened a little to ensure that enough mixture shall be given to keep the engine running after starting.

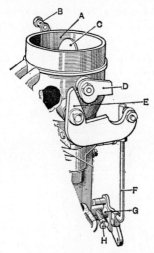

Fig. 123. Showing the interconnected air choke and throttle (Zenith).

This is done, in the case of the Zenith carburettors by interconnecting the air valve, or choke, to the throttle, so that when the choke control knob is pulled on the engine dashboard the air valve closes and the throttle opens a little. In Fig. 123 which shows part of the Zenith carburettor, as fitted to a typical car engine, the main air intake to the carburettor is indicated at (A). The automatic choke flap (C) is mounted on the choke spindle (B). This spindle has an operating lever at the end (B) which is connected to the dashboard choke control knob. At the other end of this spindle a cam plate (D) is fitted. When the choke is closed this plate engages with a lever (E) which moves to the left and lifts the connecting rod (F), so as to move the spindle (G) of the main throttle valve, to open the valve slightly. The 'closed' position of the throttle can be adjusted, by means of the spring-loaded screw (H) to alter the slow-running speed.

The Zenith Carburettors. These are made in several models, the downdraught types now being fitted to cars. They embody the well-known principles of mains and compensating jets; these are pre-determined and fixed in orifice size by the manufacturers to suit each engine type.

Fig. 124 shows one model of the VEI-type Zenith carburettor

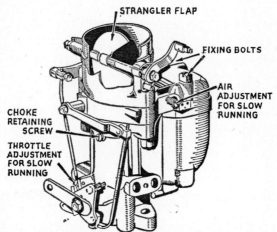

Fig. 124. The Zenith VEI-type Carburettor.

which has been widely used on production car engines and is made in the vertical, horizontal and downdraught models. It has a special design of choke or air valve which we shall designate the strangler flap. This consists of a circular-disc type air valve mounted on a spindle on one side of the geometrical diameter of the disc. As mentioned more fully, later, it has the interconnected choke and throttle linkage shown, previously in Fig. 123.

In addition this model incorporates an important feature whereby the engine is arranged to run upon an economical air-fuel mixture at low to cruising speeds but a *slightly rich full-power mixture* is supplied during the latter part of the throttle opening to the fully-open position. *When the engine is started from the cold* the strangler control on the dashboard is extended, which will result in the strangler flap closing the air-intake of the carburettor. A cam on the end of the strangler spindle will cause the connecting link to lift and open the throttle slightly when the strangler is closed. This will ensure sufficient volume and richness being obtained to give instant starting when the engine is turned over with ignition switched on. A rich mixture is necessary only to obtain the initial firing. The strangler flap is free to move on the spindle and is only held closed by the spring shown in Fig. 124.

Action After Starting. After starting, the engine speed increases, causing additional suction on the engine side of the strangler flap, forcing the latter to open and thus to admit more air. Thus, the strangler automatically provides the normal mixture for warming-up purposes. With the throttle closed down to the idling position the mixture comes from the pilot jet. With the strangler out of action and the throttle just open the depression will be concentrated on the outlet passage which will in turn be directed on to the slow running jet. Thus, petrol will be drawn from the well below the jet, measured on passing through, and meet air entering at the base of the adjustment screw. The amount of air mixing with the petrol from the slow running jet is controlled by an air adjustment screw.

At the throttle edge there is a further outlet which breaks into the slow running passage. Upon the throttle being opened from the idling position this will give an additional mixture to ensure progressive get-away from slow running.

Adjustments. The only adjustments provided are for slow-running, by means of an adjustable air screw, on the right and a mixture quantity adjustment on the lower left. The air screw gives the richer mixture and when this is correct the throttle opening screw should be moved to give the correct idling speed.

The Solex Carburettors. There are several different models of these, but most have common features and methods of adjustment. The model shown, externally, in Fig. 125 is the down-draught bi-starter one used on cars. The Solex bi-starter unit is a small auxiliary carburettor embodied in the main unit for the purpose of ensuring easy starting from the cold and good acceleration until the engine is hot, when it is cut out of action.

For slow-running purposes, after starting by the bi-starter device, a pilot jet and air supply or 'bleed' tube is provided. The richness of the mixture from the slow-running jet is regulated by means of a screw marked (*W*) in Fig. 125. When this control

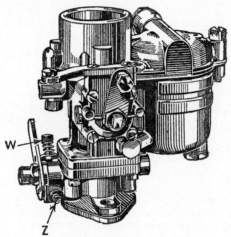

Fig. 125. The Solex Type FAI Carburettor.

is screwed in a clockwise direction it decreases the mixture strength. The amount of this mixture reaching the engine, for slow-running purposes, is regulated by the throttle stop screw (*Z*). The adjustment procedure is as follows: Run engine until it is hot. Then set the throttle stop screw (*Z*) until idling speed is on the high side. Next, slacken the volume control screw (*W*) until the engine begins to 'hunt' or run erratically. When this happens screw this in very gradually until hunting ceases. If the engine speed is too high reset the screw (*Z*) to reduce the idling speed.

The S.U. Carburettor. The S.U. Carburettor belongs to the suction-operated variable jet type, with variable choke area. Fig. 126 shows one model used on B.M.C. cars. It is fitted

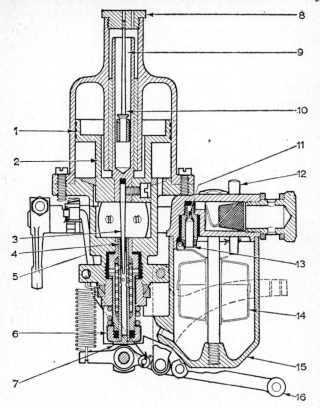

Fig. 126. The S.U. Controllable-jet Carburettor.
1 suction disc. 2 piston. 3 tapered jet needle. 4 jet orifice. 5 throttle and mixture control connecting link. 6 adjusting nut. 7 jet head. 8 oil cap nut. 9 piston rod. 10 oil dashpot. 11 needle seating. 12 float depressing plunger. 13 float needle. 14 float. 15 float chamber. 16 jet adjusting lever.

with an air cleaner and has a damper consisting of a plunger and non-return valve attached to the oil cap nut, which operates in the hollow piston rod that is partly filled with oil. It gives a slightly richer mixture on acceleration.

The adjustment of this carburettor is as follows: Run the engine until it attains its normal running temperature. Then adjust the throttle abutment screw to give a moderate idling speed. Adjust the jet to give a richer mixture by screwing the jet adjusting nut downwards, keeping the jet head in contact with it until the mixture is *too rich*, as indicated by 'hunting' and a smoky exhaust. Then screw the jet adjusting nut upwards, still keeping the jet head in contact with it, until it brings the jet to the position where the engine idles with an even exhaust and runs at the best possible speed for this throttle setting.

The correct mixture can be tested for, at this stage, by lifting up the piston a little with a pencil, to a height of $\frac{1}{32}$ inch. When this is done the engine should run a little faster. If, however, it runs much faster, this shows *too rich* a mixture. If the engine stops when the piston is thus raised it is an indication of *too weak* a mixture.

If it is found that the car runs better with the manual control pulled out, in the case of any particular make of engine this shows that a needle giving a richer mixture is required; if it runs slower then a weaker mixture needle is needed.

The needle is held by a set screw, at the side of the piston; when this is unscrewed the needle can be detached. It is important to note that the *correct position of the needle* is with its shoulder flush with the face of the piston.

The H-type carburettor, shown in Fig. 127, is fitted with an internal light spring (S) to return the piston to its lower position. It also has a small knob (8) to operate a plunger that lifts the piston when it is necessary to tune the carburettor.

The later HS model, as fitted to literally millions of front-drive small cars, while operating upon the same principles uses a nylon tube to supply fuel from the float chamber to the jet and it has a different float chamber mounting method. It now has a nylon float anchored to the lever arm; fuel connections to the lid are of the 'push-on' kind.

Sources of Trouble. The possible sources of trouble of S.U. carburettors include:

(1) The piston may be sticking and not functioning properly.
(2) There may be dirt or water in the carburettor.
(3) The float mechanism may have become deranged, and the carburettor is in consequence flooding.

Piston Sticking. The suction piston consists of the piston proper forming the choke; the suction disc, into which is inserted the hardened and ground piston rod working in a bearing in the suction chamber; and a tapered needle regulating the jet opening.

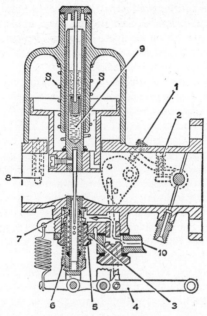

Fig. 127. The later type 'H' S.U. Carburettor (P. G. Knight).
1 jet-throttle interconnection adjusting screw. 2 throttle adjusting screw. 3 sealing cork. 4 jet lever. 5 locking screw. 6 jet adjusting screw. 7 jet gland. 8 piston lifting pin. 9 oil well. 10 fuel feed from float chamber.

If the piston is sticking, this can easily be ascertained by releasing the curved air intake pipe and then inserting a finger in the air intake and raising the piston. The piston should come up quite freely and return to its seat with a click as soon as it is released.

The piston rod sliding within its bearing is the only part which is in actual contact with any other part, the suction piston and its needle possessing a slight clearance space around them. If,

F

therefore, the piston does not return readily to its seat it is probable that the piston rod has become dry or sticky.

To free this, remove the oil cap nut to be found at the top of the suction chamber, pour in a few drops of good quality engine oil – such as an S.A.E. 20W oil – and replace the cap. In particularly obstinate cases a little paraffin may be introduced into the oil cap opening and the piston worked up and down until it is free by inserting a finger in the air inlet. *Under no circumstances should a heavy-bodied lubricant be used, and no oil must be introduced on any other part of the suction chamber.*

Water or dirt can be eliminated by first releasing the curved intake pipe, then, with a pencil, raising the piston so that the jet can be seen. Flood the carburettor by holding up the float chamber needle and note whether petrol issues freely from the jet. If it does not, the foreign matter blocking the latter can usually be got rid of by starting the engine and opening the throttle. Then momentarily block the air inlet by placing the hand over it, keeping the throttle open until the engine commences to race.

The petrol filter is situated behind the large hexagon nut at the junction of the petrol pipe to the float-chamber lid and is released by uncoupling the petrol pipe union, by unscrewing this large hexagon nut. The filter should never be cleaned with rag; always employ a stiff brush and petrol.

Remember when replacing the filter that the helical spring must first be introduced into the filter housing and that the thimble-like filter has its open end bearing against the union piece.

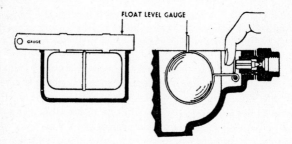

Fig. 128. Float gauge to check fuel level in float chamber.

Fuel Level in Float Chamber. An occasional cause of trouble is that due to the level of the petrol being too high or too low, so that apart from the risk of flooding in the former case the mixture strength can be seriously affected and the engine operation impaired. It is therefore necessary to check the petrol level when the engine has been in long service or when being overhauled. All carburettor makers now supply fuel-level checking gauges, a typical example being that shown in Fig. 128 for a model having a spherical float and a hinged-lever operated fuel shut-off valve, the latter being tipped with rubber. In this case the float gauge is placed on the machined casing joint of the carburettor.

Carburettor Adjustment and Tuning. The driver of a car will be concerned mostly with the necessary adjustments of his carburettor for obtaining the maximum efficiency from the engine under all running conditions, combined with ease of starting from the cold and slow-running qualities. It will here be necessary to say a few words on the subject of carburation in order that the reader may appreciate the object of the adjustments.

The petrol engine will work on a fairly wide range of petrol-air mixtures, namely, from the richest (in petrol) of 8 to 10 parts of air to 1 part of petrol by weight, to the weakest mixture consisting of 18 to 20 parts of air to 1 of petrol. Now, there is only one mixture which gives maximum power, namely, one of about 13 parts of air to 1 part of petrol. Whilst this mixture is the most powerful it is not the most economical as reckoned in 'miles per gallon'; this is the reason of the relatively bad petrol consumption of *car engines tuned for racing purposes*. In order to obtain the *greatest mileage per gallon* of petrol it is necessary to use a mixture on the weaker side, namely, about 16 or 17 parts of air to 1 part of petrol. Incidentally, for complete combustion or burning of the fuel, the mixture strength is about 15.

If one tunes for petrol economy alone, it is necessary to sacrifice a little power (and therefore acceleration and maximum speed); this loss of power amounts to about 10 per cent on the average. The best all-round mixture is one of 14 to 15; the petrol consumption is only 5 parts in 100 greater, and the power drop only about 5 per cent, an amount unnoticeable in driving a car. Applying the above principles to carburettor tuning, a jet opening or jet is chosen which gives a fraction less than maximum power – as measured, say, by maximum speed on the level.

Maximum Power Devices. It should here be mentioned that in most modern carburettors provision is now made for increasing the mixture strength at three-quarters to full throttle opening, in order to give maximum power, whilst providing economical mixture at smaller throttle openings.

Measuring Petrol Consumption. A good practical method of checking the carburettor in this case is by a measured petrol consumption test. To do this fill the petrol tank (with the car standing on a level piece of ground) to a given level – as measured by a dipstick or fuel gauge (for longer runs). Then after noting the speedometer reading, run the car for an hour or two, and on returning to the original spot, note the speedometer mileage and the quantity of petrol you have to pour into the tank to bring the level to its original value. If the difference in speedometer readings is, say, 52 miles and you have to pour in 2 gallons of petrol, the mileage per gallon will be $52 \div 2 = 26$.

Cars having two-level taps or reserve tanks can readily be arranged for such a test by using in one tank a measured quantity of petrol, and running the car until the supply is used up.

Testing for Weak Mixture. A good reliable method of testing for weakness of mixture is to run the car on the level, and with the throttle at a given setting (temporarily rigged up for the purpose). Then flood the carburettor with a makeshift device, e.g. a Bowden carburettor 'tickler', or with a long stick rigged up for the purpose. Note whether the speedometer shows any increase of speed; if so, this is a sure indication of a previous weak mixture setting of the carburettor; the obvious remedy is an increase in jet size. The test should be carried out at about 15 to 20 m.p.h., to ensure the 'main' jet being in operation.

With a weak mixture the engine will work sluggishly at low speeds, sometimes misfiring or running jerkily, further, the acceleration will be poor; very weak mixtures will occasion 'popping back in the carburettor'.

For these and other carburettor tests it is important first to *check the ignition timing*.

Testing for Rich Mixtures. From what has been said it will be evident that one good method of checking for too rich a mixture setting of the carburettor is to note whether the petrol consumption is excessive for the make of car. The following is a rough guide to the average petrol consumptions of modern cars with correctly set carburettors.

PETROL CONSUMPTIONS OF MODERN CARS

R.A.C. Horsepower	7	8	9	10	12	14	18	20	26
Miles Per Gallon	40 to 50	42 to 45	38 to 42	35 to 38	30 to 35	27 to 32	24 to 26	22 to 24	18 to 22

Rich mixtures may be revealed by running the engine with both wheels jacked up and the brakes applied so as to simulate a load upon the engine. The gearbox-driven speedometer will show the equivalent road speed. If the throttle be set at a given position (by a block under the accelerator pedal) and the speed noted, the jet can be reduced in size until the speed just begins to drop. The jet size will then be about right. *Too rich a mixture* gives a *pungent odour from the exhaust* and a sooty deposit on a piece of white paper held near the exhaust outlet. The colour of the exhaust flame – which can be seen at night – is bright *yellow for rich mixtures* and *bluish-white for weak mixtures*. For the correct mixture it is an *intense light-blue colour*.

Carburettor Troubles. Carburettor troubles may be divided into two classes, namely, those caused by mechanical defects (Fig. 129), and those due to wrong adjustment or the presence of foreign matter in the petrol.

Before concluding that the carburettor is the cause of poor performance, difficult starting, inability to run slowly, etc., it is important to make certain that the ignition system and timing are correct, the valve stem clearances right, engine compression good and, in general, that the rest of the engine is not the cause of the trouble.

Mechanical Troubles. One of the occasional mechanical items giving rise to leakage of petrol at the jet and flooding of the float chamber is a *leaky needle valve*. In this case the conical valve end does not bed properly into its seating with the result that petrol continues to flow into the float chamber all the time the tap is on. If, as is usual, this leakage is slight, the excess *petrol will drip from the jet*.

The remedy is to grind the needle on to its seating with valve grinding compound, or, if worn very badly, to replace the needle and true up the seating in the lathe or with a special conical rose-bit tool. When replacing the re-seated needle, it will be necessary to re-adjust the petrol level in float chamber. *Leakage from the float chamber and main jet* is also caused by a piece of dirt getting on the needle valve's seating and thus preventing the valve from closing properly.

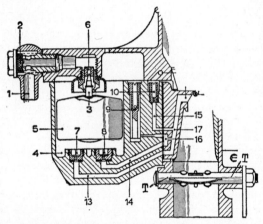

Fig. 129. Showing possible causes of carburettor troubles.
1 leaky fuel inlet. 2 filter plug joint faulty. 3 worn float needle. 4 dirt in base of float chamber. 5 punctured float. 6 worn float needle valve seating. 7, 8, 9 and 10 dirt in control jets. 13 and 14, dirt in fuel passages. 15, 16 and 17 fuel passages partly choked. *T* throttle spindle and bearings worn – causing air leakage.

Another mechanical trouble liable to happen on any car is that of a *punctured float*. This is usually due to the presence of a pin-hole or defective soldering; prolonged usage will also tend to wear the metal through near the balance weights. The symptom of a punctured float is the constant flooding of the carburettor. To ascertain whether the cause is due to the float or needle valve, turn off the petrol, remove the float and shake it; if punctured you will be able to hear the petrol swishing about inside. Upon careful examination you will be able to find the leak; otherwise heat the float by placing it under the surface of some hot water and note where the bubbles escape. Incidentally this is a good means of getting rid of the petrol inside; when the leak is found keep this part of the float above the surface of the hot water. Having found the leak, it can readily be soldered over.

Worn balance weights and needle collar mechanism, used in earlier models, will cause an alteration in the level of the petrol, the latter becoming higher as the balance weights and needle collar wear.

In such a case the only remedy is to renew the worn balance levers, or to re-set the needle collar on its needle.

In modern carburettors the vertical movements of the float operate the fuel needle valve, either direct (as shown in Fig. 129 for the Zenith 30VM model) or by the float operating a small hinged lever, so that the float force is multiplied at the valve seating. Recently, float *needle valves* have been *tipped* with *synthetic rubber*, e.g. Viton, greatly to extend their leakless life.

A loose needle seating will cause petrol leakage or dripping; sometimes the seatings become a little slack, or unscrewed, due to vibrational effects, and therefore require tightening up.

Leaky petrol unions are generally due to the presence of the dirt on the coned joints, or to a distorted joint. If, after tightening, leakage still occurs, the cone and its seating should be trued up by grinding in with a fine abrasive. As a makeshift measure, when on the road, smear the outside of the joint with yellow soap (as this is insoluble in petrol) and bind with several layers of insulating tape. Fibre washer type joints found to be leaky will require new washers.

In the case of automatic carburettors having *sliding pistons or sleeves* worked by the suction of the engine, the effect of long usage is to cause relative wear between the sliding parts due principally to the grit in the air drawn in. The carburettor will then work indifferently, the piston or sleeve failing to rise to its full extent owing to leakage past it. *The engine will not then give its full power or run slowly*. A new piston or sleeve of the oversize type must then be fitted.

The throttle is another source of mechanical trouble. If of the butterfly type, its bearings will in time, become slack, allowing a leakage of air from outside; the engine will then not run slowly. Further, a slackness in the throttle bearings is apt to cause 'hunting' of the engine, whereby the engine is constantly varying its speed over a given range with the throttle lever set.

Starting Difficulties. In the case of engines which are difficult to start, the valve tappet clearances when the engine is cold should be checked and the battery ignition tested for operation by rotating the engine by hand, and watching for the spark at the plug; the latter is removed and laid sidewise on the cylinder for this purpose. If the trouble is thus traced to the carburettor, first try flooding the jet by depressing the float. If this fails to start the engine when the latter is cranked with switch on, the jet may be stopped with dirt or water. To test for this, remove the plugs and inject a little petrol into each cylinder. If on cranking the engine – the plugs having been replaced, of course – it fires, runs for a few turns, and then stops, this is a sign of a starved jet. Remove the jets and clean out the float chamber.

Incorrect adjustment of the starting unit, e.g. the pilot jet, is often the cause of poor starting. If the engine will not start in *very cold weather,* the petrol may be condensing in the inlet passages. It is then a good thing to wrap a hot flannel round the inlet part of the carburettor or inlet manifold. A piece of iron, bent to fit around the manifold and heated in the fire is another good device for starting. Sometimes the injection of petrol into the cylinders will get over the trouble.

Another frequent cause, is excessive use of the air choke. This gives too rich a mixture. Now, switch off, open the choke and crank the engine with the throttle full open; then try again.

Slow Running Troubles. In many engines in which starting is not difficult they tend to race and will not run slowly. The cause may be: (*a*) *worn valve guides*, causing leakage of air past the valves, thus giving too weak a mixture in the cylinder; the use of valve stem sealers, e.g. the Flexigas or S.U. types is advocated in such cases. Most modern overhead valve engines (see Fig. 45) now employ special *oil sealing washers* – usually of Neoprene rubber – for the valve stems; these washers also tend to prevent air leakages past the valve stems. (*b*) Air leaks past the carburettor flange or inlet manifold joints, due to faulty gaskets or loose nuts on the joint studs or screws. (*c*) *The slow-running* or *pilot jet* may be set for too weak a mixture – or it may be choked. The remedy in the former case is to increase the jet size or reduce the air supply. (*d*) *The throttle stop* may be set so that the throttle does not close and so permits too much mixture to pass. The stop should first be adjusted so that the engine races and with the engine running it should gradually be closed until the engine ticks over slowly. Do not adjust for too slow a top speed for with the engine cold it will not run satisfactorily. (*e*) The throttle in the case of some engines requires to be open by about $\frac{1}{3}$ to $\frac{1}{2}$ for starting; if opened too wide there will not be enough suction on the jet to draw up the petrol. In cases of difficult starting it is always advisable to close partially the main air supply; an air choke is fitted for this purpose.

Engine Misfires at Various Speeds. Assuming the ignition is working satisfactorily, misfiring may be due to: (*a*) water in the float chamber of jet well; (*b*) dirt in the main jet; (*c*) a choked petrol filter or (*d*) air lock in the petrol pipe.

Loss of Power. Loss of engine power, traceable to carburation, is due to (*a*) throttle not opening to its full extent due to accelerator mechanism being incorrectly adjusted; (*b*) starvation of petrol by too small a jet, choked filter or air lock; (*c*) too rich a mixture – this may be checked in the manner previously outlined under the heading 'Rich Mixtures'; or (*d*) the inlet pipe washer partly obscuring the inlet orifice.

Poor Acceleration or Pick-up. The causes of poor acceleration are similar to those given in the previous paragraph. The best practical method of tuning the carburettor in such cases is gradually to increase the size of the jet, give the car a road run and note its 'pick-up' and maximum speed on the level until the best results are obtained. See that the mixture is not too rich, the jet being the smallest which will give good acceleration.

Mechanical Fuel Pumps. A typical mechanical petrol pump is the A.C. one. The diaphragm providing the movement for the pumping action receives its motion from the rocker arm; the latter bears on a cam formed on the engine camshaft.

The earlier S.U. petrol pump was fitted with a glass bowl above which in the pump casing there was a gauze filter to trap any solid matter in the fuel. When any sediment was seen to have accumulated in the glass bowl the latter was readily removable, by unscrewing a knurled hand-nut under the bowl and swinging the securing stirrup aside. The gauze screen and sealing cork washer could be removed and the former cleaned, at the same time.

Fig. 130 shows the A.C. fuel pump and filter as used on the Hillman Imp and many other cars. The various components are indicated and described in the caption below. Briefly, the action is as follows: An eccentric cam on the engine camshaft moves the elbow lever to and fro against the action of the spring (10). The end (11) of this lever moves a flexible diaphragm (16) down, while a spring returns it upwards. This up and down movement creates a pumping action in the chamber above the diaphragm, such that on the downward stroke petrol is drawn into the space above the diaphragm from the inlet pipe (19) and *via* the non-return valve (17). On the spring-return upward stroke this petrol

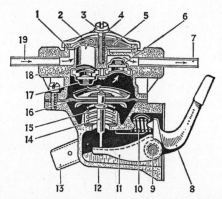

Fig. 130. The A.C. fuel feed pump and filter (Hillman).
1 cover gasket. 2 filter cover. 3 cover screw. 4 washer. 5 filter gauze. 6 delivery valve. 7 delivery pipe to carburettor. 8 engine-operated pump lever. 9 lever bearing. 10 lever return spring. 11 pump arm. 12 pump casing. 13 hand priming lever. 14 pump pull rod to diaphragm. 15 diaphragm return spring. 16 flexible diaphragm. 17 inlet valve. 18 top body. 19 fuel inlet pipe.

is forced out past the non-return valve (6) and into the pipe (7) which is connected with the carburettor inlet union. In the top of the chamber there is a gauze filter through which the fuel from (19) passes before it enters the valve (17) opening.

When the engine has been at rest for some time it is usually necessary to operate the pump by hand, using the priming lever (13) to give a few strokes to the diaphragm independently of the lever (8).

Maintenance. When working properly, the pump should supply petrol at a pressure of about 3 to 5 lb. per sq. in. This should be be measured with a gauge, but for the owner-driver a simple test is to disconnect the carburettor end of the delivery pipe (7) and let the end go into a small vessel, such as a jam-jar. Then crank the engine by hand and observe if there is a definite spurt from the end of the tube (7), at each working stroke – which is once every two engine crankshaft revolutions; if so the pump is working properly.

External pipe connections to the pump should be checked regularly for signs of leakages. The filter gauze should be cleaned every 2,000 miles and at the same time the filter chamber must be cleaned. To do this first remove the screw (3) and cover (2), taking care not to damage the cover joint (4), since an air leak here can stop the pump from working.

After a long period of operation the diaphragm may need inspection, for wear, damage, hardening or cracking; failure of the pump to operate satisfactorily after a long period of service may be due to one of these causes. All seals and gaskets should be renewed at this same period. The two valves – which are interchangeable – may also then need renewal.

It should be mentioned that for motor garage test purposes a special A.C.-Sphinx bench test stand is supplied. In this case the fuel pump is removed from the engine and mounted on the bench test stand, the delivery of the pump for a given number of strokes being measured.

Electric Fuel Pumps. The other important type of fuel pump is the electric one using a solenoid operated plunger. Fig. 131 shows the S.U. electric fuel pump, as used on all B.M.C. cars, in partly dismantled view.

The only maintenance necessary is the occasional removal and cleaning of the filter *B*; the latter is inserted into the bottom of the pump body and is removed by unscrewing the hexagon nut shown below. When removed it should be cleaned in petrol with a bristle brush; rag or cloth should never be used.

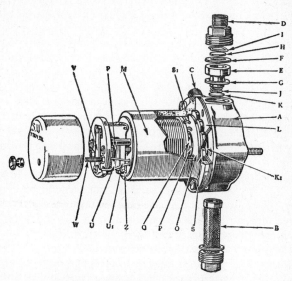

Fig. 131. The S.U. Electric Fuel Pump.

Should the pump fail to work, first attach a length of wire to any part of the pump body and temporarily attach the other end to the body of a 12-volt bulb. Then disconnect the lead from the pump terminal and touch the centre contact of the bulb with it, keeping the bulb well away from the pump. If the lamp lights this will indicate that there is the necessary current at the terminals, so that it is the pump's mechanism that is at fault. Failure of the lamp to light shows that the current supply is at fault. If the trouble is in the pump remove the wire from the terminal and then the bakelite cover, which is retained by the terminal nut, shown on the left in Fig. 131. Attach the lead of the test bulb on to the terminal screw and touch the centre contact of the bulb with the lead to the pump. If the contact points are in contact and the bulb does not light it is very probable that the contact points have become dirty and require cleaning.

The contacts can be cleaned (Fig. 132) by drawing a strip of clean notepaper between them, whilst they are held lightly together. This operation should be carried out every 3,000 miles.

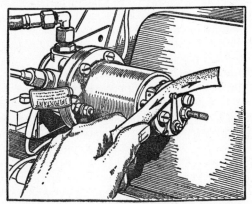

Fig. 132. Cleaning the contacts on S.U. Fuel
Pump (B.M.C.).

If the contacts are found to be badly pitted, a B.M.C. Dealer should be consulted.

On the other hand, if the points are not making contact, see that the tips of the inner rocker (U) are in contact with the magnet housing. If they are not, it is an indication that the armature has failed to return to the end of its normal travel. To cure this loosen the six screws which attach the magnet housing to the pump body and make sure that the diaphragm is not sticking to the face of the magnet housing. The hinge pin (Z) should then be removed and the six retaining screws tightened up again. The tips of the inner rockers will probably now be found to be making contact with the face of the magnet housing; if not, it will be necessary to remove and dismantle the whole magnet assembly to see if any dirt has caused a jam.

If the pump becomes noisy this shows that an air leak is taking place on the suction side of the pump. If so, check the level of the petrol in the tank and see that it is not too low; also check all the unions and joints, making sure that the filter union and inlet unions are airtight. If the connections to the pump are in order and the trouble persists, it is probable that an air leak has developed somewhere in the petrol feed pipe between the tank and the pump. The best way to test whether this is so is to replace the feed pipe by a short length of temporary piping, the mouth of which can be inserted in a can of petrol. If the pump then functions properly it is obvious that a leak has developed somewhere in the feed pipe.

Should the pump continue beating without delivering petrol it is very probable that some dirt has become lodged under one of the valves, in which case they should be dismantled by unscrewing the top or delivery union and lifting out the valve cage, when they can be cleaned and re-assembled.

If, however, the unit struggles to pump and becomes very hot, it is probable that the pipe line has become obstructed or that the filter has become clogged.

Air Cleaners and Silencers. All modern cars are fitted with devices connected to the carburettor main air intake pipe, for cleaning the incoming air of dust particles. At the same time these air cleaners also silence the air flow; earlier designs of air cleaner were notably noisy in operation. The popular type used on many British home-market cars is of cylindrical shape, having an oil-wetted wire mesh type of air filter at one end, the main body of the cylinder forming the silencer. Every 5,000 to 6,000 miles the air cleaner should be removed from the engine and its wire mesh end immersed in a shallow bath of petrol (Fig. 133), then dried and re-oiled by immersion in a pan of engine oil. The cleaner should be hung up and allowed to drain before re-fitting to the engine.

If the air filter is allowed to become dirty the air flow to the engine will be reduced and a loss of power will result.

Another oil cleaner used on some home and all export British cars is shown in Fig. 134. Known as the oil bath type it traps most of the solid particles in the incoming air in an oil bath (*D*). The partly cleaned air then passes upwards through a gauze filter (*F*), and finally downwards along a vertical air-silencer passage (*H*).

Fig. 133. Cleaning the filter element of air cleaner.

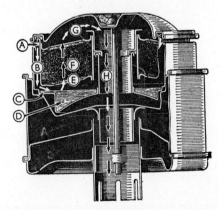

Fig. 134. The oil bath type of air cleaner and silencer.

A	air entry.	*E* entry to gauze filter.
B	air passage.	*F* gauze filter.
C	oil bath shelf.	*G* clean air chamber.
D	oil reservoir.	*H* air exit passage.

The oil picked up from the oil shelf (*C*), by the air automatically oils and washes the filter element (*F*).

The filter can readily be dismantled for cleaning and oil replenishing by removing a wing-nut on top and lifting off the top cover and filter element. Any sludge found in the oil container should be removed and fresh oil supplied to the oil bath (*D*) to the correct level. It is recommended that this type of oil cleaner should be dismantled for inspection every 2,000 miles; or in dusty climates, every 1,000 miles. The filter element should be washed in a paraffin bath, allowed to drain and dry, and then oiled before replacement.

The Paper Element Air Cleaner. This type has largely replaced the felt element filter on automobile engines, except for export models and known dusty air operating conditions.

The filtering element consists of an annular-shaped pleated paper unit which, on account of the pleats, presents a relatively large air filtering area. A special kind of paper impregnated with a certain substance and having excellent fine filtering properties is used for the element (Fig. 135). The air to be filtered flows

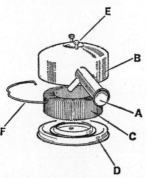

Fig. 135. The paper-element air cleaner (Austin).

through the inlet pipe (*A*), into the outer metal chamber (*B*), whence it passes radially inwards through the paper element (*C*) and flows out from the central bore of the element to the carburettor. The element is held by the spring (*F*) between the top of (*B*) and the top of the base member (*D*) by means of rubber sealing rings. Provision is made for removing the filter bodily by undoing two set bolts (*E*). In some designs a single central wing nut holds the outer metal chamber.

Every 3,000 miles or so the paper element should be removed and shaken to remove any surface dust and the interior of the chamber and base plate cleaned. The life of a filter element is about 10,000 miles. after which it should be removed and a new element fitted in its place.

Care should be taken, when cleaning at 3,000 miles, not to damage the paper element; for this reason only very low pressure compressed air should be used when this method is employed.

In certain recent cleaners provision is made to swivel the air inlet (*A*) (Fig. 135) so that it draws hot air from the vicinity of the exhaust pipe or manifold, for winter driving conditions. For summer conditions the inlet member can be swivelled away, so as to take in cooler air.

CHAPTER 5

THE RADIATOR AND COOLING SYSTEM

THE radiator is one of the items of a car requiring occasional attention. The filler cap should be removed and the water level inspected before each long run. The water in the radiator must evaporate when hot, so that, apart from any source of leakage, it should be replenished occasionally.

Use only 'soft' water, such as filtered rain-water, for filling; and filtering is to eliminate solid matter. If 'hard' water is used the fine water passages between the air cores will be liable to choking from the sediment formed and the efficiency will then be impaired.

When the radiator has been filled to just below the level of the overflow pipe and the engine started and warmed up, the effect of the expansion of the water will be to cause some to overflow through the overflow pipe.

General Maintenance of Cooling System. Normally, the cooling system requires little attention beyond the regular topping up of the water level in the radiator and an occasional inspection of the rubber hose joints for signs of water leakage. At regular intervals the water should be drained out and the radiator and water passages flushed out with plenty of clean water, in order to get rid of solid deposits; usually, this is done every 6,000 miles.

The cooling fin passages should be kept quite clean as any dirt or solid objects in the air spaces, e.g. dead insects, will reduce the cooling efficiency of the radiator.

The holding down nuts of the bolts or studs securing the radiator casing to the chassis front cross member should be checked every 6,000 miles or so for tightness. Similarly, the stays from the back of the dashboard panel to the top of the radiator should be checked to see that the tensioning nuts are tight.

Other items that should occasionally be inspected or attended to, are (1) The fan belt, for tightness. (2) The fan pulley bearings (lubrication). (3) The cylinder head joint nuts. (4) The thermostat, for efficient operation. The principle of the modern cooling system is shown in Fig. 136, the arrows indicating the directions of flow of the water or other coolant.

In Fig. 137 the chief components of a modern car cooling system are clearly shown; the arrows indicate the directions of cooling water flow in the various parts of the system.

Briefly, the cold water at the bottom of the radiator flows upwards into the cylinder water jacket *via* the lower hose connection. Thence it becomes heated by the metal of the cylinder

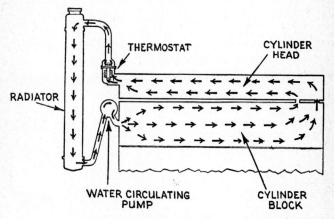

Fig. 136. Principle of modern cooling system (Vauxhall).

and, as it is then lighter, it rises to the top of the water jacket and flows along the upper hose connection to the top tank of the radiator and downwards through the water cooling spaces of the latter to the bottom, where it commences the next cycle of movement. In modern systems the circulation of the water is assisted by a water pump or impeller, which gives it a greater velocity and therefore improved cooling, enabling a smaller size of radiator to be used than for unassisted 'thermo-syphon' cooling systems. Another improvement is the insertion of an automatic water temperature regulator – usually in or near the upper hose connection – and known as the *thermostat*.

In the cooling system shown in Fig. 137, hot water is tapped off from the cylinder head water space for circulating through the car interior heater whence it flows back to the suction side of the

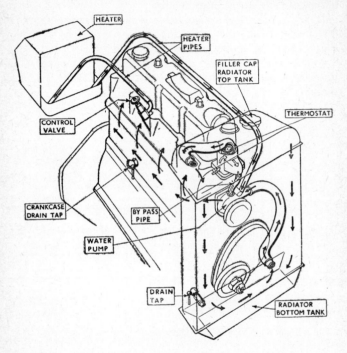

Fig. 137. Cooling and car interior heating water system (Austin) car.

water pump. There is a shut-off screw-down control valve for cutting out the heater. They have nothing to do with the actual cooling system, however.

Pressure Cooling Systems. Ordinary cooling systems having air vents open to the atmosphere allow the water to boil at 212° F. If, however, the cooling system is sealed from the atmosphere and supplied with a spring-loaded valve which opens at some higher pressure than atmospheric the water will, if allowed, boil at a higher temperature than 212° F. Thus for a pressure of 4 lb. per sq. inch above atmospheric, water boils at 223° F.

Many modern car cooling systems are pressurized, with valves to open at 4 to 10 lb. per sq. inch in British cars and 13 to 15 lb. per sq. inch in recent American cars. The higher operating temperatures obtained, by raising the boiling point allows the engine to operate more efficiently and smaller radiators can be used. In pressurized systems the radiator filler cap (Fig. 138) is made an air-tight fit, and has two valves, namely, (1) a vacuum valve which opens to the atmosphere when the engine cools down, to prevent excessive pressures in the system and (2) a pressure

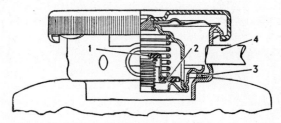

Fig. 138. Radiator cap with pressurizing valve (Vauxhall).
1 vacuum valve seat. 2 pressure valve seat. 3 filler cap seat. 4 overflow pipe.

valve which opens at a given pressure above atmospheric to the atmosphere. The radiator cap in this system is provided with a special bayonet joint and sealing washer.

Detailed Maintenance of the Cooling System. The points requiring maintenance attention are indicated by the letters on the illustration of the Ford Consul cooling system in Fig. 139. These will now be dealt with.

(B) *Fan Belt*. This must be kept at its correct tension and the belt pulleys, after a long period of service, examined for wear, to ensure that the belt does not 'bottom' on the pulley and therefore slip, in spite of its normal tensioning. The method of adjusting the belt tension in the case of a Morris car is shown in Fig. 140. The tensioning pulley is that on the dynamo – shown on the right – and tensioning is done by undoing the nut at *A* and the one at *B*, when the dynamo can be moved bodily to the right to tighten the belt. In this and most other cases the tension is correct when the longest side of the belt can just be deflected to the right through one inch, as shown in Fig. 140.

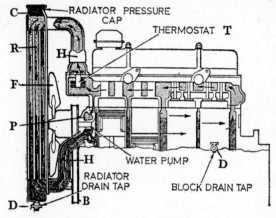

Fig. 139. Illustrating cooling system maintenance items.

(*C*) *Radiator Cap*. This should be kept tight on its thread, more particularly with the pressure system caps, to ensure that no pressure is lost. The sealing washer must be in good condition.

(*D*) *Drain Cocks*. There are usually two cocks, namely, one on the cylinder block and the other at the bottom of the radiator. These must both be opened when draining the cooling system and they should be kept free to open and close. Check after filling that the cocks do not leak.

(*F*) *Cooling Fan*. Ensure that none of its blades is bent and that the common fan-pump impeller bearings are lubricated, through the grease plug provided for this purpose.

(*H*) *Hose Connections*. The hose clips should be checked every 1,000 miles or so for leakages and if found the clip screws should be tightened accordingly. After long usage or if previously the rubber is found to be damaged or has deteriorated, the hoses should be renewed.

(R) *The Radiator*. Keep the air flow cores or spaces quite clean and free from insects, and solid matter. Fill, only with rain or 'soft' domestic water. Maintain the water at the top level and flush out – when necessary – as described later.

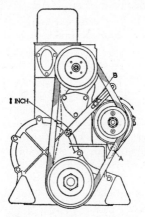

Fig. 140. Method of adjusting fan belt tension (Morris).

(T) *The Thermostat*. The purpose and operation of this component is described later. In regard to its maintenance this unit seldom needs attention and it usually operates satisfactorily over long periods. If, however, it should fail to work properly, the engine may either overheat or run too cool and lose power. It is therefore advisable to test the thermostat when the engine is decarbonized or given a top overhaul, by immersing it in a glass jar of water provided with a thermometer. The engine manufacturers always state the proper opening temperatures of their engine thermostats so that these can be checked by the heated water method. If found to be appreciably above or below this temperature another thermostat should be fitted.

Cooling System Capacity. It is useful to know how much cooling water is used in the complete system of any car. In modern cars, with their high efficiency radiators, the quantity of water varies from about $\frac{7}{8}$ gallons (7 pints) to $1\frac{1}{8}$ gallons (9 pints) per 1,000 c.c. of engine capacity.

Cleaning the Radiator. If dirty or muddy water has been used, the radiator should be flushed out immediately an opportunity presents itself. It is good practice to wash out the radiator, every 6 to 8 months, by inserting the nozzle of a hose-pipe in the filler-spout, leaving the drain tap open so that there is a regular flow of clean water through the system. If the engine has a water circulating pump, the engine should be started and the flow from the hose-pipe adjusted so that it just does not overflow the filler-spout. After 5 minutes the system will be well cleansed. *If hard water has been used,* it is advisable to scour out the scum and sediment by first running out the water from the cooling system, closing the drain tap and filling the radiator and the rest of the water system with *a saturated solution of ordinary washing soda* (sodium carbonate) or caustic soda (lye).* Then run the engine with the spark retarded until it is thoroughly warmed up. Switch off, and leave the system for several hours to cool down. Finally, run off the soda solution and flush out several times with clean water to get rid of every trace of the soda solution. The 'running water and hose' system is the most efficacious means of eliminating the latter. When applying this method *be careful not to let the soda solution touch any of the paint or varnish of the body-work*, as it may otherwise attack the finish.

In motor garage practice, special radiator cleansing solutions, containing rust inhibitors (or preventers) are now employed. The engine is run for a definite period with the solution in the cooling system, instead of the usual water. Afterwards, the solution is drained off and the system flushed out with clean water.

Back flushing of radiators, using the reverse flow direction is now much used in the routine servicing of vehicle radiators, for cleaning out solid particles.

Repairing Radiators. Small leaks in radiator elements can usually be repaired by soft soldering, but it is necessary to drain the water from the radiator before this can be done. A finely

---

* Soda solution should not be used if aluminium parts, e.g. cylinder heads, are used in the cooling system.

pointed blow-lamp flame, such as that obtained from a small spirit torch, will be found convenient for this purpose.

It is inadvisable to attempt to stop radiator leaks by putting so-called 'radiator sealing compounds' in the radiator; the very small water-spaces will in time be stopped up and the cooling thereby seriously interfered with. Sometimes, however, an external repair can be made by means of 'cold solder' – a preparation sold in lead tubes for repairing metal parts.

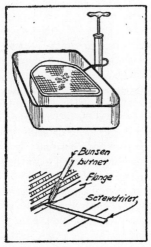

Fig. 141. Illustrating (above) the method of testing a radiator element for leaks and (below) method of repair.

When a radiator has been seriously bent and damaged, it is usually sent back to the makers to be rebuilt and to have a new section or core inserted. This is an expensive procedure, but another method of repair is practical. The radiator is rebuilt by removing the outer shell covering the body, and the top and lower water tanks, which will then expose the centre tubes or core for repair. To test the radiator, plug the inlet, outlet and filler-cap, place in a bath of water and connect a tyre pump to the overflow tube. Pump in air, which will cause bubbles to issue from the leaking tubes. The outer shell is first removed from the body by unsoldering the lugs. To expose the tube ends remove the top and lower water tanks. This is done by unsoldering the holding flange and bending it up. To do this work efficiently a bunsen gas-burner is used, an ordinary blow-lamp will not do, as the flame should be concentrated in one spot, and care must be taken to avoid melting the solder holding the tubes. As the solder melts, carefully lift the flange up by levering with a thin screw-driver (Fig. 141). The lower tank flange may be unsoldered and bent up in a similar manner. Both ends of the radiator tubes are now exposed. The faulty tubes are straightened by running a stout rod, of suitable size, through them. Expand both ends of the damaged tube bell-mouthed with a punch and clean the expanded ends bright with a sharp knife. Slide a thin-walled copper tube to a the faulty tube; the former should be a good fit and should project $\frac{1}{16}$ inch beyond each end of the expanded outer tube. Run solder into the joint between the bell-mouthed and the inner tube. Finally replace the top and lower tanks by carefully bending and soldering the flange back into position. Replace the outer shell and solder the lugs holding the shell to the body.

Frosty Weather Precautions. In frosty – or rather, freezing – weather it is necessary to ensure that the water in the radiator and cylinder jackets does not freeze, for the act of freezing causes a sudden expansion which may fracture the cylinder jackets and burst the radiator. If the garage is not heated *run out the water* after putting the car away. The radiator can be filled with fresh hot water when it is necessary to use the car again. This ensures that there is a minimum of 'sediment', and facilitates starting from the cold.

If the draining of the water system is not convenient, the car being used daily a good make of radiator lamp of the Davy or miner's safety-lamp pattern such as the 'Everwarm' should be placed inside the bonnet, and the outside of the latter, and also the radiator, covered with rugs or blankets. These lamps are quite safe and reliable in action. Electric heaters that plug into a mains supply are good alternatives; these take little current.

Whenever the car is left standing for more than an hour or two in the open, the radiator and bonnet should be covered with a rug or muff.

Anti-Freeze Solutions. To obviate the use of radiator heating appliances, whilst permitting the car to be left in unheated garages or in the open, in freezing weather it is usual to use, instead of water in the cooling system, a solution of water and some other chemical possessing the property of not freezing under the worst winter conditions.

In the past, solutions of glycerine or denatured alcohol in water, have been used as anti-freeze liquid. In each case the addition of the agent lowers the freezing point of the solution by an amount that increases with the proportion of anti-freeze agent.

A much more convenient method of using a proprietary brand of anti-freeze solution is now employed. A typical example of such a solution is that of *ethylene-glycol*, a 30 per cent solution having a freezing point about 26° F below that of water, i.e. approximately the same as a 30 per cent alcohol one. Modern ethylene-glycol anti-freeze liquids are usually made to rigid specifications, e.g., the Government DTD.779 one. This contains an inhibitor against corrosion of light aluminium alloy heads or barrels, but for automobile use another inhibitor to prevent corrosion of cast-iron cylinder passages is included. These are used in 20 per cent solution giving protection against freezing down to −3° F. A 25 per cent solution protects down to −18° F, i.e. 50° of 'frost'.

Procedure. First empty the cooling system and then flush through with water. Next, inspect all hose clips and cylinder head nuts for tightness.

Then half-fill the cooling system with soft water. With proprietory anti-freeze solutions divide cooling system capacity by 4 to give the correct quantity of anti-freeze to add, for protection from freezing down to about −25° C.

Next add this quantity of anti-freeze to the water already in the radiator system and fill to the top with soft water. Replace radiator cap and start up engine, and run until cooling water is warmed up. Then inspect level in radiator and, if necessary top up with a 25 per cent anti-freeze solution. Should the level fall afterwards when the car is in use always top up with the same percentage solution.

Care of the Circulating Pump. The earlier type of centrifugal water pump, has been replaced by the water impeller that is driven by the fan pulley shaft. In regard to both types the only important item of regular attention in this case is that of lubricating the pump spindle. A grease nipple or cup is provided for this purpose.

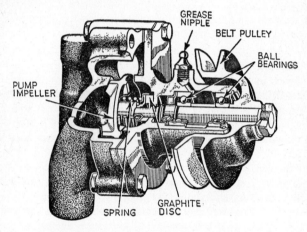

Fig. 142. Combined fan pulley and pump (Austin).

In the combined fan pulley and water pump unit (Fig. 142) the pulley shaft is extended rearwards and has a water impeller at the rear end. The shaft runs on a pair of ball-bearings which are lubricated at regular intervals by means of a grease gun through a nipple provided for this purpose – as shown in Fig. 142.

The water in the pump casing is prevented from leaking past the shaft towards the fan pulley by a carbon (graphite) disc seal, which is held against the right face of the pump casing by means of a light compression spring.

Should any leakage of water occur at the fan pulley it will, no doubt, be due to this carbon block having worn down, but it can be stated that this type of water seal has a very long useful life.

The Thermostat. Usually, the thermostat which is situated between the cylinder head and radiator upper tank requires no attention.

Two different thermostat systems are used, namely, (1) That in which the thermostat is situated in the upper water hose so that when its valve is closed when cold, the flow in the system is stopped and (2) *The by-pass type* which when closed allows a small amount of water to flow from the top of the cylinder jackets to the lower water connection.

In the former method the thermostat shuts off the radiator when the water in the system is cold, thus allowing the water in the cylinder jackets to heat up quickly. In a typical system the thermostatic valve starts to open at 155° to 165° F and becomes fully open at 180° to 185° F, thus allowing hot water from the cylinders to flow to the top of the radiator. With pressure systems the thermostats are arranged to open at rather higher temperatures, namely from about 170° to 175° for pressures of 4 to 6 lb per sq in. and from 177° to 183° for those from 10 to 14 lb per sq in. In the by-pass method there is always a limited circulation through the jackets, but not through the radiator when the water is cold. When hot enough the thermostat allows the radiator to come into action.

The thermostat (Fig. 143) consists of a kind of thin metal

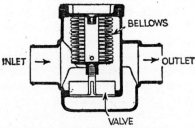

Fig. 143. Typical thermostat unit.

bellows or 'concertina', having some volatile liquid, such as ether, inside. When heated the bellows, under the vapour pressure effect, expands axially and in doing so moves a conical valve off its seating in the water circuit.

A more recent thermostat makes use of the expansion of a melting wax element to open the valve to allow the cooling water to circulate from the radiator to the cylinder water jackets. Fig. 144 illustrates the wax pellet type used on various car engines.

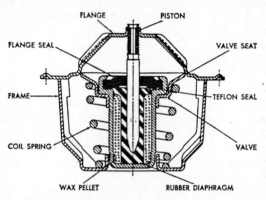

Fig. 144. The wax pellet thermostat used on modern car engines.

It has a wax pellet which is connected through a piston to a water flow valve, such that when the pellet is heated to the predetermined temperature the wax melts and pressure is exerted against a rubber diaphragm which forces the valve to open downwards and allow the hot water from the radiator to pass through the valve opening to the cylinders. When the water temperature falls the wax hardens and contracts; this allows a coil spring to close the valve so to shut off the water in the radiator from the cylinders.

This type of thermostat is made in different models, to open at specific temperatures and one of its special features is that it enables the engine to warm up quickly in cold weather and gives efficient regulation of the water temperatures.

The thermostat, when operating satisfactorily, allows the engine to warm up fairly quickly from the cold and shuts off the radiator when the engine cools down. There is, however, *a risk of the radiator freezing up* when driving in very cold weather, soon after starting from the cold, as then, the radiator is shut off from the cylinder jackets until the thermostat valve opens.

As the thermostat valve is closed when the engine is cold it is advisable to fill the radiator slowly in order to prevent an air-lock. Topping up, however, may be done in the usual manner.

Do not use excessive force when removing the radiator hose or the thermostat may be damaged, when the thermostat is fitted in the top hose connection. Do not use a hose-sealing compound or free movement of the valve may be interfered with.

In event *of failure of the bellows* the valve springs fully open, so that the full water flow is assured.

Some Useful Radiator Hints

(1) If the radiator leaks avoid any of the so-called radiator leak preventers; these tend to clog up the radiator passages and cause overheating. The only satisfactory remedy is to repair the radiator.

(2) Never put cold water into a 'hot' radiator, when you discover the engine is overheated or the level too low. Wait until it cools or you can be scalded, and the cylinder may be cracked.

(3) Examine the rubber hose connections for internal 'kinking' or peeling; the flow of water may seriously be impeded in such cases.

(4) Never oil the rubber hose connections to facilitate replacement; oil has a deleterious effect on rubber. Use soap and water to get the connection in place.

(5) If the engine is found to be 'frozen' do not attempt to start it or you will damage the cylinders, pump or radiator; the best thing is to remove the car to a warm building and allow the water to thaw gradually.

(6) Keep the radiator (outer) air cores quite clean, i.e. free from insects, dust, etc., for efficient cooling. Do not use metal to clean out obstructions or you may injure the very thin metal of the cores. Use a soft wood stick, or bristle brush with paraffin, or water.

(7) When the radiator has been connected up after decarbonizing the engine, or an overhaul, first check that all hose joints are

tight after filling the radiator. The joints should again be examined when the engine is hot.

(8) Use clean rain water or that from a water softener to fill the radiator, to prevent internal deposits.

(9) To prevent corrosion of the internal parts of the cooling system use a proprietary grade of corrosion inhibitor fluid. About $2\frac{1}{2}$ oz. of sodium benzoate per gallon of cooling water will prevent any rusting or corrosion.

Cooling System Troubles and Remedies

(1) SYSTEM RUNS TOO HOT

Possible Cause	Remedy
Too little water in system.	Check for leakages and replenish water.
Ignition too retarded or advanced.	Check ignition timing.
Fan belt loose or bottoming in pulley.	Tighten or replace worn belt.
Radiator cores partly clogged.	Empty water out and reverse flush.

(2) SYSTEM RUNS TOO COOL

Thermostat stuck open.	Reset or replace thermostat.

(3) RADIATOR NEEDS FREQUENT REPLENISHMENTS

Radiator cores or tanks leaking.	Recondition radiator.
Water circulation pump leaking.	Check water seals.
Hose joint leakages.	Examine rubber condition. Tighten clips.
Cylinder head joint leaking.	Renew gasket. Check nuts for tightness.
Cylinder block expansion (Welch) plugs leaking.	Renew plugs after cleaning around housings.

Radiator leakage can readily be located by placing a clean sheet of paper, e.g., newspaper, under the car overnight and examining it for location of water drops in the morning.

CHAPTER 6

THE CLUTCH

OF the different types of clutch in present use there are two important classes, as follows: (1) the Single Plate Clutch, and (2) the Multiple Plate Clutch. These will be dealt with in the order named.

Single Dry Plate Clutch. In this now common type there is a single metal plate on the gearbox shaft engaging with two driving plates faced with annular discs of friction material, such as Ferodo, mounted one on either side of the steel disc member. The clutch pressure between these driving and driven discs is maintained either by a single central spring or a series of six or eight spiral springs arranged evenly around the circumference of the disc.

The general layout of a single plate clutch is shown in Fig. 145; whilst this illustration serves to indicate the components and operation of the clutch it is not to be regarded as typical of the later designs of clutch as described in Volume 3 of this series of Motor Manuals.

The clutch plate consists of a thin circular disc of steel F to which the friction material circular discs G are riveted. The plate F is riveted to a steel boss E provided with a splined hole permitting it to slide on the gearbox primary shaft extension D and to rotate with the latter. The end of this shaft A is provided with a spigot B running in a ball race mounted in the engine flywheel C. The right-hand face of the latter engage with the left-hand face G of the friction material and there is another annular steel plate member J with which the right-hand friction disc G engages at the same time. These driving members and the double-faced driven member F are held into engagement by means of springs located on the studs L and provided with adjusting collars and lock-nuts at K. There are usually about six of these pressure spring units, spaced equally around the flywheel. The clutch is disengaged by depressing the clutch lever which carries an arm *R*, a fixed position clutch lever shaft bearing (shown below *R*) being employed for this purpose. The curved outer end of *R* presses against the right-hand face of the thrust ring withdrawal

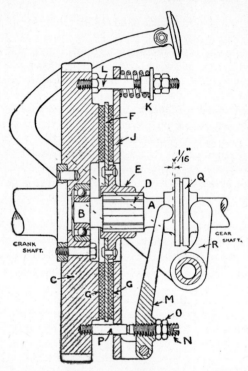

Fig. 145. Illustrating principle and components of dry plate clutch.

member *Q*, which contains a ball thrust bearing and the other face communicates its movement to the curved end of another lever *M*, with a pin bearing below, formed integral with the outer pressure plate *J*. Movement to the left of the lever *M* causes the plate *J* to be moved to the right, since the portion of *M* near the adjusting nuts *O* forms the fulcrum; this disengages the clutch.

The stud P is fixed in the flywheel. Usually, there are three clutch release levers similar to M, spaced evenly, i,e. at 120° apart, so as to communicate a uniform withdrawal pressure on the member J; these levers rotate with the flywheel and pressure plate. In practice a free movement of $\frac{1}{16}$ inch is allowed between the end of M and the thrust-washer member Q.

This type of clutch requires very little attention, beyond the *lubrication of the spigot bush*, or central guide, in the flywheel member. In some modern clutches the spigot has a ball-bearing in the flywheel which is lubricated automatically.

The clutch engagement collar, which is operated by the clutch pedal, should also be kept well lubricated with engine oil; in some cars this item is oiled automatically from the engine crankcase; in other instances a self-lubricating graphite washer is employed. The type of single plate clutch known as the *Dry Plate Clutch*, as its name implies, does not require any lubrication. If any oil gets on the clutch friction surfaces, slipping under load may occur.

Friction Material Wear and Clutch Slip. After a long period of usage the friction material of the clutch plates wears down until it becomes too thin for reliable service. This wearing of the friction material may be accentuated by a driver who makes a habit of slipping the clutch on numerous occasions or who adopts the inadvisable practice of *resting his foot on the clutch whilst driving* the car over long distances. As the frictional material wears, the amount of free play in the clutch pedal increases; this play is usually taken as the indication of clutch plate wear. Further, when the surfaces have worn down a certain amount the rivet heads become flush with these surfaces and noisy clutch engagement occurs.

If a dry plate clutch slips without showing signs of wear this is due probably to grease on, or glazing of, the friction material; the remedy for this is to wash the plate in petrol and to roughen the surfaces with a wire brush.

Bonded Clutch Linings. Instead of riveting the friction discs to the clutch plate, these are now bonded to the plates by a special process which results in as good or better union than by the riveting method. In particular, these bonded linings are applicable to high revolution clutches where trouble may be experienced between the rivets due to centrifugal force, causing disintegration. The bonded lining gives a greater area than the riveted one; moreover, there are no discontinuities over its surface, by rivet recesses.

Relining Clutch Plates. The process of refacing worn clutch plates is as follows: First obtain moulded replacement friction discs from the car manufacturers or a firm of friction material suppliers. The old friction material should be removed from the steel plates by punching out the rivets; as these are generally of aluminium they can be driven right through the central steel

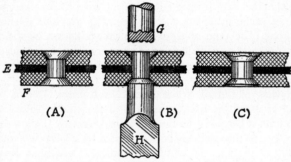

Fig. 146. Method of riveting clutch friction disc.

plate. After cleaning the latter thoroughly and testing for dead flatness on a surface plate, correcting for any distortion by hammering, one of the new friction discs should be clamped at two or three places to the steel plate, accurately in its central position and holes drilled through the steel plate and friction material with a drill the same size as the holes in the plate. This procedure should be repeated for the other friction disc. Next, as shown at (A) in Fig. 146, countersink each side of the friction disc with a rose-bit type of countersink tool used in the drill chuck. Having selected the correct size of countersink rivet to fit the holes in the steel plate, check the amount of countersinking in the friction disc holes; the heads of the rivets should lie below the surface by about $\frac{1}{16}$ inch or more, according to the thickness of the friction material. The shank of the rivet should project sufficiently to enable the riveted portion to lie below the surface by the same amount as the head. A suitable riveting tool is shown at *G* in diagram (B), Fig. 146; below the rivet head is supported by a steel member, known as a 'dolly', as shown at (H) Commence riveting by hammering lightly and centrally on the punch (G) to expand the aluminium evenly into the countersunk portion of the hole, until the final result is as shown in diagram (C), Fig. 146. If a hammer is employed for riveting, the first blows should be struck centrally on the rivet shank in order to expand the latter so as to obtain a firm fit in the steel plate; afterwards the metal around the periphery of the rivet end should be hammered with the ball-end or 'peen' of the hammer so as to spread the metal outwards to fill the countersunk portion.

Alternatively, hollow aluminium or copper rivets are used instead of solid ones, and a special punch is required for riveting up these.

Multi-Plate Clutches. Similarly to single plate clutches, multiple ones require an occasional adjustment for wear of the material. The makers usually provide an adjustment so that the clutch pedal movement remains the same, the plate wear being taken up by screw adjustment.

In the case of the earlier models Morris car, the clutch consisted of four friction surfaces, comprising the rear face of the flywheel, and both faces of a floating plate, the forward face of the clutch pressure plate. Six clutch driving pins pass through the flywheel, the floating and the pressure plate. The driven surfaces comprise a *double line of cork inserts*, in two steel plates, the latter being mounted on a toothed driving hub keyed to the gearbox driving shaft.

This clutch ran in oil obtained from the engine. With this design, after the first 2,000 miles of running the friction surfaces 'bed' together and the clutch pedal may develop more 'free' movement than is desirable. Special provision is made in the hub of the clutch pedal whereby the pedal in the car can be adjusted.

If the clutch shows signs of slipping, this may be due to the clutch pedal being in incorrect adjustment, or to the breaking of one of the clutch springs.

Clutch Pedal Adjustment. It is usual to allow a small amount of free movement of the clutch pedal, when the clutch is engaged; according to the type of clutch this movement, measured at the pad on the pedal, is from ¾ to 1 inch. Provision is made in the clutch operating linkage for adjusting this clearance, usually by a screwed member engaging a tapped hole in its adjoining member; a lock nut is provided for securing the adjustment. Fig. 147 illustrates the Morris Minor 1000 clutch pedal

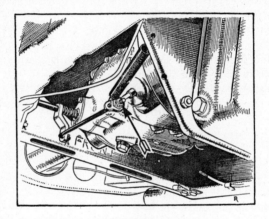

Fig. 147. Clutch pedal adjustment. (Morris Minor 1000).

adjustment which is done by adjusting nuts at the end of a screwed-end link, as indicated by the arrow. The correct free pedal movement is ¾ inch. After adjusting the screwed-end link the lock nut should be tightened securely.

The clutch free pedal movement, in the case of the Humber Hawk car is illustrated in Fig. 149. In this example the connecting link between the clutch pedal elbow lever and the clutch operating lever consists of two members, one of which is screwed and provided with adjusting nuts to alter the effective length of the combined link. The oil nipple lubrication points for both the clutch and brake-lever bearings are also shown in Fig. 149. The correct free movement of the pedal pad is 1·0 inch.

Fig. 148. A useful tool for removing
Morris clutch springs (Terry).

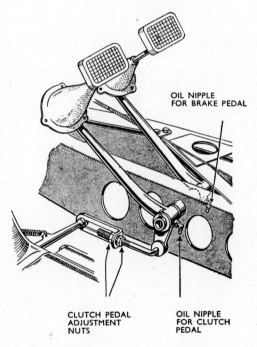

OIL NIPPLE
FOR BRAKE PEDAL

CLUTCH PEDAL
ADJUSTMENT
NUTS

OIL NIPPLE
FOR CLUTCH
PEDAL

Fig. 149. Clutch pedal adjustment (Humber Hawk III).

Hydraulic Operation Clutches. The hydraulic method of clutch operation is illustrated and described on page 56. It is usual with this method to adjust the *free travel* on the clutch release arm which, of course, has a much smaller movement than the clutch pedal. Thus, in the case of modern Ford cars the free travel is $\frac{1}{16}$ in; this is the clearance between the end of the adjusting nut (Fig. 150) and the clutch release arm, with the retracting spring disconnected. The *free movement* is the distance the clutch pedal moves before the hydraulic pressure begins to operate the clutch, but this movement is measured as described earlier. After making this adjustment the lock nut should be tightened securely.

To avoid clutch operation troubles the fluid in the combined hydraulic brake and clutch reservoir must be maintained at the level recommended – and usually marked – by the manufacturers.

The Borg and Beck Clutches. These clutches, of American

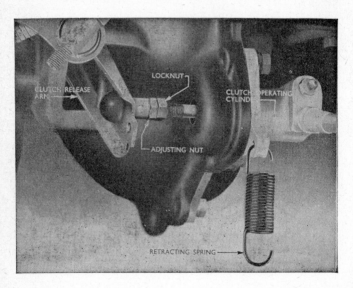

Fig. 150. Hydraulic clutch adjustment (Ford Consul and Zephyr).

design, are widely used on British cars, typical instances being the Austin, Morris, Standard, Hillman and Humber cars.

The principal components of this single plate dry disc clutch, with their names, are illustrated in Fig. 152, whilst the four main units, in the case of the Morris clutch, are shown in Fig. 151.

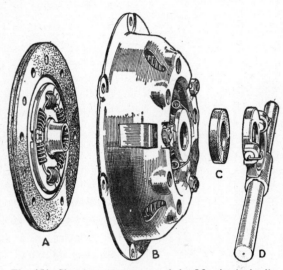

Fig. 151. Showing components of the Morris single disc clutch. *A*, friction faced clutch plate with spring drive; *B*, clutch casing; *C*, graphite thrust washer; *D* clutch withdrawal shaft and trunnion member.

No provision is made for adjustment for clutch material wear, the operating levers being located in position during manufacture. The adjusting nut on the clutch is locked in place and should only be disturbed when new parts are fitted as replacements. The driven plate assembly *A* (Fig. 152) has a splined hub, and flexible steel driven plate *C* to the outer diameter of which are fixed the friction discs. This plate is attached to the splined hub by a spring mounting which acts as a shock-damper. The clutch withdrawal unit *C* and *D* employs a graphite disc thrust bearing mounted in a cup attached to the throw-out fork and a release plate J is attached to the inner ends of the release levers L by means of retainer springs K. Each release lever is mounted on a floating pin P. The outer ends of the eye-bolts extend through

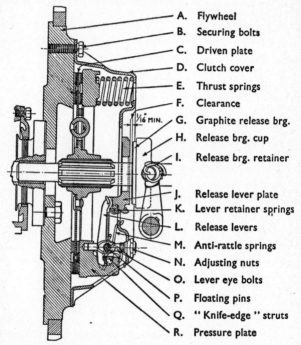

A.	Flywheel
B.	Securing bolts
C.	Driven plate
D.	Clutch cover
E.	Thrust springs
F.	Clearance
G.	Graphite release brg.
H.	Release brg. cup
I.	Release brg. retainer
J.	Release lever plate
K.	Lever retainer springs
L.	Release levers
M.	Anti-rattle springs
N.	Adjusting nuts
O.	Lever eye bolts
P.	Floating pins
Q.	" Knife-edge " struts
R.	Pressure plate

Fig. 152. The Borg and Beck clutch, in sectional view.

holes in the clutch cover and have adjusting nuts N to locate each lever correctly. The outer ends of the levers engage the pressure plate lugs by means of struts Q which give knife edge contact between the lever ends and pressure plate lugs. Thus, in operation, the pressure plate R is pulled away from the driven plate C, compressing six coil springs E which fit between the plate R and clutch cover D. When foot pressure is released from the clutch pedal the springs force the pressure plate forwards against the driven plate, gradually and smoothly until there is a positive drive to the gearbox shaft.

Clutch Running Adjustments. There is only one adjustment necessary during the life of the friction facings, namely, to take up the effects of wear which would, otherwise, limit the clutch pedal movement. As the driven plates wear, the free movement of the clutch pedal diminishes. When it is reduced to about $\frac{1}{2}$ inch – as measured at the pedal pad – it is time to restore the free movement to the pad; this should be 1 inch in most Borg and Beck clutches. This amount of free movement corresponds to a minimum clearance at F (Fig. 152) of $\frac{1}{16}$ inch.

To restore this free movement of the clutch the adjusting nuts, and lock nuts on the lower end of the clutch lever should be adjusted, the nuts afterwards being tightly 'locked'.

If the total travel is too much, slacken off the locknut at the top of the clutch lever and adjust the stop screw as required. Over-travel of the release bearing leads to solid coiling of the thrust springs and causes undue stresses on the clutch mechanism; under these conditions the graphite disc will wear rapidly.

Dismantling and Re-assembly of Clutch. Whilst this is not usually considered an operation for the driver-mechanic, it is not a difficult one. The clutch unit, removed from the engine, should be placed with the pressure plate resting on two wooden blocks. A block of wood is then placed on top, as shown in Fig. 153, so that it rests on the spring bosses. Pressure is applied by means of a hand or power press ram to the cover, when the three adjusting nuts can be removed. Upon releasing the pressure, gradually, the clutch springs will extend to their full length. The cover plate can then be lifted off so that all parts are available for inspection.

To remove the release levers, grasp the lever and eyebolt between the thumb and fingers so that the inner end of the lever and the threaded end of the eyebolt are close together, keeping the eyebolt pin seated in its socket on the lever. The strut can then be lifted over the ridge on the end of the lever, so that the eye bolt can be lifted off the pressure plate.

After cleaning the dismantled clutch components they should be carefully inspected and any parts found to be worn should be replaced by new ones. The clutch is assembled by placing the pressure plate on the two wooden blocks on the press bed, placing

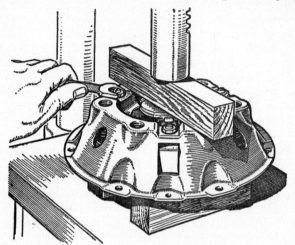

Fig. 153. Dismantling the Borg and Beck clutch.

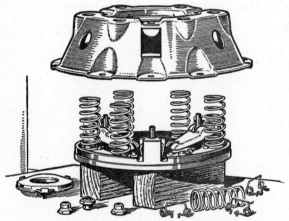

Fig. 154. Re-assembling the Borg and Beck clutch.

the springs on it in a vertical position (Fig. 154) and seating them on their locating bosses. After assembly of the release levers, eyebolts and pins, etc., lay the cover over the parts, taking care that the anti-rattle springs are in position. Place a block of wood across the cover and apply pressure with the press to compress the springs, at the same time guiding the eyebolts and pressure plate lugs through the correct holes in the cover. Make sure that the thrust springs are seated properly. Replace the eyebolt nuts and then release the pressure on the press ram.

It should be mentioned that the final setting of the release levers should be done with the aid of the special gauge plate supplied by the clutch manufacturers.

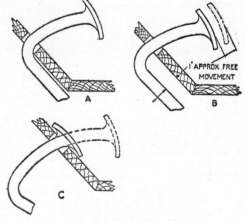

Fig. 155. Clutch pedal positions.

Total Clutch Pedal Movement. The total movement of the clutch pedal is the sum of the free pedal movement and that required to operate the clutch mechanism, in order to give the full disengagement of the clutch. Thus, with the usual 1 inch free pedal travel, corresponding to $\frac{1}{16}$ inch between the lever plate $\mathcal{J}$ (Fig. 152) and the face of the thrust bearing G, and the operating clutch release movement of $\frac{5}{16}$ inch, the total movement will be about 4 to 6 inches. The normal disengagement of the pedal is shown at A, in Fig. 155 and the position when the pedal free play is taken up, at B; the point of clutch engagement is indicated by the dotted lines at C and of full disengagement by the full lines at C. After a clutch on a new car has operated for 500 to 1,000 miles, the *bedding down of the friction surfaces* will necessitate *a small re-adjustment of the clutch mechanism.*

The Diaphragm Spring Clutch. This new design is replacing the types previously described. It uses a single concentric large diaphragm instead of the several compression coil springs of the other type, to actuate the pressure plate. This clutch has several advantages over the previously described type, as follows: (1) It has fewer components. (2) Operates with reduced pedal pressures and gives a smoother engagement. (3) The clamping pressure of the diaphragm spring does not alter during the life of the clutch, so that clutch slip cannot occur. (4) Due to the circular form of all of the parts a better static balance is obtained. (5) The clamping load is not affected by engine speeds. (6) Due to absence of levers and pins, much reduced wear.

Fig. 156 shows the principle of the Borg and Beck clutch, as

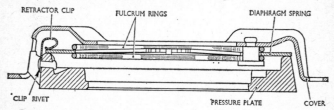

Fig. 156. Principle of the Borg and Beck diaphragm spring clutch.

used on the Vauxhall cars. The diaphragm spring has a number of radial slots over its central portion (Fig. 157) but is plain over its outer periphery. When the clutch unit is mounted on the engine flywheel the diaphragm spring, of normal conical shape, is flattened to provide the clamping pressure on the clutch driven plate. As distinct from the conventional clutch, the clutch pedal system operates through the release bearing direct on to the central portion of the plate. Near the outer (plain) portion of the plate a fulcrum is provided, in the form of a pair of rings so that pressure on the diaphragm spring at the centre, towards the fly-

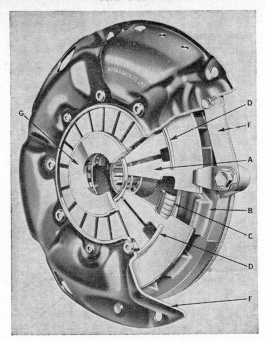

Fig. 157. The Borg and Beck diaphragm spring clutch, in part section. *A* diaphragm spring. *B* pressure plate. *C* torque spring. *D* fulcrum rings. *E* steel drive straps (cover to pressure plate). *F* casing.

wheel, forces the pressure plate away from the flywheel and thus frees the friction plate from the engine drive.

Maintenance. The clutch can be operated hydraulically, as with the previously described type, or by means of a Bowden-type inner cable inside a nylon-lined casing, as in the Vauxhall Viva. In either case, adjustment for the free travel of the clutch-operating fork is provided at the clutch end. Thus, in Fig. 156 the adjusting nut is used to give the correct free travel at the clutch fork; this should be 0·16 in. at the outer end of the fork.

The fork ball should be grease-lubricated at long intervals, at which time the clutch pressure plate friction face should be inspected for signs of wear or scores. The clutch spigot bearing in the flywheel is of the oil-impregnated kind and therefore needs no attention. The Bowden cable is lubricated during assembly and is sealed at its ends and so needs no lubrication in service.

Clutch Troubles, Causes and Remedies.

The three chief kinds of clutch trouble likely to be experienced after an appreciable period of service are, as follows: (1) *Clutch Slip*. (2) *Clutch Judder*, or *Fierceness*. (3) *Clutch Spin*, and (4) *Clutch Rattle*.

(1) *Clutch Slip*. The experienced driver can readily detect this, but to those not familiar with this trouble a good method is to run the engine, depress the clutch pedal to disengage the clutch, holding it out whilst the hand brake is applied, strongly.
Then, with the engine accelerated release the clutch, gradually. If the engine is gradually brought to rest there can be no clutch, slip, but if the engine continues to run, this is a sure indication of clutch slip.

(2) *Clutch Judder or Fierceness*. In this case upon releasing the clutch pedal after gear engagement, the drive is taken up suddenly or with a pronounced snatching effect – known as 'judder' – no matter how carefully the clutch pedal is released.

(3) *Clutch Spin*. If, after releasing the clutch pedal with the gear in neutral the driven plate does not come to rest quickly, the primary shaft of the gearbox will continue to spin and gear changing will prove difficult. In some cases, after the engine has been started it is found to be difficult to engage first gear for starting off; this is due to clutch plate spin. In some clutches a clutch stop, or brake, is fitted to stop this clutch spin.

(4) *Clutch Rattle*. Clutch noises or rattle are due to worn components or to some broken member; the possible causes are given in the Table on page 209.
Having explained the principal clutch troubles that may occur, it is now proposed to tabulate the chief causes and suggested remedies, with special reference to clutches of Borg and Beck design.

DIAGNOSIS OF CLUTCH TROUBLES

Clutch Trouble	Cause	Remedy
Clutch Slip	Insufficient pedal clearance.	Adjust pedal.
	Oil on clutch faces.	Clean with petrol or fit replacement.
	Clutch facings badly worn.	Fit replacement.
	Pressure springs too weak.	Fit correct springs.
	Pressure plate broken.	Fit replacement.
	Toggle mechanism too tight (or seized).	Use penetrating oil and work until free.
Clutch Judder or Fierceness	Pedal sticking.	Dismantle and clean.
	Linings badly worn.	Renew.
	Carbonized oil on clutch faces.	Clean or renew.
	Clutch disc distorted.	Renew.
	Clutch gear shaft splines worn.	Renew shaft.
	Release levers too light.	Clean and lubricate.
	Release levers wrongly adjusted.	Adjust again.
	Bent withdrawal fork.	Fit replacement.
	Pressure plate broken.	Fit replacement.
Clutch Spin	Incorrect pedal adjustment.	Re-adjust.
	Release levers wrongly adjusted.	Re-adjust.
	Oil on lining.	Clean and roughen.
	Distorted driven plate.	Renew.
	Clutch disc splines tight.	Remove and free.
	Clutch pilot (spigot) bearing too tight.	Examine and remedy as required.
	Loose clutch facings.	Renew.
Clutch Rattle	Worn or broken release levers.	Renew.
	Broken toggle springs.	Renew.
	Excessive play in clutch splines and on shaft.	Renew.
	Excessive wear in pedal mechanism.	Renew.

Useful Clutch Notes

(1) Never drive with the foot constantly on the clutch pedal – this is known as 'riding the clutch pedal'. This practice results in unnecessary wear of the friction material and slack in the clutch mechanism.

(2) If the clutch 'drags', this may be due to bad adjustment of the clutch or pedal, a worn spigot bearing, gummy or sticky friction surfaces, or to bent or warped discs.

(3) If the clutch pedal is adjusted so that it touches *the back* of the toe-board of the car before the clutch is fully engaged, clutch slip will occur, and the friction material will wear fairly quickly.

(4) If the clutch pedal is adjusted so that the foot pedal portion touches *the front* of the toe-board before the clutch is fully disengaged, gear changing will become difficult; the gears may be easily injured in this case.

Hydraulic Clutches. These are used in the simpler type of automatic transmission systems and act in the same manner as centrifugal clutches, which are disengaged when the engine runs slowly but are engaged when it is accelerated to a speed of about 800 to 1,000 r.p.m.

A typical hydraulic clutch has a casing member (*A*) and (*C*) (Fig. 158) which is driven by the engine crankshaft; and an

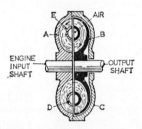

Fig. 158. Principle of the hydraulic clutch, of fluid flywheel.
A and *C* two-piece engine-driven casing. *B* torus member attached to output or gearbox input shaft. *D* air annulus space.

inside paddle or torus member (*B*), attached to the gearbox-drive or output shaft. The casing is filled with a light oil. At lower engine speeds, due to the friction of the gears in the gearbox, the member (*B*) remains stationary, while the casing (*A–C*) rotates around it. However, when the engine is accelerated to about 700 to 1,000 r.p.m. the fluid inside begins to drag the paddle around and as the engine speed is increased the output shaft of the paddle is eventually driven positively. Thus, we have a smooth and gradual take-up of the power by the gearbox gears.

Maintenance. Apart from checking that the casing joint and the oil seals around the output shaft are not leaking there is no other attention necessary, but should the unit have been dismantled, and reassembled it should be filled fully, by removing a plug or plugs on the casing. This will ensure that the unit is properly balanced, so that no vibrations can occur, when in operation.

CHAPTER 7

THE GEARBOX AND GEAR CHANGING

THE most widely used gearbox in this country is the synchro-mesh or 'easy-gear' change one, controlled by either a lever mounted on the top gearbox or by one arranged under the steering wheel on the steering column. The usual type has four forward and one reverse gear with synchromesh on the top (4th), 3rd and 2nd gear ratio, as a rule, and ordinary dog-clutch change on bottom (1st) gear. In the case of American designed and certain mass-produced British cars, e.g. the pre-1960 Ford, Standard and Vauxhall ones, only three forward speeds are fitted.

More recently *overdrives*, e.g., the Laycock, de Normanville, and Borg-Warner types have been fitted to several British makes of cars.

A further step in simple-operation transmissions has been the two-pedal control, i.e. accelerator and brake, but no clutch, pedal type of which typical examples are the Manumatic, Newtondrive, Standrive and Smith two-pedal electromagnetic clutch, systems. Such systems are termed *semi-automatic* ones.

Fully-automatic systems, used in this country include the Roverdrive, Smith electromagnetic, Hydramatic and Borg-Warner. These transmissions are fully described and illustrated in the 6th edition of Motor Manual Volume 5. *Modern Trans-mission Systems*.

In each design, maintenance and adjustment instructions are provided by the car manufacturers using these transmissions, so that no further reference is given, here, beyond certain driving instructions and some general remarks on two-pedal control system maintenance.

In the present considerations the less difficult maintenance and overhaul items, only, are dealt with, since the complete dis-mantling, reassembly, adjustment and final testing are outside the scope of the owner-mechanic and, with modern gearboxes, are the concern of the specialist.

Apart from the periodical lubrication of the gears, the gearbox seldom gives the owner-driver any trouble during the first 30,000 miles or so, if the car has been used carefully. As we have already considered the question of gearbox lubrication in Chapter 2 it will not be necessary to dwell further on this subject.

It should, however, be reiterated that the regular lubricant replenishment of the gearbox, and the initial (500 miles) and

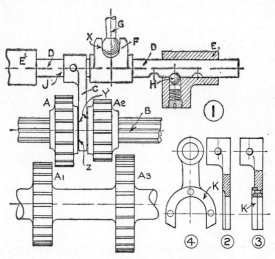

Fig. 159. Gearbox components.
(The lettered components are referred to on page 216)

occasional (5,000–6,000 miles) emptying and flushing out of same are important to quiet, trouble-free operation of the gears.

Gearbox Troubles. After bad usage or very long service, certain troubles are liable to develop, and although the amateur mechanic can tackle some of these it is better, as a rule, to obtain the services of a suitable motor garage or the makers of the gearbox. The principal troubles which occur may be enumerated as follows: (1) Refusal of Gear Lever to Change Gears, or Gears

Jump out of Mesh. (2) Noise when Changing Gear. (3) Continuous noise on the Indirect Gears, with Vibration. (4) Oil Leakage from Bearings.

In most cases rectification of gearbox trouble involves the dismantling of the components and in this connection the detailed instructions of the manufacturers as given in their workshop manuals must be consulted.

Gear Slipping and Gear Stiffness. Gears which, after changing, sometimes jump out of mesh, leaving the engine in neutral, are either only partially engaged after gear changing, or have their operating forks and locking plungers badly worn. In the former case, *slipping is due to the gear lever not being pushed right home* when gear changing. In this case the gear only slips at rare intervals.

The gears, after changing, are held into mesh by means of small plungers kept in position by means of springs, as shown at *H* in Fig. 159; the movement of the gears is accomplished by the selector rods and forks engaging with collars. The principal objects of the plungers are to ensure the full width of the teeth of each gear being in contact with the teeth of the meshing gear, and, further, to lock the sliding gear members in this position.

If a gear frequently jumps out of mesh whilst the car is on the road, it may be on account of these locking plungers or the gear-shift forks being worn; the only remedy in these cases lies in the replacement of these parts.

Other causes of gears jumping out include the following: (1) Worn gear teeth. (2) Worn teeth on engagement dogs. (3) Weak or broken selector springs, on ball or plunger gear lock. (5) Worn ball or plunger. (5) In the case of steering column gear lever method, incorrect adjustment of connecting mechanism or wear in working members of same.

Replacing Selector Rod Balls. When it becomes necessary to remove a selector rod, which is located in position by means of a spring-loaded ball, it may be difficult afterwards, when reassembling to get the ball back in position. This can, however, be done quite easily, by the use of a thin rod, as shown in Fig. 160. It holds the ball while the latter is being pushed down on its spring. This operation is done while the fork is in position in its gearbox. Check afterwards to see that the selector rod works and 'locks' properly. Make sure that no balls are dropped into the bottom of the gearbox, or trouble will occur when the gears are operating.

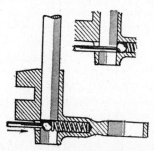

Fig. 160. Method used for replacing spring-loaded balls for selector rods.

Noise when Changing Gear. This is one of the commonest of gearbox troubles, and, assuming that the driver knows how to change 'up' and 'down' correctly, it may *be due to the clutch stop* (as fitted to earlier car and at present some commercial models) *being incorrectly adjusted*, i.e. allowing the clutch to spin. In this case the main gear shaft to which the clutch member is attached keeps spinning, and on the driver endeavouring to change gear, the teeth rub over one another, causing the noise mentioned. The remedy is a closer adjustment of the clutch stop.

Another cause is that of *a sticky clutch*, the gearbox connected plates of which being dragged round by the engine plates when the clutch pedal is depressed. The remedy is to flush out the clutch with petrol, and, if not of the dry-plate type, to introduce fresh lubricant of the correct consistency.

If a gearbox has been badly used, as when a poor driver constantly makes noisy gear changes, the edges of the sliding gears and those of the fixed gears on the engagement side become burred or chipped and will not mesh without an extra effort on the gear lever. In such a case a noisy change will always result, and the only remedy in the former case, is to dismantle the

gearbox, take out the gears and have the burrs removed by grinding on a dish-shaped emery wheel.

To test for the above-mentioned fault remove the gearbox
cover, and feel the engaging edges of the gear teeth; the presence
of burrs will at once be apparent to the touch.

Gear Engagement Faults. A frequent cause of incorrect
adjustment in gear boxes occurs when the gear lever does not
slide the gear wheel to be engaged sufficiently far to obtain full
width tooth engagement, the result being as shown at B in Fig.
161. This fault and its cure may be illustrated by reference to
Fig. 159. The sliding gears A and A_2 are moved into or out of
engagement with the layshift gears A_1 and A_3 by means of a
flat-sided fork C fixed to the selector bar D, sliding in bearings EE
in the gearbox casing. The selector bar D has a bracket containing
a slot F with which the ball end of the driver's hand gear lever G
engages. If the groove in between wheels A and A_2 becomes
worn or the side of the fork C wears or if the slot F for the gear
shift lever is worn there may be sufficient backlash to prevent the
fork C from sliding the gears A and A_2 into full tooth width
engagement with their mating gears A_1 and A_3.

Usually there is a ball-stop H in the gearbox casing E which
engages with notches or cups in the selector bar D to lock the
gears in their correct engagement positions.

Wear at X in the slot F, at Y on the side of the fork and Z on
the gear wheel fork groove will usually be found after long periods
of service; the result is increased wear between the gears A, A_1,
A_2, and A_3, due to only partial engagement of the teeth; the
gears also run with more noise. The remedy is to take up the
wear by grinding down the side of the fork member C as in (2)
Fig. 161, and fitting a mild steel packing piece as at (3) and (4) to
increase the width of the fork. The packing piece is riveted with
countersunk rivets. If the fork member is hardened it must be
softened to enable the rivet holes to be drilled. After fitting the
packing piece it may be necessary to grind its outer face down a
little in order to give the correct sliding fit in the gear wheel
groove. The fork member should then be case-hardened over its
two parallel faces K. Any backlash between the gear lever ball
end and the slot F may be taken up either by filing out the sides

of the slot F and silver soldering packing pieces of cast steel or by removing gear lever, heating the ball end to redness and hammering it sufficiently to expand it so as to just fit the slot F. It should then be trued up with a smooth file and polished with emery cloth before case-hardening.

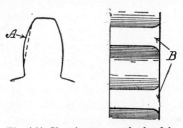

Fig. 161. Showing two methods of detecting wear in gears. A, wear on face of tooth; B, sliding gear that does not fully engage with its members. (Note there is no wear on right.)

Noisy Gearbox. Some earlier cars, even when new, were noisy on their second, third and other indirect gears, due to faulty design and machining of the gears. Usually the gear shafts were relatively long, and 'whipped' under load; in some cases the shapes of the gear teeth were incorrect for noiseless running.

Before *checking the gearbox for noisy operation* make sure it has the correct amount of recommended lubricant.

If the engine is operated, with the gear lever in neutral, the main gear shaft and layshaft will rotate, one pair of constant mesh gears then being in engagement. If these gears are worn, noise may occur, but this will disappear when the clutch is depressed – the gears then stopping. Another possible cause of this 'neutral' noise is that of worn layshaft bearings.

If the rear wheels – or one wheel only – are jacked up, the front wheels being chocked to prevent movement, the noise emitted by each set of gears as it is engaged can be tested for. It should, however, be noted that the noisy operation of the intermediate gears may be due to worn layshaft bearings and not, necessarily, to worn gear teeth.

Another common cause is lack of lubricant or the use of an unsuitable lubricant – namely, one which is too 'solid', so that the gears cut tracks, or too thin a gear oil, allowing metallic contact of the teeth.

Worn bearings will allow radial movement of the gears and, therefore, bad meshing of the gear teeth.

If, in the case of a car which was previously quiet on its gears and kept well lubricated, noise develops in the course of time, it is advisable to remove the gearbox from the chassis and dismantle it on the bench. Examine the gear fork levers, gear teeth and test for slack in the bearings. As gear shafts run on ball or roller bearings, it is possible to eliminate any bearing slackness either by fitting new ball or roller bearings, or, if the latter are adjustable, to take up the wear.

Oil Leakage from Gearbox. Oil leakages may be due to one of the following causes: (1) Overfilling with lubricant. (2) Worn main or layshaft bearings. (3) Faulty oil seals on bearings. (4) Faulty top or end gearbox casing joints. (5) Loose drain plug.

The fault of overfilling, i.e. filling to a level above the maker's recommended one, should be avoided since oil may leak into the clutch unit and there cause clutch slip. Moreover, too much oil in the gearbox will result in a loss of power in transmission through the gearbox, owing to oil churning.

Notes on Gearbox Removal. Whilst it is not possible, here, to give detailed instructions on this subject, some notes for the general operation of gearbox removal may prove helpful to those concerned. These notes refer to the widely used engine-clutch-gearbox combination unit, as shown in Figs. 162 and 166. It is best to jack the car and use axle blocks to hold it as high as the jacking will allow; better still, the operation may be carried out over a pit. The procedure is then briefly as follows:

Disconnect the forward end of propeller shaft at the joint flange and tie up the forward end of the shaft.

Support the engine under the flywheel or clutch case and remove the rear gearbox supports on the cross-member of the chassis frame. Each type of support must be examined beforehand, to ascertain the best method of disconnection. Disconnect

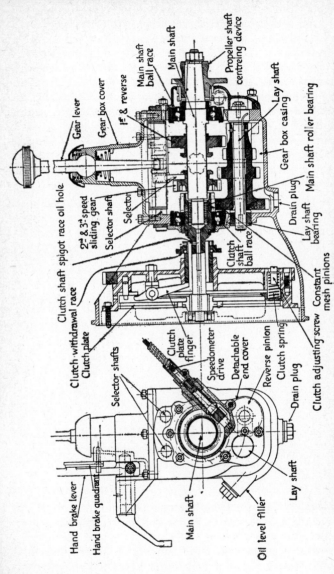

Gear lever

Gear box cover

1st & reverse

Main shaft ball race

Main shaft

Propeller shaft centreing device

Lay shaft

Gear box casing

Clutch shaft spigot race oil hole

2nd & 3rd speed sliding gear

Selector shaft

Selector

Main shaft roller bearing

Drain plug

Lay shaft bearing

Clutch withdrawal race

Clutch plate

Clutch shaft ball race

Constant mesh pinions

Clutch plate finger

Speedometer drive

Detachable end cover

Reverse pinion

Clutch spring

Clutch adjusting screw

Selector shafts

Hand brake lever

Hand brake quadrant

Main shaft

Oil level filler

Lay shaft

Drain plug

Fig. 162. A simple three-speed gearbox and clutch unit, to illustrate usual notation employed.

219

the hand-brake front mechanism and tie up the brake connecting rod. Usually, also, the starter motor must be removed.

As the clutch unit comes away with the gearbox, it is necessary to disconnect the clutch pedal assembly – usually by removing a nut on the end of the clutch cross shaft and sliding the latter with its assembly out. The nuts around the flywheel part of the crankcase must now be removed and the speedometer cable disconnected by unscrewing the nut on its outer casing.

At this stage a careful inspection should be made to make sure that there are no other external connections to the gearbox clutch assembly. The gearbox can then be moved rearwards and lowered to the ground.

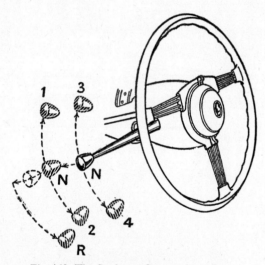

Fig. 163. The Sunbeam-Car steering column
gear lever positions.

Steering Column Gear Change Lever. In American and many, but not all, modern British cars the steering column gear control lever and quadrant is used. This method necessitates a somewhat complex mechanism between the control lever and gearbox, having certain wearing members and adjusting devices.

In some cases links with hinged ends are used; in others cables and links.

Each particular design requires it own special method of adjustment in cases where the gearbox has been removed.

A typical example of a modern change speed control mechanism is that of the Sunbeam car shown in Figs. 163 and 164. The former illustration is of the gear control lever positions. Thus, when starting from rest, the clutch is depressed and the lever is moved from the lower neutral 'N' position to '1' and the clutch released. To get into the second gear the clutch is depressed and the lever moved right across to the '2' position. For changing up to the 3rd gear ratio it is necessary to lift the lever upwards towards the steering wheel and at the same time move it across to '3', with the clutch depressed. The top or 4th gear position requires the lever to be moved across to '4'. For getting into reverse 'R' the lever is placed in the lower 'N' position, and the knob on its end pulled out and then moved to the 'R' position on the right. In all cases gear-changing is accompanied by initial declutching and eventual releasing after the gear lever is in the correct position.

Referring to Fig. 164 which shows the gearbox actuating mechanism, it should be mentioned that this is carefully adjusted and 'locked' at the manufacturer's before the car is dispatched to the purchaser. Only in the case of accidental damage or dismantling should re-adjustment be necessary.

To re-adjust the control cable, slacken off the inner cable fixing in the gearbox end of the cable; use two spanners to avoid kinking the cable. Next, put the gear change speed lever H in neutral, swing the selector lever L to midway position and push the lever H forwards, thus engaging 1st gear in the gearbox. With the change speed lever in 1st gear make sure that it is secured against the stop, i.e. towards the pedals, without operating the reverse stop, by inserting a suitable piece of wood between the change speed lever and steering wheel rim.

With the left hand grip the selector lever L on the gearbox and move it forwards and rearwards, noting the amount of movement by marking the inner cable with two pencil marks to the rear of the fixing (Fig. 164). The movement shown by the marks should

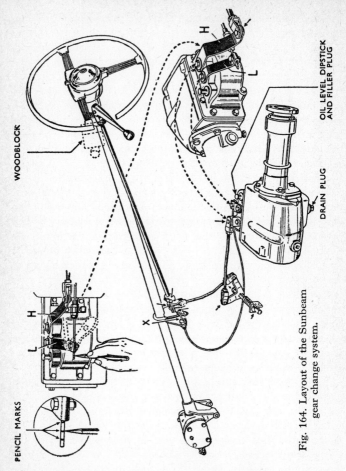

WOODBLOCK

OIL LEVEL DIPSTICK AND FILLER PLUG

DRAIN PLUG

PENCIL MARKS

Fig. 164. Layout of the Sunbeam gear change system.

then be bisected by a third pencil mark. Move the lever *L* until the central mark registers with the rear edge of the fixing and tighten it in this position, again using two spanners. The cable will then be in its correct adjustment.

Lubrication. The various pin joints of the change speed mechanism on all cars thus fitted require periodical lubrication with the oil can. In Fig. 164 the smaller arrows indicate the lubrication points which should be oiled every 2,000 miles, with engine oil; the control cable, also, must be kept well oiled.

The Synchromesh Gearbox. In this improved gearbox two or more of the engaging gears are fitted with a special device to ensure quiet and easy engagement of the gears.

It is not proposed to describe the synchromesh gear in detail, since this is done in Vol. 3 of this Series, but merely to outline its method of operation. It consists of a conical clutch operating in

Fig. 165. Showing principle of synchromesh
gears.

conjunction with a positive tooth clutch in such a way that the latter is brought up to the same speed as that of the gear with which it has to engage before the actual engagement takes place. It is made up of an inner hub and an outer ring. Teeth on the inside of the ring mesh with teeth on the outside of the hub at all times. In the neutral position (Fig. 165) the central location of the ring on the hub is maintained by six steel balls, held in a groove in the ring by means of springs; these can be seen in Fig. 165 which shows the spring-loaded steel ball at (*A*), the outer member (*B*) containing the dogs or teeth to be meshed with the gear on the right and the inner member (*C*) having the internal cone or clutch. The hub has an internal bronze section at each end which fits the conical steel flange on either second or top gear. When a change is made either to top or second gear the

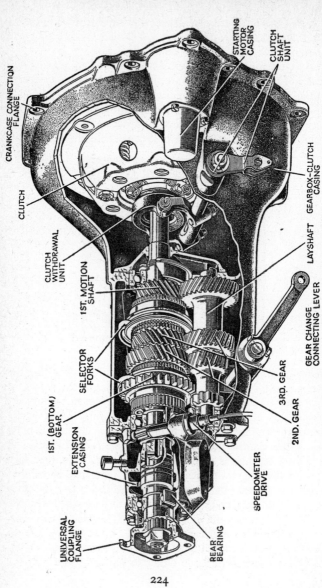

CRANKCASE CONNECTION FLANGE

STARTING MOTOR CASING

CLUTCH SHAFT UNIT

CLUTCH

CLUTCH WITHDRAWAL UNIT

1ST MOTION SHAFT

GEARBOX-CLUTCH CASING

LAYSHAFT

GEAR CHANGE CONNECTING LEVER

SELECTOR FORKS

3RD. GEAR

1ST. (BOTTOM) GEAR

2ND. GEAR

EXTENSION CASING

SPEEDOMETER DRIVE

UNIVERSAL COUPLING FLANGE

REAR BEARING

Fig. 166. The Austin four-speed synchromesh gearbox and clutch unit.

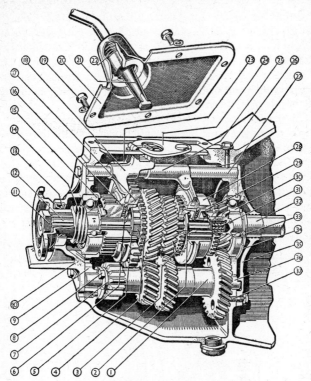

Fig. 167. The Austin car four-speed synchromesh
gearbox components.

1 laygear.
2 front thrust washer.
3 third speed wheel, syn-
   chronizing cone and
   coupling sleeve, mounted
   on bush.
4 second speed wheel, synchronizing cone and
   coupling, mounted on
   bush.
5 rear thrust washer
   (steel).
6 synchronizing springs and
   balls.
7 layshaft steel thrust
   washer (rear).
8 layshaft thrust washer
   (bronze).
9 gearbox case.

10 gearbox rear cover.
11 third motion shaft nut.
12 third motion shaft.
13 rear oil seal.
14 speedometer wheel.
15 rear ball bearing.
16 second speed synchron-
   izer.
17 first speed wheel.
18 first and second speed
   fork.
19 top cover set screws.
20 top cover.
21 change speed lever.
22 change speed lever
   spring.
23 reverse fork.
24 change speed gate with
   interlock arm.

25 third and fourth speed
   fork.
26 fork rod locking pin.
27 forward speeds fork
   rod.
28 third and fourth speed
   coupling sleeve.
29 third and fourth speed
   synchronizer.
30 front ball bearing.
31 front roller bearing.
32 first motion shaft.
33 spring ring for first
   motion shaft.
34 spring ring for front ball
   bearing.
35 front cover.
36 layshaft.
37 front cover screw.

synchronizing device moves as a unit until the bronze section of the hub engages with the conical flange of the gear; the speed of the two then becomes equal, and as the change is completed the internal gear or ring of the synchronizing unit is released from its centrally located position on the hub, and the internal teeth engage in the teeth of the top or second speed gears, as the case may be; there is, therefore, no clashing of the gears.

The maintenance of synchromesh gearboxes is practically as simple as for plain ones, but it should be noted that if the gearbox cover is removed, *the outer ring of the synchronizer should not be moved forward* of its inner hub; otherwise the six steel balls previously mentioned will fly out under the influence of the pressure of their springs. To replace these usually means dismantling the gearbox and the use of special equipment to get the balls back into their proper positions, as described in the next section.

Synchromesh Unit Assembly. The six balls and springs require special guides to assemble them into the speed synchronizer. Fig. 168 shows the method for the Austin gearbox, illustrated in Fig. 166.

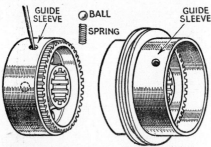

Fig. 168. Re-assembling synchromesh unit.

The guide is a sleeve of the same width as the coupling sleeve, and the machined part of the guide bore is slipped over the synchronizer and then rotated until the hole coincides with one of the six sockets in the synchronizer. A spring and ball are then inserted into this hole and the guide rotated to retain them in position. This procedure is repeated for all six springs and balls. The guide is then pushed farther along the synchronizer splines and followed up closely with the gear coupling sleeve. The splined part of the guide fully depresses the balls against their springs and then, as the coupling sleeve replaces the guide the balls find their location in the coupling sleeve groove.

The Layshaft. This shaft usually rotates in plain or needle bearings in the case of smaller gearboxes and ball or roller bearings in the larger sizes. In the Austin A40 and 90 gearboxes the layshaft gears have Clevite plain bushes which are a press fit in the gear holes and a running fit in the layshaft. A thrust washer is provided at each end to allow end 'float' of 0·001 to 0·003 inch.

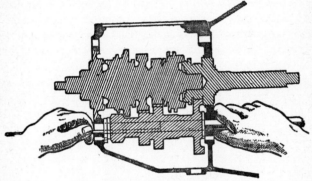

Fig. 169. Lowering the laygear to free the 3rd motion shaft (Austin).

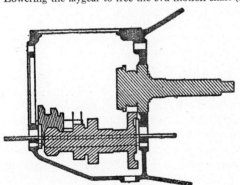

Fig. 170. Lowering the laygear to clear the 1st motion shaft.

The layshaft of the B.M.C. gearbox can be lowered to allow the gears to come out of mesh with the gear assemblies on the shafts above, i.e. the first and third motion shafts, by unlocking the plain layshaft and driving it endwise, following it up with a small diameter stiff rod in order to prevent it from dropping into the gearbox casing below, and to hold the thrust washers in position. Once the layshaft has dropped on to the thin rod (Figs. 169 and 170) the upper gear cluster can be withdrawn through the aperture on the left, having of course, first removed the end cover screws. If it is desired to remove the layshaft, it is necessary only to withdraw the thin rod, manipulating the reverse gear by hand to clear same. The reverse gear is secured by a set screw *A* (Fig. 171); upon removal of this the shaft can be tapped out.

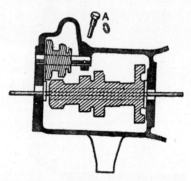

Fig. 171. A reverse shaft locating screw.
The laygear moved out of line to allow
reverse gear to be positioned.

Lubrication. It is important to use only the approved oil of the manufacturers. At the end of the first 500 miles the oil should be changed, draining the used oil through the plug orifice below whilst the oil is still warm.

Instead of having a separate plug for replenishing the gear oil, and dipstick, the two can be combined, as shown in Fig. 172 for the Riley 4/72 car. It is necessary first to lift up the carpet and remove the rubber cover over the gearbox cover shown at *C*.

Every 5,000 miles the oil should be completely changed. A

dipstick indicates the oil level. The capacity of the gearbox is 4 pints. The preselector rack should be oiled occasionally.

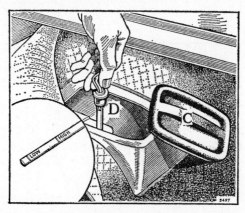

Fig. 172. The Riley combined gearbox filler and dipstick.
C – gearbox cover, D – dipstick.

The Pre-selective Gearbox. In this type, as fitted previously to the Armstrong-Siddeley, Daimler and other cars, the gear selecting lever and dial are arranged on the steering column, the gears themselves being of the epicyclic pattern with separate controlling bands or brakes. Gear change is effected by depressing a control pedal taking the place of the usual clutch pedal, and releasing it when the gear pre-selected, i.e. the gear to which the steering column lever is pointing, is automatically engaged (Fig. 173).

Operating Pre-selective Gears. *In regard to the operation of the Wilson pre-selective gears* fitted to the cars previously mentioned, the following notes may be found useful.

As previously mentioned, the lever on the steering column pre-selects the gears, and the movement of the pedal allows the gear to change itself. It will be seen, therefore, that any one gear can be selected while the car is running on another, the selected gear only being put into use when the control pedal is operated.

It is usually preferable when changing gear to go from one

gear to the next, either immediately above or below the one in use. It is, however, sometimes necessary to engage, say, second gear when the car is actually running in fourth, as, for example,

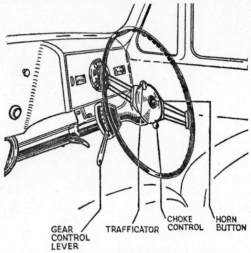

GEAR   TRAFFICATOR   CHOKE   HORN
CONTROL   CONTROL   BUTTON
LEVER

Fig. 173. Armstrong-Siddeley pre-selector
gear and other driver's controls.

in a mountain district, where a very acute turn on a narrow road is followed by a stiff incline. On such occasions the engine should be accelerated before the control pedal is allowed to return to its normal position, so as to ensure a smooth engagement.

Before starting the engine it is advisable to pre-select neutral and operate the control pedal to be sure that no gear is engaged. Depress the pedal to the full extent of its travel.

As soon as the engine has been started and slightly warmed up, move the selector lever into the first gear or reverse position as may be required, fully depress and release the pedal and the car will glide away. When or before it is desired to change the gear, move the selector lever into the gear desired, but until the control pedal is depressed and released, no actual change of gear will take place.

Other gears are operated in the same manner. *When stopping* always pre-select neutral on the dial and depress and release the control pedal.

Failure to depress the pedal fully may cause it to return without changing gear. It will then be found harder to depress the pedal once again, but this will not harm the gears in any way.

When running normally *the control pedal can be used as a clutch pedal* and will only allow the gear to change itself when the selector lever has been moved and the pedal fully depressed. When partly depressed, it will always act as a clutch pedal. It is important to remember that the gear will not change unless the control pedal is depressed right to the end of its travel; the action of the pedal returning to its normal position engages the individual clutch on the gearbox.

Coasting. To coast down long hills select the top gear and depress control pedal; then release the accelerator pedal. Keep the control pedal fully depressed until ignition warning light shows that the engine revs. have fallen to the idling speed. Then gently release the control pedal; the engine is thus disconnected from the transmission.

Fig. 174. Armstrong-Siddeley gear quadrant.

Maintenance and Overhaul. In regard to the overhaul, repair and adjustment of this type of gearbox, although the latter is as reliable and gives the same length of service as the ordinary types, when it eventually becomes necessary to service the preselective gearbox it is advisable to have this work done by the firm's service agents. It may be mentioned that detailed instructions, with illustrations, for timing and adjusting the gears and toggles were given in the 4th and 5th editions of this volume.

Two-pedal Semi-automatic Transmission Operation. As mentioned earlier, this system, which once was popular on certain cars, dispenses with the clutch pedal for all gear changing operations and employs only the accelerator and brake-pedals. The driving of a car is thus simplified and after a short period of instruction drivers of the usual three-pedal clutch-gearbox transmission can readily adapt themselves to the two-pedal system.

The synchromesh gearbox is used and the clutch is engaged and disengaged automatically during gear-changing operations.

At the same time the engine speed is controlled, automatically, so that when a gear change up or down is made the engine crank-

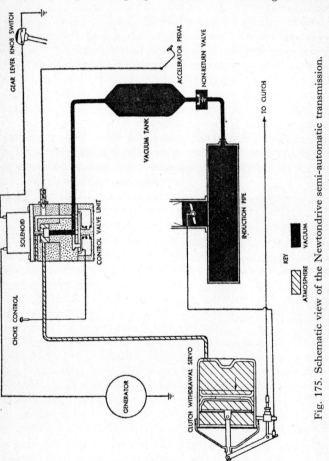

Fig. 175. Schematic view of the Newtondrive semi-automatic transmission.

shaft and the gearbox driven shaft both rotate at the same speed. Provision is also made for a gradual take-up during the clutch engagement.

The various components and circuits for a typical semi-automatic transmission, namely, the Newtondrive, are shown in Fig. 175. The vacuum and atmospheric air pressure circuits are denoted by the black and cross-hatched areas, while the electrical circuits are shown by the fine lines. As depicted, the clutch is being re-engaged by the vacuum-servo piston rod during a gear-changing operation.

It is necessary, in place of the usual torque converter to use either *a fluid flywheel or a centrifugal type of clutch*, so that whenever the engine is running below a certain speed the drive to the gearbox is disengaged. It is thus possible to leave the gear lever (or gearbox gears) in any of the forward or reverse speed positions without the car moving under the engine power, the hand or foot brake should of course be applied while the car is at rest.

Starting Procedure. The starting procedure is first to place the gearbox in the low gear gate slot, then release the brake and press the accelerator pedal down, gradually, when the drive is taken up by the centrifugal clutch and the car will move forward.

Changing Gears. To change up to the next higher gear, the gear lever knob is held in the hand so as to *depress an electrical button switch on top of the knob*, and while depressed to move the gear lever to the next gear position, afterwards releasing the switch. The engine speed will automatically adjust itself to the equivalent road speed and a smooth clutch re-engagement of the clutch – which has been disengaged by the act of depressing the gear lever knob switch – will occur.

The procedure for changing down to the next lower gear is the same as for changing up and the engine speed for this operation is synchronized automatically to that of the gears, making it *unnecessary to use the accelerator during gear changing*. The only time the accelerator need be used to adjust engine speed during a gear change is when a rapid change down to a lower ratio is desired.

Town Driving Positions. It should be emphasized that under town traffic driving conditions there is no need to put the gear lever in 'Neutral' when stopping, it should however be placed in the low gear slot used for normal starting from rest. The only occasion when 'Neutral' is used is for starting the engine from the cold.

Bringing Car to Rest. Whatever gear lever position is in use, the car can be brought to rest without moving the gear lever to 'Neutral', merely by releasing the accelerator pedal and applying the brake. The engine will then continue to idle, without transmitting its drive to the gearbox, irrespective of the gear lever position.

Maintenance. The maintenance items generally include the vacuum-servo operating system, the electrical system; clutch adjustment after long periods of operation and the lubrication of the bearings and pins of the operating mechanism. Where an hydraulic clutch linkage is employed, as in the Manumatic control system, this will require the checking of the fluid level in the supply reservoir or tank at 1,000 mile intervals and the lubrication, at 5,000 miles intervals of the slave cylinder, after cleaning same, with Rubberlube grease.

Should the control system fail to operate correctly, the manufacturer's instruction book should be consulted, before attempting to make any adjustments on the screwed members provided for this purpose, e.g., the carburettor controls. Since the ordinary and centrifugal clutches and also the synchromesh gearboxes used in these control systems are the same as for ordinary three-pedal systems, the maintenance of these items, with certain minor exceptions, is the same for both systems.

The Roverdrive Controls. This British fully-automatic transmission system (described in Vol. 5 of this Series) is more simple and compact than the corresponding American systems.

It comprises (*A*) a torque converter giving a low speed ratio of $2 \cdot 18:1$; (*B*) a vacuum operated clutch to enable easy changes from 'Neutral' to 'Drive', 'Emergency Low' and 'Reverse'; (*C*) an ordinary two-speed and reverse gearbox and (*D*) a separate overdrive unit giving a top gear step-up ratio of $1 \cdot 3:1$.

The simple dashboard control lever has a small gate marked 'Drive', 'Emergency Low' and 'Reverse'. The 'Neutral' position is intermediate between the 'Drive' and the two other positions.

In this position the engine can be started by its motor, but not in the other positions.

The small gear knob has a press-button switch on top which, on being depressed before moving the gear lever, energizes a solenoid, which opens a valve and through a vacuum-servo unit puts the clutch out of engagement. Release of the button causes the clutch to re-engage the drive to the gearbox. With this system no clutch pedal is necessary, the only control of engine and car speed being the large accelerator pedal. The kick-down switch, operated by depressing the accelerator pedal to its full extent, enables the overdrive to be cut out, thus giving a lower gear ratio for fast acceleration and hill-climbing.

Driving Procedure. The engine is started with the gear lever in neutral and the hand brake 'on'. To start the car the gear lever knob button is depressed and the lever moved to the 'Drive' position. The knob button is released so that the engine drive is through the converter to the neutral gearbox gears position. Next, the engine is accelerated, during the primary stage of which the converter acts as a fluid flywheel, but subsequently the drive is taken up positively at the top gear starting ratio of 10·2:1. When the car reaches 30 m.p.h., and the throttle is half-open, then the overdrive is engaged, as explained previously. The same procedure is employed when using the 'Emergency Low' gear for very steep hills, or starting from rest on hills. This gear is also recommended for use when descending steep hills.

The converter casing is supplied with oil from the engine oil system, the total capacity of the engine sump and converter being 3 gallons.

Automatic Transmission Systems. In view of the increasing use of these systems and more particularly for smaller cars, e.g. the B.M.C. 1100 and Minicars, the following brief notes may be of interest to the owner–driver.

The more widely used systems in this country include the General Motors Hydramatic, the Borg-Warner – used on certain B.M.C. and Ford larger cars, the B.M.C. and the Automotive Products Company's system used on B.M.C. 1100 and Minicars.

The Borg-Warner system has been chosen in order to illustrate the general principles, method of driving and maintenance.

In common with all American and most other makes of automatic transmission, this system consists of an engine-driven *torque converter* which may be regarded as a kind of hydraulic clutch (described previously) and a fluid device for increasing the gear ratio for starting off from rest and at lower speeds on the road. This converter is coupled to the engine output shaft and in turn drives the *mechanical gearbox transmission unit*, which almost always consists of at least *two separate epicyclic gear units*, in which the selected gear ratios are obtained by means of brake bands on the epicyclic gear drums and, usually, one or two multi-plate clutches. When the required gear is selected by the driver by moving a small lever over a marked quadrant, or by pressing a selector button, and the driver presses the accelerator pedal gradually downwards, the selected gears to provide the gear ratio are engaged by means of hydraulic pressure acting on small pistons in their cylinders in the gearbox.

Fig. 176, which is given for explanation purposes, shows the schematic layout of one model of the Borg-Warner transmission members, which includes a front clutch (A), torque converter (T) which drives through to epicyclic gears. There is another clutch at (C) and three brake bands, at (B), (D) and (E), respectively.

It is not proposed to describe the various operations to obtain the desired gear ratios, since this subject is more fully dealt with in Volume 5 of this Series, but to indicate the method of driving a car fitted with this transmission.

Driving an Automatic Transmission Car. The first thing to be done is to study the driver's selector lever and its scale. In the present example, the lever scale is marked P, N, D, L and R, denoting, respectively, Park, Neutral, Drive, Low and Reverse.

When starting off from rest with a car fitted with this transmission, the gear selector should be in the P or N position, with the engine just idling, and *the hand brake on*: this is most important, with all automatic transmissions, otherwise the car will begin to creep along. It should, however, be mentioned that in recent transmissions there is a locking pawl which automatically locks the car against forward or backward movement. This applies, only, when the lever is in the P position. When in N the hand brake must be on.

To start off, place the selector lever in the D position, release the hand brake and depress the accelerator, when the car will start off in its lowest gear ratio. As the accelerator pedal is further pushed down the gears will automatically be changed, first to 3rd and then to Top and the car can then be driven without further attention at cruising to the maximum road speeds. When the accelerator is released gradually, the gear ratios are automatically changed down to the lowest one.

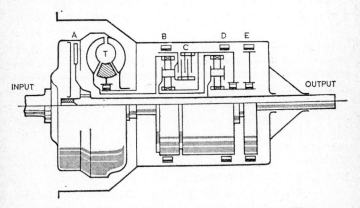

Fig. 176. Arrangement of the components of the Borg-Warner automatic transmission.
A front friction clutch. *B* front brake band. *C* clutch. *D* middle drum unit brake band. *E* rear drum unit brake band. *T* torque converter, showing the reactor member and free-wheel (shaded).

When it is required to keep the car in *low gear*, as when travelling up steep inclines, the selector lever is placed in the L position, this position is also good for engine-braking down steeper hills. The road speed should be below 35 m.p.h. when using this gear ratio.

If, when in *top gear* it is desired *to change down* to the intermediate ratio the accelerator pedal is depressed downwards as far as it will go, when the gears change automatically. Usually the '*kick-down*' switch does not operate above about 55 to 60 m.p.h.

To stop the car, leave the lever in the D position and apply the foot brake until the car comes to rest; then place the selector lever in the N or P position.

To reverse the car place the lever in the R position. It is recommended that the left foot be used at the same time on the foot brake when manœuvring in confined places.

If the engine requires *an emergency start*, due to a flat battery, it can be started by pushing or towing, but must be in the N or neutral gear; it must not be towed at more than 25 m.p.h. The ignition should be switched on and the lever placed in the L position.

In the event of *an accident* to the car it can be towed in the N position, but if the *transmission breaks down*, then it is necessary to disconnect the propeller shaft, or to lift the rear wheels and tow the car backwards.

Maintenance of Automatic Transmissions. Except for occasional inspection of the fluid level in the transmission casing and lubricating the external selector mechanism, there is little that the owner-driver can do if any faults occur internally. These can only be dealt with satisfactorily by a mechanic trained to service such transmission systems.

In the case of the Borg-Warner Type 35 automatic transmission which is made in this country and fitted to many makes of car, e.g. B.M.C. and Ford cars, the transmission casing has a filler tube with breather and dipstick, just forward on the bulkhead – in B.M.C. cars. The car should be driven on to a level surface with the engine and transmission at normal running temperature. Select P and allow the engine to idle for two minutes. With the engine still idling in P, withdraw and wipe the dipstick with a clean, non-fluffy cloth or paper. Insert the dipstick and withdraw it immediately. If necessary, add fluid to bring the level to the high mark. The difference between the low and high marks on the dipstick is 1 pint and the total casing capacity is 11 pints, which includes $5\frac{1}{4}$ pints for the torque converter. The dipstick has two marks, namely, for 'High' and 'Low', respectively. It is recommended that inspection for topping-up should be at 3,000 miles periods.

CHAPTER 8

THE PROPELLER SHAFT AND BACK AXLE

The Propeller Shaft. The earlier spherical front universal coupling and the fabric disc type, dealt with in previous editions of this book, have been replaced entirely by the modern Hooke's joint metal universal and in some instances by the Layrub rubber block pattern, although the latter is used more in commercial vehicles.

The modern propeller shaft has a metal universal coupling at the rear and a similar front coupling combined with a sliding-type of splined shaft and hole unit, to allow for lateral movement of the propeller shaft under the vehicle's spring action.

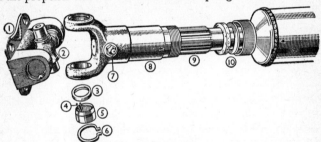

Fig. 177. Front end of propeller shaft, showing universal coupling and splined sliding joint.

1. flange yoke.
2. spider.
3, 4 and 5. needle bearing assembly.
6. spring ring.

7. oil nipple for splines.
8. sleeve yoke.
9. splined end of propeller shaft.
10. dust cap with steel and cork washers.

Fig. 177 shows the Austin front end universal coupling and sliding unit in partly dismantled form to illustrate the components of the coupling.

The propeller shaft itself is of tubular construction and is welded at the front end to the splined shaft unit which can slide in a splined hole in the rear universal fork or yoke (8). A nipple is provided for lubricating the splines.

The star member of the coupling (2), has needle roller bearings (4) at its four ends and these are lubricated by oil or grease gun through another nipple; for this purpose the star member (Fig. 178) is drilled with oil channels so that lubricant enters at the centre and flows along the four drillings to the bearings.

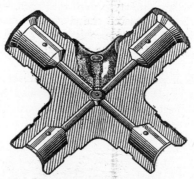

Fig. 178. The universal coupling star member, showing oil or grease passages.

Maintenance Attention. If the three nipples previously mentioned are lubricated at regular intervals the couplings and splined joint have a long trouble-free life. If neglected, or after long service, wear may occur (a) on the thrust faces of the star and its housings, (b) in the needle roller bearings or (c) on the splines.

Wear on the thrust faces may be detected by pushing the star endwise in each of its 90° positions; alternatively, the assembled universal joint may be tested by lifting it in the two axial directions of the star bearings. Bearing play is indicated by circumferential movement of the shaft relative to the flange yokes; this test includes also wear clearance on the sliding splines.

Disconnecting the Propeller Shaft. It is generally advisable to jack up the rear end of the car and then support the end of the car on blocks. Then the front end of the shaft should be supported by a wooden strut or tied up from above on the chassis whilst

the four nuts and bolts are removed from the flange yoke (1), Fig.
177. The rear flange yoke is detached in a similar manner. Then,
the dust cap (10) at rear of the splines should be unscrewed by
hand and the splined sleeve yoke slid forwards by about $\frac{1}{2}$ inch
towards the propeller shaft, to free the pilot flanges.

Fig. 179. Tapping the joint to extract
the needle bearing unit.

Dismantling the Couplings. The dismantling procedure for
the widely used Hardy-Spicer couplings, as fitted on Austin

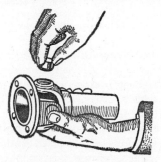

Fig. 180. Removing a bearing cup
complete with its needle rollers.

'A' series cars is illustrated in Figs, 179, 180 and 181. The same
general procedure is used for both front and rear couplings.

Clean away the enamel from all the snap rings and bearing
faces, to ensure easy extraction of the bearings.

Remove the snap rings by pressing together the ends of the rings and extract with a screwdriver. If the ring does not come out easily, tap the bearing face lightly to relieve the pressure against the ring.

Now, holding the joint so that the splined sleeve trunnion is on top, tap the radius of the yoke with a lead or copper hammer (see Fig. 179), and it will be found that the bearing will begin to emerge. If difficulty is experienced, use a small bar to tap the bearing from the inside, taking care not to damage the race itself. Turn the yoke over and extract the bearing with the fingers (see Fig. 180), being careful not to lose any of the needles.

Repeat this operation for the other bearing, and the splined yoke can be removed from the spider (see Fig. 181).

Fig. 181. Separating the joint.

Examination and Reconditioning. The items most likely to exhibit signs of wear are the star journals and the needle bearing races. As no replacement oversize journals or stars are provided it is necessary to replace the complete star and bearing assembly, but if there should be any ovality in the trunnion bearing holes, this would prevent the bearing outer races being a light driving fit – as they should be, in the yoke holes. In this case new yokes must be fitted, i.e. a completely new coupling. The propeller shaft fixed yoke (rear), should only be renewed if the wear in the bearing holes is appreciable, since it means a new propeller shaft.

In regard to the splined members a total of 0·004 inch circumferential movement, measured on the outside diameter of the spline, is the maximum allowed. Before re-assembling the coupling and splined members see that the needle *roller bearings are filled with oil* and *the splines well lubricated* all along their mating surfaces.

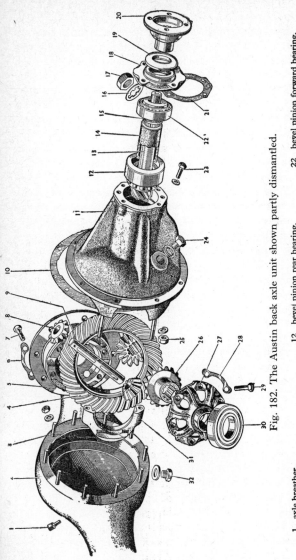

Fig. 182. The Austin back axle unit shown partly dismantled.

1 axle breather.
2 axle case.
3 carrier stud.
4 crown wheel.
5 differential case (L.H.).
6 crown wheel bolt lockwasher.
7 crown wheel securing bolt.
8 differential pinion.
9 differential pinion shaft.
10 gear carrier joint washer.
11 gear carrier.

12 bevel pinion rear bearing.
13 bevel pinion.
14 pinion sleeve.
15 bearing adjusting shim.
16 bevel pinion lockwasher.
17 bevel pinion nut.
18 end cover.
19 dust cover.
20 pinion flange.
21 end cover joint washer.

22 bevel pinion forward bearing.
23 end cover bolt.
24 oil filler plug.
25 crown wheel bearing cap nut.
26 differential wheel.
27 differential case (R.H.).
28 differential case lockwasher.
29 differential case securing bolt.
30 crown wheel bearing.
31 crown wheel bearing end cap.
32 axle drain plug.

It should also be noted that the oil seals, i.e. the cork washers and washer retainers are tapped into position on the inner ends of the journals or pins of the star member before assembling the coupling; it is usually advisable to renew these cork washers.

Long-life Universal Couplings. In order to reduce the maintenance attention for these couplings new designs are now in use which require no lubrication over very long periods of service; typical couplings of this kind are fitted to recent Vauxhall cars. The Hardy-Spicer extended-life coupling has components, including needle bearings, which are precision-cleaned before assembly and have a nylon-base end washer for each bearing. A special chemically compounded grease ensures adequate lubrication, while a metal-clad rubber boot entirely seals the bearings from extraneous matter, e.g. dirt, salt, water, etc.

The American Ford cars employ such couplings, which require no attention under about 36,000 miles.

The Back Axle Unit. This unit comprises the final drive gear, which is usually a bevel pinion meshing into a crown (bevel) wheel, the differential gear, the two half or jack axles, the bearings for the gears and axles, adjustment devices, oil seals, the back axle casing and brake drum end plates (fixed).

A complete back axle unit in dismantled form is given in Fig. 182, the various numbered parts being indicated in the caption below. The mechanic will be able to identify and acquaint himself with each of the components, and should then be in a good position to understand the servicing of the back axle.

The back axle is not likely to give trouble to the car owner, at least during the first 25,000 miles of its life, provided it has been kept properly lubricated. Instructions for lubricating this unit are given in Chapter 2. It is important to emphasize the necessity of draining off the lubricant once every year (or every 10,000 miles) as small particles of metal from the teeth of the gears may become dislodged and find their way into the working parts. After flushing out with special flushing oil, and draining, re-fill with fresh lubricant to the level of the filling plug.

Removal of Back Axle. It is usually advisable, when making major repairs to adjustments to the back axle, to remove it bodily from the chassis. The rear part of the frame should first be jacked or otherwise lifted up and secured in the raised position. It is best to remove both the rear wheels and brake drums at this stage, leaving the brake shoes and back plate in position on the axle casing. The brake drums are held to the hub flange by countersunk screws, which should be removed. Next, uncouple the

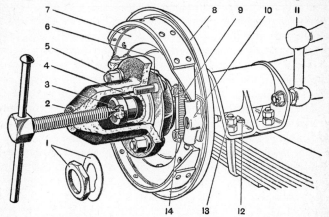

Fig. 183. Method of removing wheel hub of Austin back axle.

1 hub lock-nut and washer.	8 brake back plate.
2 hub extractor.	9 brake shoe return spring.
3 extractor adapter.	10 brake shoe adjuster.
4 axle tube.	11 shock absorber arm.
5 wheel stud and nut.	12 rear spring centre bolt.
6 hub.	13 spring clip securing nuts (later
7 brake shoe.	replaced by Simmonds nuts).
	14 brake back plate securing nut.

front end universal coupling of propeller shaft. Then detach the rear spring attachments to the axle casing and spring shackles.

The Austin 'A' series back axle (Fig. 183) is of the three-quarter floating type, having a flange attached to the outer end of each half-axle. The latter can be drawn out of the casing by gripping the flange outside the hub and pulling it by hand. If it proves to be tight it can be prised, gently, with a screwdriver blade inserted between the flange and the hub. Care should be taken of the paper washer. This will leave the hub (6) Fig. 183, with its four studs in position.

Having removed the half axle the wheel hub retaining nut is accessible. This nut is locked in position by a tab washer, the tab being bent up against one of the flats on the nut; the tab should be knocked back and the nut removed. It is necessary to use a screw-type extractor (Fig. 183) to force the hub off the axle tube.* The special adaptor (3) provided by the makers is recommended for use with the extractor (2). The latter has a flange to fit over the hub studs and is held in place by two of the wheel studs. By screwing up the centre pointed-end screw of the extractor the hub and double-row ball bearing together with the washers and oil seal will be withdrawn. The bearing can then be tapped out of the hub, using a drift, if it is to be screwed.

The other components of the back axle, e.g. the bevel pinion, crown wheel and differential assembly can be dismantled without difficulty if the illustrations in Fig. 182 are first studied.

Fig. 184 illustrates how the back axle of one model Armstrong-Siddeley car is removed. The rear spring attachment is by means of the pin C, which secures the clip B to A. D is the shackle-link; E, the shackle pin; G, the Silentbloc rubber bush; H, the tab-washer, and F, the places requiring regular lubrication. The rear spring brackets are held to the axle casing by the pivot pins C, which are provided with an oil lubrication nipple. The centre clips which hold the rear spring and through which the pivot pin passes should not be disturbed, except when necessary, as were the clips to be released, the separate leaves would be difficult to replace without special apparatus. *If a spring must be removed,* the bottom clip should be undone and the side of each leaf marked to ensure centralization when re-assembling. To re-assemble compress the middle leaves in a vice, taking care that their centre dents fit into each other, and then secure the leaves with their end-clips. Add the upper and lower leaves and plate, the spring gaiters helping to keep the leaves flat. The rear springs must be held a little out of centre in the vice to enable their central clip to be fitted.

Back Axle Troubles. The following are the principal troubles which eventually may occur during the life of a car: (1) Excessive Noise in the Differential or Bevel Pinion and Crown Wheel.

* See also Figs. 286 and 287 for other hub extractors.

(2) Broken Half Axle. (3) Leakage of Lubricant into Brake Drums. (4) Leakage of Lubricant from Plugs in Casing. (5) Wear in the Ball or Roller Bearings.

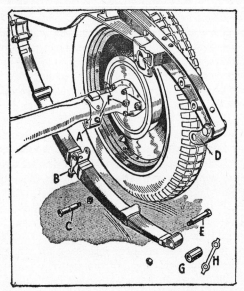

Fig. 184. Back axle, illustrating method of removal.

Noisy Back Axle Unit. The chief causes of noisy operation are, as follows: (1) Insufficient lubricant in the back axle casing or use of an unsuitable, e.g. too thin, lubricant. (2) Bevel pinion and crown wheel badly worn or incorrectly adjusted. (3) Bearing (ball or roller) worn or damaged. Before investigating the cause of a noisy axle, make certain that *the noise heard* is *not due to the gearbox or to exhaust system vibration.* The subject of back axle lubrication is dealt with in Chapter 2.

Perhaps one of the most common causes of noisy operation is that of incorrect meshing of the bevel pinion and crown wheel teeth, so that this should be one of the first items investigated.

If the gear teeth are not badly worn, and the cause is one of incorrect teeth meshing, the maker's instructions or a sectioned illustration of the final drive unit should be obtained, to ascertain the particular method of adjustment of the gears. In this connection, however, the following notes may be found useful:

Meshing of Pinion and Crown Wheel. In regard to the general subject of bevel drive back axle adjustment Fig. 185 (1) indicates a crown and bevel wheel correctly located to each other, whilst in diagrams (2) and (3) they are incorrectly located.

Gear makers always turn the peripheries of the crown and bevel wheels at an angle, the line WK coinciding with the peripheries of both wheels being at right angles to the line YZ, which is the line bisecting the angle of the drive and always intersecting the axes of rotation of both wheels.

Now since the teeth of any bevel wheels of whatever angle of drive have different pitches at different parts of the tooth, it is obvious they should gear together so that those points on the tooth of one wheel which are at a certain pitch from each other must gear with points on the teeth of the mating wheel which have the same pitch. If the pitch does not coincide at any one point along the length of any tooth or pair of teeth it will not coincide at any other point on the tooth, and the result will be the same as though one geared together two ordinary straight tooth pinions having different pitches to each other. Obviously there will be sliding instead of rolling motion (which correct tooth form gives) and resultant friction, wear and noise.

In Fig. 185 (2) the bevel pinion is pushed up in the line of its axis towards the crown wheel to get a deeper mesh and points on the wheels (marked by a dot) which have the same pitch are not meshing with each other, while in Fig. 185 (3) the crown wheel has been moved towards the bevel pinion to get the full mesh and again points on each wheel of coinciding pitch (marked by dots) do not mesh together.

Therefore to ensure true pitch mesh if one moves the bevel pinion up one must also move the crown wheel towards it. The ratios of the amount each wheel is moved will be the same as the ratios of the gear. If the gear is 4 to 1 one must move the crown wheel four times the distance the bevel wheel is moved if the end thrust wear on each is equal, i.e. the wear of the thrust bearings, because moving the bevel pinion alone along its axis would require it to be moved four times the distance (to get in full mesh with the crown wheel), as one would have to move the crown wheel along its axis to get the same full mesh.

It will be seen therefore that true equal pitch meshing can only be effected by moving both wheels in the ratio of their gear ratio. One need not measure the amount the wheels move since the surface of the peripheries as made square with tooth lines gives us the necessary indication. All that is required is to move the

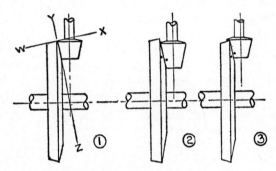

Fig. 185. Back axle bevel drive adjustment.

wheels so that a 6 inch straight edge rule, laid across both wheels as at *W-X* in Fig. 185 (1), lies touching both surfaces of the peripheries for the whole of their length.

Many different arrangements are provided by the makers for making both adjustments, i.e. adjusting the crown wheel nearer the pinion, and the pinion up towards the crown wheel. The diagram Fig. 186 shows one method of using shims on either side of the bearings carrying the differential cage, which also carries the crown wheel. Reducing the number of shims at *A* and increasing them at *B* moves the crown wheel towards the bevel wheel.

The other method, generally used, is by the use of screw adjusters on either side of the axle inner bearings. With these the differential unit with its crown wheel can be moved sidewise in relation to the bevel pinion.

Complete Adjustment of Crown Wheel and Pinion.
When a back axle has been dismantled and reassembled, or a new crown wheel and bevel pinion is fitted, four distinct procedures are involved, namely:

(1) Correct location of the pinion.

(2) Preloading the pinion bearing.

(3) Adjusting the differential bearing preload.

(4) Adjusting the backlash between the gears.

Complete instructions for these operations are given in the car manufacturers' service manuals, but the following brief information will be found useful in regard to Items (1) and (2).

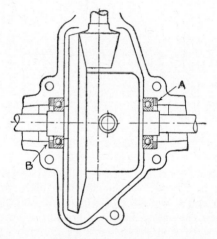

Fig. 186. Method of adjusting bevel gear mesh
with crown wheel.

Typical Adjustments. Fig. 187 illustrates a typical final drive unit with the spiral bevel pinion shaft mounted on Timken tapered roller bearings spaced apart by a distance piece in the front portion of the axle casing. The inner ends of the half axles which are splined to fit into the differential mounting are also on roller bearings. In order to adjust the mesh of the pinion gear into the crown wheel, thin liners or shims are fitted at the back of each inner bearing race. These shims are selected to give the correct degree of gear mesh, without end play of the bevel pinion shaft or its bearings. It should be noted that the inner races of the lower bearings are a press-fit on the differential bosses.

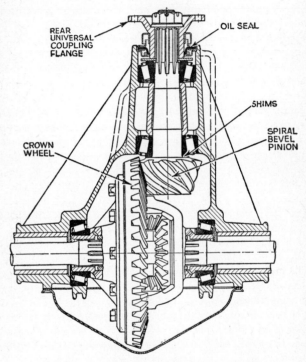

REAR
UNIVERSAL
COUPLING
FLANGE

OIL SEAL

SHIMS

SPIRAL
BEVEL
PINION

CROWN
WHEEL

Fig. 187. Adjustment of final drive gears, fitted with
Timken roller bearings.

In the more recent final drives the taper roller bearings are preloaded to a torque of 6 to 8 lb. in., adjustment being effected by the insertion or removal of shims between the pinion sleeve and the inner races of the roller bearings; this adjustment, however, is the work of an expert.

When double-row ball bearings are used for the bevel pinion shaft it is usual to adjust the pinion mesh in the crown wheel by a screw adjuster which moves the pinion member bodily towards or away from the crown wheel.

Pinion Bearing Preloading. Typical methods of adjusting the bevel pinion and differential unit in the case of a car having semi-floating half axles are shown in Fig. 188.

The bevel pinion unit is located accurately in mesh with the crown wheel by means of spacer and adjusting shims. The differential assembly is adjustable sidewise, by means of the adjusting nuts shown outside each tapered roller bearing.

The bevel pinion is mounted on pre-loaded taper roller bearings. The inner race of the rear bearing is a tight press fit on the pinion. The inner race of the front bearing is a close sliding fit on the pinion stem. The outer race of each bearing is pressed against a shoulder recessed in the carrier. The adjustment of the pinion along its axis is by means of shims placed between the pinion rear bearing inner race and the pinion head. A splined universal joint flange marked F in Fig 188 is fitted to the pinion stem by a special self-locking nut which bears against a special washer. Tightening the pinion nut compresses the spacer shown between the inner race of the front bearing and a shoulder on the pinion shaft.

The object of this compressible spacer is to preload the pinion bearings, to obviate initial wear effects and to prevent the inner race from rotating.

The amount of preload is measured by the turning effort or torque of the pinion nut. In most modern cars this preloading torque is from 12 to 20 lb. inch; a torque wrench is used for this purpose.

Backlash between Crown Wheel and Pinion Gears. It is important when adjusting these mating gears to allow the correct amount of free play, or backlash between the teeth of these gears.

The correct backlash is given by the car manufacturers and usually lies between 0·004 and 0·008 inch.

Backlash is adjusted by moving the differential crown wheel assembly bodily sidewise by means of the shims or screw

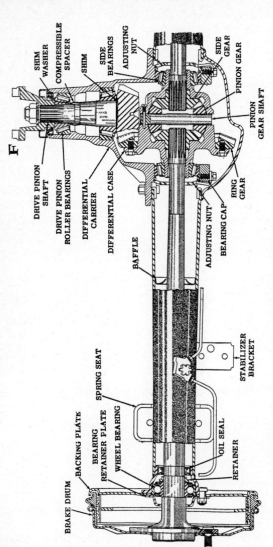

SHIM

WASHER

COMPRESSIBLE
SPACER

SHIM

SIDE
BEARINGS

ADJUSTING
NUT

SIDE
GEAR

PINION GEAR

PINION
GEAR SHAFT

F

DRIVE PINION
SHAFT

DRIVE PINION
ROLLER BEARINGS

DIFFERENTIAL
CARRIER

DIFFERENTIAL CASE

BAFFLE

ADJUSTING NUT

BEARING CAP

RING
GEAR

SPRING SEAT

STABILIZER
BRACKET

BACKING PLATE

BEARING
RETAINER PLATE

WHEEL BEARING

OIL SEAL

RETAINER

BRAKE DRUM

Fig. 188. Rear axle assembly, showing shim and adjusting ring methods of gear adjustment (General Motors).

adjustment means provided on either side of the two bearings, as shown in Fig. 188.

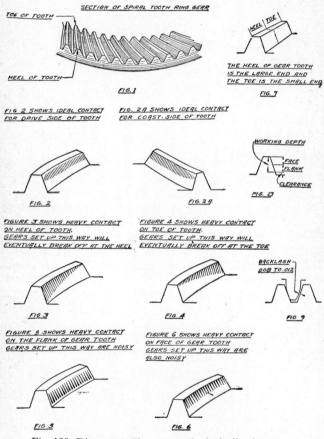

Fig. 189. Diagram to illustrate method of adjusting gear teeth and to show results of incorrect meshing.

Appearance of Gear Teeth.

The appearance of the contact regions of the bevel and crown wheel teeth are a sure indication of the accuracy, or otherwise, of the alignment or meshing of these gears.

Referring to Fig. 189 the appearances of the contact areas of the gear teeth are clearly shown. These contact regions are readily revealed by painting the surfaces of the teeth thinly with white lead paint before meshing them. As these diagrams are practically self-explanatory it is necessary, only, to draw special attention to (Fig. 2) in Fig. 189 which shows the ideal contact area and location in the case of spiral and plain bevel gears, for the drive side of the tooth. The names of the teeth regions are given in (Figs. 7 and 8) and the usual amount of backlash in (Fig. 9).

Broken Axle. This is not an uncommon trouble in the case of cars which have seen several years' service. Records made by the Royal Automobile Club show that broken axle shafts accounted for about 16 per cent of all car breakdowns, in 1947; dropping to 7·5 in 1958 and then to 3·0 per cent in 1964, due no doubt to better design and the use of higher tensile and fatigue strength shafts. Fracture of one of the two half axle shafts which convey the drive from the differential members to the road wheels is due to 'fatigue' of the metal; this fatigue is caused by the repeated stresses to which the shaft is subjected, namely, bending and torsion. In time the metal structure is altered and weakened, until finally the shaft breaks clean through. Back axles of the semi-floating type, in which part of the car's weight is carried by the half axles, instead of by the wheels direct, are more apt to fracture than those of the three-quarter and full-floating type.

The symptom of a broken back axle shaft is the failure of the car to move when a gear is engaged and the clutch released. To ascertain whether the clutch is not slipping – for this will cause a similar effect – get someone to look under the car and note whether the propeller shaft is turning. If of the enclosed type this test will not, of course, be applicable; in this case jack up each wheel in turn and, with one of the gears engaged, see if the engine can be turned by the wheel; if not, it points to a broken shaft. Spare half axles can be obtained from the manufacturers or their agents and fitted without much difficulty, but the inner broken member must be removed, and this usually means dismantling the axle. If, however, the other axle shaft is removed, a rod can usually be inserted from this end and the broken part driven out. When replacing a broken axle, it is advisable to consider the fitting of a new axle in place of the unbroken one also, for the latter may fracture before long if left in place.

With semi-floating axles it is necessary to remove the road wheels from the keyed tapered shaft ends, and as the hubs are usually a tight fit on the shafts it is advisable to use a wheel-puller of the type sold by motor accessory dealers (*vide* Fig. 287). If at all refractory, paraffin or turpentine should be poured around the joint, and when the wheel-puller is screwed up fairly tight, a sharp tap with a heavy hammer on the end of the centre screw over the axle will usually release the wheel hub. In bad cases of wheels refusing to come off their axles, the judicious application of a blow-lamp flame followed by an application of paraffin and a wheel-puller will have the desired result.

Removing Typical Half-Axle Shaft. The following is an

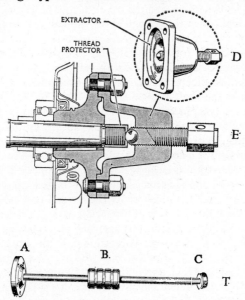

Fig. 190. Tools and method of removing half-axle shaft (Hillman, etc.).

account of the method for removing the half-axle shafts on Hillman, Sunbeam and certain other makes of Rootes Group cars.

To remove the brake backing plate, oil seal, dust excluder and hub the tool shown at (D) in Fig. 190 is fitted on to the brake backing plate in the manner shown at (E) in Fig. 190. When replacing the splash guard (not shown in Fig. 190) it should be fitted into the bearing recess with its recessed centre inwards.

Fig. 190 shows (below) the extractor tool as supplied by the manufacturers for removing the half-axle from the axle casing. This tool has a flange (A) which fits over the wheel studs and is fixed by nuts; it has a sliding weight (B) on its shaft and a fixed collar (C) on the right-hand end. When in position on the wheel stud flange the weight is moved sharply along so as to strike the collar, repeating this procedure until the half axle is released from its splined end fixture and can be withdrawn along the axle casing.

Leakage of Lubricant, Slipping Brakes. After long periods of running, oil from the back axle may find its way past the outer axle shaft oil seal washer, and thence *get into the brake drum*, thus causing the brake shoes to lose, partially, their gripping properties. If, on removing the rear wheels, any oil is found in the brake drum itself – particularly round the axle – this is a sign that the oil seal washer around the axle shaft on the inside of the bearing requires renewal. Other possible sources of oil leakage are those due to the filler plug not having been screwed down sufficiently and to the back axle casing joints nuts becoming slack.

In regard to *the oil seals* of the back axle these are fitted at the front of the bevel gear unit, to each half axle and to the outsides of the outer wheel ball races.

The earlier felt washer oil seals are now replaced by combination oil seals, using leather or synthetic rubber rings with a spiral spring coiled in the form of a ring to apply enough pressure to the contact ring that bears on the revolving shaft. (Fig. 191.)

Whenever the axle assembly is dismantled the oil seals should be examined and any faulty ones replaced.

The new seals should be fitted the correct way round, i.e. with their plain faces against the oil seal housing faces of the outer stationary members. The oil seals must be quite clean before use; they may be oiled lightly before insertion. It is a good plan to use a tube with a true end to push the oil seal along its shaft for insertion in its housing.

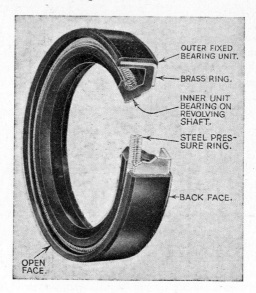

Fig. 191. Typical modern oil seal.

Lubrication of Back Axle. The axle casing is filled to a certain level with the recommended, lubricant – as given in the Owners' Manual – and after a new car has run for about 1,000 miles it should be emptied, while warm, and refilled with fresh lubricant.

The actual topping-up inspections vary among different cars. Some makers recommend inspection every 1,000 miles while others state each 3,000 miles, but most agree that the casing be drained out every 8,000 miles and then refilled with fresh lubricant. The usual arrangement is to have a square- or hexagon-headed plug at the back of the casing, which when removed acts both as a filling hole and a top level indicator. But do not fill or replenish the lubricant when the car is laden, or a quite different level will result.

Broken Gear Teeth. As distinct from worn or incorrectly meshed bevel and crown wheel gears a noisy back axle may also be caused through chipped or broken teeth on the gears; in some cases much worn bearings will cause gear fracture. Cases have occurred in the past of the bevel pinion teeth fracturing owing to non-alignment of its teeth with those of the crown wheel, to an insufficient amount of mesh – so that all the driving effort comes on the tops of the gear teeth, or to a piece of metal, broken off some part inside the axle casing, getting between the gear teeth; once this commences the rest of the teeth may quickly become damaged. This is another reason why it is necessary, periodically, to run out the lubricant from the back axle, for any chips or detached pieces of metal will usually drain out with the lubricant.

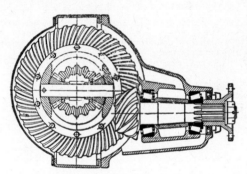

Fig. 192. Hypoid bevel gear, using
Timken roller bearings.

The Hypoid Type Spiral Bevel Pinion. Many modern cars are fitted with this type of bevel pinion, which is illustrated in Fig. 192, as it has certain advantages over the ordinary axle level type.

It is more sensitive to misalignment effects, however, and therefore requires careful adjustment; it also needs efficient lubrication with a special grade of 'Hypoid' oil. The Timken bearing outer races are made a press fit into the housing and the inner race of the rear bearing is also a press fit on the shaft. The inner race of the forward bearing is a lighter fit, in order to facilitate adjustment.

A spacer, with bearing adjustment shims, is fitted between the bearing races. This enables the whole pinion shaft assembly of bearings and the universal coupling flange to be clamped up solidly by the nut shown on the right, in Fig. 192. Gear engagement is assured by the maintenance of close tolerances of the components or *by shims* interposed between the inner race of the rear bearing and the shoulder on the pinion shaft.

Back Axle Troubles and Remedies. The following summary of the more common back axle troubles and methods of curing these, may be found useful:

(1) Noisy Rear Axle

Possible Cause	Remedy
Worn pinion or crown gears, or both.	Renew pinion and crown wheel. Note: Examine differential gears for wear or backlash (excessive). Replace if excessive.
Incorrectly adjusted mesh between pinion and crown wheel.	Re-adjust by methods described in this chapter.
Broken or damaged gear teeth.	Replace gears concerned and re-adjust mesh.
Lack of sufficient back axle lubricant.	Replenish.
Lubricant too 'thin'.	Use recommended grade of lubricant.
Worn or damaged bearings.	Replace with new bearings.

(2) Lubricant Leakage from Back Axle

Worn or defected oil seals.	Replace with new seals.
Axle casing filled above proper level.	Drain surplus from axle casing.
Breather pipe or vent choked.	Examine and clean out.

CHAPTER 9

THE BRAKING SYSTEM

THE brakes are among the most important items of the car, for the safety of the occupants may depend upon the efficiency of the braking system.

It is well worth while to make a regular habit of inspecting the brakes and making any adjustments found necessary.

Most modern makes of car are provided with ready means of adjustments to the brakes, the adjusting screws or nuts being placed in accessible positions.

In the absence of more explicit instructions, the braking system can usually be followed by tracing the rods, tubing and connections from the foot brake pedal and hand brake lever, respectively, to the brake drums. If there is any doubt as to which lever, or rod, is connected to, say, the foot brake pedal, get someone to operate the pedal whilst you watch the rods or levers that are moved by this operation.

Minor Adjustments and Maintenance Notes. Assuming the car has been purchased new, the chassis will have had road tests, and the brakes correctly adjusted as a result.

After the first 1,000 miles or so the brake friction material, which when new had a rough surface, will have bedded down to a fairly smooth condition. As a result, the brake operating mechanism will show a certain amount of free movement.

The free movement can be taken up by the particular adjustment method provided by the car manufacturers and described in their operator's manual. In the earlier cars, the usual method of adjustment was by a wing-nut or similar threaded member at the end of the braking mechanism, conveniently placed at the front end of the car. The wheels were jacked up and the adjusting screw tightened until the wheels were just free to rotate, i.e. the brake drums just clear of the brake shoes. In all modern cars the adjustment for taking up brake lining wear *is on each of the four wheel brake drums* and, usually, it is not necessary to jack up the wheels for this purpose; the method used is explained later.

It is here important to note that *no adjustments* should be made to the brake actuating mechanism, e.g. the rods, levers or cables,

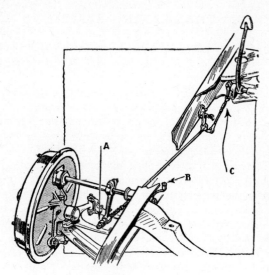

Fig. 193. Earlier front wheel brake mechanism.
A adjusting screw; *B* greaser;
C adjusting turnbuckle.

when taking up brake shoe wear. The only occasion when this is permissible is if any of the brake mechanism is seriously worn or damaged.

Equal Braking. *It is important* when adjusting brakes to check whether, when the foot (or hand) brake is applied, the brake in each wheel drum goes on equally. Sometimes one finds that one of the brakes is effective before the other comes on; this not only reduces the efficiency, but causes undue wear of one of the brakes. After adjusting the brakes with the road wheels jacked up, and ensuring that both are free when the brake pedal or lever is released, get someone gradually to apply the brake pedal or lever and test whether one front wheel is 'braked' before the other; if so, the adjuster at the brake drum end must be slackened back a little. Repeat for the rear wheel brakes.

In all modern braking systems there are compensating devices to ensure that the braking effort is applied equally to each of the rods or cables leading to the front or rear brake cam levers.

Cam-operated Brake Shoes. The earlier design of brake consisted of a pair of friction-lined brake shoes, as shown at (*A*), in Fig. 194 which were hinged at (*B*) and held together by a spring

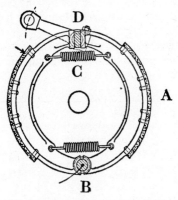

Fig. 194. Principle of the cam-operated brake.

(*C*) against a flat-sided cam (*D*) which was attached to the brake lever arm (*E*). When the brake pedal was depressed the mechanism moved the arm (*E*) and caused the cam to force the two brake shoes apart against the brake drums, not shown in Fig. 194.

Other Brake Shoe Expanders. Whilst the cam type of brake shoe expander has been widely used and is still retained in certain commercial vehicles, it has been largely replaced by the axial wedge and the hydraulic piston expanders. Examples of the former are the Girling and Bendix brakes and of the latter the Lockheed and Girling ones; further reference to these is made later.

Lubrication Notes. Cam-operated Brakes. *The brake mechanism pins* and their bearings should be kept free from mud and dirt, and well greased; it is better to use grease for the rocking shaft arm pins and bearings than oil, in order to keep out water. Some mechanics prefer, after dismantling, cleaning, greasing, and replacing the pins, to plaster the outside of the joint with grease to keep out dust and water.

Apart from lubricating the mechanism pins, the rocking shafts on the brake drums should be kept lubricated through any connections provided, unless self-lubricated bearings are used,

Cam-type Brake Troubles. With the kind of brake-operating mechanism shown in Fig. 194 *shoe faces* upon which the cam acted *become worn* in time, so that the braking effect was reduced. In this case the remedy consisted in screwing hard steel pads on to the worn faces – after truing them – so as to restore the brake to its original efficiency. This method has been used more recently for certain commercial vehicle brakes of the cam-actuated type; it is illustrated in Fig. 195.

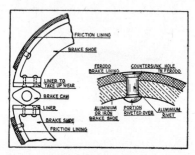

Fig. 195. Showing method of taking up wear in cam-operated brake shoes, and (right) the fitting of new brake lining.

Another trouble experienced was that of *brake shoes sticking on*, after the pressure on the brake pedal had been released. This was usually caused by rusting of the camshaft due to ingress of water over a period of service so that the shaft could not be turned in the brake plate bearing. The remedy was to jack up the wheel of the defective brake and inject some paraffin into the bearing to free it, as the wheel was turned to and fro; afterwards the bearing was lubricated with thick oil.

Relining Brake Shoes. The internal type of brake has two or more malleable iron, pressed steel or aluminium alloy brake shoes, the outer cylindrical portions of which have strips of friction material, such as Ferodo, riveted to them (Fig. 195). The procedure for relining brake shoes is as follows: New brake linings can be obtained either bent to shape for certain standard makes of car or in strip form in various widths and in rolls. In the latter case the length of strip should be about $1\frac{1}{2}$ inches longer than the final length required. Clamp the lining to the shoe with the $1\frac{1}{2}$ inches overhang but with the other end in the same position as that previously obtained with the old lining. Next, drill the holes for the end rivets at the pivot pin side rivets from inside and through the holes in the shoes; the correct size of drill for the rivets should be used. In regard to the rivets these may be of copper or aluminium and of the same diameter as the holes in the shoes. Solid copper rivets bored to about one-half their length are sometimes employed; they are fastened by expanding the hollow part with a special punch. Aluminium rivets are very convenient to use, however, and the solid type is preferable. The rivets should be made equal in length to the combined thickness of brake shoe and lining plus $\frac{1}{8}$ inch. The outer surface of the lining – which comes against the brake-drum – should have its holes countersunk to provide for the sinking of the rivet heads below the surface. This can be done with a twist drill of the same diameter as the rivet head, a suitable depth stop can be provided by means of a piece of thick brass bushing held to the twist drill with a screw. The drill end should project so that the countersunk hole is $\frac{1}{16}$ inch greater in depth than the rivet head.

It should, however, be pointed out that with properly shaped or moulded linings for standard sizes of brake shoes the stretching procedure is unnecessary, the linings being clamped in position, with woodworkers' clamps, and all the holes drilled in succession.

When the old linings have to be removed, prior to fitting new ones, the head of the rivet inside the shoe should be chiselled off and the rivet punched out by means of a flat-ended punch used from the brake shoe side.

Brake Shoes and Bonded Linings. The brake shoes have been made in the form of machined malleable iron castings, but the modern method is to employ steel pressings. The shoes are of tee-section and the flanges are drilled to take the rivets that hold the friction lining to the outer periphery of the shoes.

The disadvantages of riveted linings are: (1) the time taken to rivet them in place, special machines being used in routine brake servicing; (2) the loss of braking efficiency when the lining wears down to the rivet heads.

To overcome these drawbacks, the more recent brake linings are bonded by a special process direct to the outer surface of the shoe, no rivets being employed. The bonding is as effective as the previous riveting and the method has the further advantage of giving a large effective braking area, due to the absence of

Fig. 196. A squeaky brake silenc-
ing device. This is clamped tightly
around the outside cylindrical brake
drum.

rivet-head holes; the life of the lining is also increased thereby. A typical example of a bonded brake shoe is the Girling pressed steel one, to which Ferodo brake lining is bonded.

Squeaky Brakes. With some makes of car application of the brakes results in a somewhat annoying squeaking noise. This noise is usually caused by the vibration of the metal of the brake drum, the metal being insufficiently stiff to prevent this. In such cases, if another strong steel band be clamped tightly around the outside of the brake drum, as shown in Fig. 196, the trouble will be cured. In some cases excessive end-play of the brake shoes causes the latter to bear on the sides of the brake drum when the brakes are applied, thus causing noisy operation. Water or dirt finding its way into the brake drums will also cause squeaking, but this will cease after a few applications of the brake. Badly

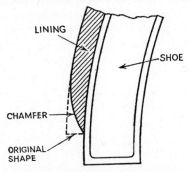

LINING

SHOE

CHAMFER →

ORIGINAL SHAPE

Fig. 197. Chamfering end of brake lining to stop 'squeal'.

worn brake linings, resulting in metallic contact of the rivets or metal of the shoes themselves, are also the cause of squeaking.

In the case of brakes normally quiet in operation, but which squeak after standing for some time out of use, the cause is generally that of *rust formation* within the brake drums. As previously stated, this noise generally stops after a few applications of the brakes. If, however, it still persists, a few drops of graphited oil or some graphite powder should be applied to the inside of the brake drum; most brake materials, such as Ferodo, are little affected by small quantities of lubricant.

Modern car brakes are sometimes *prone to brake squeal* and it cannot be said that this trouble is thoroughly understood or has been fully solved by the designer. Many expedients have been tried and good results obtained in some instances.

One method that has proved effective is to chamfer the ends of the brake lining, as indicated in Fig. 197; this gives a smoother shoe engagement and one less liable to start drum vibration.

Brake squeal in the case of the Austin car which occurred in some instances was cured by drilling a hole of $\frac{3}{16}$ inch diameter in each brake shoe and slotting this hole, as shown in Fig. 198. The web at the leading edge of each shoe was stiffened by welding struts across.

In some cases the use of a bonded brake lining will cure the trouble. In others, the use of a small quantity of graphite, namely, about the size of a pea for each half lining effected a cure. The

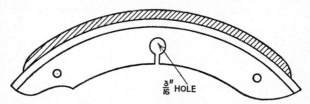

Fig. 198. Another remedy for brake squeal.

nature of the material of the brake-lining has an influence upon brake squeal *A special lining material will often cure 'squeaks'*.

The use of external tension steel bands is, as previously stated, a cure for some brake squeals.

Brake Fade. This term is used to describe the condition which results in a car continuing to move after appreciable application of the brakes has reduced its speed considerably. Brake fade occurs also after a car has descended a long hill with the brakes on, and the brakes are then applied in an emergency.

The chief cause of this trouble is believed to be one of reduced friction effect on account of the heat developed during previous braking affecting the brake linings. Other causes include brake drum wear with embedding of the metal particles in the brake lining; scored brake drums, bad cooling of the drums and distortion, due to light construction of the drums, e.g. bell-mouthed distortion.

The remedy for brake fade is principally that of selecting a braking material which will not lose its frictional properties at high braking temperatures and will not cause drum score, e.g. Raybestos C.P. compressed segments made of asbestos fabric without metal wires.

As is mentioned more fully later, the disc-type of brake has much better anti-fade qualities than most of the drum-type brakes.

Brake Shoe Material Wear. With more recent drum-type brakes it is usually advisable to *take up the wear* of the brakes about once every 5,000 miles or when the brake pedal movement exceeds about 1 inch. There are, however, recent designs of brakes, e.g. the Girling Hydrastatic, which are self-adjusting and therefore do not require this periodic attention.

When the car is new the brake floor pedal usually has a free downward movement of $\frac{1}{4}$ to $\frac{1}{2}$ inch, according to the make of brake, but as the road mileage appreciably increases it will be found that the free travel increases until eventually the brake pedal, in its 'Off' position, tends to approach the floorboard, so that it cannot apply the brakes satisfactorily. Before this is allowed to occur, i.e. when after full application of the brakes the pedal is only just clear of the foot-board, the brake shoes will need relining.

Depending upon how the car is used by its driver the actual period, with drum-type brakes, at which the brake shoes should be relined varies from about 25,000 to 40,000 miles, according to the size of car and the performance factor of larger ones. In some instances, as the results of the Consumers' Association road tests have shown, the life of brake shoe materials can be as high as 90,000 miles for the rear brakes and 80,000 miles at the front for small cars, of the *rear drive kind*. With *front wheel drive* cars the braking is more severe on the front wheels, the usual brake-lining life being about 24,000 to 30,000 miles. With high performance cars the brake material wear is much greater than for normal touring cars.

For *disc-type front brakes* the life of the brake-pads is relatively short, namely, from about 12,000 to 25,000 miles. In some exceptional cases lives up to about 50,000 miles have been obtained.

Brake 'Judder' or Chatter. This pronounced chattering effect, the braking counterpart of clutch 'judder' is generally traceable to the front steering and springing system, for the severe braking forces cause heavy loads on the steering members and spring ends. Should any slackness exist in the bearings of these systems, brake 'judder' may occur during strong braking application.

To some lesser extent, the brake lining, if badly fitted will contribute to this trouble. Typical minor causes include protruding rivet heads, lining not properly riveted to shoe, square ends to the linings (*vide* Fig. 198 for cure) and linings too long on their shoes.

Oil on Brakes. If, when the brakes are properly adjusted and there is plenty of operating movement on the brake pedal (or lever), the brakes do not act satisfactorily, the cause of this trouble may be oil or grease on the friction material; the lubricant in this case may have leaked past the axle oil seals, or have been unintentionally injected through excessive lubrication of the brake parts. Water leaking into the brake drums causes a similar effect to oil, but this effect works off in time.

In such cases the friction material should be washed with petrol and its surface rubbed with a wire brush; the other parts should also be cleaned and the cause of the presence of the oil or grease in the brakes ascertained.

Hand Brake Adjustment. In all modern cars an adjustment is provided – usually on or close to the hand brake lever – for taking up the effect of wear in the actuating mechanism. The car manufacturer's instruction book should be consulted beforehand, to ensure that the method of adjustment is understood.

A typical arrangement is shown in Fig. 199 for making the adjustment in question. In the footboard of the driver's compartment will be found a hole, through which access is obtainable to a wing-nut or hexagon-headed bolt. It is necessary to jack up the rear wheels and adjust the wing nut or bolt until the wheels, when spun, just begin to bind on their brake shoes. The adjuster should then be released sufficiently to enable the wheels to just run quite freely.

The hand brake system shown adjusts both sets of rear brake shoes in unison, but equalizers (see Fig. 199) are provided to ensure that both sets of shoes are applied equally; the equalizing adjusting nuts seldom require attention after once having been set. It is advisable before adjusting the hand brake to *lubricate the brake mechanism*, e.g. any pins, such as those on the rear axle casing for equalizing the brake pulls.

Hand Brake Failure to Hold. In cars which have seen a good deal of service, the hand brake lever may fail to engage, or

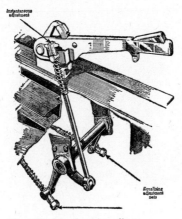

Fig. 199. Hand brake adjustment (Morris).

remain in the 'on' position although the brake shoes or band may operate satisfactorily. The cause of this trouble is to be found in the teeth of the brake-ratchet sector being worn, or the ratchet pawl itself being worn blunt. In the former case before removing the sector, measure the radius R (Fig. 200). The teeth can then be filed to the shape shown (or to that of the unworn teeth); if the sector is case-hardened, the file will not touch it, so that it must be softened first, by heating to cherry redness and allowing to cool slowly in ashes or sand. If the ratchet pawl is worn, it should be softened as described, and filed to the shape of the sector teeth. It can be hardened again by heating to a cherry red colour and plunging in water; after cooling, polish one part and lay the pawl on a piece of heated metal until the polished surface changes its colour to a straw tint; then plunge into water, and the proper degree of hardness will have been obtained.

Rattling Brake Mechanism. An annoying rattling noise sometimes develops in older cars which have been much used and can often be traced to the brake rods leading from the rocking shaft (near the gearbox) to the back axle. The cause of the noise is usually found to be wear in the pins and holes in the fork ends.

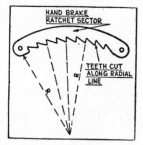

Fig. 200. Showing how to mark out and file the teeth of hand brake sector.

As a temporary cure, a light tension spring can be tied at one end to the brake rod and at the other to some convenient point on the chassis, so as always to take up the backlash; if such a resistance is introduced, the brake rods are no longer free to rattle. The best thing, however, is to reamer the oval holes in the forks and fit over-size pins; any side slackness can be taken up with thin washers. The parts should be well greased before re-assembly.

Brake Drums. Some types of brake drum are more liable to wear than others, whilst light section soft pressed steel drums may distort or become scored in service.

The hard cast iron and lined steel drums of rigid construction, providing smooth wearing surfaces appear to give the best service.

Certain grades of asbestos brake linings when used with pressed steel brake drums which become heated to an appreciable extent in service, tend to cause brake drum scoring.

Distortion and (or) wear may produce the following defects in brake drums, namely, (1) Tapered or bell-mouth effects, (2)

Barrel shape and (3) Scored braking surfaces. Each of these effects results in loss of braking efficiency and, in the case of (3) of increased wear in the brake linings.

Another defect of light section drums is that of vibrations, when the shoes are applied, causing the 'brake squeal' effect previously mentioned.

Worn brake drums should be trued on a centre lathe, or on one of the garage 'brake lathes', either by turning with a tungsten carbide-tipped steel tool or by grinding so as to leave a smooth truly cylindrical surface. Only a minimum of metal sufficient to just 'true' the surface should be removed.

Before turning or grinding the drum a steel band should be clamped to the outside of the drum, to prevent tool or grinding wheel vibration marks.

Before replacing a worn or trued up brake drum it should be tested on its wheel, for concentricity; if any out-of-centre effect is present, wheel 'tramp' or vibration will occur.

Brake Adjustments. There are so many different systems of four-wheel brakes – mechanical, hydraulic and vacuum – that it is not possible, to give here, explicit directions for adjustment applicable to all types. The manufacturers' special instructions should always be consulted. A full account of the various types of four-wheel brakes in common use is given in *The Mechanism of the Car* (Motor Manuals, Volume 3).

The usual symptom of incorrectly adjusted four-wheel brakes is the tendency, when the brakes are applied, of the car to draw to one side of the road. It will be found that *the car is always drawn towards the side on which the brake is operating in advance* of the others, i.e. of the brake which comes on first.

In the case of mechanically-operated four-wheel brakes, all four wheels must be jacked up at the same time, each wheel being raised by the jack and lowered on to a substantial block of wood, so that the wheels are clear from the ground. Next, lubricate all working parts, and work the foot brake pedal several times to assist the oil in finding its way to the bearings. Get someone to operate the foot brake pedal whilst you examine the rocking shafts and other working parts to see that these work freely.

Note the amount of movement of the foot pedal before the

brakes come on. If appreciable, adjust the brakes by the method provided in each case.

To equalize the braking, the brake shoes must be adjusted individually at their hubs, afterwards locking the adjusting screws securely, unless self-locking screws are used.

Some General Hints on Brake Adjustments. Before attempting to adjust brakes the following checks should be made:

(1) Check the front wheel bearings for wear and if found, take them up.

(2) Examine the steering joints for any signs of 'play' and if found, rectify.

(3) Make a road test of the braking system, noting the foot pressure effort and the braking distance to stop from, say, 30 and 40 m.p.h. Compare with the table on page 307. The tyres should be inflated to their correct pressures for these tests and the ground dry.

(4) After adjusting the brakes make a final road braking test from different speeds to ensure that everything is satisfactory.

(5) After these tests check whether the brake drums are cool, as they should be; if heated, the shoes are too closely adjusted to their drums.

Poor Braking due to Water Ingress. In one or two cases of cars built some years ago, it has been found that whereas the braking systems were quite satisfactory on dry roads, yet when the car had been driven for an hour or two in heavy rain conditions the brakes were not only less efficient but one brake tended to come on before the others, causing the car to swerve across the road.

The cause was traced to water getting into the brake drums but to a greater extent to one particular (front) drum.

Cable-Operated Brakes. Certain earlier mechanical braking systems employ strong steel cables in place of tie rods to actuate the brakes. In such cases the movements of the arms fixed to the brake rocking shaft are transferred to the brake-operating lever or mechanism inside the brake drums by means of a cable inside an outer casing, one end of the latter being fixed to the chassis frame and the other to the drum (Fig. 201). The cable lengths are not adjustable, the necessary adjustment being provided at

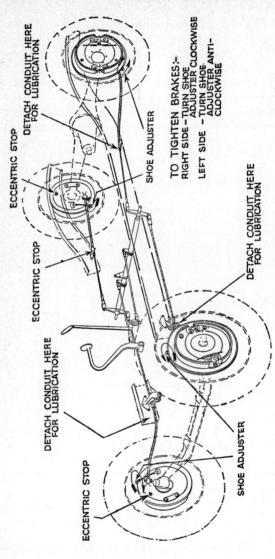

ECCENTRIC STOP

DETACH CONDUIT HERE FOR LUBRICATION

SHOE ADJUSTER

ECCENTRIC STOP

ECCENTRIC STOP

DETACH CONDUIT HERE FOR LUBRICATION

DETACH CONDUIT HERE FOR LUBRICATION

ECCENTRIC STOP

SHOE ADJUSTER

TO TIGHTEN BRAKES:—
RIGHT SIDE – TURN SHOE ADJUSTER CLOCKWISE
LEFT SIDE – TURN SHOE ADJUSTER ANTI-CLOCKWISE

Fig. 201. The Bendix single anchor cable-operated braking system. In a later type a single lubrication nipple is used for the cables.

the rocking lever arm ends. In the case of cable-operated brakes becoming stiff in action the cables and their casings should be examined and the brakes worked, noting whether the cables are quite free – as they should be – in their casings. If otherwise, the cables should be cleaned with paraffin and then greased at the places where they enter their casings.

After long periods of service it may be found that the cables have stretched appreciably and most of the adjustments provided on the rocking shaft levers have been taken up. It is then necessary to fit new cables, complete with casings and end fittings; these are usually standard for each make of car. In other cases new cables only can be fitted. These should be of identical lengths

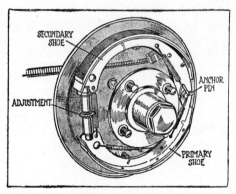

Fig. 202. The duo-servo brake mechanism.

for the front and back pairs of brakes. If the cables are pre-stretched before insertion they will not stretch any farther during the life of the car. The method of giving cables an initial stretch is by means of a special lever-tool, with which a pull of the order 250 to 310 lb. can be applied.

An example of a cable-operated brake is shown in Fig. 202, in which the outer casing is depicted on the left between the titles 'secondary shoe' and 'adjustment'; the cable itself is shown under the upper brake shoe. In cases of appreciable cable stretch the slack can be taken up with the aid of the special cable adjuster.

Adjusting Duo-Servo Brakes. As a large number of cars were fitted with the Bendix due-servo type of brake, an account of the adjustment of these brakes will be given.

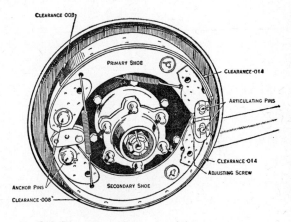

Fig. 203. Illustrating adjustment of duo-servo brakes
(the shoe clearances are also indicated).

To those who are not quite familiar with these brakes it may be stated that there are two brake shoes connected together by a floating type of hinge pin and operated at their other ends by means of the brake cam. When the latter is moved, the appropriate brake shoe is applied and the friction force of this reacts through the moving hinge pin on to the other shoe, thus giving an increased braking action. In effect, as there is a definite limited movement of the shoes in the direction of the brake drum's rotation, some of the energy of the car is used to apply the brakes, thus giving a servo action. This type of brake requires a smaller pedal pressure than the normal fixed hinged shoe type and it operates equally well in either direction of motion, giving a powerful braking action.

The adjustment of this type of brake can best be illustrated by taking an actual example (Fig. 203).

The procedure is as follows:

(1) Jack up all four wheels. Check to ensure that the brake pedal,

cross-shafts and all other parts of the brake operating gear return freely to, and are tight against, their stops when in the 'off' position.

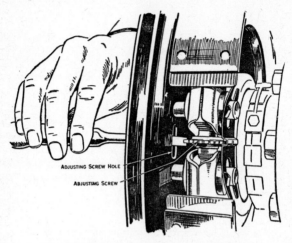

Fig. 204. Method of adjusting serrated wheel for taking up the wear of the shoes.

(2) Remove the adjusting screw-hole cover from the backing plate on the fixed brake disc wheel member. This discloses the serrated adjusting wheel.

(3) With a screwdriver inserted through the adjusting screw-hole (Fig. 204), turn the notched wheel of the adjusting screw so that the movement of the notches is away from the centre of the brake drum until the brake just drags, i.e. the hand must always be moved towards the centre of the axle to tighten the brake.

(4) Equalize as follows: Pull the hand brake lever on by two notches until the tightest wheel can be turned by hand. Tighten the other wheels gradually until all four wheels are the same.

(5) Eccentric stop for secondary shoe. This is located on the rear wheel at the bottom of the backing plate and on the front wheel at the top of the backing plate. It is usual to adjust

this eccentric stop after about 15,000 miles of running. For this the adjusting screw should be slackened off so as to free the brake entirely. Then slacken off slightly the lock-nut of the eccentric stop and turn the eccentric in the direction of rotation of the wheel (when the car is travelling forward) until the brake drags. Then slack off slightly until the brake is just free and tighten up the lock-nut. Afterwards, proceed as described in (3).

Brake Shoe Clearances. In regard to the shoe clearances, for re-lined shoes or re-adjusted ones, these should be checked with a feeler gauge. With correct anchor pin and other adjustments properly done there should be about twice as much clearance between the drum and the brake lining at the adjusting screw end of the shoes as at the anchor pin end. When checked there should be 0·008 inch clearance at the anchor end and about 0·014 inch at the adjusting screw end (Fig. 203).

The Floating Wedge-Type Brake. In this type, instead of moving the brake shoes outwards against the brake drum with a cam or lever device, they are actuated by means of a wedge and inclined plane unit. A typical example is that of the Bendix Cowdrey brake, the operating device of which is shown in Fig. 205. The central unit consists of a pair of floating rollers in a

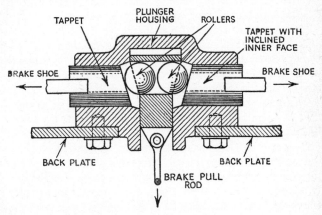

Fig. 205. Principle of the wedge-type brake.

housing terminating below in an eye member to which the actuating brake rod pull is attached.

Sliding in the metal housing shown is a pair of cylindrical plungers, or tappets having inclined faces held in contact with the rollers by the brake shoe springs (not shown). The outer ends of the tappets are slotted to engage the ends of the brake shoes.

It will be seen that when the brake rod is pulled downwards the housing carrying the rollers moves downwards and thus causes the rollers to force the two tappets apart, thus applying the shoes to the brake drum. The advantages of this type of brake are that (1) the actuating mechanism from the brake pedal is much simpler than for the cam-type and (2) a reduced brake pedal effort is needed.

Typical Braking System. Fig. 206 shows a typical braking system using the Bendix Cowdrey method of brake shoe operation. It will be observed that the brake pull rods act in the directions of the wheel axes and that single tie rods are used to connect the two front brakes and the two rear brakes to the foot pedal.

Adjustment of Braking System. In regard to the *front compensator,* the rod end of the lever A (Fig. 206) should be set forward about $\frac{13}{16}$ in. by adjusting the lengths of the two front cables.

Similarly, the *rear compensator lever A* should be set back about 1 in. by adjusting the rear brake-operating rods.

Having set the front and rear compensators, see that the hand brake is in the 'full off' position and adjust the length of the hand-brake cable C so that the lever D is about 29° to the vertical. Re-couple the rear cable at B or B^1, adjusting the length to just take out all play without altering the lever D.

The hand brake should be applied several times to ensure that the rear operating cable is properly bedded down to the abutment bracket.

In regard to the *central compensator*, the length of the push rod E should then be adjusted by loosening the lock-nut F so that the clearance between the stop G and swing link H is about $\frac{1}{16}$ in. at the front brake-rod side. Then, re-couple the front brake rod, adjusting the length to take out play from the front compensator and without disturbing the centre compensator.

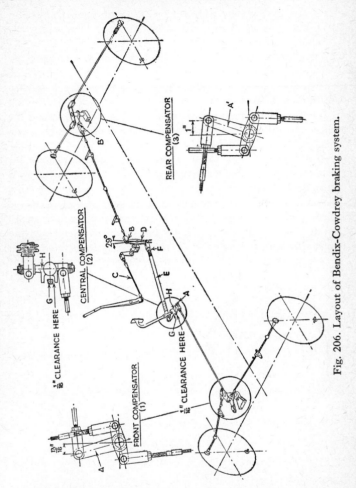

Fig. 206. Layout of Bendix-Cowdrey braking system.

The hook-up is now correctly set and the brakes should be released until the wheels are just free, which should be at approximately 6 notches or 'clicks'.

Taking up Shoe Wear. The only normal maintenance adjustment necessary to take up brake shoe wear is as follows:

(1) Screw up the shoe adjusters on the drum plates until tight, by rotating these in a clockwise direction. This applies the shoes hard on to the drums.

(2) Slack back each adjuster by three-quarters of a turn, i.e. by six notches, or 'clicks'.

It will be noticed that it *is unnecessary to jack up the wheels* when adjusting these brakes.

If, after a short road test the drums are found to be warm the adjusters on these drums should be slackened back by one or two notches.

After the first 25,000 miles the brakes should be dismantled for inspection and overhaul; the linings will probably be found worn down to the rivets, greasy, or glazed, and new replacement shoes should then be fitted. After overhaul, the working surfaces of the brake parts should be cleaned and greased with graphite grease during re-assembly. It is important when re-assembling the brake shoe springs to see that *the red painted spring* is fitted to the secondary brake shoe. It is easy to remember the correct side if

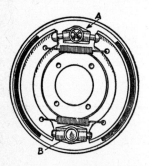

Fig. 207. Components of the
Girling brake.
(Left) brake shoe assembly.
(Left Bottom) the expander unit.
(Right Bottom) the adjuster unit.

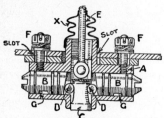
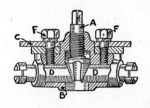

it is noted that it is on the tail side of the arrow that shows the direction of rotation of the wheel, as viewed on the top side. After assembling all the parts the shoe adjusting screw should be tightened right up by rotating in a clockwise direction. The centralizer bolt, with its nut slackened must then be tapped to centralize the shoes and locked with its nut.

The shoe adjusters should finally be slackened off a few clicks until the wheels are just free to rotate.

Adjusting the Girling Brake. This previously much-used mechanical brake belongs to the same class as the Bendix Cowdrey in having a cone and roller lateral-action expander to operate the brake shoes. Referring to Fig. 207 (upper illustration), the brake shoes have a fulcrum at A and are expanded by the wedge device at B. The latter unit which is shown in detail in the lower left illustration consists of a cone C pulled by the brake operating rod E having a water seal cover K. When E is pulled the cone C forces the rollers D outwards. These rollers engage the inclined faces of the plungers B, the other ends of which are slotted to engage the ends of the brake shoes, so that the latter are forced outwards against the drums.

The housing A is held lightly on the back plate by nuts and spring washers F so that it floats between the brake shoes, which are thus self-centring. When the shoes are removed the pins G hold the plungers in their housings.

The adjuster unit which is fixed to the back plate C by its housing B has two plungers D, with slotted outer ends and inclined faces on their inner ones. They are held apart by the adjuster A. The housing B is mounted on the back plate by means of the bolts F; these must not be disturbed when adjusting the brake.

The adjusting member A has a conical end with four flat faces. It is screwed in or out of the housing by means of the screw adjustment shown, a squared end – accessible from outside the brake back plate – being provided for actuating this screw.

To adjust the brake it is unnecessary to jack up the wheel for the adjuster A is merely screwed in a clockwise direction as far as it will go when the brake will be hard on. The adjuster is then unscrewed back by one full notch when the proper shoe

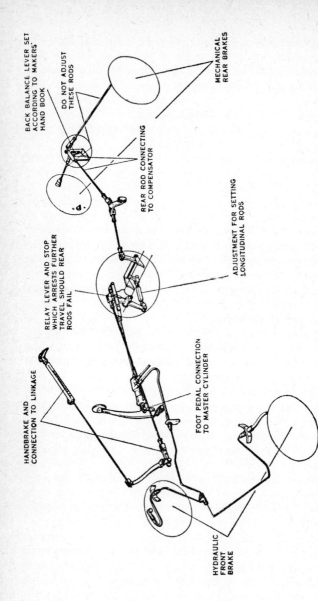

BACK BALANCE LEVER SET ACCORDING TO MAKERS' HAND BOOK

DO NOT ADJUST THESE RODS

MECHANICAL REAR BRAKES

REAR ROD CONNECTING TO COMPENSATOR

RELAY LEVER AND STOP WHICH ARRESTS FURTHER TRAVEL SHOULD REAR RODS FAIL

ADJUSTMENT FOR SETTING LONGITUDINAL RODS

HANDBRAKE AND CONNECTION TO LINKAGE

FOOT PEDAL CONNECTION TO MASTER CYLINDER

HYDRAULIC FRONT BRAKE

Fig. 208. Hydraulic front and mechanical rear brake, as used on some independent front wheel suspension cars.

clearance is given. After adjustment in this way depress the brake pedal down hard once or twice in order to centralize the shoes in the drums. The brake operating mechanism pin bearings should be lubricated at the time the brakes are adjusted.

Hydraulic Braking Systems. The mechanically-operated types of brake in previous cars have been largely replaced by the hydraulically-actuated ones in modern cars. In some cases, however, after independently sprung front wheels were adopted, it was found that there were difficulties in arranging for mechanical front brakes, so that it became the rule to fit *hydraulic front* and *mechanical rear brakes*; a typical example of such an arrangement is given in Fig. 208 which shows, also, the various connections, adjustments, etc.

Two principal makes of hydraulic brakes are used in British cars: the Lockheed and the Girling. Both types operate upon the same principle, namely the production of considerable hydraulic pressure, by foot pedal movement, which is transmitted by piping to brake cylinder and piston units on each road wheel; the movements of the pistons apply the actuating pressure to the brake shoes. The advantages of this system are: (1) equal braking pressures are applied to each wheel brake, (2) increased braking effort is produced, and (3) absence of the usual brake mechanism, e.g. rods, joints, rocking shafts. However, the hand brake must be operated mechanically, as far as the rear brake cylinders are concerned.

There are two methods of brake shoe operation, namely, the *two-cylinder* and *single-cylinder*. In the former type each brake shoe has its own actuating brake cylinder, thus providing two *leading shoes*. In the latter type, which is used on the rear wheels, a single hydraulic cylinder is employed, with provision for a mechanical device to operate the same brake shoes. The two-cylinder type is used on the front wheels only.

The Lockheed hydraulic braking system includes a *single master cylinder unit* having a piston operated from the brake pedal. Oil under pressure from this master cylinder is arranged, by means of special pipe lines, to operate pistons in cylinders on each of the brake drum units. The movements of these pistons give the necessary brake shoe operation.

Referring to Fig. 209, showing the principle of the wheel brake units, there is an oil-filled cylinder A having two pistons B which are forced apart by oil pressure and operate directly the brake shoes E.

Independent hand braking is provided for in some designs by means of a cam F operated mechanically.

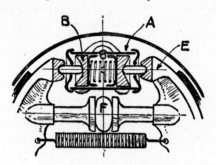

Fig. 209. Principle of Lockheed hydraulic brake.

The principle of the master cylinder is illustrated in Fig. 210. Here the brake-pedal operated lever G causes the piston H to move from left to right. This causes a pressure in the cylinder J, which is transmitted, through a spring loaded valve K, to the pipe lines leading to the brake drum cylinders. It is usual to maintain an oil pressure of about 8 lb. per square inch in the system, through the agency of the valve K.

An important feature of the system is the compensation for leakage or temperature expansion or contraction effects. A small hole L is arranged in the wall of the cylinder so that, when the brake pedal is in the 'off' position, there is a free communication between the oil in the cylinder J and that in the outer reservoir.

A Typical Braking System. The arrangement of the master cylinder, oil piping and brake units of the Morris Minor car is shown in Fig. 211.

In these cars which have independent front wheel springing each brake shoe on the *front wheels* has *a separate wheel cylinder*, thus providing two leading brake shoes with automatic compensation. On the rear wheels a single wheel cylinder, which is operated hydraulically by the foot brake and mechanically by the hand brake floats on the brake plate and actuates two shoes, viz., a leading and a trailing shoe in both forward and reverse directions.

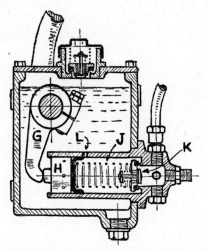

Fig. 210. Principle of the master cylinder.

A Girling Master Cylinder. A good example of a modern unit is that of the Girling Type CV which is fitted to many B.M.C. systems and also to other makes of car. Fig. 211 shows the unit in sectional view with the important components indicated and described below. This unit operates on the same principle as that shown in Fig. 210.

The reservoir (A) is filled to a certain marked level with special oil, known as Girling Crimson Brake Fluid. In an emergency oil to Specification SAE.70.R3 can be used.

For the Lockheed hydraulic brakes the correct oil is Lockheed Genuine Brake Fluid. These oils are unaffected by extremes of climatic temperatures.

In most cars of today the clutches are operated hydraulically,

the same oil being used for both braking and clutch systems.
The two reservoirs are then located together under the engine
bonnet (Fig. 212).

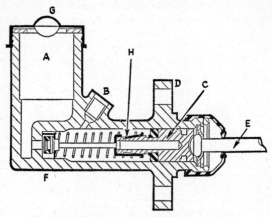

Fig. 211. The Girling type CV master cylinder.
A reservoir. *B* outlet pipe to brake lines. *C* plunger. *D* fixing flange.
E brake pedal pull rod. *F* pressure valve. *G* air vent. *H* spring thimble
holder for plunger parts.

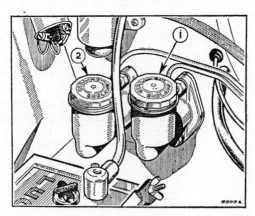

Fig. 212. Fluid reservoirs for hydraulically-actuated clutch and
hydraulic brakes.

Brake Pedal Free Play. The brake pedal should have the correct amount of free movement. In this example there *must be ½ inch of free movement* at the brake pedal pad before any resistance is felt. When, however, this free movement becomes excessive and the pedal can be depressed so that it is close to the floorboard, this is a certain indication that adjustment is necessary.

Brake Shoe Adjustments. In the case of the earlier type hydraulic brakes as fitted to Morris and Austin cars (and certain other makes) the front brakes had a separate adjustment for each brake shoe, but only a single adjustment for the rear brake; this is still the practice for full hydraulic braking systems, using shoe-and-drum type brakes.

With these earlier brakes it was necessary to jack up the wheel of the brake to be dealt with, using chocks under two of the other wheels, and then to remove the hub cap. This exposed two holes in the brake drum, through which screws could be seen (Fig. 213).

Fig. 213. Adjusting earlier type Austin and Morris front brakes.

To take up brake lining wear a screwdriver was inserted and the screw, in each case, was turned in a clockwise direction until the shoe locked solid. Then the screw was rotated anti-clockwise

K

until the brake drum was just free – usually this was one notch back.

In the case of the rear brakes a similar adjustment was made to each single adjusting screw.

With later hydraulic braking systems it is also necessary to jack up the wheels, but not to remove the hub caps, since the adjusting square or hexagon-headed bolts are on the back plate. To adjust each shoe, turn the bolt head in a clockwise direction until the shoe begins to bind on the brake drum; then slacken it back until no resistance is felt. Fig. 214 shows the two square-headed adjusting shoes in the case of the Girling brakes fitted to B.M.C. cars, for front brake adjustments.

Fig. 214. Adjusting B.M.C. front brake, the arrows show the two square-headed adjusters.

As previously mentioned, there is only one adjuster for the rear brake, this being a similar square-headed bolt on the back plate; it adjusts both brake shoes at the same time.

Earlier Lockheed car hydraulic *brakes* were adjusted, as follows: Jack up the wheel in question and spin to see that it is quite free. On the back plate there are two hexagonal adjusting bolts (Fig. 215). These, when turned with a spanner, actuate snail cams inside the brake drums, such that, when the bolt heads are turned in the directions shown in Fig. 215, they move the brake shoes towards the brake drums until they lock in the drum, after which they are slackened back until no drag is felt when the wheel is rotated.

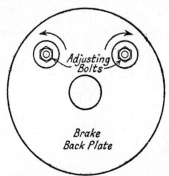

Fig. 215. Adjustment of Lockheed
hydraulic front brakes.

Later Lockheed brakes employ the same arrangement as for the Girling, namely, at the front two leading shoes with two fixed hydraulic cylinders while at each of the rear wheels there is a leading-trailing brake shoe combination actuated by a single floating brake cylinder unit.

Adjustment of the front brakes is made, after raising the front wheel of each in turn by means of a square-head screw adjuster which when turned anti-clockwise on the right-hand brake, as seen from inside facing the brake plate, until the shoe is hard on its drum. Then gradually release the screw until there is no rub when the wheel is turned. For the left-hand brake turn the screw clockwise to take up the wear. The rear brakes are adjusted, similarly, by a single square-headed screw, turned clockwise to take up any wear.

After long periods of service, when a major overhaul is due, it is advisable to dismantle the master cylinder and to renew all the rubber parts, e.g., the piston master and secondary cups, washers and rubber dust seal boot. Similarly, the wheel cylinders should be removed and dismantled, cleaned thoroughly and new rubber caps fitted. When reassembling the cylinder parts they should be perfectly cleaned and then dipped in brake fluid and assembled 'wet'.

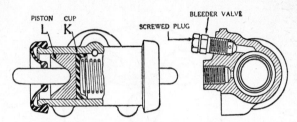

Fig. 216. Typical wheel brake cylinder *K* and piston *L*. The right-hand view shows the bleeder-valve on wheel brake cylinder.

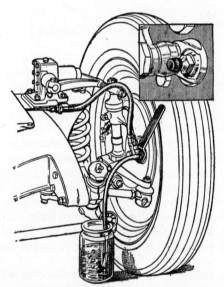

Fig. 217. Eliminating air from hydraulic braking system by the bleeding process.

Bleeding the Hydraulic System. It is very important to get rid of all air in the oil system; otherwise the brakes will not operate satisfactorily – provision is made to expel any air in the system by means of small screw taper-end valves on the brake cylinders. An example of an air-bleed valve is shown at (1) in Fig. 218 (Lockheed).

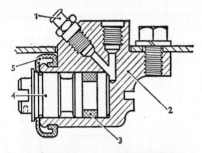

Fig. 218. Front hydraulic brake cylinder.
1 bleeder screw. 2 cylinder. 3 taper seal. 4 piston. 5 rubber boot.

In motor garages bleeding of the system is carried out with a pressure bleeding unit which has the advantage of keeping the master cylinder full of fluid while the bleeding operations are carried out; the bleeding pressures must not exceed 20 lb per sq in. or damage will be done to the master cylinder reservoir.

For the owner-driver the operation can readily be carried out with a length of rubber tubing and a glass jar, as shown in Fig. 217.

To bleed the system, unscrew each bleeder screw in turn and attach the rubber tubing – first making sure it is clean – and then using the brake pedal as a pump, give it a sharp push down and allow it to return upwards, slowly. Get someone else to watch the tube outlet fluid for air bubbles. Repeat the pedal strokes until all air has been expelled, and then screw down the air-bleed valve. Repeat the operation for all the brake cylinders.

Afterwards test the system by firmly depressing the brake pedal, when, if all air has been expelled, a strong resistance will be maintained. *Do not use* the *expelled oil* again since it contains air bubbles.

Note. A special key is supplied for unscrewing the valves. These should only be given two or three turns to open.

Hydraulic Brake Shoe Wear. Brake shoe linings should be examined when the car is completely overhauled after long service. If oil-coated or glazed, they should be cleaned with petrol and roughened with a file. If the linings are found to have worn thin, new ones should be fitted.

Girling Hydraulic Brakes. These operate upon the same principle as the Lockheed ones, and employ a master cylinder and separate wheel cylinders and shoe-operating pistons. The same general maintenance and air-bleed instructions apply to these brakes.

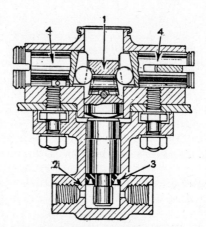

Fig. 219. Girling hydraulic wedge-
action brake.

Apart from this type there is also the Girling hydraulically-operated floating wedge expander brake, which is identical to that illustrated in Fig. 207 (lower L.H. diagram), but the braking pull on the wedge unit is supplied by oil pressure on a piston in a cylinder unit which replaces the brake pull rod (Fig. 207). In this model an extension of the plunger (1) runs into the cylinder (2) and is fitted with a rubber piston cup (3). The flexible hose connection and bleed screw are carried into the cylinder cover and the inclination of the tappet faces is such that a *push action* is given to the plunger. This causes the brake shoe actuating sliders (4) to move outwards.

In addition, for rear brakes only, there is a combination hydraulic and mechanical operation brake unit. The hydraulic part acts in a similar manner to that just described but through the central orifice of the piston assembly there passes a rod which is attached to the wedge unit at one end and to the hand brake operating mechanism at the other or outer end. Thus, the wedge unit for applying the brake shoe expansion movement can be actuated, independently, by the foot pedal hydraulic or hand brake mechanical effort.

Dismantling the Brake Drum Unit. The dismantling of the Girling brake drum unit for fitting new brake shoes, or general examination, is accomplished by, first, jacking up the car and removing the road wheels.

Next the brake drums are removed, by unscrewing the countersunk screws. To dismantle the brake all that is required is a large screwdriver, to prise one shoe out of the groove in the wheel cylinder piston. Both shoes and pull-off springs can now be removed, leaving the wheel cylinders and pivot pins in position on the back-plate. Do not detach these units from the back-plate. Do not overstretch shoe pull-off springs when removing shoes. To prevent loss of brake fluid, slip an elastic band over the wheel cylinder pistons to hold these in place. The back-plate should then be cleaned and the wheel cylinders checked for leaks and freedom of motion. The adjuster should also be checked for easy working.

To fit replacement shoes, first attach shoe springs to shoes. Be sure that the springs are between the shoe webs and back-plate, otherwise the shoes will not be flat on back-plate. Keep all grease off linings and do not handle linings any more than necessary. Place the shoes with springs attached against back-plate. Shoes have half-round slots at one end. Fit these slots to the *pivot pin*, then insert the other end of *one shoe* in the *wheel cylinder piston*. Place the screwdriver under the web of the remaining shoe and against the back-plate. Ease the shoes into the grooves on the pistons.

When fitting replacement shoes a new set of springs should also be used. To ensure correct clearance between shoes and drums, where adjusters are fitted, bring the shoes tight to the drum, and then slack off until the wheel just spins freely.

In connection with the *rubber seals*, these are of natural rubber and are affected, detrimentally, by mineral oils, so that when handling these seals it is important to protect them from mineral oils or grease.

The hydraulic system uses special Wakefield–Girling brake fluid (crimson).

Hydrastatic, Self-Adjusting Brakes. In this type the brake shoes are self-adjusting and require no attention until the linings are worn down. They differ from ordinary brakes in that the brakes shoes are in constant light contact with the drums; there are no pull-off springs and no clearance. The very slight drag is scarcely detectable.

The brake employs two shoes hinged on a fulcrum pin at the bottom. At the top is a simple wheel cylinder very carefully roll-burnished in its bore, and containing a pair of opposed short pistons. The outer end of each piston has a slotted projection which engages the tip of the adjacent brake shoe. At the back of each piston is a special form of cup washer, and the pistons are separated by a light spring. At the bottom of the shoes, close to the fulcrum point, is a light tension spring. This is called the 'Bias' reducing spring, and its purpose is mainly to hold the shoes together sufficiently to prevent any tendency of the tip of the leading shoe to grab, and to balance the outward pressure of the wheel cylinder spring. No adjustment for lining wear is necessary or provided for, as this is done automatically with this type of brake. All that is required is for replacement shoes to be fitted when the old linings are worn out.

Hydraulic Brake Troubles and Their Causes. The following is a summary of the various possible troubles liable to occur after much service or neglect, in the case of the Lockheed hydraulic brakes of the general type fitted to modern cars, e.g. the B.M.C's and other makes, together with their contributory causes:

(A) *Brake Pedal Travel Excessive (Requires Pumping).*

(*a*) Brake shoes require adjusting.
(*b*) Leak at one or more joints.

(*c*) Master-cylinder cup worn.

(B) *Brake Pedal Feels Springy.*

(*a*) System requires bleeding.
(*b*) Linings not 'bedded in'.

(*c*) Master cylinder fixing loose.
(*d*) Master cylinder cup worn.

(C) *Brakes Inefficient.*

(*a*) Shoes not correctly adjusted.
(*b*) Linings not 'bedded in'.
(*c*) Linings greasy.
(*d*) Linings of wrong quality.

(*e*) Drums badly scored.
(*f*) Linings badly worn.
(*g*) Wrongly fitted cup fillers.

(D) *Brakes Drag.*

(*a*) Shoes incorrectly adjusted.
(*b*) Shoe springs weak or broken.
(*c*) Pedal spring weak or broken.
(*d*) Hand brake mechanism seized.

(*e*) Wheel cylinder piston seized.
(*f*) Locked pipe line.
(*g*) Filler cap vent hole choked.

(E) *Brakes Remain On, when Pedal Pressure Removed.*

(*a*) Shoes over-adjusted.
(*b*) Hand brake over-adjusted.
(*c*) No free movement on pedal.

(*d*) Compensator port in master cylinder covered by swollen rubber cup, or incorrect adjustment of push-rod.
(*e*) Swollen wheel cylinder cups.
(*f*) Choked flexible hose.

(F) *Car Pulls to One Side, when Brakes Applied.*

(*a*) Greasy linings or water in drums.
(*b*) Distorted drums.
(*c*) Tyres unevenly inflated.
(*d*) Brake plate loose on the axle.

(*e*) Worn steering connections.
(*f*) Worn suspension linkage.
(*g*) Different grades of lining fitted to individual wheels.

(G) *Brakes Grab, when Applied.*

(*a*) Shoes require adjusting.
(*b*) Drums distorted.
(*c*) Greasy linings.

(*d*) Broken or loose road spring.
(*e*) Scored drums.
(*f*) Worn suspension linkage.

Hydro-Mechanical Brakes. In modern cars with independent front wheel suspension, as mentioned earlier in this chapter, the mechanically-operated brake is unsuitable on account of the rise and fall of the wheels and it is necessary for the simplest connections to be used for the operating mechanism. It had therefore become the practice to use hydraulic brakes for the front wheels and mechanically-operated ones for the rear ones. An account of the system is given in Volume 3 of this Series, so that the maintenance and adjustment of these brakes need only be considered here.

The hydraulic system is maintained in the manner previously described, the principal items being: (1) Periodical replenishment of brake fluid in the master cylinder, and (2) Adjustment at the brake drums to take up lining wear effects. The foot and hand (piston-grip) brakes both operate mechanical brakes in the

Fig. 220. The Girling hydro-mechanical brake adjustments
1 front brake shoe adjuster cams.
2 brake bleed nipple.
3 brake shoe adjuster.
4 brake shoe cylinder anchor bolt.
5 cylinder connecting pipe.

rear wheel drums. In the Girling system these are of the floating wedge-roller pattern, described previously.

It is important that the brakes are only adjusted at the brake drums for wear and that the brake linkages are not disturbed, except for replacement or for major overhaul purposes, when the maker's detailed instructions should be followed. The front brakes (Fig. 220) are adjusted by first jacking up the front wheels clear of the ground. The hexagon-head adjuster bolts on the brake back plates should then be fully released. Next, one of these bolts should be turned in a clockwise direction until its brake shoe just touches the brake drum. It must then be carefully adjusted until just free of the drum. This operation is then repeated for the brake shoe of the other adjuster bolt. The wheels should then be spun by hand to check that the shoes are clear of their drums.

It may be mentioned that the adjusters actuate snail cams which bear on the shoes, the cams being moved towards the shoes by clockwise rotation of the adjusters.

The rear brakes are adjusted by turning the square-head adjuster on each rear brake back plate in a clockwise direction, to take up lining wear effect, until a resistance is felt. The adjuster is then turned back by two 'clicks'. After adjustment, the brake pedal should be applied hard two or three times to centralize the shoes.

The Girling hydraulic front brakes of this system, as shown on the left in Fig. 220, are of the *two leading shoe type*, having high braking efficiency.

Disc Brakes. Although old in their conception, since F. W. Lanchester patented a disc brake in 1902, it is only more recently that this type of brake has been introduced, primarily, in racing cars where maximum braking efficiency and torque are required, but later to several proprietary makes of car.

The disc brake's advantages over shoe-type drum brakes can be summarized as follows:

(1) They have excellent anti-fade qualities, especially where brake diameters are limited, due to better cooling, the caliper operation method, etc.

(2) Due to the relatively large area of friction material that can be used, if required, the useful life of the brake units is much longer than for drum-type brakes.

(3) Equal braking effort in forward and reverse gear.

(4) Lighter and smaller brake units for the same brake-effort.

(5) Light brake pedal pressure for powerful braking, if with servo devices.

(6) Quick and simple adjustments and friction shoe unit replacement.

(7) Less service attention needed, due to (6) and to the smaller number of working parts.

Typical disc brakes included the Dunlop, Girling, Lockheed,

Lambert and Chrysler. Since these brakes are described in Volume 3 of this Series, present considerations will be confined to a brief outline of the operating principles and to brake adjustment and maintenance.

The principle of the disc brake is that of a steel or cast-iron disc attached to the wheel which is to be braked. Two braking pads consisting of circular or sectionally-shaped metal, lined with friction material, are arranged, one on either side of the brake disc. Fixed 'caliper' units are mounted to carry these braking pads, and it is arranged for each pad to be applied with equal force towards the disc. Thus, since these forces are equal and opposite, a balanced system is obtained. The brake pads are operated by hydraulic pressure on a piston in each case and provision is generally made to take up any brake pad wear, automatically.

Two different designs of disc brakes, namely, the Dunlop and Girling are shown in Fig. 221 at (A) and (B), respectively, with their principal components annotated.

The Dunlop brake employs a fixed caliper unit covering only a small area of the brake disc; the friction pads are of $2\frac{1}{4}$ inch diameter and are applied to the brake disc by hydraulic pressure on pistons of rather smaller diameter.

The standard pad clearance from the brake disc is 0·010 inch, this clearance being maintained automatically.

To dismantle a brake unit it is necessary to remove only four set screws.

Maintenance of this type of brake consists in always keeping the hydraulic system full of hydraulic fluid of the recommended grade. The system is freed of any air – which would interfere with the brake operation – by a bleeding method similar to that used with hydraulic brakes of the drum type. The air bleed vents, are arranged on the caliper units and can be identified in Fig. 221 (A) and (B).

The Girling disc brake employs sector-shaped friction pads, actuated by hydraulic pistons. These pads can readily be removed (Fig. 222) by first unscrewing the two setscrews that hold the retainer plate and then taking out the pads. In this way the friction surfaces can readily be inspected for wear effects. The

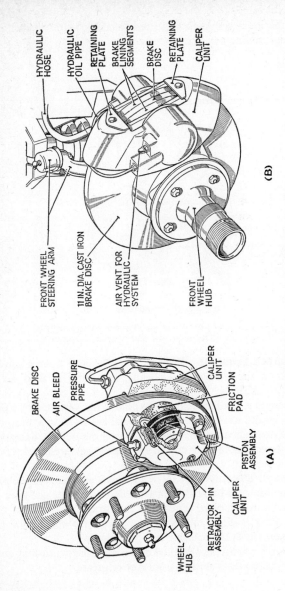

HYDRAULIC HOSE
HYDRAULIC OIL PIPE
RETAINING PLATE
BRAKE LINING SEGMENTS
BRAKE DISC
RETAINING PLATE
CALIPER UNIT

FRONT WHEEL STEERING ARM

11 IN. DIA. CAST IRON BRAKE DISC

AIR VENT FOR HYDRAULIC SYSTEM

FRONT WHEEL HUB

(B)

BRAKE DISC
AIR BLEED
PRESSURE PIPE
CALIPER UNIT
FRICTION PAD
PISTON ASSEMBLY
CALIPER UNIT
RETRACTOR PIN ASSEMBLY
WHEEL HUB

(A)

Fig. 221. Disc brakes. (A) Dunlop. (B) Girling.

hydraulic braking system will need 'bleeding' after dismantling and reassembling any of its members.

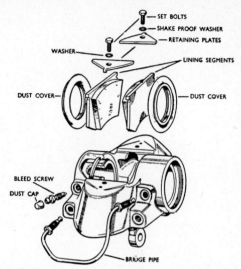

Fig. 222. Components of Girling disc brake, showing brake pad lining segments and hydraulic cylinders.

Lockheed Front Disc Brakes. These operate upon a similar principle to the Dunlop and Girling, but differ in their detail design (Fig. 223).

The friction pads should be inspected for wear every 6,000 miles or so and when the friction material has worn to a thickness of $\frac{1}{16}$ in. the pads must be renewed. During the renewal operation it is important not to allow any oil or grease to get on to the friction pads.

To remove a pad, take off the road wheel, and remove the two split-pins from the brake caliper while depressing the pad springs and remove the springs. Then, lift the friction pads out of the caliper using a slight rotational movement. *Do not depress the brake pedal* whilst the pads are being removed.

Clean, thoroughly, the exposed end of each piston, making sure that the pad recesses are free from rust or grease.

Siphon off sufficient fluid from the master cylinder to bring the level to about one-half full to allow for return of the fluid when the piston is placed back into the caliper. Check that the relieved end of each piston is correctly positioned.

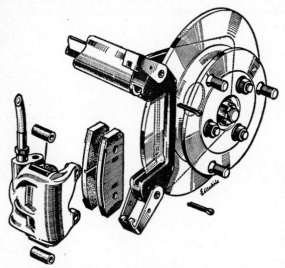

Fig. 223. Components of Lockheed disc brake.

When replaced, as described, finally depress the brake pedal two or three times to adjust the brakes and then top up the master cylinder.

Girling Friction Pad Renewal. The procedure is as follows: First remove the road wheel. Remove the spring clips from the friction pad retaining pins and take out the pins. Then lift the friction pads from the caliper. *The brake pedal should not be depressed* during this operation. Next, siphon off the fluid in the master cylinder secondary tank, to allow for the displacement of the fluid when the piston is replaced with the new pads. Finally, depress the brake pedal two or three times to re-position the pistons and then top up the master cylinder to $\frac{3}{4}$ in. below the top of the filler cap.

Servo-operated Hydraulic Brakes. Owing to the fact that the brake pedal pressure with front disc brakes is greater than for shoe-type brakes it is usual or optional to employ a vacuum-servo unit to provide some of the brake operating effort. A typical system is that of the Girling as illustrated in Fig. 224, where the vacuum servo unit *B* is installed between the four-way connector

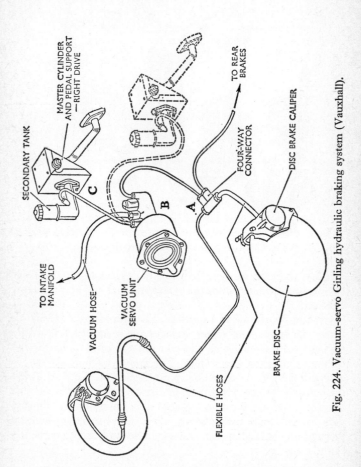

Fig. 224. Vacuum-servo Girling hydraulic braking system (Vauxhall).

A and the master cylinder-pedal unit *C*. Normally, without the unit *B* the two other units *A* and *C* are connected direct by a single fluid pipe. The dotted unit shows the master cylinder unit for opposite-hand drive cars.

The vacuum-servo unit contains a larger piston which can slide in a cylinder. The piston rod is connected direct to the master cylinder hydraulic control plunger and there is a return spring between this side of the piston and the cylinder end, on that side. Vacuum supply from the intake manifold is connected to the piston rod side of the servo piston. The foot brake moves the plunger towards the servo cylinder and opens an air valve which causes air pressure on the other side of the piston which supplies most of the effort to move the plunger along to operate the brakes.

Maintenance. The only maintenance attention is that of keeping the vacuum connecting pipe to the intake manifold connections tight and to renew the cellular air filter element inside the cylinder cover when it is dirty. It cannot be cleaned and so must be replaced by a new element.

Useful Hints on Braking. The golden rule to observe with the braking system is to use the brakes as seldom as possible. That is to say, when slowing down, take the foot off the accelerator in good time, allow the car to coast, using the engine as a brake, and only apply the foot brake when the speed has dropped fairly low.

Avoid jamming on the brakes on all occasions; it is only in an emergency that the brakes should thus be used. Excessive braking is one of the chief causes of tyre wear. When the car is descending a stiff hill, put the gear lever in bottom gear, do not switch off the engine, open the throttle a little to avoid excessive suction in the cylinders causing the crankcase oil to get past the piston, and let the engine act as a brake.

Finally, remember that excessive braking or jamming on of the brakes will not only wear the brakes out sooner, but apart from increased tyre wear, will also cause transmission wear.

Testing Braking Performance. The practical method of judging the efficiency of the braking system is to measure the distance required to bring the car to rest from a given steady speed by means of a steady normal effort on the footbrake. Generally speaking, the shorter the distance in question, the more efficient the brakes.

Special brake testing machines are used in the larger service works, for checking the efficiency of the brakes. The car is driven on to a ramp with its tyres resting upon pairs of serrated rollers. The brake pedal is depressed with a certain number of pounds load and held in that position. The effort, or torque, required to just rotate each wheel under this brake pressure is then measured with a torsion device; in most cases the torque required is indicated on a large graduated dial. The reading obtained enables the brake efficiency to be estimated for each of the four brakes. In another well-known machine, viz., the Weaver automatic brake tester, the car is driven on to the ramp at a definite speed, e.g. 8 m.p.h. and the brakes applied whilst on the ramp or platform. The braking torque at this speed is then recorded on four vertical tubes filled with coloured liquid, so that it can at once be seen whether all four brakes are of equal efficiency, and whether they come up to the requisite standard for the vehicle.

Braking Efficiency. In connection with the practical method based upon actual road tests, it is necessary to have some standard whereby the performance of various braking systems can be compared, and therefore the technician uses the acceleration due to gravity (32·2 feet per second per second) as the standard. Thus, if a car can be brought to rest at the retarding rate of 32·2 feet per second per second, it is said to have a 100 per cent braking efficiency.

The maximum efficiency occurs when the braking force is equal to the car weight, when the deceleration becomes g ft sec, per sec and the efficiency is then 100 per cent.

Braking Stopping Distances. The distance in which a car can be brought to rest from any steady road speed will depend upon a number of factors, e.g. the braking efficiency, condition and inflation pressure of the tyres, head resistance of the car, nature of the road surface and whether wet or dry, the adhesion factor, etc.

Tests have shown that the resistance to sliding experienced by a car on the road may be equal to or even greater than the total weight of the car when braked violently. The stopping distances will also depend upon the condition or adjustment of the brakes and in this connection the accompanying table, based upon practical road test results may be found useful.

STOPPING DISTANCES AND BRAKE EFFICIENCIES

Condition of Brakes	Stopping Distances in Feet from m.p.h.						Braking Efficiency* per cent
	20	30	40	50	60	70	
Perfect	15	32	60	95	135	182	100
Excellent	17	37	68	107	154	207	80
Very Good	19	43	77	122	178	245	70
Good	22	50	90	142	210	290	60
Fair	27	62	108	170	245	337	50
Poor	35	75	133	215	310	415	40
Bad	45	97	175	280	392	512	30

* Approximate.

Modern Car Braking Performance. The results of car braking tests carried out by the Road Research Laboratory on a production model of a high performance car fitted with vacuum-servo assisted hydraulic disc brakes on all four wheels, when driven at various speeds on a dry aerodrome runway surface, stated to be in good condition, are given in the accompanying table.

MODERN CAR BRAKING TEST RESULTS

Car Speed (m.p.h.)	20	30	40	50	60	70	80	90	100
Stopping Distance	22	47	82	129	185	252	330	416	515

A useful instrument for testing brake efficiency on the road is that known as the Ferodo Brake Tester. It is fitted on to the dashboard and used during the normal running of the car. In principle it acts as a pendulum-type accelerometer, or retarder. It has three windows marked 30 per cent, 50 per cent and 60 per cent, and whenever the brake is applied the coloured shutter corresponding to the actual brake efficiency appears at its window. The shutters are returned out of sight by means of a lever on the side of the indicator. The instrument should be set 'level' when first fitted; to ensure this a pointer and scale are provided on the left side of the dial. By adjusting the levelling pointer to small marks above or below the black arrow efficiencies of 20 per cent and 70 per cent can be indicated.

Official Brake Test Standards.* The minimum standards required for practical tests made by examiners are as follows:

The inspection will comprise two parts, (i) the condition and security of the mechanism and the means of operation, (ii) the effectiveness of the brakes in bringing the vehicle to rest and holding it on an incline. As regards the first, the tester should satisfy himself on the following points:

(*a*) Brake rods and/or cables are in good condition, are working freely and do not rub or chafe on other parts.

(*b*) Bolts and clevis pins are not excessively worn and are secured by nuts or split pins as the case may be.

(*c*) Hydraulic systems are free from leaks in pipes and cylinders and, so far as can be judged by the feel on application of the pedal, are free from air and are properly adjusted.

(*d*) Handbrake pawls and ratchets are not excessively worn and hold the lever securely in the 'on' position.

(*e*) Foot pedals and hand levers have a reasonable amount of reserve travel when fully applied.

(*f*) There is no visible evidence of oil leakage round the brake drums or hubs which might indicate that the linings have become affected.

(*g*) There is no other visible defect on the vehicle likely to affect the braking adversely.

Vehicles with a braking performance to the standards given in the table should be regarded as meeting requirements.

In regard to these braking tests it is recommended that these should be carried out in one or other of the following ways:

(*a*) by using such a brake-testing apparatus as may be suitable in relation to the vehicle to test whether the performance of the braking system conforms to the operational braking requirements;

* Ministry of Transport. Compulsory Vehicle Tests. See Appendix.

(b) by driving the vehicle on a road or in any other suitable place and operating the braking system while it is being so driven to test whether the performance of that system conforms to the operational braking requirements.

Braking Tests. The prescribed braking tests can be made on a brake testing machine in the testing station using a machine of the kind referred to previously in this chapter or with a decelerometer, such as either the Ferodo or the Tapley brake tester. Alternatively, tests may be made by driving the car on the road at suitable speeds and operating the brakes to test whether the performance conforms to the usual braking requirements.

The later Regulations prescribe certain minimum braking efficiency values, based upon the maximum braking force developed by the brakes at certain given road speeds. The efficiency is then expressed as the *braking force divided by the total weight of the loaded car* at the time of the tests.

The following are the minimum braking efficiencies as officially prescribed for motor-cars:

Motor-cars, Four Wheels. Brakes operating on all four wheels, by brake pedal	50 per cent
Motor-cars, Four Wheels. Hand brake, only	25 per cent
Three-wheel Vehicles. Brake operating on all three wheels	40 per cent

Driver's Tests. The car driver can obtain a good idea of the efficiency of his brakes, before submitting his car for Official Tests, by measuring the stopping distance from a given steady road speed. Thus, for the Official minimum brake efficiencies, previously mentioned, the stopping distances for a car running at a steady speed of 30 m.p.h. on a dry flat road, the following are the maximum stopping distances:

Brake Efficiency (per cent)	50	40	25
Stopping Distance from 30 m.p.h. expressed in feet	62	75	108

CHAPTER 10

THE SUSPENSION SYSTEM

THE springs have a heavy duty to perform and are constantly in action when the car is on the road. Not only are the spring leaves flexing under the action of road bumps and hollows, but they slide a little over one another under this flexing action. At the same time the shackle and anchoring pins rock in the shackle or spring bearings.

Spring Maintenance. The earlier semi-elliptic front springs have now been replaced in most cases by large-coil or torsion bar ones, although the rear springs are mostly of the leaf pattern. Another improvement that has been made is to substitute, so far as possible, special rubber bushes for the gunmetal ones previously used for the spring eye and shackle bearings. As these rubber bearings depend upon the torsional distortion of the rubber itself, there is no sliding motion and therefore no lubrication is needed. The maintenance of the leaf spring unit has therefore been simplified, although it must be added that there are still cars in service having gunmetal or porous bronze bearings that require oil- or grease-gun lubrication through the nipples provided for this purpose.

Leaf Springs. The laminated, or leaf spring is still employed to a large extent for front transverse and rear suspension systems, although the use of coil and also torsion bar rear springing systems has increased more recently.

In the earlier designs of leaf spring no provision was made for lubricating the blades, friction between these being relied upon to provide a certain damping action. In more recent leaf springs various means have been used to obviate the necessity of interleaf lubrication – which, previously, was an additional maintenance operation to that of lubricating the bronze bush bearings of the spring-eyes and shackles.

In some instances *rubber* is used between the spring blades, to provide silent operation and avoid lubrication attention. When artificial rubber is employed the outside edges of the blades can still be sprayed with thin oil since this rubber is both oil and petrol proof.

Sometimes, as in certain Austin cars, there are *zinc interleaves* between the spring blades and lubrication of the blades is provided for by a central oil nipple. Thus, some Austin car rear springs were provided with an oil nipple in the centre of the spring clamping plate below the spring (and back axle tube to which the spring is clamped). These spring blades should be lubricated every 1,000–2,000 miles, with engine oil, until the oil is observed exuding from the laminations.

In other instances the blades were made slightly concave or flat, but with oil or grease grooves, to enable the laminations to be lubricated and to retain the lubricant. It was usual to enclose such springs in specially-fitted *leather gaiters,* in order to retain the lubricant and to prevent dirt from entering the spaces between the laminations.

In more recent Vauxhall cars the rear springs have polythene inserts in the form of buttons at the ends of some of the spring blades.

Some of the later Ford cars have anti-rust-coated blades which when assembled provide the necessary lubrication. Rubber pads are fitted in the ends of the longer blades to provide a bearing surface and also prevent squeaks. These inserts are not affected by penetrating oil.

Leaf Spring Maintenance Attention. The periodical attention required for rear leaf springs depends somewhat upon the design of the laminated springs, in so far as lubrication attention is concerned. The springs should be examined for lubrication gun nipples at the shackles or spring assembly centres; also for indications of rubber bushes, if the manufacturers' manuals are not available.

The principal items of maintenance attention, as shown in Fig. 225 for the Morris Minor car include: (1) The spring blade clips. (2) The back axle clamping screws and nuts. (3) The spring bushes, and (4) The shock absorbers.

Under normal operating conditions the nuts on the spring blade clips and also the back axle U-bolts should be checked for tightness after the first 500 miles – when the car is new – and thereafter every 4,000–5,000 miles.

Fig. 226 illustrates the earlier Vauxhall rear spring unit components, showing how these items are located relatively to one another. An examination of this illustration will prove helpful, in

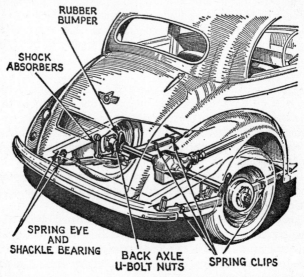

RUBBER
BUMPER

SHOCK
ABSORBERS

SPRING EYE
AND
SHACKLE BEARING

BACK AXLE
U-BOLT NUTS

SPRING CLIPS

Fig. 225. Rear suspension system maintenance items (Morris Minor).

regard to spring maintenance. It will be observed that rubber bushes are fitted to the fixed shackle pin and the two spring-eye bearings. Also, as with most other rear springing systems a rubber block 'bumper' is provided to prevent damage to the back axle casing under extreme conditions of vertical springing movement. The spring shown is provided with rollers at the individual blade ends of the four upper leaves, in order to reduce sliding friction.

The rubber bushes of rear leaf springs require no attention, other than a careful examination and check for rubber deterioration or bush slackenings in their housings. The method of removing a defective rubber bush is described later in this Chapter.

Examination of Leaf Springs. When a car is given a major overhaul after a long period of service, the springs should be dismantled from the chassis and then taken apart for examination. The procedure for a typical example, namely, the Morris Minor (Fig. 225) is, as follows:

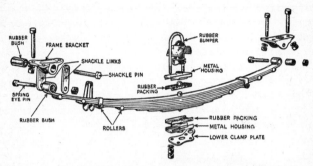

Fig. 226. Components of rear leaf spring unit.

Slacken off and remove the three spring clip bolts, distance pieces and rubber packings.

Release the locknut and nut from the spring centre bolt and remove the distance piece and bolt. The spring leaves can now be taken apart.

After removal and thorough cleaning with paraffin or detergent solution, examine each leaf thoroughly for signs of cracks or breakage. Replace any leaves that have these defects. (See also p. 318.)

Check the centre bolt for wear or distortion, since this bolt locates the spring on its axle pad.

Check the spring blades for correct camber, if possible against spare blades; flattened blades can either be re-set by a qualified spring-smith or replaced by new blades from Agent's stock.

Reassembling. Place the blades together in their correct order, locating them with the centre bolt. The dowel head of the bolt must be on top of the spring.

Fit No. 5 leaf with its clip on the forward side of the dowel bolt.

Replace the spring clip packings, clip distance pieces and bolts.

It should be noted that the Morris Minor springs have rubber bushes and rubber interleaving, so that it is important that the interleaf spaces should not be lubricated, although squeaky springs may be sprayed externally with Lockheed brake fluid or with a water-graphite solution.

Modern Rear Leaf Springs. The general practice adopted in most recent cars is to use fewer blades in the springs and to dispense with any bronze bushes, using only the Silentbloc type or other rubber bushes for the spring eyes and shackles. There is thus no lubrication needed.

Fig. 227 illustrates the Vauxhall Velox rear spring and, below, some details of the spring clip, the previously mentioned polythene buttons which in this case are located near the ends of the 2nd and 3rd blades. Also shown on the right in Fig. 227 are the rubber-type front hanger and rear shackle bushes.

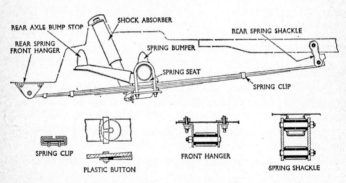

Fig. 227. The Vauxhall Velox rear leaf spring and its components.

It may be mentioned that the smaller Viva car rear springs have only two blades; the intermediate Victor car has three blades.

The method of securing the rear spring to the rear axle is shown in Fig. 228, in which the axle casing end is shown at (A) and the four spring blades at (10). The spring blades and their rubber pad insulators are attached firmly to the axle (A) by means of two U-bolts with their nuts and locking plates at (6) and (7). Above the axle is the rubber bumper (1) which is secured by the clips (2).

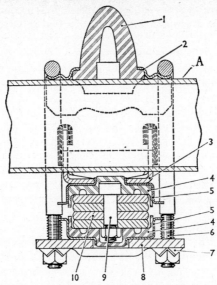

Fig. 228. Method of attachment of rear leaf spring to rear axle unit.
1 bumper. 2 bumper retainer. 3 spring seat. 4 insulator pad. 5 insulator
pad retainer. 6 U-bolt. 7 nut locking plate. 8 U-bolt spacer. 9 centre bolt.
10 rear spring.

After long service the spring units should be removed from the
car, as described later, and the spring *blades inspected for cracks*;
also for loose rivets on the clips. It may be necessary to replace the
rubber bushes, insulator pads, the rubber bumpers and polythene
buttons.

Removing Rear Spring Units. The general procedure is well
illustrated by the Vauxhall Velox spring shown in Fig. 227; it is
as follows:

(1) Raise and support the rear end of the car so that the spring
'hangs' from it.

(2) Remove the road wheel.

(3) Unscrew the U-bolt nuts and take off the bumper clip and
bumper; then swing the U-bolt clear of the spring.

(4) Jack up the rear axle free of the spring and remove the
insulator pads and retainers.

(5) Remove the nuts and shackle plate. Withdraw the shackle and pin assembly and lower the rear end of the spring to the floor.

(6) Remove the front hanger-pin nut.

(7) Support the front of the spring and remove the nuts securing the hanger plate and hanger and pin assembly to the body.

(8) Finally lift away the spring.

Reassembly of the Rear Spring. In general the installation of the rear spring unit is the reverse procedure to that of its removal, but the spring with its insulator pads and bumper should be refitted to the rear axle member tightening the U-bolts right up to the manufacturer's recommended torque, e.g. about 16 lb. ft. in the spring shown in Fig. 227. This final tightening should be done before the weight of the car is on the spring. The shackle and front end bush pins must be replaced the same way round as when they were taken out, but their nuts should not be tightened until the weight of the car is on the spring.

When a rear spring has been taken apart, before reassembling it a new centre pin [item (9) in Fig. 228], should be fitted.

Removal of Shackle Bushes. To remove a continuous gunmetal bush a screw-type extractor tool should be used; alternatively, a stepped steel drift and hammer.

In the case of one type of Austin rear shackle, shown in Fig. 229, the upper bearing consists of a phosphor-bronze two-part bush. After the upper bolt has been removed each half can be driven out of the frame housing by inserting a narrow drift through the hole in the other bush so as to bear against the inner end of the bush. After fitting new bushes – to replace badly worn ones – the shackle pin should be well greased before insertion and the nuts tightened securely, using lock washers. When correctly fitted there should be no side play in the shackles but the latter should not be so tight that it is impossible to move them to and fro.

If of the *Silentbloc rubber bush pattern* having an inner and outer metal casing enclosing the rubber, the bush is removed from the spring eye with the aid of a bolt, nut and tubular distance piece, as shown in Fig. 230. There is a special tool made on this principle,

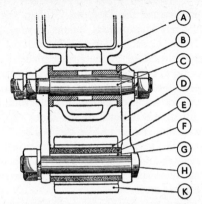

Fig. 229. Rear spring shackle of Austin car.

A chassis frame.
B phosphor-bronze bush.
C steel shackle pin.
D shackle link.

E Silentbloc outer bush.
F Silentbloc rubber.
G Silentbloc inner bush.
H Silentbloc shackle pin.
K spring eye.

which can also be used for inserting new bushes. In removal, or replacement, pressure must only be applied to the outside metal bush.

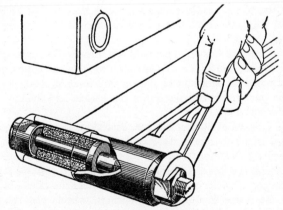

Fig. 230. Removal of rubber bush from spring eye.

Spring Examination for Defects. Springs that have been in use over relatively long periods should, during a major overhaul of the car, be inspected for possible defects. This necessitates complete *dismantling* of the spring blades. The ordinary type of leaf spring is dealt with as follows: Grip the spring in a strong vice with the jaws opposite the spring centre. Then knock off the outside leaf clips using a hammer and drift. If bolts and nuts are fitted, the removal of the inner clips is a simple matter; otherwise these clips must be knocked off.

Upon opening the vice jaws the spring blades can be removed, individually. They should be degreased and dried before examination for defects. The usual defects are cracked or broken blades and flattened leaves.

In the case of cars that have been used on racing tracks or bad roads it is not uncommon to find broken blades – pieces of the latter are often seen on our roads. It is therefore important to examine the blades carefully and to replace all broken blades with new ones.

When replacing the spring in the vice it is advisable to use a rod of the same diameter as the spring's central clamping bolt, having a tapered end to locate the blades; afterwards the proper bolt can be inserted without damage to its threads.

If a spring fractures on the road, a temporary repair – sufficient to get one to the nearest garage – may be made by lashing, with rope or wire, one or more tyre levers above and below the spring blades.

If the fracture – as often happens – is through the centre of the spring blades, and is due to a loose spring clip, the latter should be slackened off sufficient to allow a tyre lever or spanner to be inserted between it and the top of the blades, and the clip nuts then tightened up.

The Causes of Spring Noises. Squeakiness, traceable to the springs, is usually due to water and dirt having found their way between the blades; if rust has formed, this must be removed by opening the leaves and injecting paraffin. *To open the leaves,* jack the car up at the chassis frame – not under the axles – so that when the frame is elevated the springs, wheels and the axle actually hang under their own weight from the frame. There is then the least amount of compression on the springs, and the blades tend to open. A screwdriver or special spring opening tool should then be used to open the leaves still further.

Another cause of spring noise is *looseness of the spring clips*. Wear between shackle bolts and their bearings is yet another cause of spring rattle; excessive side-play between the shackles and the spring eyes will also result in noise.

The latter trouble can be cured by tightening the nut on the shackle bolt. If tightening the nut does not cure the rattle, the cause is probably that of wear in the spring eyes and shackle bolts, When tightening the shackle bolt nut, care should be taken to *avoid excessive clamping*, for this will restrict the free action of the spring and may result in the upper blades breaking.

Worn shackle pins must be replaced with oversize ones, the spring eye bushes, if not worn appreciably, being reamed out to suit.

The modern method of *curing squeaky springs* is to jack up the car by the chassis frame so that the wheels hang clear of the ground and the spring leaves open a little. Graphited thin penetrating oil is then injected by spraying between and along the edges of the spring blades, using the patent spray gun provided for this purpose; the residual graphite serves as a lubricant and to protect the mating surfaces of the leaves against any further rusting. When the shackle pins are of the lubricated type and provided with grease gun nipples these should be greased every 200 to 300 miles.

Spring Flattening. Cars which have been overloaded habitually over long periods, or have been in continuous use for several years, will usually 'settle' on their springs.

The material of the springs, being in a constant state of repeated loading and vibration, tends to 'fatigue', and to yield after a certain period of use. The result is that the blades flatten and the car sinks lower on to its springs.

In the case of earlier front springs of the semi-elliptic type, this flattening effect may affect the steering, *and cause wheel wobble*.

It is an easy matter to ascertain whether a spring has flattened, by examining the shackle link.

It is, however, the practice to check what is known as the 'Rear Spring Trim Height', namely the distance between the rear spring bumper and the under part of the body or frame, with the car unladen. The manufacturers will supply this trim height dimension for any of their cars.

One remedy for flattened springs is to obtain the services of a reliable blacksmith, namely, one who is used to setting springs and tempering them, to re-set the springs. It is helpful to make a stout wire template of the correct shape of, say, the upper blade, corresponding to the normal shackle position, and to get the smith to work to this template. Otherwise, it is usual to instruct him to 'set' the springs up, say, 1 inch or 2 inches, as the case may be. Before leaving the springs with the smith make a template on a piece of board by drawing an outline of the flattened spring with a lead pencil, so that the amount of setting can be checked afterwards.

It may be mentioned that there is an hydraulic tool, known as the Porto-Power, that is used in motor garages for spring removal and replacement; and for various other purposes.

Independent Front Wheel Suspension. There are two broad groups into which modern front suspension systems fall, namely, (1) The wishbone and large coil arrangement and (2) The wishbone and torsion bar. These and certain other variants of them are described in Volume 3, so that here the maintenance and adjustment items, only, will be considered.

The Wishbone and Coil Spring Method. This independent springing method has almost entirely replaced the leaf spring in motor-cars, but there are examples of cars which still use the transverse leaf spring in conjunction with the double wishbone system.

Fig. 231 illustrates the principle of the coil spring suspension system for the front wheels. In this method the stub axle carrying the wheel hub forms part of the king-pin unit (*BB*); it also has a steering arm but this is not shown in the illustration. This unit is provided with hinges (*B*) at each end for the upper and lower radius arms shown; their inner ends are hinge-mounted to the chassis frame. Between the two arms is mounted a large diameter helical coil spring which serves to take part of the car's weight and

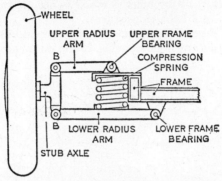

Fig. 231. Illustrating the principle of the wishbone-and-coil
front suspension system.

to do the work of the previous leaf spring. Thus, when the wheel
hits a road bump the wheel and its mechanism moves upwards
to compress the spring, eventually returning the wheel to its
original level position. The use of the longer lower arm is to keep
the wheel as nearly as possible vertical for medium road inequali-
ties, but for large road bumps the wheel inclines, somewhat as
shown in Fig. 232, unless rubber bumper stops are provided.

This springing method enables each front wheel to be sprung

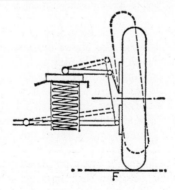

Fig. 232. Action of front suspension system on a bumpy road
as inicated at F.

L

independently of the other – which is not the case with the previously used leaf spring systems.

Austin Front Suspension. The type of suspension used in certain Austin cars is shown in Fig. 233, in which the various parts

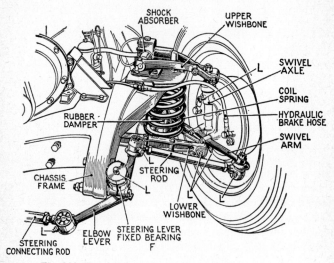

Fig. 233. Front independent coil suspension system and part of steering system (Austin).

are annotated while the lubrication nipples are indicated by the letters *L*. The illustration also shows the near-side parts of the steering mechanism with a fixed bearing on the chassis frame at *F*. The swivel axle carrying the swivel pin and upper and lower bushes in which the swivel pin works is shown in more detail in Fig. 234. It will be observed that the swivel pin is secured at each end to the upper and lower wishbone members, while the swivel axle is free to rotate on the swivel pin under the steering mechanism control.

The items of maintenance attention include: (1) The lubrication of the working pins and their bearings at the appropriate grease nipples. (2) The periodical topping up of the hydraulic shock absorbers, with suitable oil and the replenishment of the axle bearings grease at intervals of about 5,000 miles, but an excessive amount of grease should be avoided.

Wear of Members. The components of the independent front wheel suspension system which are liable to wear after long periods of service include: (1) The swivel pin and its bushes. (2) The shock absorber bearings. (3) The wishbone arm rubber bushes. (4) The wishbone arm screwed bush assembly – which is a metal-type bearing.

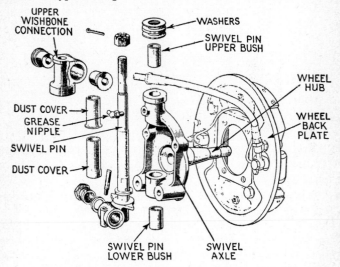

Fig. 234. Components of swivel axle unit (Austin A.40).

As the inspection of these parts for wear, their dismantling and replacement by spare parts is outside the scope of this volume, the manufacturer's service manual should be consulted for the detailed procedure to be followed.

Suspension Lubrication Points. In the case of cars on our roads of various makes and years of age, most are provided with oil or grease nipples for lubricating the outer and inner wishbone arm bearings and also the king-pin bearings. Usually these should be lubricated once every 2,000 miles.

Later car models employ special rubber bushes for the wishbone arm bearings, but many still use oil or grease nipples on the top and bottom of the king pin. Fig. 235 shows the Wolseley 16/60

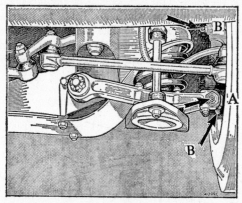

Fig. 235. Lubrication of Wolseley front suspension bearings.

wishbone arm and king-pin lubrication points. Here, there is a grease nipple (A) for the outer end of each wishbone arm and two points (B) for the king pin.

More recent cars have dispensed with all suspension lubrication points by using rubber bearings for all of the wishbone ends and nylon-steel cup and ball bearings for the king-pin ends, which are first charged with a special long-life grease and the whole unit enclosed in a rubber boot, of special design, to exclude dirt and water. Such bearings (Fig. 236) need lubricating once every 30,000 miles.

Note: It is better to jack up the front wheels when using the grease gun to lubricate king-pin bearings; the grease will then penetrate better.

Removal of the Coil Spring. The general method adopted in most cases is to jack up the front end of the chassis until the wheels are just clear of the ground. The wheel on the side to be worked on is then removed.

Next an additional jack is placed under the lower spring pan (Fig. 237) and is operated until the hydraulic damper levers are clear of the rebound rubber block. The lower fulcrum bolt is removed and the hub unit swung upwards and rested on a suitable block of wood. The jack is then released from the spring pan and the wishbone assembly pushed down when the coil spring can be removed.

In the case of *the Austin front suspension* the front of the chassis is jacked up and wooden blocks placed under the frame side member to the rear of the suspension unit.

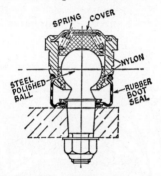

Fig. 236. A 'sealed-for-life' suspension or steering arm bearing.

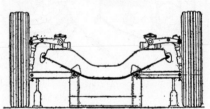

Fig. 237. Removing the coil spring on M.G.
1¼-litre car.

If the special spring jig is not available, the compression in the coil spring can be released by using two ⅜ inch slave bolts about 4 inches long and threaded the whole way. There are four nuts and bolts securing the bottom spring plate, fitted with self-locking nuts. Two of these bolts, diagonally opposite, should be removed and the two slave bolts (*H*) inserted. The nuts on the latter should then be screwed down tightly, as shown in Fig. 238, and then the other two main springs bolts can be removed, thus leaving only the two slave bolts and nuts. When the latter have been unscrewed sufficiently to release the compression of the spring, the slave bolts can be withdrawn and the springs and plate removed.

The coil spring can be replaced by the reverse process.

When the suspension system of a car that has been in service for an appreciable period of time is dismantled for inspection and overhaul, the coil spring should be checked for correct free length; if found to have closed appreciably the spring must be renewed.

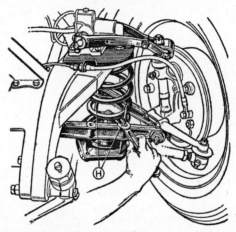

Fig. 238. Removing coil spring of Austin A.40 and A.60 cars.

The Austin A.40 coil spring has a free length of 10·54 to 10·64 inches and compressed length of 7 inches.

Coil Spring Removal Tool. A special tool for removing and refitting the coil springs is shown in Fig. 239 for use on the Humber Super Snipe front suspension.

As before, it is necessary to jack up the front cross member of the chassis and remove the wheel and shock absorber. The spring compressor supplied by the Churchill Company, is then fitted and its large nut handle turned to compress the spring enough to take the load off the spring. The four nuts which secure the spring pan to the underside of the lower link are then taken off,

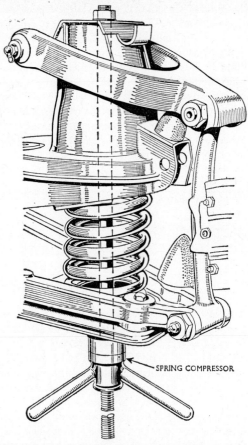

Fig. 239. Method of removing coil spring on Humber and
Hillman cars using Churchill 50D tool.

so that the spring compressor is gradually released until the
spring is fully extended and can be taken off.

Refitting of the spring is the reverse procedure but it is important to position the rubber insulator correctly at the top of the
spring and the rubber bumpers in their proper places.

Possible Faults in Coil Spring Suspension Systems.
Whilst space will not allow the detailed account of faults and their
remedies to be given, it may be useful to motor mechanics to
enumerate the principal kinds of faults liable to occur. It should,
however, first be mentioned that the chief method of checking
the suspension system for faults is to measure the wheel camber,
castor and king pin angles (see page 355) and compare the
measured angles with those given by the car manufacturers.

Faults in the suspension (and steering) mechanism are liable
to occur either as the result of an accident or through long service.
Briefly these may be as follows:

(1) Bent or distorted wishbones.
(2) Broken or weak coil spring.
(3) Worn pins and bushes.
(4) Bent stub axle.
(5) Bent or buckled chassis cross frame or front end side member.
(6) Bent hydraulic damper arms.
(7) Bent or broken king pins.

Torsion Arm Front Suspension System. Instead of using
coil springs their place can be taken by long alloy steel rods which
when twisted act as springs. The principle of this method is
illustrated in Fig. 240 which shows the lower wishbone arm (AC)
carrying at its outer end the road wheel hub (C). The other end
(A) is attached to a castellated alloy steel rod (or tube) (AB), the
other end (B) of which has castellations and fits in a bracket with
internal castellations, so as to anchor this end. When the road
wheel hits a bump the arm (CA) moves the end (C) upwards
and this twists the shaft (AB) since the end (B) is fixed. The
amount of vertical movement can be designed to meet all springing
requirements. In the diagram (Fig. 240) only one of the two lower
wishbone arms is shown; in practice both outer ends are usually
fixed to the torsion bar.

This suspension method is a simple and effective one, having
the merits of taking up far less space than the coil spring and also
requiring none of the lubricating points of the latter.

Torsion springing is used on certain Citroën cars, on the B.M.C.
Riley and Wolseley 1½-litre and Morris Minor cars and it has

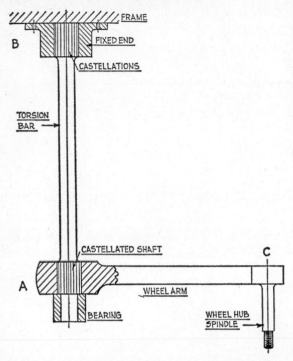

Fig. 240. Showing principle of the torsion bar suspension system.

been the standard suspension on all of the Volkswagen cars since their first introduction. In the B.M.C. cars the torsion bars are located longitudinally, as shown in Fig. 241 for the Morris Minor car, but in the Volkswagen cars the torsion members are located transversely, as in Fig. 242. Referring to Fig. 241 the front suspension comprises the upper and lower wishbone members of the previously described system. The upper wishbone is hinged to the hydraulic shock absorber, as before, but the frame side lower wishbone is secured to the outer end of the torsion bar; the rear end of this bar is fixed to a bracket on the chassis frame cross member. The inner ends of the wishbone members are anchored to the frame members in flexible rubber bushes. The

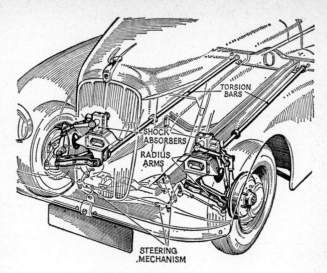

Fig. 241. Morris front end torsion bar
suspension system.

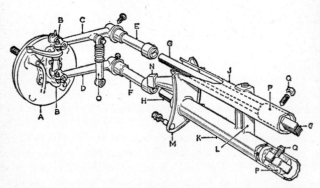

Fig. 242. The torsion bar system used for the front suspension
of the Volkswagen car.

A wheel hub and brake plate. *B* king-pin ends. *C* and *D* stub axle hinged arms. *E* and *F* parallel rods with bearings in chassis. *G* and *H* torsion bars for *E* and *F*. *J* and *K* torsion bar tubes. *L* and *M* mounts for *J* and *K*. *P* fixed collars at ends of torsion bars. *Q* screw stops to hold torsion bars. The hydraulic damper is shown at *O*.

only grease nipples provided are those at the king pin end of the wishbones.

The maintenance of the suspension member bearings is practically identical with that of the coil spring suspension ones, previously described.

Removing the Morris Minor Torsion Bars. First raise the front of the chassis and remove the road wheels. Place a jack beneath the outer end of the lower suspension arm and raise it until the hydraulic damper at the top is just clear of the rubber rebound pad.

Slacken the bolts clamping the two halves of the lower wishbone together and loosen the nut on the inner end of the arm. Remove the nut and spring washer from the lower king pin link and tap out the bolt.

Lower the jack until the torsion bar is free of its load and withdraw the bolt and spring washer securing the lock plate at the rear of the torsion bar. Then remove the nuts, bolts and spring washers securing the torsion bar hub to the frame. The torsion bar can then be disengaged from the suspension arm and lowered from the chassis. The hardened surface of the torsion bar *must* not be damaged in any way, or marked with a punch or scriber. Further, each torsion bar must be refitted to its proper side as the two bars are not interchangeable. They should have labels tied on them for identification purposes.

Trimming Torsion Bar Suspension Systems. In order to maintain the chassis (and car body) at the correct level, with torsion bar springing systems it is necessary to have some means of *adjusting the torsion bars* so as to vary the static loading. This is sometimes effected by *a screw adjuster* at the fixed end of the torsion bar which can give the latter a small amount of torsion to raise or lower the bottom wishbone and with it the wheel, when standing on the ground, relatively to the chassis frame.

In the Morris Minor cars the fixed end of each torsion bar had an arm keyed to it. The hole in the outer end of this arm was bolted through one of five holes in an adjuster plate. By selecting the right hole the car height could be altered: this operated on the vernier principle.

The Riley and Wolseley 1½-litre cars have screwed adjusters at the fixed ends of the torsion bars. The outer end of an arm fixed to the bar is adjusted by a screw, having a lock-nut, the end of this screw bearing against a fixed bracket on the frame of the car.

To adjust the trim, in order to correct any list of the car first raise the front of the car until the road wheels are clear of the ground. Suitable supports must be placed beneath the chassis and the car weight rested upon them; they should be under the forward end of the front door sills. Next place a jack beneath the outer end of the lower suspension arm and raise it until the hydraulic shock absorber arm at the top of the king pin is just clear of the rubber bumper. Care must be taken to see that the jack cannot slip. Then remove the nut and bolt securing the tie rod to the fork on the suspension arm and remove the nuts and bolts retaining the forward half of the arm. Disengage the lower king-pin link from the suspension arm and lower the jack until the load is taken off the torsion bar. Slacken the lock-nut on the adjusting bracket screw and turn the screw anti-clockwise to raise the car or clockwise to lower it.

When replacing a torsion bar in its former position or a new bar the correct adjustment can be made by reference to the dimensions shown at *A*, *B* and *C*, in Fig. 243. For the Riley and Wolseley

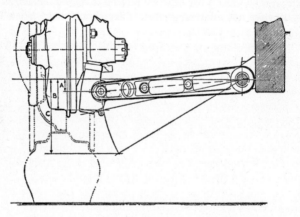

Fig. 243. Adjustment of the earlier Morris torsion bar suspension.

cars the differences in height between the centres of the lower arm inner and outer pivots should be, as follows:

(A) Full load of three passengers, $\frac{3}{8}$ in.

(B) Unladen – $1\frac{3}{4}$ in.

(C) Unladen assembly position (no load on bar), 7·5625 in.

There are 48 splines on the bar-ends, each spline giving a radial movement of the king pin of $1\frac{1}{2}$ in.

For the Morris Minor MM and 1000 cars the dimensions for (A), (B) and (C) are $\frac{3}{8}$ in., $1\frac{5}{8}$ in. and $5\frac{5}{8}$ in., respectively.

Note. It is most important when adjusting the trim of any car, whether of the torsion bar, leaf or coil spring types, to have the car standing *on level ground*.

The Shock Absorbers. The friction type shock absorbers or dampers that were fitted to previous car models have been replaced by the single and double piston type shock absorbers, e.g. Armstrong, Lucas, and Girling piston types; also by the later hydraulic telescopic or double tubular pattern. These fully enclosed dampers require little maintenance attention during their normal lives, but after long service they should be dismantled for inspection and any worn components replaced. The operating arm of the hydraulic damper is connected to the rear axle unit by means of a connecting link having rubber bushes at each end. These bushes generally require renewal after long periods of regular use.

A typical example of a hydraulic shock absorber is the Luvac-Girling shown in Figs. 244 and 245, as used on some Hillman Minx and other cars. The operating arm is connected to a pair of pistons forming a single unit, working in opposed cylinders. The system is filled with a thin oil and this requires replenishing or topping up every 10,000 miles, in order to keep the damping action effective. In *some cases this operation required the removal of the dampers* from the car, so that the levers can be worked up and down during topping up in order to expel any air in the oil system. It is also much easier to fill the dampers to the correct level namely, to the bottom of the filler plug hole when they are removed from the car. In this connection the filling of the casing to the correct level is *considered very important* from the point of view of efficient operation and allowance for expansion of the fluid.

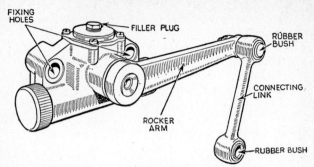

Fig. 244. Luvac-Girling double-acting hydraulic
shock absorber.

The plug and also the region around the filler plug should be carefully cleaned before removal of the plug, to prevent any dirt entering the unit.

It is not possible in the majority of hydraulic dampers for the car owner or mechanic to vary the degree of damping as the manufacturers design the damping action to suit each make of car; no adjustment is provided for its subsequent variation.

In regard to the hydraulic dampers fitted to the independent front springing mechanism of the types mentioned earlier in this

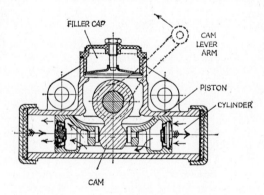

Fig. 245. Sectional view of Girling double-acting hydraulic
shock absorber.

chapter, these are so located that they *can be topped up without removal* from the chassis.

Another example of an hydraulic shock absorber for independent front wheel suspensions is the Armstrong Model 15, used on many British cars. The upper wishbone fixed bearing, which is bolted to the chassis frame, is integral with the shock absorber member, the wishbone axle being arranged by an internal linkage to operate a piston when the front wheel strikes a bump on the road.

Movement of the piston causes oil to be transferred from its cylinder to a second or 'rebound' cylinder which is fitted with a piston, by means of a pre-set 'bleed' valve and a high pressure relief valve. The former valve controls the smaller road shocks and the latter valve, the more violent shocks. The rebound cylinder and piston control and damp out the main spring movements.

Maintenance of the Armstrong shock absorber consists in periodical topping up of the hydraulic fluid every 10,000 to 12,000 miles and the checking at shorter intervals of the nuts or fixing bolts that secure the shock absorber unit to the chassis frame. The screws holding the cover plate should occasionally be checked for tightness. Usually the rear shock absorbers require removal from the chassis for replenishment purposes.

Telescopic Hydraulic Dampers. While a considerable number of cars on the road use the previously described hydraulic dampers, the more recent tendency is to employ the telescopic ones as they are more easily fitted and can also be used as anti-roll members. Typical telescopic dampers include the Girling, Newton-Bennett and Woodhead Monroe models.

Fig. 246 illustrates the Woodhead Monroe type which is direct-acting and completely sealed so that no topping-up is needed, nor is any adjustment possible. The only maintenance is that of periodical inspection of the end mountings and the rubber bushes, which can be done without any special tools.

Should a damper prove faulty it can be returned to the manufacturers' agents and a replacement fitted.

Fig. 247 shows the telescopic damper as fitted to certain B.M.C.

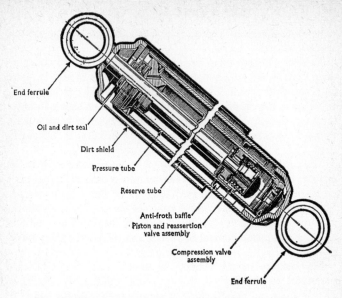

End ferrule

Oil and dirt seal

Dirt shield

Pressure tube

Reserve tube

Anti-froth baffle
Piston and reassertion
valve assembly

Compression valve
assembly

End ferrule

Fig. 246. The Woodhead Monroe telescopic shock absorber.

Fig. 247. The Morris telescopic shock absorber,
which also acts as an anti-roll device.

cars, at the rear ends, so as to act both as shock absorber and anti-roll device.

Testing Hydraulic Dampers. If, with the springs in good condition, their rear shackles free and any metal bearings lubricated the springing appears to be harsh or 'too soft', the hydraulic dampers should be first inspected for correct oil level and replenished if necessary. Should this make no difference remove the dampers from the chassis and hold them in a vice working the lever arm up and down through complete strokes. If in good order a definite resistance to motion should be felt all the time. An erratic movement or an absence of resistance indicates that the damper is faulty. In the latter case the cause may be that of

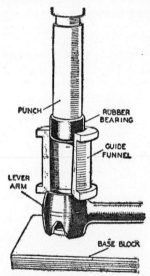

Fig. 248. Inserting new rubber bush in
shock absorber connecting link.

air in the fluid. Too much resistance indicates a broken internal part or a *seized piston*. In this case the damper should be either dismantled for inspection and repair or if too badly damaged, replaced by a new one. In all cases the *brand of fluid* recommended by the manufacturers *should always be used*, since the required damping qualities are adjusted to the particular grade of fluid.

In the instance of telescopic dampers, the fluid must be at the correct level. Usually no adjustment is provided for the motor mechanic. In this case the damper may either, if not of the sealed type, be dismantled for inspection and repair or, if badly damaged, replaced by a new one.

Fitting New Rubber Bushes. Before fitting new bushes, the holes in the connecting link (Fig. 248) should be cleaned free of dirt and grease. To insert the new bush a guide funnel is placed centrally over the hole in the link and pressure applied to the bush with a press ram or punch, after dipping the bush in *soapy water*. A quick action should be used to force the bush through the tapered guide into the boss.

CHAPTER 11

THE FRONT AXLE AND STEERING

IN view of its importance, from the viewpoint of comfort and ease in driving the car, the maintenance and adjustment of the front axle and steering system should clearly be understood and carried out.

In the case of earlier cars fitted with rigid front axles and semi-elliptic springs the front axle itself demands little attention. It is

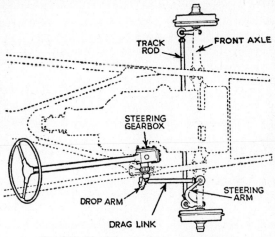

Fig. 249. Fixed front axle steering system.

simply the transverse member carrying the wheel stub axles and steering pivots; it also anchors the centre portions of the (semi-elliptic) springs. Beyond checking the security of the spring clip nuts, and the fit of the steering pivot pins, there is nothing of consequence to attend to.

Regarding the steering system itself, the various important points are illustrated and annotated in Fig. 249.

Steering System Maintenance. Commencing from the steering wheel end, it is necessary to give lubrication attention regularly to the steering column head bearing, the controls, steering gearbox, drop arm, steering pivot pins and steering cross rod bearings as outlined in Chapter 2.

These bearings – in particular those of the drop arm (Fig. 249), cross tie and steering pivots – should be protected against the ingress of water and dirt; wherever possible flexible leather covers packed inside with grease, should be attached to the steering rod joints.

Go over the nuts of the steering column, its dashboard bracket, the steering box, and pivot pins, occasionally, and tighten if necessary.

Recent Steering Systems. The independent front suspension systems have now entirely replaced the rigid front axle type shown in Fig. 249. The former systems have more bearings to be lubricated, but by the use of rubber-bushed wishbone arm bearings, only the king-pin bearings usually need hand lubrication. However, the latest tendency is to use special nylon and metal combination bearings so that, after greasing and sealing with special rubber covers, the bearings are practically sealed for life. Further information on these bearings is given elsewhere in this volume.

Taking Up Steering Play. The amount of slackness in the steering system can best be gauged by testing the amount of free movement of the steering wheel, the road wheels being on the ground – not jacked up. If this exceeds about $\frac{3}{4}$ inch on the rim, the source of the slackness should be traced, and if possible, most of the play eliminated. In this connection it is *inadvisable to have no steering play*, otherwise greater care must be exercised when driving. Most drivers prefer a little freedom, namely, about $\frac{3}{8}$ inch on the steering wheel rim.

The usual causes of steering slackness are wear in the *steering worm (or cam), wear of the worm wheel teeth, wear on the pins and in the bearings of the steering mechanism, wear on the king pins and in their bushes, and, finally, wear in the front wheel bearings.*

Worm and Wheel Steering Gear. The most serious item of wear is generally the steering worm, for a small amount of wear in the teeth gives a relatively large amount of play at the steering wheel.

In some modern cars, provision is made for eliminating this trouble by turning the worm wheel around a quarter of a revolution, so that a fresh set of teeth come into action. The steering drop arm must be detached from the worm shaft, and replaced after the new position of the worm wheel has been fixed.

Another source of steering slackness is that of *end play* in the steering worm, due to wear in its axial thrust bearings. Some designs of steering gearboxes make provision, usually in the form of an axial adjusting screw, to take up this slackness; the security nut should be locked after making this adjustment; in some cases *shims, or liners,* are provided for taking up end play of the steering worm.

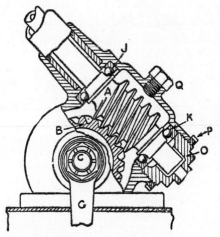

Fig. 250. Worm and wheel steering gearbox (side section).

A typical worm and worm wheel steering gearbox is illustrated in side and front sectional views in Figs. 250 and 251. The worm *A*, of hardened steel, engaged with the phosphor bronze worm wheel *B* keyed to the worm wheel shaft *C* which is carried in two bearing bushes *D* and *E* (Fig. 251) which can be readily removed and replaced when worn. The worm at the end of the steering column shaft is carried in cup-type ball bearings $\mathcal{J}$ and K engaging with corresponding cone bearings on the worm shaft. In some designs adjustable taper roller bearings are employed instead of the type illustrated. End play in the worm is taken up by means of an adjusting screw O, which after adjustment is locked in position by means of the locknut P. The supporting spigot is shown near O. Wear in the worm wheel is usually corrected for by removing the wheel from its shaft by unscrewing the castle nut M and its washer and driving the worm off the tapered end of the shaft. Usually, four keyways are provided in the worm wheel so that when wear occurs the latter can be moved round on the shaft to the next 90° position so that a new unworn portion of the worm

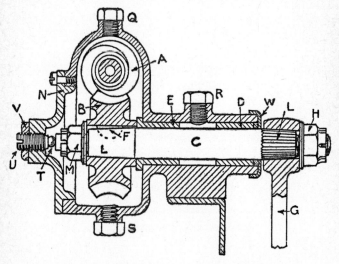

Fig. 251. Worm and wheel steering gearbox (front section).

wheel is thus brought into action. The other end of the worm-wheel shaft is either squared or castellated, as at L, and the drop arm G has similar squares or flutes; it is secured by the castle nut H.

End play in the worm-wheel shaft is taken up by the adjusting screw U which has a ball thrust I and a lock nut V. The steering gearbox casing has a removable cover N to provide access to the worm wheel. To prevent oil leakage from the casing a felt washer is inserted at the end of bearing D, and is held in position by a spun metal cover W made a press fit on the end of the casing. For lubrication purposes two hexagon plugs Q and R are provided; these must be removed in order to insert the lubricant – which is usually engine oil; a drain plug is provided at S, for periodical removal of the oil, prior to replenishment of the lubricant.

In some designs of worm and worm wheel steering the wheel can be brought closer to the worm by rotating an eccentric bush – taking the place of the two bushes D and E.

Cam Steering Gears. Each design of steering gearbox requires its own special method of adjustment and to illustrate one of these, the example of the Bishop cam steering will be considered. (Fig. 252.)

In this design the cam takes the form of a worm of special shape, attached to the steering column. A conical roller on the rocker arm engages with the space between the teeth or threads of the worm and, as the latter is rotated by the steering wheel, the roller moves in an arc, causing the rocker shaft (11), Fig. 252, to turn through the same angle. The steering drop arm is attached to the rocker shaft by a splined joint and moves solidly with it through the same angle as the rocker. The steering gear has a variable ratio from 13 to 1 in the straight ahead position, to 16 to 1 at full lock.

Maintenance. Apart from periodical replenishment of the gearbox with oil (grease should, on no account, be used) all that is required during normal service is to check the steering box clamping bolt for tightness.

Periodic Check for Wear. After much service the front axle should be jacked up and all steering joints tested by hand for wear. The steering gearbox should be checked, independently, for (a) Backlash and (b) Endplay. Endplay at the steering column is due to clearance between the worm and roller.

Backlash can be taken up by unscrewing the locknut of the adjusting screw (14) on the side cover (12) and turning the screw clockwise, afterwards locking it with the nut. After each adjustment the backlash should be checked at the drop arm. When correctly adjusted, a high spot will be noticed as a slight drag, as the arm passes the central position and no backlash can be felt.

End play is taken up by unscrewing the four setscrews on the end cover (23), placing an oil tray underneath to catch the oil from the gearbox. Shims (20) will be found between the end

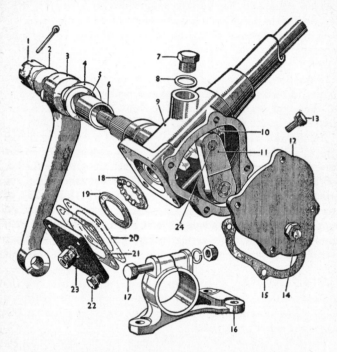

Fig. 252. Exploded view of Austin Bishop steering gearbox.
1 shaft nut and split pin. 2 washer. 3 steering arm. 4 retaining disc. 5 cork washer. 6 bush for rocker shaft. 7 oil plug. 8 washer. 9 steering gearbox casing. 10 steering column and worm-cam. 11 rocker shaft. 12 side cover. 13 set-screw. 14 thrust adjustment screw. 15 washer. 16 steering gearbox bracket. 17 clamping bolt. 18 ball and cage. 19 ball cup for cam bearing. 20 shim. 21 joint washer. 22 set-screw. 23 bottom end cover. 24 roller or peg.

cover and the flange on the gearbox. One or more of these must be removed in order to take up the end play.

The ball bearings should be examined for wear, after long service intervals, as any play in these cannot be taken up by the method outlined. Similarly, if the worm-cam is worn appreciably it may require replacement; in this case the rocker shaft peg also must be replaced.

The Marles Steering Gearbox. In this design a kind of hour-glass worm cam engages with a tooth-section roller, mounted on ball bearings. This roller is located at the end of the rocker arm, as shown in Fig. 253.

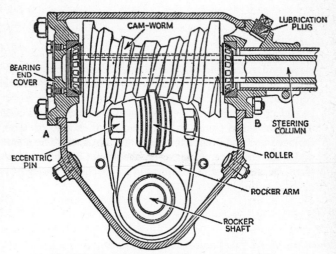

Fig. 253. The Marles 'hour-glass' steering gearbox.

Adjustment for wear is provided for, there being two separate operations, as follows: (1) Engagement between the roller and worm. (2) Adjustment of the bearings between which the worm revolves.

(1) Provision for altering the depth of mesh of the roller in the worm is made by making the pin on which the roller revolves, eccentric in the middle part, relatively to the two end parts

which are fitted to the rocker shaft. Locknuts are provided so that the pin can be locked after it has been rotated to take up wear effects. When correctly adjusted there should be a slight amount of backlash at the ends of the drop arm travel but none in the centre or 'straight ahead' position. If the roller is adjusted too tightly the steering will, of course, also be tight.

(2) In one model, the neck of steering gearbox is split and is held together by a bolt and nut. The column support is screwed into this neck. End play of the worm-cam member can be taken up by slackening the clamping bolt and rotating the column support in a clockwise direction, until the clearance is taken up. The second bolt, i.e. the one between the split member clamping bolt and the steering wheel should not be interfered with.

In a later model Marles steering gearbox, shims are provided under the bottom cover A and column support B for taking up any end play in the steering column. To effect this adjustment the column support must be withdrawn; it can be slid up the column tube after undoing the clamping bolt. This allows the shims to be removed, then one or more removed and the proper thickness thus obtained. The shims under the end cover B, however, should not be altered since they are used, by the manufacturers, to centre the cam in relation to the rocker shaft.

When correctly adjusted the worm-cam should turn freely but without any end play.

Testing Steering Gear for Backlash. *To find out exactly where the play is,* disconnect the steering connecting rod at the drop arm, and endeavour to move the lower end of the latter in a fore and aft direction; any play found here is due to slackness in the steering gearbox mechanism. If the rest of the steering mechanism be tested, whilst the steering connecting rod is disconnected, play in the pins and their bearings can readily be located.

Stiffness in Steering System. If the steering of the car on the road appears to be stiff, before inspecting the steering mechanism first ascertain that (*a*) The tyres are inflated to their correct pressures. (*b*) The steering gearbox has sufficient lubricant. (*c*) All oil or grease nipples on the bearings of the steering system have been dealt with by the lubricant gun.

If steering stiffness still persists, jack up both front wheels clear of the ground and test by rotating the steering wheel to and fro. If stiffness is felt, first localize the testing to the steering gearbox by disconnecting the end of the draglink from the drop arm. If the steering wheel then turns freely this indicates that

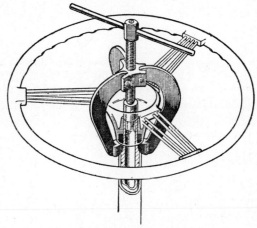

Fig. 254. Illustrating removal of steering wheel
from its column.

the trouble lies somewhere between the drop arm and the king pin bearings of the nearside wheel unit.

If, however, stiffness is found when the draglink is disconnected, this is due to the gearbox or the steering column in its housing and, in the former case may be due to lack of, or unsuitable lubricant, or wrong adjustment of the gear units. If the steering column is not free to rotate in its housing this is no doubt due to *lack of lubrication* – most probably at the upper or steering wheel end.

In general, if the steering gearbox has not previously been adjusted any stiffness in its operation will be found to be due to lack of lubrication of the gear units, rocker shaft in its bearing – usually of the plain type, or the steering column.

Removal of Steering Wheel. The usual method is to take off any attachments, e.g. the controls, and then remove the nut at the top of the steering column. A wheel puller, such as that shown in Fig. 254 is then applied and the screw rotated by the cross bar at the outer end, when the wheel will come away.

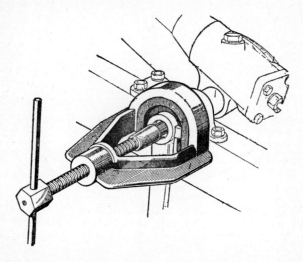

Fig. 255. Removing steering drop arm from gearbox rocker shaft.

Removal of Steering Drop Arm. The drop arm is spline-fitted to the rocker shaft of the gearbox. It can be removed, after taking off the castle nut (1), Fig. 252, with an extractor tool of the type shown. A note should be made of the position of the drop arm on the splined end of the rocker shaft; usually this is marked on the arm and rocker shaft, to ensure correct replacement. If it is not, then the two parts should be marked with centre punch dots or chisel marks.

King Pin Wear Effects. After an appreciable period in service, and more particularly if the lubrication of the king-pin bearings has been neglected, wear effects develop between the king pin and its bronze bushings in the front axle ends. One result of this wear is to allow the wheels to rock sideways so that the car cannot be steering dead ahead – more especially at the higher road speeds – without constant correction on the steering wheel.

Wear in the king-pin bushes, in either the rigid front axle or the independent front suspension systems, may be detected by jacking up the front wheels and applying pressure alternately in the directions of the arrows A and B (Fig. 256); if there is any play between the king pin and its bearings this is shown by movement

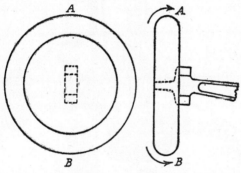

Fig. 256. Testing for king pin wear effects.

at A and B. If, however, there is any play in the wheel bearings this will give a false indication, since this amount of wheel movement will be added to the king pin play; wear in the wheel bearings should therefore be taken up before applying the test in question.

The king pin (Fig. 257) is locked in the hole in the axle end by means of a cotter pin, A; this must be pressed or driven out before the king pin itself can be forced out. It is advisable to remove the wheel from its hub before doing this, in order to reduce the over-hang weight on the stub axle member to a minimum. The bushes in the stub axle member can then be forced out in a machine press or by a screw and nut method. The king pin should then be examined and checked with a micrometer for wear, and if not found to be worn appreciably, new replacement king-pin bushes

can be pressed into the stub axle holes and the king pin used
again. The lubrication grooves and holes must be reproduced in
the new bushes in a similar manner and position to those of the old
ones. It is seldom, however, that ball or roller thrust bearings,
when fitted, need replacement.

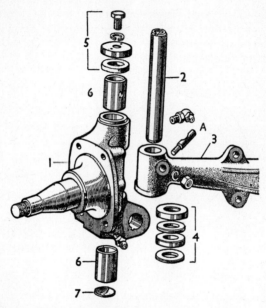

Fig. 257. Showing components of rigid front axle wheel unit.
1 stub or swivel axle. 2 king pin. 3 front axle. 4 lower thrust assembly.
5 upper set-screw and felt washer assembly. 6 king-pin bushes. 7
welch plug. A cotter pin.

In some cases the existing king-pin bushes can be reamed out a
little to true the holes and an oversize king pin fitted. This method
is often used for mass produced cars.

If, however, both the king pin and the bushes are found to be
worn both should be replaced and in case the bushes contract a
little in the pressing-in process it will usually be necessary to
ream the hole to suit the king-pin.

Fig. 257 illustrates a typical front axle, in the dismantled condition, the various parts being numbered and described below.

Referring to the king pin (2) this is locked in the front axle boss by the grooved cotter screwed pin at *A*. The upper and lower bushes that are pressed into the swivel or stub axle (1) are shown at (6). The lower bush is locked into its stub axle hole by a disc which is expanded into a groove in the hole.

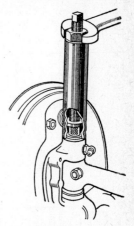

The method of extracting the king pin with the aid of a screw press type of tool is illustrated in Fig. 258. It is, of course, necessary to slacken the nut on the cotter *A* and to lightly tap same to release the locking pressure on the king pin. The screw of the extractor fits into the screwed hole left when the screw shown at (5) has been removed.

Fig. 258. Removing the king pin.

Independent Front Wheel Steering. The steering mechanism used in cars having independent front wheel springing is of different design to that for solid front axles, in being, as a rule simpler and allowing more vertical springing movement without affecting the steering action. Of the alternative steering systems the revived rack-and-pinion one is now used on some of the lighter cars, but it is not considered suitable for large cars or commercial vehicles.

Fig. 259 shows the Citroën front drive steering gear and maintenance details. It will be observed that the rack when moved sideways causes the spherical bearing units of the nearside and offside track-rods to move with it, thus actuating the steering arms of the stub axles. This type of steering gearbox is packed with lubricant before it leaves the manufacturers and it should need no further attention until the car has run about 12,000 miles. No adjustment of the gearbox should be necessary, but if tapered roller bearings are fitted to the lower end of the steering column rod any end wear can usually be taken up by means of shims on

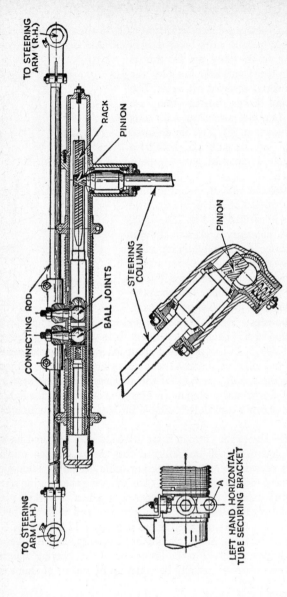

TO STEERING ARM (R.H.)

RACK

PINION

STEERING COLUMN

CONNECTING ROD

BALL JOINTS

TO STEERING ARM (L.H.)

PINION

LEFT HAND HORIZONTAL TUBE SECURING BRACKET

A

Fig. 259. The Citroën rack-and-pinion steering system.

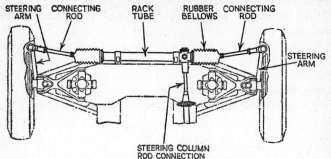

STEERING   CONNECTING   RACK   RUBBER   CONNECTING
ARM   ROD   TUBE   BELLOWS   ROD

STEERING
ARM

STEERING COLUMN
ROD CONNECTION

Fig. 260. Plan view of rack-and-pinion steering system.

the cover. After the car has completed its running-in period the
front axle should be raised on jacks and the set bolts A (Fig. 259)
at the bottom of the two split securing brackets for the horizontal
steering tube, loosened; these brackets are bolted to the underside of the body. The steering should then be worked to the full
extent of its travel in each direction; afterwards the two set bolts
must be re-locked. This will ensure that all parts of the steering
gear settle down to their best working positions.

Vauxhall Rack-and-Pinion Steering. The Vauxhall Viva car
uses two alternative steering gears, namely, the Burman and the
Cam, the latter type being shown in Fig. 261.

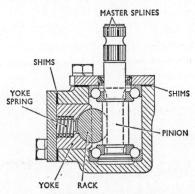

MASTER SPLINES

SHIMS

SHIMS

YOKE
SPRING

PINION

YOKE   RACK

Fig. 261. The Vauxhall Viva rack-and-pinion gearbox.

M

The complete rack-and-pinion unit, with its transverse ball-type end connections, part of which is shown in Fig. 262, is mounted on rubber support houses on the front axle cross member. The rack is supported at one end of the housing by a spring-loaded adjustable yoke which keeps the rack and pinion in engagement; at the other end the rack has a bush-type bearing. Tie rods are connected at each end of the rack by adjustable ball

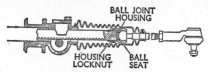

Fig. 262 Showing the rack-and-pinion and R.H. connecting rod.

joints. The helical-toothed pinion runs in ball-bearings, and shims – which are shown in Fig. 261 – are used for adjusting the bearing pre-load. Adjustment shims are installed under the yoke cover plate; these are used to take up any wear between the rack and its pinion.

The gearing units are sealed by rubber boots and charged with oil during assembly. The ball joints at the ends of the tie rods are lubricated and sealed for long period use.

Steering Transfer Box. In the later systems there is another fixed unit known as the *steering transfer box*. The arrangement of the steering mechanism is shown, schematically, in Fig. 263.

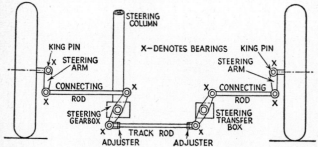

Fig. 263. The Morris steering system (shown diagrammatically).

It will be observed that the gearbox – which is of the Bishop type – has a double-ended lever attached to its rocker shaft. A similar lever is attached to the spindle or shaft of the transfer box; the latter provides a fixed bearing for this shaft. The front ends of the double-ended levers are connected by a track rod, with ball-socket joints at the ends. The other end of the steering gearbox rocker shaft lever is connected by a hinged tie- or connecting-rod to the offside stub axle arm, whilst the rear end of the transfer shaft lever is connected in a similar manner to the nearside stub axle arm. All of the rod end joints are of the ball-and-socket types.

A Typical Modern Steering System. Fig. 264 shows the steering system of the new Hillman Minx cars, with the various components described below.

The following members are mounted rigidly on the car frame: the upper single wishbone unit (12), the idler lever bearing (4) and the lower steering gearbox (17).

Movement of the steering wheel for a right-hand turn, causes the gearbox drop arm to pull the R.H. short outer track-rod (1) to the left so that the R.H. stub axle steering arm (14) – which is attached to the wheel axle member – is moved clockwise, thus bringing the axle (A) downwards and with it the wheel.

At the same time the gearbox drop-arm unit moves the arm (1) to the left, thus pulling the centre track-rod to the right: also the lower end of the idler arm (4). This, in turn, moves the shorter outer track-rod (5) to the left so that the stub axle steering arm (6) moves the axle (B) upwards to give the right-hand steering action to the road wheel.

Maintenance. In the case of the steering system shown in Fig. 264 it is necessary to lubricate all of the steering mechanism bearings, the king pins, idler lever bearings every 1,000 miles. The steering gearbox should be topped up every 3,000 miles with Shell Spirax 90 E.P. lubricant.

Cars introduced during the past ten years until about 1965 were provided with separate grease or oil nipples to the front suspension and steering mechanisms, a typical example being the Austin A.55 (Mk. 11) and A.60 cars which were provided with grease nipples for the front suspension outer wishbone arm

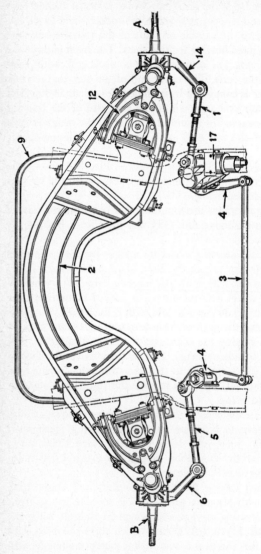

Fig. 264. Complete steering system of the Hillman.

1 outer track-rod adjuster. 2 cross member. 3 centre track-rod. 4 idler levers (fixed bearings). 5 outer track-rod. 6 and 14 steering arms. 9 anti-roll bar. 12 upper suspension link. 17 steering gearbox. A and B stub axles.

bearings, the king pins, steering track-rod and drag link ball joints and also one nipple for the rear spring shackle pins, making about 14 greasing points in all. Fig. 265 shows the front suspension and steering greasing points.

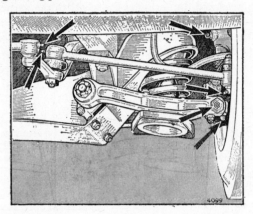

Fig. 265. Lubricating points of A.55, A.60 and certain other Model B.M.C. cars.

Subsequent British cars have progressively reduced the number of such greasing points in the front suspension and steering mechanisms until, at the time of writing, such cars as the Vauxhall models, the Hillman Imp, and most other 1966 cars have no greasing points, needing only to examine and if necessary replace the various bearing units after about 30,000 miles. (See Fig. 236.)

Some cars, however, e.g. the Morris Minor, have only two king-pin bearing nipples on the inside of each front wheel which require greasing every 3,000 miles. There is also one nipple at the end of each tie-rod.

The B.M.C. Minicars have six steering and front suspension grease nipples, namely two for the upper and lower king pins, and one for each side of the upper support arm, inner pivot. There is also a grease nipple on each rear radius suspension arm bearing. These points are greased every 3,000 miles.

The 1100 models have only two nipples for the king-pin bearings, which should be lubricated every 3,000 miles.

Front Wheel Alignment. If the front wheels were arranged with their central planes vertical, they would overhang their supports and cause severe drag on the steering. To avoid this, it is arranged for the centre of the tyre to be located under the king-pin axis, produced, by inclining the wheel to the vertical plane through the king-pin axis. The inclination of the central wheel plane to the vertical is termed the *Wheel Camber Angle*. (Fig. 266.)

In some cases, more particularly where the camber angle would

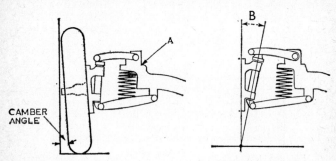

Fig. 266. The camber angle   Fig. 267. The king-pin angle b
(Austin).   (Austin).

be excessive it is arranged to incline the kin pin, so as to reduce the camber angle. The inclination of the king-pin axis to the vertical is termed the *King-pin Angle;* an examination of most cars will reveal this inclination of the ends of the front axle.

In the case of rigid front axle cars, the *camber angle* is usually about $\frac{1}{2}°$ to $1\frac{1}{2}°$, but it may exceed $2°$ in certain cases.

The *King-pin angle* is generally about $5°$ to $8°$, but may vary to $10°$ in special examples (Fig. 267.)

Apart from the king-pin inclination mentioned it is also inclined, as viewed from the side of the wheel in order to bring the point of contact of the wheel with the ground *behind* the point where the extension of the king-pin axis meets the ground. This gives the well-known effect of the castors that are fitted to the legs of furniture. Its object in motor vehicles is to assist the front wheel to straighten after making a turn.

In practice the *Castor Angle*, i.e. the angle made by the axis of the king pin with the vertical, when the car is on level ground, is usually about 2° to 4° but may be rather more, or less, in special circumstances. Apart from the wheel and king-pin inclinations mentioned the two front wheels are usually inclined towards one another at the front. This is termed wheel *Toe-in*. It is almost invariably given to rigid front axle cars and usually amounts to about $\frac{1}{8}$ to $\frac{3}{8}$ inches according to the size of wheel. In the case of independently sprung front wheels, however, there is often a 'positive' toe-in, i.e. a 'toe-out' or the wheels are kept parallel, as in certain B.M.C. cars.

It is now proposed to deal with these alignment factors in more detail.

Wheel Camber. After being in service for some time there is a possibility of the camber of the wheels changing. If it becomes greater, heavy tyre wear, cupping, etc., will result; if it decreases, there will be a greater drag on the steering.

Excessive camber can be identified by the fact that the outside of the tyre becomes worn deeply and smoothly whilst the centre of the tyre is but little affected.

The camber angle can be checked by arranging for the car to be on *a level concrete floor* and using a sufficiently large hardwood or metal carpenter's square, as shown in Fig. 269. The distances of the wheel rim at D and E should be measured accurately. If the difference between them is X inches and the wheel rim diameter is d inches then the camber angle can be estimated from the following relation:

$$\text{sine (camber angle)} = X/\text{d}$$

Checking the Camber Angle. If, after the car has been in an accident, or the front wheels have hit an obstacle very hard or if the tyres show signs of excessive side wear, the camber angle should be checked against the manufacturer's figure.

It is possible in most cars with independent front suspension to correct the camber, by taking out or adding thin metal plates (shims) between the wishbone unit mount and its attachment to the car frame, as shown at (A) in Fig. 266. An examination of the suspension will show just where to adjust the camber angle.

Fig. 268 shows, in plan view, part of the Hillman Minx front suspension, the shims being located at X between the upper link

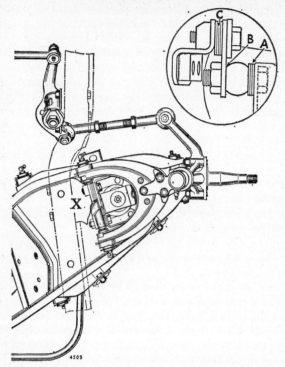

Fig. 268. Adjusting camber angle on Hillman Minx cars.

attachments and the frame cross-member. The road wheel should first be removed and then the nuts retaining the upper fulcrum to the cross-member slackened. The bolts between the brackets should next be slackened to permit selection of the shims.

To increase the camber angle move the required number of shims from position A to position B.

To decrease the camber angle remove the proper number of shims from C and add a similar number of shims to position A, or if the shims are found in position B remove from B and insert in position A. After making the adjustment tighten the nuts on their bolts securely.

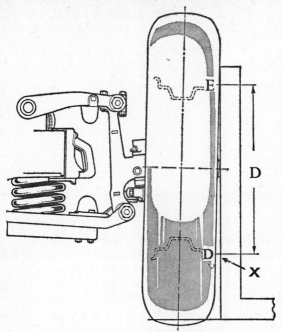

Fig. 269. Checking the camber angle.

For routine checking purposes use is made in motor garages of special wheel alignment apparatus, typical examples being the Dunlop wheel camber, castor and king-pin gauge (Fig. 270), A. V. Churchill wheel alignment gauge, Chass-O-Meter and the Bradbury gauge. The manufacturers issue full instructions for these devices, which are time-saving and accurate in use. The method of measuring camber, shown in Fig. 270, is to hold the gauge with the ends of the single and double arms against the wheel rim, with the spirit level bubbles central, when the camber angle can be read off the appropriate scale.

Mention should also be made of *optical alignment gauges* for measuring 'toe-in' and 'toe-out'. The Dunlop optical gauge is an example of this type, but is essentially for general garage applications covering small cars to large commercial vehicles.

Wheel 'Toe-in'. The exact amount of inward slant towards the front of the car, or *toe-in* of the wheels depends upon the

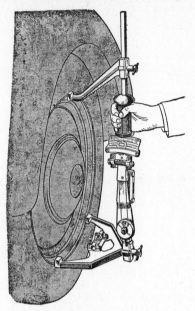

Fig. 270. The Dunlop front wheel
alignment gauge.

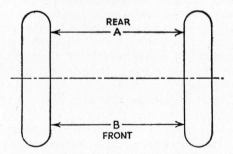

Fig. 271. Illustrating 'Toe-in'. The distance
B should be less than *A* at axle height.

design of the steering pivots, stub axles and wheels. The manufacturers generally supply information on this point by stating the distances (measured at axle height) between the front and rear of the two front wheel tyres. On the average, for medium types of cars, there is a difference of $\frac{1}{4}$ inch to $\frac{3}{8}$ inch between the front and rear, *i.e.* as shown in Fig. 271, the distance B is less than A, by this amount.

Before attempting to measure camber, castor or toe-in, *it is important* to check that there is no slackness in the front wheel bearings or steering mechanism, including the king-pin bearings; otherwise, inaccurate and often misleading results will be obtained.

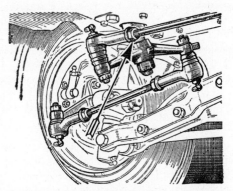

Fig. 272. Showing track-rod place of adjustment
on Morris Oxford car.

The tyre pressures should be at their correct values also. Further, it should be noted that all *measurements should be made from the wheel rims* and not the tyres, except where stated.

Usually, the track rod is screwed with left- and right-handed threads at its end connections. (See also Fig. 272). The rod is locked in its adjusted position with locknuts. When making an adjustment of 'toe-in', the front of the car should be jacked up, the locknuts slackened and the track-rod turned in the appropriate direction, afterwards checking the 'toe-in' and when correct, locking the nuts.

To facilitate quick measurements of the front and back distances between the wheels at axle level adjustable trammels of the types illustrated at (A) and (B) in Fig. 273 can be employed with advantage.

The device shown at (A) consists of two round steel bars with pointed ends at X and Y, bent as shown at A and B. The left-hand end of (A) has a piece of steel riveted to it to form a bearing for the plain part of the other bar. The end C of the latter has a

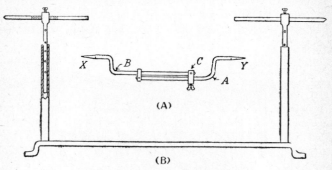

Fig. 273. Front wheel trammels.

metal block and clamping screw to secure the two bars in any desired position. If set to the rear wheel distance it can be transferred to the front and the difference measured with a short rule.

The wheel alignment device shown at (B) is rather more elaborate and is intended for garage use. It is adjustable in height and for width of the trammel points and can be used when the wheels are jacked up.

For routine garage checking purposes special graduated turntables (Fig. 274) are often used to measure 'toe-in'. These turntables, mounted on large ball bearings are let into the floor. The front wheels are located on a pair of turntables and the scales show the degrees of movement to the left and right of the amount of 'toe-in' or 'toe-out' on ahead, right and left turns; the steering wheel is used in the latter tests.

Alignment of Front and Rear Wheels. If the car has been in an accident, or has hit the road kerb severely, it is advisable

Fig. 274. The Churchill floor turntable for measuring 'toe-in' or 'toe-out'.

to check the alignment of both front and rear wheels, for the frame may have been distorted or the front axle displaced. In one method of checking the alignment, the front and rear wheels on one side are placed parallel as tested with a stretched cord, or the edge of a straight board. Then measure the distance between the other front tyre *side* and another cord stretched so as to touch both sides of the rear wheel tyre and the rear side of the front tyre. The steering wheel should be turned so that the two left wheels are parallel. If the distance between the outer front tyre and the cord, or straight-edge, corresponds to that given by the correct 'toe-in', the alignment of the front and rear wheels is correct.

Wheel Castor. *The amount of castor* of the front wheels is another important item when checking the alignment of these wheels. The king pin, as viewed from the side of car, is usually tilted forward at the bottom, the inclination of the axis of this pin to the vertical being the *angle of castor* as mentioned earlier. This angle should be measured with the normally loaded car arranged on a horizontal surface with the tyres correctly inflated (Fig. 275).

If the angle of castor is too great, the steering will become difficult and steering wobble may result; there will be a tendency for the car to drive into the gutter on a crowned road.

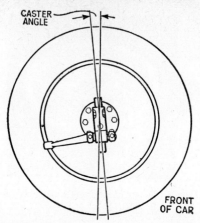

Fig. 275. The castor or caster angle.

The angle of castor of earlier fixed front axle cars may be checked by jacking up the frame of the car, removing the wheels and king pins and fitting long rods in the place of the latter. The front axle must be kept horizontal during the tests. The inclination of each rod to the vertical, as given by a plumb-bob line, can then be checked by means of a template previously marked out in degrees (Fig. 276).

For routine checking purposes it is advisable to employ one of the combination wheel alignment devices mentioned previously, as the castor angle can readily be measured and with greater accuracy than make-shift methods.

Wheel Tramp. This is the name given to excessive vertical movement of the front wheels which often occurs in older cars or those that have seen long service, or have been neglected.

The principal causes include unbalanced wheels, excessive tyre pressure or loose track-rods. These and other causes and remedies are summarized at the end of this chapter.

Wheel Shimmy. With the earlier fixed front axle cars this trouble was prone to occur after much service on the roads. It was usually due to faults in the steering mechanism, shock absorbers or the wheels and tyres.

This trouble consists of oscillations of the front wheels about

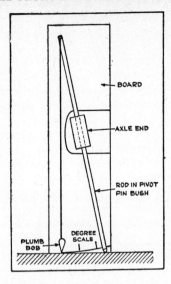

Fig. 276. Method of checking wheel
castor.

the king-pin or stub-axle joints: more particularly when ball
joints are used. These oscillations are usually uncontrollable by
the steering wheel and often originate when the wheel strikes a
road bump or pot-hole. It may become more serious at resonance
frequency of the system.

The causes include worn steering mechanism joints, unbalanced
wheels and tyres, high tyre pressures, faulty shock absorbers, etc.
These causes and their remedies are summarized at the end of this
chapter.

It may be mentioned that in some instances, more especially
with solid front axle cars, if the track-rods were too small in
diameter they were liable to vibrate sideways and thus to cause
corresponding movements on the wheels.

Notes on the Steering System

(1) When moving the car slowly in the garage, get someone to
push on the front wheels whilst you turn the steering wheel.

Never attempt to work the steering wheel whilst the car is stationary, or you may cause undue wear in the steering gearbox or bend the track-rod.

(2) Only a small amount of forward (or backward) way on the car is sufficient for operating the steering wheel.

(3) Keep the front tyres inflated to the maximum pressure the tyre manufacturers recommend. Under-inflated tyres will cause heavy steering.

(4) Never drive the car too close to the kerb; you may put your wheels out of alignment.

(5) See that the front brakes are correctly adjusted and thus put no drag on the steering.

(6) Make all adjustments to the steering mechanism with the front wheels jacked up. You can check the steering system for ease of operation in this manner and trace the cause of any stiffness.

(7) In cases of steering stiffness traceable to the swivel pin bearings this may be due to the lubricant not reaching the thrust bearing surfaces. In this case jack the wheels up and apply the lubricant, working the steering wheel to and fro. The lubricant will then find its way to the thrust surfaces since the weight of the car will be taken off these.

Steering Troubles, Causes and Remedies. The following is a useful summary of much of the information given in this chapter; it is useful for quick diagnosis of steering troubles

STEERING STIFF IN OPERATION

Cause	Remedy
Tyre pressures low.	Inflate to proper value.
Lack of lubrication, more especially on thrust bearings of king pins.	Lubricate all round, including the steering column.
Steering gearbox adjusted too tightly.	Re-adjust for free movement.
Steering column binding in its top bearing.	Re-adjust to maker's instructions.

STEERING TOO SLACK

Cause	Remedy
Steering mechanism bearings worn, e.g. drop arm, steering arm and track-rod bearings.	Adjust or renew, as necessary.

Cause	Remedy
Steering gearbox units worn.	Re-adjust to maker's instructions.
Drop arm loose on rocker shaft.	Tighten nut and check lock washer.
Steering top bearing wrongly adjusted.	Re-adjust.
Wear in front-wheel bearings.	Re-adjust.
King-pin bearings worn.	Renew.

STEERING TENDS TO WANDER

Cause	Remedy
Incorrect front or rear tyre pressures.	Inflate to correct values.
Toe-in (or toe-out) incorrect.	Check and re-adjust.
King-pin bearings worn.	Renew.
Loose wheel bearings.	Inspect and adjust.
Road wheels loose on their hubs.	Tighten wheel nuts.
Steering mechanism joints worn.	Renew or re-adjust.
Castor or camber different for each front wheel.	Check and adjust.
Track-rod ends loose.	Tighten up.
Excessive wear in steering gearbox.	Take up wear or replace gearbox.
Damaged suspension unit on one side.	
Bad unbalance of one road wheel.	Re-balance with balancing machine.
One front brake not fully clear of disc or drum.	Check and re-adjust brake shoes.

EXCESSIVE TYRE WEAR

Cause	Remedy
Incorrect wheel alignment.	Check and reset 'toe-in'.
Incorrect tyre pressures.	Inflate to correct values.
Excessive wheel camber.	Check and re-set.
Loose wheel hub bearings.	Adjust.

WHEEL SHIMMY

Cause	Remedy
Worn pins or bushes in steering linkage.	Renew or re-adjust bearing.
Worn ball joints.	Replace or take up wear.
Shock absorbers need topping-up or worn: or end bushes faulty.	Replace, re-adjust or top up.
Excessive tyre pressure.	Deflate to proper value.
Wheel hub bearings slack.	Re-adjust.
Track-rod screws end nuts loose.	Check toe-in and tighten up.
Wheel-tyre unit out of balance.	Have both rebalanced on suitable machine.

Official Steering System Tests

In connection with the compulsory periodic vehicle tests required
for vehicles three years old or more, it is laid down in the Road
Traffic Act of 1956 that all parts of the steering gear of all vehicles
must be maintained in good and efficient working order and be

properly adjusted. In order to ensure uniformity of treatment by the examiners in officially appointed garages the following minimum standards of practical tests are required for three- and four-wheeled vehicles:

(1) Track-rod, steering-arm and drag-link joints should not be excessively worn; all securing nuts and split-pins should be in position.

(2) The steering box should be securely attached.

In addition there should be:

(3) No excessive wear in king-pins and bushes.

(4) No excessive rock in the front-wheel hub bearings.

(5) No excessive play or slackness, or restriction of movement overall in the system as indicated by free movement at the steering wheel.

(6) No other visible defect on the vehicle likely to affect the steering adversely.

CHAPTER 12

THE CARE OF THE WHEELS AND TYRES

The Road Wheels. The modern car wheel is of the fully-detachable type, comprising a complete wheel which is bolted to the wheel hub by means of four, five or six studs fitted with bronze cap nuts having conical ends to bear against the recessed stud holes in the pressed steel wheel. In this case the whole wheel is detachable from the hub and a spare wheel is carried.

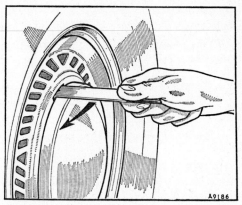

Fig. 277. Removing wheel dust cap with special tool (B.M.C. cars).

The alternative method is that of the wire-spoked wheel secured to the wheel hub by a large nut member. This type is used on sports and racing cars on account of its lightness and quickness of detaching from and assembling in position on the hub.

The usual wheel unit is provided with a large chromium plated steel dust cap. This is held by three projecting heads inside the hub and is sprung over these into the securing position. This cap is readily detached from the wheel with the aid of a screwdriver blade or special tyre tool (Fig. 277). When removed it exposes the wheel securing studs and nuts, as well as the axle greasing nipple. When replacing this cap take care not to dent it.

When removing or fixing a pressed-steel wheel the nuts should first be slackened a little in rotational order; some manufacturers recommend the opposite diagonal order, to reduce distortion effects.

Before replacing the wheel see that the hub is quite clean. The

Fig. 278. Tightening up the wheel nuts.

studs also should be clean, and it is a good plan to smear a little graphite grease on each and run the nut up and down before replacing the wheel. The wheel nuts should be tightened, fully, using the brace spanner provided. (Fig. 278.) Every 2,000 miles or so these nuts should be checked for tightness. Car squeaks or 'groans' can sometimes be traced to slack wheel security nuts.

If the rim sticks in the process of putting it on to its wheel it can usually be brought into position by means of a series of sharp kicks on the side of the tyre with the heel of the boot, the operator standing with his back to the wheel.

The Wire Wheel. The detachable wheel is one in which the hollow serrated hub of the wheel is forced on to or away from the fixed serrated male hub member on the axle by means of a large diameter nut. This type of light but very strong wheel is mostly used for sports and racing cars, since it has the additional advantage of being capable of rapid detachment and replacement, there being a single 'hammer-type' nut to operate for these purposes.

In the case of detachable wheels the fixed hubs should be kept clean. A light smear of grease is helpful in preventing sticking of the wheel and to keep out water; it will also be found beneficial in wheel changing.

Removing a Wire Wheel. The winged hub nuts used on modern sports cars, e.g., the B.M.C. models, are marked 'Left' and 'Right' to indicate which side of the car they are fitted. In the case of the L.H. wheel the hub nut should be knocked with a copper hammer in an anti-clockwise manner to unscrew, while the R.H. hub nut should be turned clockwise (Fig. 279).

Fig. 279. Method of removal of right hand wire spoked wheel (M.G.B. car).

The wheel should always be jacked up before using the hammer, or mallet and when replacing the wheel the hub nut must be hammered tightly home.

Wire Wheel Maintenance. It is advisable after taking delivery of a sports car to check the hub nuts for tightness at once and again after about 100 miles.

Before replacing a wheel the wheel hub serrations, cones and threads and also those of the axle should be wiped quite free from dirt and then coated lightly with grease, as used for the axle bearings.

Yearly Attention for Wire Wheels. Remove each wheel in turn and thoroughly clean the inside of the hubs, also the mating surfaces of the wheel axles.

Examine the wheel rim for dents and the spokes for any damage. If serious it is advisable to return the wheel to the manufacturers or a wheel specialist for rectification of the damage.

Any rusted parts of the wheel rim should be cleaned and repainted with a suitable protective paint.

The Front Axle Bearings. Earlier makes of cars were fitted with the cup-and-cone type of ball-bearings similar to those used on pedal cycles, in which there is a fixed ball race at one end and a screwed adjustable one at the other; similar type bearings were used until a few years ago on certain American cars. Their method of adjustment is similar to that illustrated and described later for tapered roller bearings.

Following the cup-and-cone bearings were the separate *deep-race* type of *journal ball-bearings,* designed to take a certain amount of end thrust. Fig. 280 shows the components of the Austin A.40 car front axle ball-bearing assembly, removed from the axle hub. (7). In this case the outer ball-bearing (5) is smaller in diameter than the inner bearing (8).

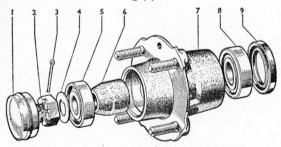

Fig. 280. Front axle components of A.40 car.
1 hub cap. 2 castellated nut. 3 split pin. 4 locating washer. 5 outer bearing. 6 distance piece. 7 hub. 8 inner bearing. 9 oil seal.

After long service these bearings should be tested for wear by the method illustrated in Fig. 282. If any positive movement of the wheel and tyre is observed the bearings – not being adjustable – must be replaced by new ones.

Taper Roller Front Bearings. In this type, the front axle unit is mounted upon a pair of taper roller bearings, as shown in Fig. 281, which are adjustable for wear. Such bearings will take appreciable side thrust in addition to the weight or radial load. The small ends of the rollers face inwards. The bearing outer or hub races are a press fit in their housings, while the inner or axle races are an easy push fit on the axle journals; this permits the cones to move on their seatings thus giving good load distribution all round the inner race.

Adjustments. When it is necessary to take up end or radial 'play' in this type of bearing the split pin on the castellated nut – which is exposed when the wheel hub cap is removed, is taken out and the nut screwed in against the key washer which abuts the inner race, until no wheel play can be felt. The split pin is replaced and the wheel given a final spin to check for both freedom of rotation and absence of wheel play on the axle.

The swivel pin of the steering swivel or stub axle is mounted on a T-type flat thrust bearing; when fitting the bearing, in order to avoid damage to the races, known as 'brinelling', a preload washer should be fitted above the top face of the axle boss; this washer should be 0·002 inch thicker than the gap in the unloaded condition.

Testing Front Bearings. When testing the front wheel bearings for play, jack up the wheel, hold the wheel at the top *A* and bottom *B* (Fig. 282) and endeavour to shake it about its horizontal diameter, i.e. towards and away from the engine. If, however, the wheel is held across its horizontal diameter *CD*, any end play found will be due to slackness in steering mechanism, In connection with the adjustment of the tapered roller type front wheel bearings, after slackening the lock-nut and disengaging the lock-washer, tighten the cone member until on testing the rotation of the wheel itself, a slight degree of binding is felt. Unslacken the cone member a little and lock the nut. Then test for freedom of rotation, for the act of tightening the lock-nut also

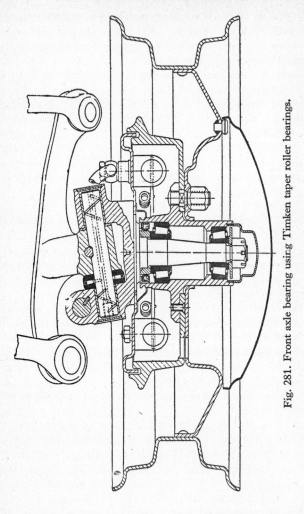

Fig. 281. Front axle bearing using Timken taper roller bearings.

tightens, slightly, the cone. The best final test with unbalanced type wheels is to place the tyre valve horizontal, when its weight should just rotate the wheel until the valve comes to the bottom.

When adjusting front wheel bearings, be sure to replace the split-pin in the locking-nut.

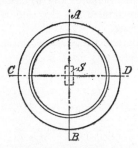

Fig. 282. Illustrating method of checking wear in front wheel bearings by rocking wheel about axis *A B*.

Lubrication of Front and Rear Axle Bearings. The front axle bearings of most cars manufactured before 1966 require lubrication additions about once every 5,000 to 6,000 miles.

Many of the later models are grease-packed for a period of about 30,000 miles, but they employ a special type of grease for this purpose.

Fig. 283 shows the New Hillman front hub after it has been dismantled for cleaning and re-greasing at a general overhaul.

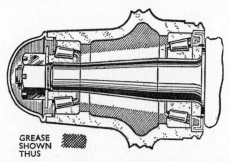

GREASE
SHOWN
THUS

Fig. 283. The front wheel hub, showing correct grease packing method (Hillman Minx).

When re-assembling the hub the taper roller clearance, to give correct running, should be 0·005 to 0·009 in. This is the proper end clearance – not the radial or journal clearance.

The grease recommended for this and the B.M.C. axles is Shell Retinax 'A' grease.

The B.M.C. more recent cars use a simple front-axle bearing greasing method. Referring to Fig. 284, after the wheel hub

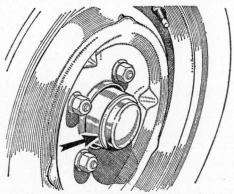

Fig. 284. Illustrating method of greasing B.M.C. front wheel bearings. The removable cap is shown by the arrow.

covers have been removed to expose the hub securing-nuts, it will be found that there is a steel cap over the end of the hub, as indicated by the arrow. This cap must be prised off with a screwdriver and after filling with grease tapped back over the hub with a piece of wood or a mallet; any excess of grease will then be forced out of a small hole in the centre of the cap.

Rear Wheel Hubs. The bearings of all cars of fairly recent date do not require any manual lubrication since they are lubricated automatically from the back axle casing lubricant supply.

Removing Front Wheel Hub. The method of withdrawing a front wheel hub is well illustrated in the case of the Austin car shown in Fig. 285, which shows the hub extractor in position. It will be noted that the boss of this tool screws on to the hub cap

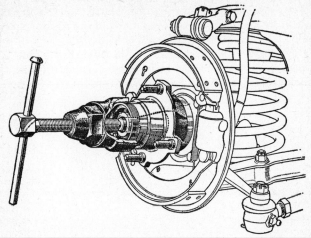

Fig. 285. Method of removing front wheel hub on Austin
car axle.

thread, whilst the pointed end of the screws engages with the
centre depression of the axle.

Tools for withdrawing wheel hubs operate upon the principle
of a locating bracket or member which is anchored to the hub
and a central fine thread screwing member abutting the axle end.
The locating bracket can be made with a flange having holes to
pass over the hub studs – on which the wheel fits – so that the
wheel nuts can secure the flanged portion of the fixed member,
as shown in Fig. 286 (B) or with split sides and clamping bolts
and nuts as at (A).

Fig. 287 illustrates a universal tool which can often be adapted
for wheel, as well as pulley withdrawal. The jaws are adjusted
by the cone nut member.

The Wheel Rims. It is important from the viewpoints of
road performance and tyre wear that the rims of the road wheels
should be free from any defects.

When a tyre has to be removed, before replacement the wheel
rim should be closely inspected for rusty patches, rim local distortion and signs of cracks – more particularly at welded surfaces.

Rusty rims should be carefully cleaned free of rust, with emery cloth or with one of the proprietory makes of rust remover and the rim then painted with a good brand of black paint.

Local indentations can often be hammered out and then smoothed off, but with the now almost universal tubeless tyre wheels it may not always be possible to ensure air-tight fitting;

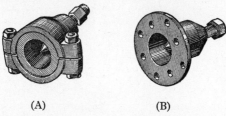

(A)   (B)

Fig. 286. Types of wheel hub extractors.
(A) front hub. (B) rear hub.

Fig. 287. Universal wheel hub extractor.

only a test with the tyre can show if the repaired rim is satisfactory.

Wheel Distortion. This may be due to the result of a crash or to striking a road kerb too hard. It can be detected by jacking up the suspected wheel and fixing up a scriber having an adjustment for the pointed end. Then check the wheel rim edge as the wheel is slowly rotated to see whether there is any side 'run-out'. If so this should not exceed $\frac{1}{16}$ in. Similarly, there should not be any radial 'run-out' exceeding the same amount (Fig. 288). Unless

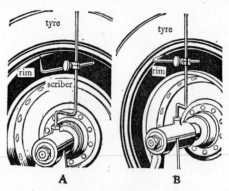

Fig. 288. Method of checking wheel rim distortion. (*A*) Radial distortion. (*B*) Lateral distortion.

the distortion comes within these limits the wheel should be replaced by a new one.

Wheel Cracks. These may develop around the edges of holes in the wheel where the fixing studs are used; around the valve hole; around welded surfaces and in the small radius corners of the wheel rim. Since it seldom pays to attempt oxy-acetylene welding repairs it is better to scrap such wheels and use new ones in their place.

Elongated Wheel Fixing-Stud Holes. These are another possible source of trouble in old cars but these can safely be rectified by fusion welding and the wheels used again.

Care of the Tyres. The earlier standard type of car tyre was of the well-base rim with inextensible wires in the beads. When fitting or removing this tyre it should *not be stretched* over the wheel rim. It is unnecessary to use force, as the wire beads can be adjusted into the rim well of the wheel and then manipulated on, or off the rim as required.

Fig. 289 shows the Dunlop tyre and illustrates the method of tyre manipulation. The cover bead cannot be pulled over the rim at (*A*) until the cover bead (*B*) is pushed off the rim shoulder (*C*) down into the rim well at (*D*). When this is done the bead (*A*) will come over the rim easily.

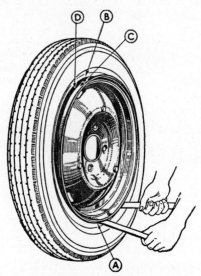

Fig. 289. Method of removing Dunlop
tyre from well-base rim.

When removing a tyre first deflate it and then push both beads off their rim seatings; this will facilitate the tyre removal, later.

The bead on the valve side should first be loosened with a tyre lever and pushed into the rim well on the opposite side of the wheel to the valve. Using a second tyre lever, about 2 inches away from the first, as shown in Fig. 289, the bead should be prised over the rim and then the rest of the bead will readily come over the rim. The tube can then be taken out and finally the cover can be taken right off the rim by using the rim well method and a lever inserted from the front between the bead and flange, pulling the cover back over the latter. When a tube is re-inserted into its cover, it should be slightly inflated before attempting to replace the tyre bead in position.

Tubeless Tyres. These tyres are now being fitted as standard to British production cars.

Fig. 290 shows the Dunlop tubeless tyre in sectional view from which it will be seen that the beaded portion is a tight fit on the specially-shaped wheel rim.

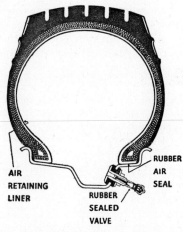

Fig. 290. The Dunlop tubeless tyre.

The base of the bead usually has a 15° taper and the load is carried on this base portion. The low flange of the rim acts as an effective stop and centring device. It should be mentioned that *tubeless tyres are not interchangeable with ordinary tyres* on the same rim and so have different size markings.

The chief advantages of tubeless tyres are, as follows: (1) They are lighter than the conventional two-element tyre. (2) They run appreciably cooler. (3) They are no more difficult to repair and are as easy or easier to fit as the conventional pattern of tyre. (4) With recent nylon cord construction they are as strong as ordinary tyres and can be retreaded equally well.

When a puncture occurs in a tubeless tyre, e.g., by a nail, the puncturing cause can be left in the tread and the car driven on for an appreciable distance as the air leakage is usually very gradual. With the inner tube tyre, if a puncture occurs this generally goes through the tube as well, so that the air leaks at a much higher rate.

The usual *gradual air leakage*, by diffusion, of the inner tube of the conventional tyre *does not occur in tubeless tyres*, so that the air pressure should be maintained over longer periods.

When re-fitting tubeless tyres special care is necessary to ensure that the rim flanges are clean and that there are no irregularities at the welded joint of the rim; any dents, or burrs on the rim should be removed, or air leakages may occur. The tyre is fitted to the wheel rim in the usual manner, using two or three tyre levers, but these should be of the smooth kind to avoid damaging the tyre bead, or wheel rim. Clean water is used to lubricate the tyre beads, when fitting the tyre. Inflation is best carried out with air from a compressed air supply line; the beads are then quickly forced against the wheel rims to make the air-tight joint.

If only a hand or foot pump is available the correct procedure is to apply a tourniquet of strong cord around the outer circumference of the tyre in the centre of the tread and tighten this with a suitable twisting bar (Fig. 291). This will compress the tread and expand the tyre beads against the wheel rim shoulders to make the air seal. The tyre should then be inflated with the valve core in position until the beads are tight against their rims. The tourniquet can then be removed and the inflation completed. It is desirable to *test for leakages* after a tubeless tyre has been fitted, *using a bath of water* and watching for air bubbles.

Repairing Tubeless Tyres. When a tubeless tyre has been penetrated by a small sharp object, e.g. a sharp flint, tack or nail, the air leakage, as previously stated will be very gradual, but the object should be removed as soon as possible. The puncture can readily be repaired by a method based upon a somewhat similar principle to the 'needle-and-thread'. In this case, the needle is a steel rod and the thread, a length of circular rubber of about twice the diameter of the puncture orifice. The needle is coated with rubber solution and inserted and removed several times, in the direction of the orifice, in order to solution the orifice. Next

Fig. 291. Method of contracting tubeless tyre into wheel rim
(Ford Motor Co).

a 'plug' of rubber 'thread' is inserted through the eye of the needle, then dipped in solution and pressed through the orifice. (Fig. 292.) Afterwards the needle is withdrawn, leaving the rubber plug in the orifice. (Fig. 293.) The surplus plug is then cut off about ⅛ inch from the surface of the tread; the repair is then complete. Special tools and rubber plugs are available, commercially, for these repairs; in this connection the Dunlop 'Reddiplug' repair kit contains everything necessary for repairing small punctures.

Alternatively, if such a kit is not available the tyre can be removed from the wheel rim and the puncture sealed, from within the tyre, with the ordinary tube repair patch. Larger orifices or tread defects should be repaired by the usual vulcanizing methods.

Finally, tubeless tyres *should be examined carefully every* 2,000 *to* 3,000 *miles* for indications of punctures or other injuries.

Radial- and Cross-ply Tyres. Modern tyres are of two chief types, viz., *Radial-* and *Cross-ply*. In the former the tyre casing

N

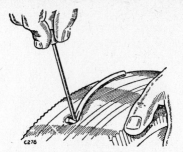

Fig. 292. Method of inserting puncture sealing plug (Rover).

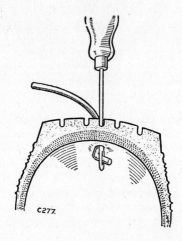

Fig. 293. Showing the plug in position, ready for
cutting off excess piece above.

cords run radially from bead to bead. In the latter kind of tyres
the plys are crossed in opposite diagonal directions.

It is a matter of *much importance not to use both types* on the
same car, except in only one particular instance, i.e. that one can
safely use cross-ply tyres on the front and radial types on the back

wheels. Under no circumstances should radial-ply tyres be fitted on the front wheels only.

The reasons for these precautions are that the two types have greatly different properties when cornering and combination of the two is considered dangerous by the tyre manufacturers.

Tyre Troubles and Their Causes. Excessive or irregular tyre wear can be due to several different causes, including incorrect inflation pressure, wrong steering mechanism geometry, i.e. camber, castor and toe-in, bad driving of the car, unbalanced wheel and tyre, worn steering mechanism and king pins, tyre impact against hard objects, etc. Some of these troubles will be dealt with, in their order.

Tyre Inflation Pressures. These will depend upon the size of tyre, the load on the tyres and the maximum speeds at which the car is driven. The car manufacturer recommends the *average pressure* to be used, and in some cases the pressures for *partly* and *fully loaded* cars and for normal cruising and regular *high speeds*. Thus, in a typical case the pressure for both front and rear tyres was 24 lb per sq in. (cold) for three occupants and speeds up to 50 m.p.h. With five occupants, the rear tyre pressures were 26–27 lb per sq in. for the same speeds but, for high speeds up to 90 m.p.h., fully laden, the rear tyre pressures were 30 lb per sq in.

Under-inflation Effects. If the tyre pressures are appreciably lower than the correct values the tyre walls will flex more and greater stress will occur on the tyre cords, causing also greater heat to weaken the casing. The results will be to cause uneven wear on the tread, reduced car performance, greater roll on curves and higher petrol consumption. Fig. 294 (A) shows the results on a tyre of under-inflation, there being a greater tread contact area with the ground.

Over-inflation Effects. The higher pressure causes greater tyre cord stresses and increased wear on the centre of the tread. It also tends to reduce the suspension comfort and to cause noisier driving. Further, an over-inflated tyre is more susceptible to cuts and bruises (Fig. 294 B).

The manner in which wrongly inflated tyres affect the life of a tyre is well illustrated in Fig. 295 which indicates the life of the properly inflated tyre by 100 per cent. It will be seen that if the

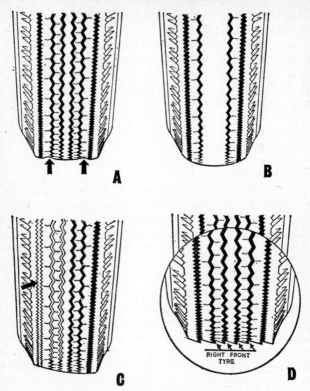

Fig. 294. Some causes of excessive tyre wear.
(*A*) under-inflation. (*B*) over-inflation. (*C*) excessive camber. (*D*) excessive 'toe-in'.

tyre pressure is 80 per cent of the correct value the tyre life is reduced by 15 per cent; if 60 per cent under-inflated the life is reduced by 55 per cent. Over-inflation has a similar effect, but the tyre would not last long if much over-inflated.

Note. Tyres inflated in cooler weather increase in pressure by 2 to 4 lb per sq in. if the car is driven hard under sunny conditions, later, in this country.

Effect of Incorrect Wheel Camber. Excessive wheel camber will cause greater wear on the outer ribs of the tyre as shown at

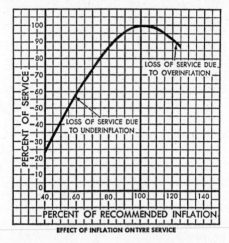

Fig. 295. Showing the effects of under- and over-inflation
pressures on the life of a tyre (Lincoln).

(C) in Fig. 294 for a case of too much positive camber. If excessive
negative camber then there will be greater wear on the inside tyre
ribs.

Toe-in or Toe-out Effects. If the toe-in is greater than the
correct distance given by the manufacturer, then as indicated in
Fig. 294 (C), the front wheel tyres will develop fins on the outside
edges, which will shorten the tread life. If the front wheels have
too much toe-out the tread ribs will show fins, but on the opposite
sides of the ribs to those shown in Fig. 294 (C).

If a car, with correct camber angle is regularly driven on a well-
cambered road, the left-hand front tyre will tend to wear more than
the other tyres.

Irregular 'Spotty' Wear. This kind of wear which sometimes
occurs on front tyres consists of irregular wear areas on the treads,
as if the tread had been touched in places with a high-speed grinding wheel. The causes are believed to be those resulting from
severe acceleration, braking, steering action and springing movements. Unbalanced wheel–tyre combinations may also contribute
to this effect. The only practical solution is to check the various

possible causes mentioned and to change the wheels around at shorter intervals, e.g. 2,500 miles.

Impact Effects. When a car wheel driven at moderate speed strikes the side of a road kerb or any other solid object the impact will often fracture the tyre casing cords, with the result that some time later the tyre will fail by a blow-out. If, therefore, after such an impact is known to occur, the tyre side shows a slight bulge, it should be removed from the wheel and if not repairable, a new tyre must be fitted.

Tread Examination. At regular intervals the tyre treads should be carefully examined for signs of cuts or other penetrations, road particles in the tread grooves, impact bruises and the presence of oil or grease. If the latter, a good application of French chalk will often prove effective. If the treads are much worn, but the tyre carcase is sound, *retreading* will extend the useful life of the tyre appreciably, but it should be remembered that *retreaded tyres should not be used at speeds exceeding about* 60 *m.p.h.*

Rear Wheel Mis-alignment. If, owing to chassis frame distortion, as a result of damage, the rear wheels are not parallel to the centre line of the chassis, serious tyre wear due to sideways drag or grinding will occur; the condition of the tyres, themselves, are an indication of mis-alignment errors.

Excessive Speeds. The rate of tread wear increases fairly rapidly with the car speed. The following figures, by The Dunlop Rubber Company, clearly emphasize this:

Average Speed			*Mileage obtained.*
30 m.p.h.	..	..	Normal.
40 „	..	..	76 per cent. of normal.
50 „	..	..	59 „ „ „ „
60 „	..	..	43 „ „ „ „
70 „	..	..	30 „ „ „ „

Other factors affecting tyre wear include: condition of road surface; road curves and gradients; and temperatures – the rate of wear being twice as fast on warm roads than on cold.

Changing the Tyres Around. In order to obtain the greatest mileage from a set of new tyres (including the spare wheel one) it is necessary to change these round at intervals of about 3,000

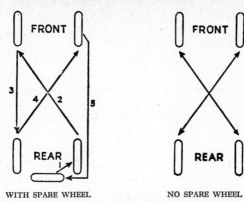

WITH SPARE WHEEL   NO SPARE WHEEL

Fig. 296. Method of changing tyres around to
obtain maximum mileages.

miles for rear drive cars and 2,000 miles for front drive ones during
their useful life. Fig. 296 shows the recommended procedure at
the previously stated intervals. If there is no spare wheel, the
two front tyres should be placed at the rear at 3,000 miles intervals.

Wheel and Tyre Balance. Of much importance in racing
cars, wheel balancing has also become an important factor in
modern high performance cars so that it is now the practice
to balance the wheel and tyre unit, so special machines, e.g.
the Dunlop, Churchill and Bradbury ones are used for this
purpose.

If the wheel unit is out of balance, road shocks of a vibratory
kind known as *tramp* and steering *shimmy* may occur. The former
trouble is due to the wheel unit being unbalanced in the radial
sense, as at (*a*) in Fig. 297 whilst the latter is due to the unbalanced
region being out of centre as at (*b*), Fig. 297.

It is now the common practice to mark new covers with *white
spots* on the beads to denote the lighter sides of the tyres. The
inner tubes are marked with *black spots* on the heavier sides of
the tubes. When assembling the tyre and tube the black and
white spots should be placed opposite, as indicated in Fig. 298,
for a Morris wheel unit.

When the complete tyre and wheel unit is tested for balance, the lighter side of the unit is revealed and the correct balance is effected by placing *lead weights*, specially designed for the purpose, on the rim's lighter side (Fig. 299). A correctly balanced wheel, in the static sense should, after spinning it, come to rest in any position.

The lead weights, for rim flanges up to 16 inch incorporate spring clips. For larger wheels, with rims of tubular flange type balance adjustment rubber is placed in the tyre casing. Some new tyres are fitted with balance rubbers before leaving the factory.

When a tyre is removed for vulcanizing repairs or a new tyre, is fitted to a 'balanced' wheel unit, it is necessary to *re-balance the unit*.

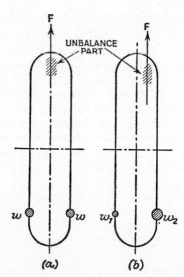

Fig. 297. Illustrating two types of wheel unbalance. (a) static. (b) dynamic. The method of balancing by the weights w_1, w_2, w are indicated.

Cuts in Tyre Treads. *Neglect of small cuts* is another fruitful source of rapid tyre deterioration, for water and grit readily penetrate and in time cause the cords to perish; eventually the cut extends, and the inner tube may blow out. For small cuts use one of *the plastic tyre stoppings* sold by tyre manufacturers; this will keep out the grit and moisture. When applying this tyre 'dough', clean carefully the inside and edges of the cut with petrol, apply solution and when almost dry force the stopping into the cut with a knife-blade. Bind a piece of paper over the stopped cut for a few hours until quite secure.

Large cuts should certainly be vulcanized at once; this can be done with a small home type vulcanizer, although most local garages undertake this work.

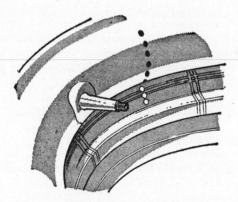

Fig. 298. Method of marking covers and tubes for balancing purposes.

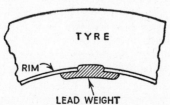

Fig. 299. Wheel rim balance weight.

It is advisable, if a cut is discovered, and the tyre is not vulcanized but only filled, to place one or more patches inside the cover, opposite to the cut; this will need wheel re-balancing.

Storing a Car. When storing a car for a long period, remove the tyres and store in a cool, dry place; otherwise jack the car wheels off the ground, and rub the surfaces well with French chalk, to remove any grease.

Punctures. When a puncture occurs, on the road, the car should be stopped and the wheel changed. If the car is driven on a partly or fully deflated tyre irreparable damage may be caused. Tubeless tyres when punctured lose their air more slowly.

Tube Repairs. Small repairs such as punctures, tread cuts, or valve troubles can be dealt with by the motorist, having the proper tools and materials but the more serious items can only be repaired by garages having commercial vulcanizing equipment. When making a repair, see that you have the proper tyre tools, and so do not damage the tyres in taking them off or in replacing. Having removed the inner tube, feel around the inside of the outer cover casing for solid particles; the punctured part of the tyre tread should be stopped or vulcanized according to the size of the cut.

Although the ordinary inner tube repair patches, having prepared raw rubber faces, are satisfactory, the neatest job is obtained by vulcanizing. A simple but efficient vulcanizer should be kept in the garage. The H.F. Jiffy vulcanizer is a small type that uses a solid methylated spirit tabloid for the vulcanizing heat. It is only necessary to clean the tube around the cut, smear over a small piece of plastic rubber, and then a strip of non-adhesive paper cloth, clamping the tube in the press provided. The tabloid is then placed in a perforated cup in the press, ignited with a match, the cap replaced over the cup and the apparatus left for about 15 minutes; the tube will then be found to be neatly and effectively vulcanized.

When fixing a patch in the ordinary way, after cleaning the surface of the tube with petrol, paraffin, a match head or sandpaper, apply the minimum amount of rubber solution and let it dry for 5 to 10 minutes before placing the prepared patch in position. After this sprinkle some powdered chalk over the patch to prevent its sticking to the outer cover; the tube can be inflated at once

A small puncture can usually be located by inflating, partially, the tube and holding different parts, in turn, near the ear, when the escaping air will be heard; a little moisture rubbed over the suspected place will verify matters.

CHAPTER 13

ELECTRICAL SYSTEM MAINTENANCE*

WHILE the subject of the maintenance, checking for faults and doing overhauls of the various units of the electrical system is an extensive one and many of the operations require the services of a motor electrician there are, on the other hand, quite a number of maintenance jobs which the owner-driver can undertake satisfactorily.

In the present necessarily limited instructions the complete electrical system of the car has been divided up into the five principal individual items or systems depicted at (1), (2), (3), (4) and (5) in Fig. 300, which shows schematically, the various basic parts and circuits of the ordinary car's electrical system. The five main items shown are, briefly, as follows:

(1) *The Battery*. (2) The Ignition System, (3) The Charging System, (4) *The Starting System* and (5) The Accessories, which include the car lighting items, horn, windscreen wipers, turn indicators (flashers), car heater, radio, electric petrol pump (B.M.C. cars), fuel and other electrically-operated gauges.

In the complete layout shown in Fig. 300, all of the current for the various electrical components is taken from the battery which is kept fully-charged by the dynamo and its regulating device, marked 'R'. The cut-out 'C.U.' prevents any current flow in the dynamo circuit when the engine is only running at idling speed, or when it is stopped. Instead of using insulated cables for the supply and return currents to the various items from the battery the return current side of each electrical component is connected to the chassis frame of the car, thus giving what is known as an 'Earth' return. This method saves all the insulated return cables that otherwise would be needed.

Hitherto, in all British cars the positive pole of the battery was

* For fuller information, consult Volume 6 of this Series (*Modern Electrical Equipment*).

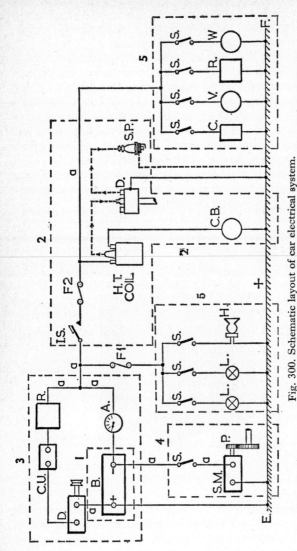

Fig. 300. Schematic layout of car electrical system.

A ammeter. *a* live cables. *B* battery. *C*, *V*, *R*, *W* car accessories (clock, voltmeter, radio, windscreen wiper, etc.). *C.U.* cut-out. *D* dynamo. (1), distributor (2). *EF* common earth. *F* fuses. *C.B.* contact-breaker. *I.S.* ignition switch. *H* horn. *L* lamps. *P* motor starter pinion. *S* switches. *S.M.* starting motor. *S.P.* sparking plug. (1), (2), (3), (4) and (5) the five basic circuits.

connected to 'Earth', but more recently it has become the practice to follow the American negative earth system.

The Battery. This, for cars, is a lead-acid battery using separate packs of positive and negative plates immersed in a solution of sulphuric acid and distilled water. Batteries are denoted by their energy-storing capacities, i.e. the number of hours required to discharge the battery at a constant current. Car batteries range from the smaller ones of 30 ampere-hours to the larger ones used in big cars, of 80 ampere-hours. The latter, e.g. will give a constant discharge current of 4 amperes for 20 hours.

The car battery must be *properly maintained*, at all times, since any failure will put the car out of action. The various maintenance items for a typical battery are illustrated in Fig. 301.

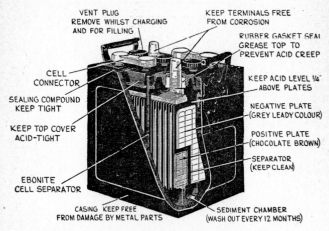

Fig. 301. Illustrating the care and maintenance of the automobile battery.

The Acid Electrolyte. The solution for a new battery is made by adding gradually 1 volume of commercial sulphuric acid of 1·835 density to 3 volumes of distilled water, to give a final cool solution of about 1·28–1·29 density at 80° F.

When a battery is in good condition the fully-charged, half-charged and completely discharged densities should be 1·28 to 1·29; 1·19 to 1·210 and 1·116 to 1·120, all at 80° F. If hotter than this temperature add 0·004 for every 10° F above and deduct the same amount for every 10° below 0° F.

The acid density is checked with an hydrometer, which can be had from any garage supplier. It consists of an outer glass tube, with a rubber tube to dip into the acid, and an inner calibrated glass float to read the acid density. It should be read vertically, as shown in Fig. 302, readings being taken for each battery cell. Any lower reading from one cell indicates a faulty cell.

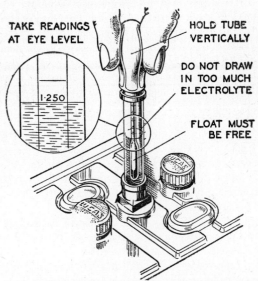

TAKE READINGS AT EYE LEVEL

1·250

HOLD TUBE VERTICALLY

DO NOT DRAW IN TOO MUCH ELECTROLYTE

FLOAT MUST BE FREE

Fig. 302. Checking acid density on Lucas battery.

Always keep the acid level just above the level of the tops of the plates. If the level drops through *evaporation*, as in hot weather, or through over-charging, use *distilled* (not tap) *water* to bring up the level. If, however, the level falls during charging when the acid is splashed out due to the 'gassing', or the acid is accidentally spilt, make up with fresh acid solution of density 1·350.

When the car is in use the battery should be checked and if

necessary, 'topped-up' every month or so. If the vent plugs are removed the acid level can be seen; the water added should be sufficient for the solution to just cover the tops of the separators. If over-filled the excess solution may be thrown from the cell during charging and *corrode the terminals*.

Note. Battery acid is injurious to the hands and clothes and it also attacks most metals.

Voltage of Battery. The condition of a battery cannot be gauged from a voltage measurement taken across its terminals, although it can be judged with a special form of voltmeter which applies an electrical load, by means of a shunting resistance, which takes a heavy current discharge for a short time. Immediately after a new battery has been charged the voltage across each cell reads 2·6 to 2·7, but after it has stood for an hour or two this falls to 2·15 to 2·20. Thus a 6-volt battery when fully charged should, after standing read 6·45 to 6·6 volts and a 12-volt one, 12·9 to 13·2 volts. After discharge, the voltage falls to about 1·8 per cell.

Maintenance of the Battery (Fig. 301). The battery should never be left in a semi- or fully-discharged condition for long. It is advisable to keep a battery trickle charger in the garage to give the battery an occasional charge when not using the car, and in winter when there is a bigger demand on the battery. Most trickle chargers give from 2 to 3 amperes and if fixed on the wall near the battery position are quite easy to use.

If the car is to be laid up for a long period the battery can be stored by the 'dry' method. To do this, the battery should first be fully charged, and the acid then drained out. The pitch seal should be removed with the aid of a hot iron and the wooden separators should be taken out, dried and stored in a dry place. The battery plates, also, should be dried. When the battery is again required, it is re-assembled, filled with acid and charged.

Every twelve months when in normal use, empty out the battery acid and wash out the sediment from the sediment wells with distilled water. Refill with fresh acid solution and charge.

Battery Terminals. The battery terminals are apt to become corroded with a green powdery deposit (copper sulphide) due to the acid creeping up the electrodes.

The terminals must be kept clean, otherwise this deposit will act as an insulator, making it difficult to get a good connection between the battery and the car leads. The terminals, after cleaning and making the cable connections, should be liberally coated with vaseline or thick grease – particularly around the electrodes where these come out of the cell cover.

Battery Troubles. *If a white deposit forms on the plates,* this is a sign that the battery has been neglected. The cause is known as '*sulphation*', lead sulphate being formed. This sulphate acts as an insulator, and reduces the effective electric charge storing capacity of the battery.

Batteries which are not too badly sulphated may often be reconditioned by charging at a very low rate, namely, from $\frac{1}{5}$ to $\frac{1}{10}$ their normal current charging value. This charging should be continued until the battery begins to gas freely when it should be discharged through a high resistance (e.g. a number of electric lamps) at about $\frac{1}{3}$ to $\frac{1}{4}$ ampere rate. Other *battery troubles* which may in the course of time occur include *internal short-circuiting* of the plates due to the breaking away of the paste from the plates and its lodgment between the plates, and *buckled plates* (due to excessive vibration or constant over-charging).

To find out which cell in a defective battery is the cause of the trouble, test each cell individually with a voltmeter. Each cell, if well charged should read 2·15 to 2·2 volts.

Battery Charging. New batteries should be charged at the rate recommended by the manufacturers. The actual rate depends upon the type and size (or ampere-hour capacity) of the battery.

The first charge rate varies from about 2·5 to 6·0 amperes, according to the type. Thus, in the case of the usual 12 volt 63 ampere hour (10-hour discharge rate) battery the initial charge rate would be about 4·5 amperes, for a period of 40 to 80 hours according to the time it had been stored since manufacture.

After the first charge, the battery can be recharged at 7 amperes, until the voltage and density show no increase after three successive hourly readings.

A battery in good condition can be given a *rapid or boost charge,* such that it is charged in half to one hour. The acid temperature should not exceed 110° F during this process. Usually, the battery is about 80 per cent recharged by this method.

The Ignition System. This system supplies the sparks in the cylinder which ignite the air-petrol mixture. It derives its electricity from the battery and uses a high-tension coil instead of the earlier magneto.

The complete coil ignition system is shown, schematically, in Fig. 303 for a four-cylinder engine. It includes the battery, the ignition switch connected between the arrows, high-tension coil which converts the low voltage from the battery supply to the very much higher voltage needed at the sparking-plug points, the contact-breaker and distributor unit, which has an engine-driven four-sided cam to operate the contact-breaker, the four sparking plugs and the various connecting cables. It will be seen that there are earth returns for the battery, H.T. coil, contact-breaker and sparking plug outer shells.

The Coil Ignition Unit. This unit contains the contact-breaker, a condenser – to prevent pitting of the contacts by the spark, a rotor arm to distribute the H.T. current to each of the sparking plugs in turn, and the distributor cover having the H.T. contacts within and the sparking plug cable terminals outside. There is a central terminal for a cable from the H.T. coil to the distributor – as shown in Fig. 303.

The Contact-breaker. This contains one fixed and one hinged arm-type pair of contacts. The engine-driven cam opens the contacts at the appropriate times, so that a spark is created by the H.T. circuit. It is important to keep the mating contact surfaces quite clean and their opening gap at the correct dimension.

In the case of the earlier model Lucas contact-breaker (Fig. 304) the contact-breaker gap was 0·012 in. To adjust the gap correctly the engine crankshaft should be turned until the contacts are fully opened. Then, the two screws securing the contact plate, as shown in Fig. 304, should be slackened. Afterwards this plate should be moved until the gap is exactly 0·012 in; as checked with the manufacturer's or a feeler gauge. This gauge should be a sliding fit between the contacts, when the latter are fully opened. The screws should then be tightened.

The more *recent Lucas contact-breaker*, shown in Fig. 305, has

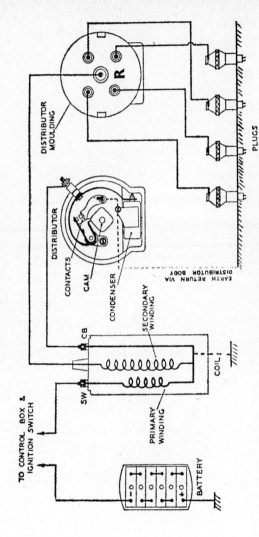

Fig. 303. Schematic layout of four-cylinder engine ignition system.

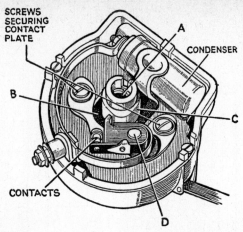

Fig. 304. Lucas contact-breaker unit, showing items of maintenance attention. The lubrication points are as follows: *A* distributor bearing. *B* automatic advance mechanism. *C* cam face. *D* contact-breaker arm pivot pin.

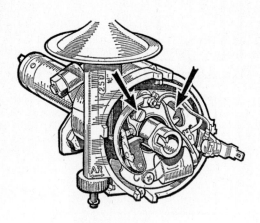

Fig. 305. Later design of contact-breaker (Lucas).

only one securing screw as shown on the left by the arrow, but there is a special shape adjusting slot as shown by the right arrow. When the screw is slackened and the contacts are fully open their gap can be adjusted by inserting a screwdriver blade in the notched slot and, for increasing the gap turned anti-clockwise; to reduce the gap turn the blade clockwise. The correct gap for this later unit is 0·016 in.

The Delco-Remy ignition equipment as fitted to Vauxhall engines has two screws, side by side, near to the moving arm of the contact-breaker. The locking screw near to the contacts is slackened and the other screw adjusted until the contact-breaker gap is correct at 0·019 to 0·021 in.

Cleaning the Contacts. Periodically, say every 5,000 miles or so, the contacts should not only be checked for the correct gap but their mating surfaces should be examined for any signs of burning or pitting. If necessary the surfaces should be cleaned with fine emery cloth (on a thin metal strip) or carborundum stone of fine grade.

It is best to remove the moving contact member and true it in the hand, using a carborundum abrasive stick as shown in Fig. 306. Do not endeavour to remove every small pit in the surface, but brighten up the latter generally and remove, on an oilstone, the small raised portions of the opposing contact.

When trimming contacts it is most important that, when finished, they should close 'dead parallel' so as to contact over their whole surfaces.

Worn Contact Breakers. When excessive wear of the contacts, the fibre cam and its bearings occur, after long service, it invariably pays to replace the whole contact breaker unit by a new one, which can be purchased at a comparatively low price from the local garage.

Lubrication of Contact-Breaker Unit. Periodically, namely, about every 4,000 to 5,000 miles, the unit requires lubrication at the places shown at *A*, *B*, *C* and *D*, in Fig. 304. The distributor bearing (*A*) should be given a few drops of engine oil – the rotor arm must first be removed, for this operation. For (*B*) use the same oil and for the contact arm pivot use a light machine oil sparingly. Smear the cam face (*C*) with a light grease, wiping off

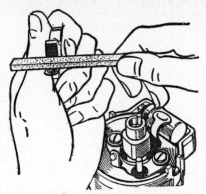

Fig. 306. Trimming the contact on contact-
breaker (Lucas).

any surplus; otherwise it may get on to the contacts and cause
trouble.

In later contact breakers the items (*A*) and (*B*) are both
lubricated at the place (*A*).

Excessive Pitting of the Contacts. The cause of excessive
contact pitting is usually a faulty condenser unit. The condenser
is readily accessible for removal or replacement; it is usually
placed in the contact-breaker casing, and is a flat, D-shaped or
cylindrical metal unit (Fig. 303 and 304). If the condenser is
suspected, examine the contacts for the presence of a yellowish or
whitish deposit – this is a sign of excessive sparking; making
certain, however, that the cause is not oil or grease on the contacts.

The quickest method of checking the suspected condenser is
to substitute a new one and then check the performance.

The Distributor. This unit, which is shown in Fig. 303, is of
the jump-spark type, the H.T. spark jumping from the end of the
rotor to each distributor metal element in turn.

After much service the cap should be removed and cleaned both
inside and out using a soft dry cloth. The inside of the insulation
of the cap should be examined for *fine black cracks* or 'spark
tracks', as these may cause ignition breakdown.

The H.T. cable terminals should be tested for sound end contacts by removal of each terminal. The correct method of making the cable connection is by threading the bared conductor through a brass washer and bending the wires out.

The rotor should be pulled off the drive shaft end, cleaned and examined for excessive wear at the curved metal plate edges, where the spark leaps across to the distributor contacts. If much eroded a new rotor arm should be fitted, since the sparking gap with a worn arm will be too big. The H.T. cables to the sparking plugs are liable to perish after long usage. They should therefore be examined for cracks; if any are found new cables should be used.

Before replacing the cap see that the central spring-loaded carbon brush is satisfactory and works freely in its holder.

The H.T. Coil. If trouble arises with the ignition system and the other items enumerated have been checked and found correct, it may be the coil that is at fault. One method of testing is as follows: Remove the H.T. terminal on the coil from its push-in connection on top of the H.T. coil. Hold the H.T. cable so that the terminal is about $\frac{1}{4}$ inch away from its post, and crank the engine round with the ignition switch on. Sparking should be strong and uniform. If *weak or irregular*, a new coil should be fitted, and the same test applied as a check. In making the above test, it is important to keep the fingers at least 3 in. from the terminal.

A quick method of checking the H.T. coil, if a new one can be loaned for the purpose, is to substitute this for the suspected one and then test the engine performance.

Timing the Ignition. As described more fully in Volume 4 of this Motor Manual Series, it is necessary for the ignition spark to occur a few degrees of engine crank angle before the piston reaches the end of its compression stroke. This angle depends upon the combustion system, the compression ratio and type of fuel used and so is different for the various designs of engines. Therefore, it is important to know the actual ignition advance angle before one is able to time the moment of ignition for any particular engine. This angle is given in most car owner's manuals.

In a few instances of somewhat earlier engines the ignition is timed with the contact-breaker contacts opening on *top dead centre* for ordinary grades of fuel and compression ratios. For higher compression ratios, namely, 7·5:1 to 8·5:1 the ignition timing is usually 5° to 7° before top dead centre.

When premium grade fuels are used, ignition timings of 6° to 10° before top dead centre are usually recommended. In cases of doubt, the top dead centre method should first be used and the car performance tested. The ignition can then be advanced in small steps and the performance checked, until the best results are obtained.

Principle of Timing Methods. It is necessary, firstly to crank the engine until the piston of No. 1 cylinder (nearest to the radiator) is at the top of its compression stroke; this is the stroke when both valves remain closed. Secondly, since the ignition spark occurs when the contact-breaker contacts open, it is essential that this opening occurs at the manufacturer's ignition advance angle. The crankshaft (flywheel) must therefore be turned back by the amount of the ignition advance degrees.

In practically all modern cars either the flywheel or the crankshaft belt pulley is marked with two marks, or notches, namely one to show the top dead centre (T.D.C.) and the other the advance angle. These marks are brought opposite fixed marks on the engine top casing or on the timing gear case. We shall now consider examples for some of the popular British cars.

B.M.C. Cars. (Figs. 307 and 308.) All more recent cars use the crankshaft pulley and timing case mark method. There is a half-round groove on the back flange of the pulley and three 'pointers' on the timing gear casing. The long pointer, when opposite the pulley groove indicates the T.D.C. of No. 1 piston and the other two pointers indicate 5° and 10° before T.D.C. For the Austin A60 engine the timing advance angle is 5° for the higher compression engine (8·3:1) and 6° for the lower 7·2:1 engine, on regular grade petrol. For premium grade fuel – on the 8·3:1 engine the angle is 10°.

If the contacts do not open at the proper angles they can be made to do so by either (1) turning the knurl-headed screw (*S*) on the contact-breaker casing in the advance (*A*) or retard (*R*) direction, or (2), for larger angle adjustments by slackening the

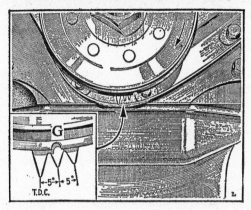

Fig. 307. Method of timing ignition on B.M.C. engines by means of half-groove on crankshaft pulley rim and three pointers on the timing gear case.

Fig. 308. Timing adjustments on B.M.C. engines. A–R directions for ignition advance and retard. N distributor unit clamping nut. X micrometer scale. S knurl-headed adjusting screw.

distributor nut (N) and moving the complete distributor unit about the distributor shaft drive axis, as shown also in Fig. 309 for one of the Hillman engines.

A simple method, which shows at once when the contacts open, is to connect a 12-volt bulb holder and bulb between the low-tension terminal on the distributor outside casing, at its contact-breaker end, and any good earth point on the engine. Then when the contacts are together the bulb does not light but as soon as the contacts begin to open the bulb lights.

To advance the ignition timing the unclamped distributor casing should be turned in the opposite direction to that of the cam's rotation. In the scale on the Lucas distributor units every full division represents 5° and one such division is equal to 55 clicks of the knurled adjuster against its control spring.

The Vauxhall Cars. In these cars the engine has a steel ball embedded in the flywheel rim and when this ball is opposite a notch in the aperture near the top of the flywheel casing, the ignition advance is obtained. The aperture in question is normally covered by a detachable cap.

The Ford Cars. The method for the Ford Anglia and Prefect engines is to set the No. 1 piston on its T.D.C. (compression stroke) by aligning the notch on the crankshaft pulley with a timing mark on the cylinder front cover. Then slacken the screws securing the distributor engraved plate to the cylinder head and line up the 'O' mark on the plate with the mark on the cylinder head. Then tighten the screws again. Next, apply a light pressure to the rotor arm, clockwise, and slacken the distributor clamping bolt and turn the distributor body anti-clockwise until the contacts are closed. Then, turn the body clockwise until the contacts begin to open and tighten the clamping screw bolt. This will give the recommended ignition advance angle of 5°.

For Ford Consul and Cortina engines when the notch on the crankshaft pulley aligns with the lower (outer) timing mark on the cover the ignition advance is 6°. There is a special design of distributor for high-compression engines using fuels of 95 octane and above and another design for high compression (8·7:1) engines using lower octane fuels. Also, a different distributor for engines with 7·3:1 compression ratios. All use the same static timing previously mentioned, but provision is made by a graduated scale to alter the timing to suit special conditions, e.g. higher altitudes.

Humber Engines. The ignition timing of the Humber New Hawk engines is such that the contacts should begin to open at T.D.C. to 2° A.T.D.C. on premium fuels. Adjustments are made by the timing lamp method, using pointers on the crankshaft pulley and timing cover to give the T.D.C. There is also a vernier scale adjuster to give special timings. One division on the scale equals 4° of crank angle and one turn of the knurled adjusting head equal 3 crank degrees.

B.M.C. Mini- and 1100-Car Timings. Owing to their transverse front-drive engines these cars do not use the notched pulley and timing cover methods for indicating the T.D.C. piston position. Instead, there is a cover on the top of the clutch housing which, when removed reveals the flywheel rim and starting gear teeth. It is necessary to use a mirror to time the engine. Thus, when the engine is slowly turned on its compression stroke the mark 1/4 will come opposite a small pointer just below the top of the clutch housing. This shows the T.D.C. of No. 1 piston. If, now, the engine is turned slowly the 5° and 10° marks will be seen. The correct timing for the Mini-Minor engine is 7° B.T.D.C. for regular fuels and, with the special premium fuel distributor available the timing is on T.D.C. For the 1100 car engines the timing is 3° B.T.D.C.

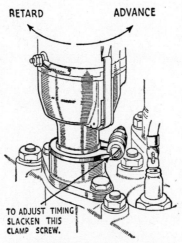

Fig. 309. Method of timing Hillman
engine ignition.

The crankshafts of these engines can be turned by using a spanner on the crankshaft pulley nuts.

The Sparking Plug. Modern sparking plugs seldom, if ever, give any trouble under about 10,000 miles of service, provided that they are looked at every 2,500 to 3,000 miles.

The plugs should be examined for any of the faults indicated in Fig. 311 but, usually, it will be found that only the insulators will need cleaning and the plug sparking points re-adjusted to the recommended gap.

The plug should be inverted and petrol poured in. Then with a fine but stiff wire, work around the inside insulation and plug shell to loosen any carbon. Then empty the petrol, refill and empty again.

The plug points gap should be set either with the maker's gauge (Fig. 310) or with a feeler gauge. For 14 mm. plugs, which

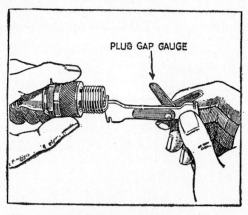

Fig. 310. Combined plug gap tester and electrode setting tool (B.M.C.).

are now universal in car engines, the usual British plug gap is now 0·025 in. for B.M.C. engines, 0·023 to 0·028 in. (Ford) and 0·028 to 0·032 in. (Vauxhall).

Sparking plugs should be changed every 10,000 miles, to ensure efficient and reliable engine performance.

When altering the plug gap always bend the electrode or 'point' attached to the metal shell – never the central point.

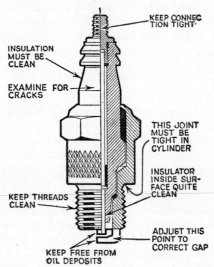

Fig. 311. Illustrating maintenance of the sparking plug.

Colour of the Plug Insulator after Service. If the insulator is a dry, yellowish grey colour with a coating of light fawn powder this shows that a fuel having tetraethyl lead has been used.

If the insulator is brown, the electrodes grey and the plug body relatively clean, the engine conditions may be regarded as satisfactory.

Overheated plugs are revealed by a dry fawn-to-white insulator, with the electrodes eroded at the tips. A black shiny deposit on the insulator and electrodes is a sign of too cool a plug. A wet black deposit of a solid or semi-solid nature indicates cylinder or piston wear, the oil getting past the piston into the combustion chamber.

A useful device for checking the condition of sparking plugs, known as the Champion Plugometer, consists of an anodized aluminium plate having five divisions, each one of which has a hole for insertion of a plug, and also a picture, in colour, showing the different appearances of plugs. It is necessary, only to match the plug and picture, and then read off the appropriate remark, e.g. Normal, Worn, Oily, Burned, Petrol Fouled. The device has a built-in plug points adjuster and feeler gauges.

Ignition Troubles and their Remedies

(1) *Engine Fails to Start*

Having verified that the carburettor is not at fault, there being a good supply of petrol to the float chamber, and no air leaks past the valves or inlet pipe joints, the following items of the ignition system may be the cause: (*a*) The contact breaker rocker arm stuck in its bearing. (*b*) The ignition switch 'off'. (*c*) The H.T. distributor brush broken. (*d*) A particle of dirt or layer of grease bridging the contact breaker points; or (*e*) The H.T. coil broken down. (*f*) The distributor cap or cover cracked or 'tracked' between the metal contacts. (*g*) The condenser short-circuited inside. (*h*) The rotor arm cracked or the metal tongue badly eroded by sparking action. (*i*) Wet plugs, i.e. the electrodes bridged by oil or petrol. Too long usage of the choke may be the cause of wet plugs. In this case remove the plugs and dry out over a gas flame. (*j*) Battery run down.

The ignition switch should be examined to see that it functions correctly.

Too big a gap at the contact breaker points or dirty contacts often makes starting difficult.

If the sparking plug gap is too great, there will be no spark at low engine speeds.

The battery should be checked for acid density and voltage, as a practically run-down battery will prevent the engine starting. Note whether the ammeter shows 'discharge' when you switch on; if so, there should be current flowing in the ignition system. *Loose or corroded battery terminals* will prevent current from flowing from the battery. If the battery is exhausted, the engine can be started by connecting another charged battery in parallel with it, afterwards removing the latter.

The high tension cable from the ignition coil to the distributor may become disconnected or earthed; this will prevent starting of the engine.

If the preceding tests fail it is possible that the H.T. coil has broken down internally. If everything else has been checked and the trouble traced to the coil, try a new or substitute coil in its place. If the contact breaker cam unit drive from the engine has slipped, the ignition timing will have altered and starting will be rendered impossible.

(2) *Engine Misfires or Runs Irregularly.*

Intermittent firing at the plugs is usually due to (*a*) oily or dirty plugs or broken porcelain; (*b*) dirty or incorrectly adjusted contact breaker points; (*c*) loose H.T. connections to plug, or perished insulation which occasionally shorts to earth; (*d*) weak contact breaker spring; (*e*) distributor cover 'tracks' between contacts; (*f*) loose H.T. cable connections in distributor cover; (*g*) faulty condenser; (*h*) loose L.T. connection or connections; (*i*) one or more H.T. cables loose or detached from their plug connections; (*j*) H.T. cables deteriorated, thus sparking occasionally to metal of engine (earth); (*h*) sparking plug gaps too great.

When the engine fires intermittently, short-circuit the terminals of the plugs in turn with a screwdriver (Fig. 312); in the case of the cylinders which are firing correctly, short-circuiting their plugs

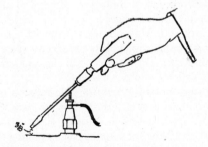

Fig. 312. Showing method of ascertaining which cylinder is misfiring by short-circuiting the sparking plug with a screwdriver.

will cause a sudden drop in the engine speed. 'Shorting' the defective plug will, of course, make no difference to the running of the engine.

To check a suspected plug: remove from the cylinder, connect up its H.T. cable and lay the plug on to a fairly clean part of the cylinder, holding it in place by the insulated cable end. Get someone to crank or motor the engine and watch for a good spark at the plug points. No such spark indicates a faulty plug.

Should a faulty plug be suspected replace with a new one, but if this does not operate in the engine cylinder the fault is in the H.T. cable or its connections.

The Dynamo. The purpose of the dynamo is to keep the battery charged all the time the engine and car are in use. The circuit, as shown at (3), in Fig. 300 consists of the battery, dynamo, a cut-out device and a current-and-voltage, or voltage regulator. Here we are concerned only with the dynamo and cut-out.

Fig. 313 shows the various components of a modern dynamo, in their respective positions, as dismantled. It is of the two-brush type and consists of four main units, namely, the end cover on the left, carrying the brushes, the armature, the casing carrying the field coils and the right end cover. The two covers are secured to the casing by the two long bolts and nuts shown below. There is a porous-bronze bearing at the left and a ball-bearing at the right for the armature shaft.

Car dynamos are made with maximum outputs from about 18 to 30 amps with maximum controlled voltages of about 13·5 at about 2,000 r.p.m. armature speed.

Dynamo Care and Maintenance. From the exploded view in Fig. 313 the various components are clearly shown. Of these the principal ones that may require maintenance attention include the *commutator brushes*, and the *bearings*.

The Commutator and Brushes. The dynamo casing has a cylindrical clip which acts as a dust cover over the commutator and brush gear. Upon releasing the clip screw the clip can be slid along so as to expose the interior, thus enabling the commutator to be cleaned by wiping with a piece of cloth (Fig. 314 (*A*)) and the brushes to be removed for inspection or replacement (Fig. 314 (*B*)).

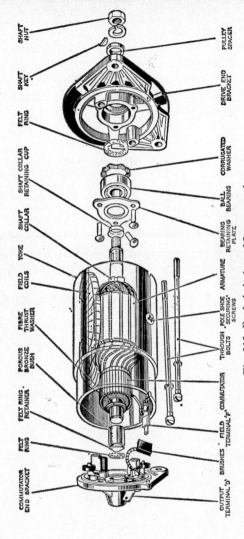

SHAFT NUT

SHAFT KEY

FELT RING

SHAFT COLLAR RETAINING CUP

YOKE

FIELD COILS

FIBRE THRUST WASHER

POROUS BRONZE BUSH

FELT RING RETAINER

FELT RING

COMMUTATOR END BRACKET

OUTPUT TERMINAL 'D'

BRUSHES

FIELD TERMINAL 'F'

COMMUTATOR

SHAFT COLLAR

THROUGH BOLTS

POLE SHOE SECURING SCREWS

ARMATURE

BEARING RETAINING PLATE

BALL BEARING

CORRUGATED WASHER

DRIVE END BRACKET

PULLEY SPACER

Fig. 313. Exploded view of Lucas car dynamo.

Once every 5,000 miles or so, remove the dust cover from around the commutator part of the dynamo, and see that the brushes and commutator are not worn unduly. The dust which collects inside the dynamo should be blown out with a hand bellows or compressed air blast. It is advisable to clean the segments of the commutator by holding a piece of clean rag moistened with petrol against them whilst the dynamo is rotated by hand.

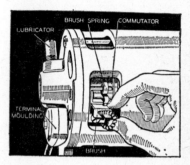

Fig. 314. (*A*) cleaning the commutator. (*B*) removing a dynamo brush.

The better method, however, is to insert a flat, thin strip of wood, about 1 inch wide, the end of which is covered with a piece of heavy cotton cloth moistened with petrol. Start the engine and, with the brushes lifted or removed, press the cloth end against the commutator. If the latter remains black or rough, it should be smoothed and brightened with a piece of No. 00 (fine) sand paper attached to a suitable piece of stick. Do not use emery cloth or paper; after cleaning, blow out all dust with a pair of bellows.

The brushes should be examined, and any hard greasy glaze removing by filing. It is important to see that the brushes bed properly on to the commutator surface.

The brushes should slide up and down freely in their guides. If they are found to be sticking clean them with petrol first and then, if necessary, smooth with a fine file.

The brush spring tension must be correct. If too light, sparking may occur; if too great, excessive wear and heating will result.

The brush spring tension should be tested with a spring balance. (Fig. 315.) The correct tension for British car dynamos is from about 15 to 30 oz. according to the design and size. For the Lucas model shown in Fig. 313 the tension is from 15 to 25 oz. If the tension is too low, a new spring should be fitted. *If pronounced sparking occurs* at the brushes when the engine is running, remove and examine the brushes; if glazed or badly worn, replace

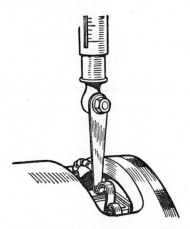

Fig. 315. Testing the tension of the brush springs with a spring balance.

with new ones. If, on the other hand, the commutator is worn, it may be necessary to remove the armature and turn the commutator in the lathe, finishing with a polished surface. For the best running and output results, the mica stops between the copper segments should be undercut with an old hack-saw blade (Fig. 316). If the mica projects above the segments, *sparking will usually occur*.

The Bearings. After long periods of usage the armature shaft bearings may be found to have worn appreciably. Usually, this will not occur under 30,000 to 40,000 miles of service. The porous-bronze bush should be pressed out of its housing in the

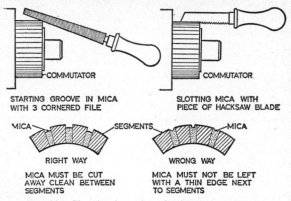

STARTING GROOVE IN MICA
WITH 3 CORNERED FILE

SLOTTING MICA WITH
PIECE OF HACKSAW BLADE

MICA — SEGMENTS — MICA

RIGHT WAY

WRONG WAY

MICA MUST BE CUT
AWAY CLEAN BETWEEN
SEGMENTS

MICA MUST NOT BE LEFT
WITH A THIN EDGE NEXT
TO SEGMENTS

Fig. 316. Showing how the mica insulation of the commutator is under-cut with file and saw-blade.

dynamo end plate and a new one inserted, using a shouldered mandrel between the press ram and end plate.

The ball-bearing should be pressed out, after knocking out the bearing retaining-plate rivets. When a new ball-bearing is fitted it should be packed with a high melting point grease and the grease retaining washers replaced, as before.

Lubrication. The modern car dynamo has a ball-bearing at the driving end and a porous-bronze self-lubricating bearing at the armature end. The latter bearing was previously lubricated by a felt pad saturated with a thin grease, e.g. H.M.P. grease, a spring being used to press the pad on to the shaft.

Every 10,000 miles the lubricator should be unscrewed, the felt pad and its spring lifted out and the lubricator half-filled with grease.

Modern car dynamos use porous-bronze lubricated bearings at the brush cover end and 'grease-packed for life' ball-bearings are fitted at the other cover end.

The brush end bearings should be given three or four drops of engine oil every 6,000 miles (Fig. 317) although in the case of Vauxhall cars the period is now 12,000 miles: if in any doubt consult the owner's manual.

The Belt Drive. It is essential to maintain the dynamo driving

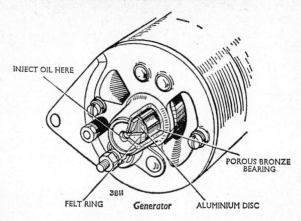

Fig. 317. Lubrication of dynamo plain bearing (Humber Hawk).

belt at the correct tension. Usually, this belt also drives the water pump and cooling fan. The method, as previously mentioned, is illustrated in Fig. 140 on page 183.

The belt should not be too tight, otherwise the bearing on that side will wear appreciably. Neither should it be too slack or the dynamo may not charge sufficiently.

A common cause of a dynamo failing to charge correctly is that of the belt bottoming on its pulley. If the bottom surface appears to be much polished, this is a sign of belt slip.

The Cut-out. This unit, shown at *C.U.,* in Fig. 300, connects and disconnects the battery to and from the dynamo when the engine has stopped or it is operating at idling speeds. When the ignition switch is switched on the 'discharge' red warning bulb glows but, as soon as the cut-out operates, showing that the battery and dynamo are connected electrically, the red bulb ceases to glow.

If the cut-out does not operate, the battery will discharge through the dynamo windings to earth, with the ignition switch 'Off' or 'On'. The cause of this failure may be: (1) Weak pull-off spring. (2) Sticking contacts. (3) Bent contact arm. Before servicing a cut-out, always disconnect one pole of the battery.

Should the battery discharge quickly whilst the car is not in use, the cut-out should be inspected for one of the above possible defects. If the contacts stick, a gentle tap on the moving arm will usually separate them.

The contact surfaces should be quite clean and bright. If dirty they must be cleaned. A satisfactory method is to place a strip of fine emery cloth between the contacts and, whilst pressing the latter together, to draw the cloth through, two or three times.

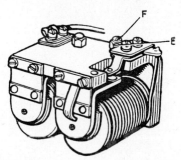

Fig. 318. Adjusting the cut-out on the
Lucas R.F. 95 regulator (B.M.C.).

The cloth should then be turned over and the procedure repeated, in order to clean the other surface.

The usual contact gap measurement is about 0·015 in.

Referring to Fig. 318, if the cutting-in speed is too high, the cut-out may be adjusted by slackening the locknut E and turning the adjusting screw F slightly in a clockwise direction to raise the voltage and anti-clockwise to lower it. The correct voltage, across the terminals marked 'D' and 'E' on the control box when the cut-out begins to operate should, in this case, be from 12·7 to 13·3.

Locating Faults in Constant Voltage Control Dynamos. The following table shows the usual symptoms of troubles liable to occur with Lucas voltage control dynamo equipment, their possible causes and suggested remedies.

The Starting Motor. The starting motor very seldom gives trouble and requires a minimum of attention. The usual types of starting motor are provided with sealed self-lubricating bearings.

DYNAMO FAULTS AND REMEDIES

SYMPTOMS	PROBABLE FAULT	REMEDY
Battery in low state of charge, shown by lack of power when starting.	Dynamo not charging, indicated by ammeter failing to show charge reading when running with no lights in use, due to: Broken or loose connection in dynamo circuit or regulator not functioning.	Examine charging and field circuit wiring. Tighten loose connection or replace broken lead. Particularly examine battery connections. If trouble persists, have equipment examined by a Service Depot.
	Dynamo giving low or intermittent output, indicated by ammeter showing low or intermittent charge reading, when running steadily in top gear, due to:	
	Loose or broken connections in dynamo circuit.	Examine dynamo wiring. Tighten loose connections or replace broken lead. Particularly examine battery connections.
	Commutator or brushes greasy.	Clean with soft rag moistened with petrol.
	Brushes worn, not fitted correctly.	Replace worn brushes. See that brushes 'bed' correctly.
	Regulator not functioning correctly.	Have equipment examined by a Service Depot.
Battery over-charged, shown by burnt-out bulbs and frequent need for topping up.	Dynamo giving high output, indicated by ammeter giving high charge reading when lights are in use, due to:	
	Regulator not functioning correctly.	Have equipment examined by a Service Depot.

Periodically test the holding-down or attachment bolts for tightness and also the connection from the battery.

The same methods of armature and brush maintenance apply as in the case of the dynamo.

In regard to the Bendix pinion, the square thread on the starting motor armature shaft, along which the pinion travels, *should not be greased*, but kept quite clean. The presence of grease prevents the pinion from engaging with the flywheel teeth. If, therefore, *the motor merely speeds up*, and hums, *without the pinion engaging the flywheel teeth*, this is a sign that the pinion screw thread is held by oil or grease. Washing with paraffin will cure the trouble. Petrol should not be used.

It is advisable, every few thousand miles, to grease the flywheel teeth, lightly, with a motor grease.

The electrical connections to the starting motor are simple as, will be seen from Fig. 319.

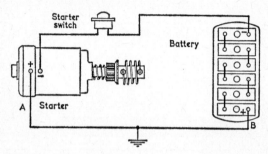

Fig. 319. Circuit for starting motor. *AB* is the earth return path.

Starting Switch. Although the starting switch is shown separately in Fig. 319, in practice there is a small switch on the instrument fascia which takes a small current, but this is used to actuate a relay bringing into operation a more powerful switch on the motor casing to take the very large starting current, of a few hundred amperes.

Should *the motor fail to start* on depressing the switch, first ensure that the switch is making good contact. Next examine the battery to see whether it is charged up. Finally, make certain the battery and switch connections are tight, and the latter are not corroded. The earth connection of the battery (i.e. the positive lead) should make good contact with the metal of the chassis frame, and the motor casing should also be well earthed.

Check whether the switch is at fault by short-circuiting it with a piece of starter cable.

To test the starter, the headlamps should be switched on and the starter switch operated. If the lamps go dim, but the starter does not respond this indicates that current is flowing to the motor windings, so that the starter pinion must be jammed in the flywheel toothed ring; in this case the procedure described later should be followed.

If, however, the lamps do not dim on operating the starter switch, check that the latter is functioning properly. If in order, check the battery connections of the starter circuit and those at the switch and starter. Failure to start after these checks indicates an internal fault in the starter itself.

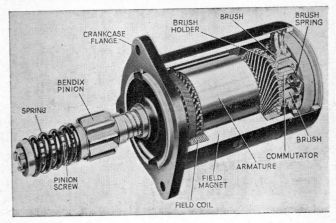

Fig. 320. The Lucas starting motor type M.418G.

Should the starter operate sluggishly, this is due either to a fault in the starter itself, a low battery or to a bad connection in its wiring circuit.

When using any starting motor, never depress the switch whilst the engine is running; make sure the engine, has stopped first. If you look at the oil pressure gauge or ammeter, the reading will give you an indication as to whether the engine is running or not; *broken flywheel teeth* are traceable to non-observance of the afore-stated rule.

If *the starter pinion jams,* put the gear lever into high gear and rock the car forward and back until the Bendix pinion disengages; the switch should, of course, be 'off'.

The Lucas starting motor armature shaft is provided with a

square-ended extension (Fig. 321) so that in the event of a jammed starter pinion a spanner can be applied to the shaft and the latter freed.

After long service it is necessary to check the brushes for wear and, if necessary, to renew these.

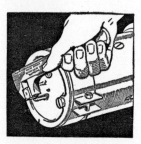

Fig. 321. Freeing jammed
starter.

The commutator also will need cleaning, but it is here important to note that *the mica of the commutator must not be undercut.*

Particulars of electrical tests for dynamos, control and cut-out units, and starting motors are given in Volume 6, of this Series.

Starting Motor Troubles, Causes and Remedies. The table gives in (on page 427) convenient form much of the information on Lucas starters previously referred to, and it will enable starter troubles to be diagnosed and rectified quickly.

The Lighting System. It is not possible in the present general brief account to give detailed instructions on the electrical system maintenance.

Every car driver, however, should make a point of studying the manufacturer's wiring diagram of his car, so that in the case of trouble he will have a good idea of where to look for the fault. The best plan after acquiring the car is to take the wiring diagram to the car and trace every wire shown, on the car itself.

About every 10,000 miles of running go over the various wires and their connections to the lamps, dynamo, cut-out, switches, fuse and battery; see that none of the cables are frayed, and make sure the screw connections are tight.

STARTING MOTOR FAULTS AND REMEDIES

CONDITION	PROBABLE FAULT	REMEDY
	If engine cannot be turned by hand, then fault is due to a stiff engine.	Locate and remedy cause of stiffness.
	If engine can be turned by hand, then trouble may be due to:	
	Battery discharged.	Start by hand. Charge battery either by a long period of daytime running or from an independent electrical supply.
Motor sluggish or fails to move engine.	Broken or loose connection in starter circuit.	See that connections to battery, starter and starter switch are tight and that cables connecting these units are in order.
	Starter commutator or brushes dirty.	Clean.
	Brushes worn, or not fitted correctly.	Replace worn brushes. See that brushes 'bed' correctly.
	Starter pinion jammed in mesh with flywheel.	Rotate squared end of starter shaft with spanner.
Starter operates but does not crank engine.	Pinion of starter drive does not engage with flywheel, due to dirt on screwed sleeve.	Clean sleeve with paraffin.
Starter pinion will not disengage from flywheel when engine is running.	Starter pinion jammed in mesh with flywheel.	Rotate squared end of starter shaft with spanner.

In the case of the now universal single-pole system of wiring, the metal part, or frame of the car, forms the return lead to the battery. In the earlier and present American cars the *negative pole* of the battery is always *earthed*, so that the positive lead is insulated. In later British cars *the positive pole is earthed*.

More recently, with the substitution of alternating current generators for dynamos there has been a growing tendency in British cars to return to the negative earth system.

It is important to *make sure that all 'earthed' parts make good metallic contact with the frame* since failures are often traceable to faulty earthing.

Cable Identification. The manufacturer's wiring diagram indicates the colours of the various cables by means of figures alongside the wiring lines and an identification table on the side or foot of the diagram, so that the cables to the various components can readily be traced.

In modern wiring systems, the insulated cables in the low tension or battery circuits do not connect directly with their components; instead, *detachable cable connections* are fitted near each component.

Tracing Troubles. The best indication of the lighting system functioning properly is that of the ammeter reading when the lights are switched on. Its needle should show the normal discharge reading according to the number of lights switched on, e.g. 4 to 8 amperes. If an excessive discharge is shown, this indicates a bad leakage of current somewhere; the cause must be investigated.

If the *ammeter shows no charge*, the causes may be either (1) a blown fuse in the dynamo field; (2) a broken connection in the dynamo–battery circuit; (3) defective ammeter; or (4) run-down battery.

The regulator control or fuse box should first be examined, and if it is found that the fuse has blown, endeavour to trace the cause; it will be found that there is a short-circuiting of one or more of the cables somewhere, or that a 'live' wire has accidentally been earthed.

Never replace a fuse until you have first ascertained the reason for its having blown and rectified the trouble.

Test the circuit for loose or broken connections, and for short-circuits.

Insufficient illumination, in the case of the lamps, may be due to (1) dirty reflector or cover glass; (2) improperly focused bulb; (3) battery run down. Having verified that items (1) and (2) are in order, check the voltage and density of the battery.

If the lights gradually become dim, this is a sign that the battery is becoming exhausted.

A frequent cause of the ammeter failing to show a reading is a faulty cut-out in the dynamo circuit. If, when the engine is running at a speed corresponding to 15 to 20 m.p.h. on top gear, the ammeter gives no reading, remove the dust cover of the cut-out and touch the armature; if it clicks into position on the magnet poles, the ammeter should then read correctly. See that the armature contact is clean and properly adjusted.

If the lights glow too brilliantly or burn out, the cause may be a blown main or battery fuse (owing to a short-circuit), allowing the dynamo to supply the lamps direct. In this case at once stop the engine, or run it only at a slow speed until the trouble can be remedied.

In some systems the dynamo current regulator may not operate satisfactorily, and, instead of preventing a current increase at high engine speeds, actually allows it to occur.

If the lights flicker, the cause will be found in a loose connection or contact in the lighting circuit. A loose bulb-holder, rusted earth connection (in single-pole systems), or a loose terminal connection will account for this flicker.

If one lamp fails to light when switched on, either its bulb filament has broken or there is a broken connection between the lamp and the switch.

The fault-finding table on page 437 will be found useful when endeavouring to trace trouble in the lighting circuit.

The Fuses. These protect the circuits in case, due to faulty components, the 'live' current in any circuit short-circuits to earth. Then, the fuse blows and cuts off the current so that it cannot burn out the faulty components.

In most of the smaller to medium British cars, notably those fitted with Lucas equipment, only two fuses are fitted, namely one fuse of about 35 amps. to protect the circuits controlled by the ignition switch, when it is 'On' and the other fuse which protects all circuits, e.g., the lamps, brake lights, instrument lights, etc. when the ignition switch is 'Off'. Usually, as shown in Fig. 322, two spare fuses are provided in the fuse block: the last mentioned fuse is usually of 50 amps.

Alternatively, in most of the larger cars several fuses are fitted, so that it is easier to find the faulty individual circuit when trouble arises. A typical example of such a fuse box is that of the Vauxhall Velox and Cresta which have fuses for the following circuits: (1) The heater, radio and cigarette lighter. (2) The brake stop lights, direction indicators, oil and ignition warning lights, windscreen wiper and reverse lamps. (3) The car interior light,

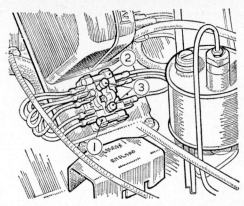

Fig. 322. B.M.C. car fuse block. (1) fuse terminal A1 and A2.
(2) fuse terminal A3 and A4. (3) spare fuses.

electric clock, and luggage boot lamp and, finally, (4) For the tail
lights, number plate light, panel lights and clock bulb for illumination. All four fuses are mounted in a rectangular box and are of
25 amp. each.

Volkswagen cars have a four-fuse box on the instrument panel,
for the ignition, lighting, windscreen and direction indicator
switches and certain lights and another two-fuse box beside the
fuel tank for the headlamps and their dimmer switch.

Circuit Breakers. These take the place of certain fuses and
operate on the principle of any excessive current heating a coil
which causes a bimetal strip to break the circuit of the excessive
current. When the fault is cured, the same device protects the
circuit against any future fault. Thus, it acts as a permanent non-
destructible fuse.

Whenever a fuse blows or a circuit breaker operates – which it
does by vibrating – the fault should be traced and rectified before,
in the former case, the new fuse is inserted.

Direction or Turn Indicators. The original British indicators
were known as 'trafficators' and since some cars still on the roads
are fitted with these devices some brief notes are given. The
'trafficators' are of the solenoid-actuated swing-arm type and
fitted inside with red lights.

The only attention in regard to maintenance is to apply one or two drops of sewing-machine oil to the moving arm bearings (Fig. 323). Care should be taken not to give more than this quantity of oil as it may affect the electrical connections. The Lucas 'trafficators' are held in their 'off' positions by means of a spring, but the arms can be moved by hand, for lubrication purposes. Alternatively the arm can be moved out by means of the switch and, supporting the arm by hand the switch can be moved to the 'off' position.

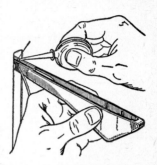

Fig. 323. Oiling the traffi-cator arm hinge.

In more recent cars the trafficator has been replaced by *a flashing lamp system,* such that when the driver wishes to make, say, a right-hand turn he operates a switch lever on the steering wheel centre before making the actual turn. This causes a white side-lamp type of light at the front right-hand side and a red or orange light on the same side, but at the rear, to switch on-and-off repeatedly, until the switch is moved to its central 'Off' position.

In all cases there is an *indicator light,* or two lights, on the fascia or panel which light up and flash, in order to show that the flashing indicators are working properly; if the indicator lights do not flash the cause should be investigated.

The flasher unit is of small dimensions and is contained in a cylindrical case which is spun over the base; the latter has three flat strip terminals with tapped holes for cable screw connections. In another model the flat strip terminals plug into a corresponding socket.

Checking and Maintenance. Should the flasher system fail to operate, first check the lamps for broken filaments. Next, with the aid of the wiring diagram (Fig. 324) check all the circuit connections.

Finally, switch on the ignition and (*a*) check with a voltmeter that the flasher unit terminal B (Fig. 324) is at the battery voltage (6v. or 12v.), to earth, (*b*) connect together the flasher unit terminals B and L and then operate the direction indicator switch. If the flasher lamps now become illuminated this will show that the flasher unit is defective.

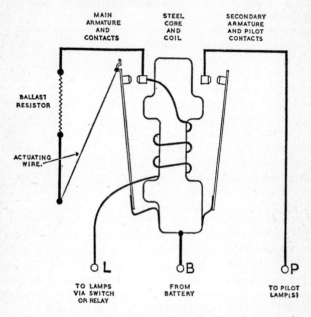

Fig. 324. Electrical diagram, showing flasher unit parts and connections.

As the flasher unit is sealed in its container it is usually advisable to fit a new unit, but the container can be removed by pressing up the spun lip and the contacts examined and, if necessary, cleaned or re-set. In some cases this has effected a cure; the container can then be replaced and spun over its base member.

The flasher unit should be carefully handled as it is sensitive to shocks and may fail to operate if dropped. The unit should be mounted horizontally or vertically, as advised by the manufacturers.

Care of the Lamps. Always keep the bulbs and cover-glasses of the lamps clean; rain and mud are apt to obscure the illumination.

The reflectors of the headlamps should be kept clean and polished. As these reflectors are usually of silver-plated copper, the silver being relatively soft, care should be taken in cleaning them. Use only a soft rag, and one of the silver polishing liquids or powders. Polish with a soft cloth, such as Selvyt. Wadding damped with methylated spirit makes a good silver cleaner.

Chromium-plated reflectors need only be cleaned with a damp cloth and polished with a soft cloth.

Focusing and Levelling the Headlamps. The maker's instructions should be followed carefully on these points. From the relatively large proportion of badly adjusted lamps one sees on the road, it is evident that the drivers have neglected these points. Incorrectly adjusted lamps, apart from giving bad illumination, are apt to cause inconvenience to others on the road.

There are usually two adjustments provided for the headlamps, namely, (1) focusing the bulb, and (2) for beam direction, up and down and sideways. In all but the more recent *pre-focus bulb type* headlamps, provision is made in the bulb-holder unit for moving the bulb nearer to or farther away from the reflector, to increase or diminish the beam spread. The correct position is that which provides a bright and long penetrating beam covering the usual road width.

Pre-focus Bulb Headlamps. Fig. 325 shows the Lucas pre-focus bulb type of headlamp, as used on many makes of British cars, in the partly dismantled state. The light unit is attached to the fixed portion of the lamp by three spring-loaded attachment screws, the top one of which is also used for making vertical adjustments to the lamp beam. The two other screws are also used for horizontal adjustments to the beam.

To remove the light unit, unscrew the retaining screw at the bottom of lamp rim and remove the rim and also the rubber dust-excluder ring; the three spring-loaded screws are then revealed. Press the light unit inwards against the spring tension and turn it anti-clockwise, when the unit will be removable.

To replace a lamp. Twist the back shell (Fig. 325) anti-clockwise and pull it off, when the bulb can be withdrawn. Insert the new bulb in holder so that the slot in the periphery engages the projection in holder. Press the bulb into place and twist it anti-clockwise to engage its catch.

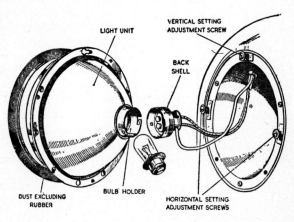

Fig. 325. Pre-focus bulb headlamp (Lucas).

Setting the headlamp beam. The lamps are adjusted so that the main beams are parallel with the road surface. The plated lamp rim and rubber ring must be removed to reveal the three adjusting screws (Fig. 325) which are then used to make the required vertical and horizontal adjustments.

It should be mentioned that this type of headlamp is provided with double-filament bulbs, controlled by a foot switch, on the left side of the clutch pedal, to dip the lamp beams, for anti-dazzle purposes.

The general procedure for practical alignment of the headlamps is to arrange for the car to stand on level ground at 25 ft. from a vertical wall, preferably white or with a white screen for each head-lamp, mounted on the wall. The car should be carrying its normal load and its tyres should be inflated to the correct pressures. The vertical and horizontal adjusting screws are turned until each beam is parallel to the longitudinal axis of the car. The centres of each bright area of concentrated light should be separated by the distance between the centres of the lamps on the car and the height of the centre of the bright areas should be the same as the height of the centre of each lamp above the ground, as indicated for the Lucas-type headlamps, in Fig. 326. It is usual to cover one head-

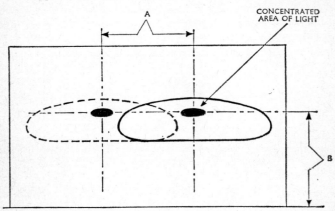

Fig. 326. Method of checking alignment of headlamps. For this test the car must be on level ground and square to the wall. *A* distance between headlamp centres. *B* height of lamp centres above ground.

lamp while the other is being adjusted. If two vertical chalk marks are made on the wall at the same distance apart as the centres of the headlamps, and a horizontal chalk line is drawn at the height of the centres of the lamp – as indicated by the dotted lines in Fig. 326, these lines will simplify the alignment procedure.

Final Road Tests. After adjusting the lamps by the wall test method it is advisable to take the car out on the road and with the car directed parallel with the latter to check the combined lamp beams for (1) distant penetration (2) full road width illumination; it is sometimes found necessary to readjust the lamps a little to suit the driver's position, number of passengers and individual requirements, (3) the dipped beam illumination and direction.

When making road tests choose a level and preferably uncambered road and make a test for non-dazzle, or beam height, by walking from a distance towards the car and noting the beam of each lamp in turn. Any dazzle indicates that the vertical adjustment is incorrect.

Sealed Beam Headlights. In these the headlamp bulb is sealed within a glass container the back of which is silvered inside to provide the reflector, while the front is a fluted cover glass, so that the complete unit is in itself a sealed headlamp. This unit is mounted in a lamp casing to which it is attached by a metal ring and outer cover. To remove the sealed beam unit (Fig. 327)

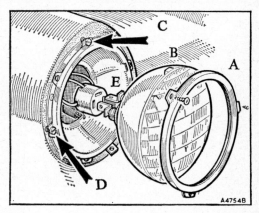

Fig. 327. Sealed beam headlamp, showing method of beam adjustment. *A* lamp cover. *B* sealed beam unit. *C* vertical and *D* horizontal adjusting screws. *E* plug and socket.

remove the three retaining screws securing the inner light rim and then take off the rim assembly. Finally, pull the unit forward and disconnect the three-pin socket to release it from the backshell. These headlamps have one vertical beam adjustment screw at the top of the lamp and one screw for horizontal adjustment, on the left-hand side at centre level.

The lens front portion of the sealed beam unit has three projecting lugs near the outer edge, for use when aligning the beam, with the use of a garage optical device, known as a *Beam Aimer, or Aligner*. This provides accurate adjustment of headlamps, without using the previously-mentioned wall tests.

FAULT-FINDING TABLE FOR THE HEADLAMPS

LAMPS
- —Insufficient illumination.
  - —Lamp badly set on bracket.
  - —Bulb discoloured through use.
  - —Out of focus.
  - —Dirty reflector or bulb.
  - —Battery exhausted.
- —Light when switched on, but gradually diminishes.
  - —Battery exhausted.
- —Brilliance varies with speed of the engine
  - —Battery exhausted.
  - —Acid level low.
  - —Battery connection loose or broken.
- —Lights flicker
  - —Loose connection.
  - —Lamp adaptor contacts faulty.
- —Lights out
  - —Battery exhausted.
  - —Broken or loose connections.
  - —Lamp filament broken.

Locating Wiring Faults. Fig. 328 illustrates a simple method of ascertaining whether a length of wiring cable, in place on the car, is faulty; the upper and lower illustrations refer to the double- and single-pole wiring systems respectively. In the former case

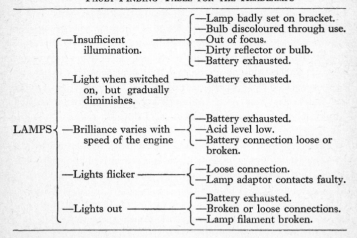
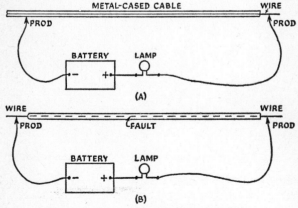

Fig. 328. How to test for a defective electric lighting cable.

a test lead with a flash lamp or ordinary battery and a test lamp (or voltmeter) is connected as shown to the outer metal casing, and the inner (based) copper wire; if there is a short-circuit between the two the test lamp will light up; otherwise the cable is not defective. In the latter case, one pole (the positive) is earthed to the frame, and the test lead is attached to the bared copper wire of the suspected cable. If the latter is defective, i.e. earthed to the frame, the lamp will light, for the circuit will be completed; this is a good method of testing for a short-circuited cable.

The same method can be used to test for a broken cable, the two test leads being connected, one to each end of the suspected cable. If the lamp fails to light, the cable is broken or disconnected in between. [Fig. 328 (B)]

Windscreen Wipers. The electric wiper, which has replaced the vacuum type in all recent cars, consists, basically, of four separate units: (1) The electric motor. (2) The gear or mechanism in the motor case, (3) The power transmission system and (4) The wiper blades.

Fig. 329 shows a typical windscreen wiper of the cable-rack

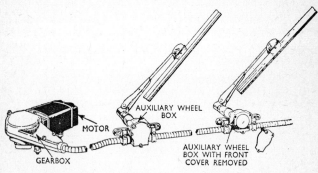

Fig. 329. Cable rack-and-pinion type windscreen wiper.

operating kind. The small electric motor consumes about 2 to 3 amperes at 12 volts and through a small gearbox revolves a wheel at the required speed. This wheel operates a connecting rod the other end of which is hinged to one end of a special type of grooved cable which acts as a rack which moves to and fro. It is connected within an outer cable to a gear wheel at each auxiliary gearbox, a simple mechanism which gives the to-and-fro motion to the wiper rubber-ended blade.

Maintenance. The windscreen wiper seldom experiences trouble, but if it should either *refuse to operate* or to start, the connections at either end of the 'live' supply cable should be examined for tightness, and also the 'earth' connection. Since the gearbox, cable-rack and the auxiliary gearboxes are grease-packed during assembly at the manufacturer's works they need *no periodic lubrication*. If the car is used frequently the *blade rubbers* will need replacing about once a year. Poor wiping action, apart from worn rubbers, may be due to insufficient pressure on the windscreen or to deposits, c.g. tar spots, dirt or car polish on the glass; if so, remove with petrol or methylated spirits. Should the *cable-rack not work freely* this may be due to a kink in the casing. This can be checked by applying pressure with a spring balance to the disconnected end, at the gearbox. It should not require a greater pull than 6 lb. to slide the rack freely.

If the motor is suspected, it can be checked with a moving coil voltmeter connected across the 'live' supply terminal and a sound earth. If the motor is satisfactory a reading of 11·5 volts will be shown.

In all motor-driven wipers a *limit switch* is located in the motor gearbox; this provides the correct parking position for the blades, when not in use. An adjustment for this is fitted in the gearbox and is accessible from outside.

The Lucas-type wiper blade holder has an internally-splined boss which fits over splines on the driving crankshaft. Just near to the boss is a spring clip which when raised enables the blade unit to be taken off its splines, so that it can be *refitted in another position*, when needed.

PERIODIC VEHICLE TESTS, LIGHTING EQUIPMENT

The statutory requirements, laid down under the Road Traffic Act, for the compulsory tests of motor vehicles state that, in so far as the lighting equipment is concerned, and in accordance with the provisions of the Road Transport Lighting Act, 1957, and Road Vehicles Lighting Regulations:

Lighting Equipment and Reflectors

(a) *Headlamps*, *Spotlamps*, *etc.* (all lamps having bulbs over 7 watts)

It should be established that either:

(i) these lamps are permanently directed downwards so that, with the vehicle on level ground, an observer whose eye level is 3 ft. 6 in. from the ground 25 feet or more distant from the vehicle would not be dazzled, or

(ii) the vehicle is fitted with a dipping mechanism which will operate so as not to dazzle an observer placed as at (i) and that this mechanism works satisfactorily.

(b) *Other lamps and reflectors*

A certificate should be withheld if the *obligatory* side lights and rear lights and reflectors are not in working order, or to the number required by the law, or of the size or in the position required by the law.

CHAPTER 14

MAINTENANCE OF THE COACHWORK, UPHOLSTERY, ETC.

It is important to maintain the good appearance of any car by regular attention, if only to obtain the best second-hand value of the car.

The earlier paints, varnishes and cellulose enamels have given way to quicker drying coatings – primers, undercoatings and finishing coatings – obtained from synthetic resins and other products, which give much harder and longer endurance coatings, which retain their colour much better than hitherto.

Maintenance of coachwork and outside metal parts involves washing down, drying and final polishing of the painted surfaces.

Washing Down. For ordinary maintenance procedure, it is important *never to leave mud* on the car to dry; always wash off with a copious supply of water whilst the mud is still soft.

A good big sponge or fine water spray are probably best for washing the car down. The dirty parts of the car should be dabbed with the sponge full of water, squeezing some of the latter out over the surface. *Never rub the surface* whilst washing down, but always adopt *the principle of flowing the dirt off with plenty of water*; otherwise the grit will have an abrasive action: Alternatively, the hose-type car brush can be well recommended.

If a hose is used for washing down, do not use a greater water pressure than will carry the water six inches beyond the nozzle; excessive pressure drives the grit rapidly across the varnished surface and scratches it. The hose should, preferably, be fitted with a variable jet nozzle, which by a turn of the hand will give a jet varying from a fine spray to a 'solid' jet.

When washing a car down, wash the lower parts of the chassis first, namely, the wheels, front and rear axles, bumpers, etc.

Unless the coachwork has been finished with a wax-type of polish, the use of a *domestic* or special *car washing detergent* in the washing water is a definite advantage, since it dissolves any grease on the surfaces and will leave a better finish than water alone; usually, it is not so necessary to 'leather off' the surface after washing down.

A different sponge should be used for the wheels, back and front axles, brake drums and the other lower parts of the car for grease is apt to get on to the sponge; this grease would dull the upper parts. Rinse the sponge out frequently whilst washing the car down to get rid of the abrasive grit.

It is most important always to dry, thoroughly, the bodywork after being out in the rain or washing down, otherwise light spots and stains may be formed on the varnished parts. The best method is to soak and then wring out *a piece of chamois leather*, and go lightly over the wet surface of the car. The leather will effectively absorb all the moisture and leave the surface quite dry, clean and polished. It has been proved by the writer, that if a car is washed down in clean or detergent water and 'leathered off', and without using any car polishes, it will *retain its original new condition for several years,* assuming that the original finish was satisfactory,

Care of the Body Finish. As mentioned earlier, it is possible to maintain the bodywork finish over a period of years by regular washing down and 'leathering off', but in many cases it is neither convenient nor possible to do this, so that unless the car is washed and polished at a garage, the surfaces will become dull, 'bloomed', or spotted. In such cases the use of one of the better long-life proprietary polishes, mentioned later, is advisable.

Some of these 'polishes' are advertised both to clean and polish the dirty surfaces but since some sort of fine abrasive is necessary to remove dust or mud deposits and deep stains, such polishes would appear doubtful; some are known to remove part of the surface coating, as shown by the coloured stains on the cloths used.

Assuming that a good wax polish is used, e.g. Simoniz or Johnsons, the car must first be washed down and 'leathered off' before applying the polish with a soft cloth, e.g. mutton cloth. Areas of about one to two square feet should be treated with the polish and afterwards polished, rather than larger areas.

For cars that have to be left out in the open air much of their life, it is advisable to use one of the recent silicon wax polishes, e.g. Autobrite or Turtle. If properly applied the surfaces treated will not only be unaffected by rain and dust, but will retain their polished condition for several months. When, eventually, signs of 'bloom' or dullness appear, the bodywork should be washed down and repolished.

Removing Tar Stains. These stains can be removed by rubbing the places with either turpentine, petrol or paraffin.

Care of Polished Metal Surfaces. The nickel plating on earlier cars, which required a certain amount of maintenance attention, has been replaced by *chromium plating*, needing little attention.

If the plating is rain spotted or dirty it need only be rubbed over with a damp cloth. Should it be very dirty, however, warm soapy water will quickly restore its lustre.

Chromium-plated bumpers and similar plated parts can be maintained bright by using a car wax polish, lightly rubbing this afterwards. *Metal polishes should on no account be used* on chromium. The plated layer is very thin and the abrasives in these polishes will soon reveal the base metal.

The more recent stainless steel body trims, require nothing more than the occasional application of a damp cloth.

Glass Windscreens. These may be cleaned with soap and water, a detergent solution, or metal polish. Tar and insect marks can be removed with petrol or benzole, or scraped off with a safety razor blade or the edge of a coin. A piece of chamois leather wetted with water and then wrung out is another effective medium for cleaning glass windscreens.

A good car windscreen and window cleaner is the liquid preparation known as Windolite. This is applied and rubbed over with a cloth. When dry it is rubbed off, leaving a perfectly clean polished effect.

Care of the Upholstery. Leather upholstery should be kept free from dust. The material can be preserved and polished by using a good leather reviver preparation or leather polishing wax. If the leather dulls, the surface can be improved by sponging with a weak solution of egg albumen: when dry, rub vigorously with a stiff brush.

Dull leatherwork may be revived by washing with castile or curd soap and lukewarm water. Afterwards go over the cleaned surface with clean water, absorbing the surplus moisture with a sponge or chamois leather. A little neat's-foot oil rubbed over the surface with a piece of soft rag usually revives the appearance. Imitation leather should be treated in the same manner as leather.

Oil, petrol, or benzole should never be used on the leather upholstery. If the leather becomes spotted with oil or grease, remove with rectified benzine on a cotton wool pad; alternatively ordinary rubber solution rubbed over the spot with the finger will remove the stain.

For ordinary non-leather upholstery, the use of a vacuum cleaner is recommended. Spots on the fabric can be removed with one of the better known household dry cleaners. When the cleaner has evaporated, apply, judiciously, a hot iron wrapped in a wet cloth. Dirty parts can be cleaned with a damp cloth.

The Roof Lining. If dirty, a damp cloth can be used to clean; but if obstinate, water with a little soft soap should be used. Do not soak the lining. Further, on no account use petrol or any other spirit cleaner.

Care of the Hood. Canvas or fabric type hoods are cleaned with soap and water; rubberized material should not be cleaned, locally, with petrol. Hoods which have become leaky can be waterproofed with proprietary makes of solution sold by local garages.

A preparation for waterproofing a fabric-type hood is made by dissolving 3 oz. of beeswax in $\frac{1}{8}$ to $\frac{3}{4}$ pint of petrol in a closed container – to avoid evaporation effects – for about 24 hours; the solution should be agitated at intervals to assist the dissolving action. When the wax is dissolved the solution should be applied to the hood with a stiff brush, working briskly over the surface, so as to give a long-enduring coating.

Modern all-weather car hoods are made of a synthetic or plastic material which is water, oil and petrol proof. This type of hood is cleaned by brushing well with a soap-and-water solution to remove any dirt and then flooding over with clean cold water.

Carpets. Floor carpets can be kept free from dust with a vacuum cleaner or stiff bristle brush. Periodically, they should be removed and beaten to get rid of all dust. Oil or grease stains can be eliminated with a good carpet soap; small stains can be got rid of with petrol or benzene.

Car carpets are frequently attacked by clothes moths, especially when stored for periods. This may be prevented by spraying the carpets with a suitable insecticide, such as Flit, and then closing all the car windows for several hours.

Body and Door Rattles. Loose holding-down bolts, slackened hinge screws, worn or badly adjusted door stops (these are usually in the form of rubber blocks), loose mudguard stay bolts, broken bonnet securing clips, insecure hood frame clips and even running-board stays are among the more frequent causes of these rattles.

Door rattles can usually be eliminated by adjusting the door stops on the door frame. It may, sometimes, be necessary to pack these out in order to take up door play, in the closed position.

To minimize bodywork rattles the various nuts on the bolts concerned should be tightened at six-monthly intervals.

Lubrication of Bodywork Items. The door lock hinges should be oiled occasionally.

The door lock slides should be greased slightly.

The earlier sliding roof runners after cleaning with petrol for dirt and congealed grease should be given a light smear of graphite grease.

The engine bonnet catch pin bearings and catches should also be greased to ensure easy operation.

It is a good plan to lightly grease the metal runners of the adjustable seat slides; the securing screws should also be checked for tightness.

CHAPTER 15

DIAGNOSING ENGINE TROUBLES EASILY

THERE are so many possible causes of engine trouble that some motorists frequently become hopelessly confused when their engine stops, refuses to start, or runs unsatisfactorily. It is quite a straightforward matter, however, to examine, systematically, the possible causes and by a *Process of Elimination* to arrive at the cause.

There are three principal causes of engine trouble which may be classified under the headings: (1) Mechanical, (2) Ignition, and (3) Carburation. Of these, the last two are the more common. Obviously, it is important to ascertain to which class the fault belongs, and then to examine the causes in detail. Engine troubles embracing the three classes mentioned can be analysed into three principal groups as follows: (*A*) *The Engine Refuses to Start;* (*B*) *The Engine Stops;* and (*C*) *The Engine Runs Unsatisfactorily.*

Before dealing with these groups, it should be mentioned that carburation troubles are, generally speaking, the easiest to deal with, and their cause should usually be ascertained first. A careful examination of the external working parts of the engine whilst it is cranked around will sometimes reveal such mechanical defects as *broken valve or valve spring, a stuck valve,* incorrectly adjusted valve, broken or slipping or coil ignition drive coupling, etc.

(A) The Engine Refuses to Start. Ascertain first whether the cause is Carburation or Ignition. *A good spark at the plugs indicates carburation trouble. Refusal to spark* when petrol is injected into the cylinders through the sparking plug holes *indicates ignition trouble.*

Having ascertained whether the cause falls under the heading (2) or (3), above, we can proceed to diagnose the trouble as follows:

446

(1) *Carburation.* Petrol tap (if fitted) shut off; No petrol in tank; Air lock in petrol pipe; Water in base of jet; Dirt in jet orifice; Needle valve of float chamber sticking; Throttle too far open; Throttle disconnected; Too much air through carburettor; Pilot jet blocked; Choked petrol filter; Fuel pump not operating.

(2) *Ignition* (*a*) No spark at plugs. Broken cable. Contact breaker arm sticking; Dirty contacts; Wrong plug or breaker gap; Distributor detached or dirty; Battery exhausted; Battery disconnected; Switch off; H.T. Coil shorted inside; H.T. coil cable disconnected.

(*b*) Spark at H.T. cable end. No spark at plugs. Defective plug; Soot insulation; Broken insulation; Points bridged by oil or dirt.

(B) The Engine Stops. Test whether cause is Carburation or Ignition, as in (*A*).

(1) *Carburation.* Petrol run out; Choked jet; Water in jet; Filter choked; Broken petrol pipe; Fuel pump diaphragm broken; Filter or valve blocked; Punctured float; Needle not free; Throttle disconnected; Fuel in tank, run out.

(2) *Ignition.* One of the items enumerated previously under heading (*A*) (2) Ignition.

(3) *Mechanical.* If carburettor is functioning and there is a good spark at the plugs, the cause is a mechanical one. [*Good Compression*]: Controls out of order; Stripped timing gears; Slipped coil ignition drive; Engine seized. [*Bad Compression*]: Valve sticking; Broken valve; Stretched valve; No valve tappet clearance; Broken spring; Insufficient lubrication; Broken piston or connecting rod; Rings gummed up.

(C) Engine Runs Unsatisfactorily.

(1) *Misfires. Intermittent Sparking.* Plug insulation sooted; Oily plug points; Dirty contact breaker points; Broken H.T. carbon brush; Faulty cable insulation. Plug gaps too large.

[*Regular Sparking*]: Valve sticking or broken; Mixture too weak, or rich; Water in carburettor; Partly choked petrol filter; Air leak in inlet pipe; Leak in petrol pipe; No vent hole in petrol tank cap.

(2) *Loss of Power*. (*a*) *Regular*. Poor compression (worn valves, piston and piston rings): Throttle control out of adjustment; Ignition timing incorrectly set; Wrong valve tappet clearance; Valve faces pitted or burnt; Weak or broken valve spring; Wrong mixture strength (carburettor); Choked silencer; Valve timing wrong; Gear too high; Excessive carbon deposit; Lack of engine oil; Valve sticking in guide regularly; Cylinder head joint leaking; Throttle will not open fully.

(*b*) *Irregular*. Valve sticking occasionally; Carburettor mixture regulation faulty; Petrol supply intermittent; Brakes adjusted too close.

(3) *Engine Runs too Hot, and Knocks*. Excessive carbon deposit; Obstructed radiator; Insufficient water in radiator; Insufficient lubrication; Spark too far advanced or retarded; Mixture too rich or too weak; Fan belt slipping or broken; Water pump broken; Bent fan blades; Thermostat valve stuck.

(4) *Engine, Temperature Normal, but Knocks*. Spark too far advanced; Loose connecting rod bearings; Slack piston; Excessive backlash in engine gears; Excessive tappet clearance; Unsuitable sparking plugs.

(5) *Engine Fires Occasionally Only*. Sooted or oiled plugs; Dirty contact breaker points; Bad insulation; Dirty distributor; Mixture too rich or weak; Choked petrol feed; Water in jet; Valve sticking; Dirty petrol filter.

(6) *Engine Misses at High Speeds*. Unsuitable sparking plugs or insulation defective: Spark gaps too large; Dirty distributor or distributor points (jump spark); Weak ignition distributor spring or defective H.T. coil; Contact breaker gap too great; Contact arm sticking; Pre-ignition; Cracked distributor head; Bent valve stem; Incorrect carburation at high speeds (mixture too rich or too weak); Defective petrol supply.

(7) *Poor Hill Climbing and Low Maximum Speed*. Engine requires overhaul; Excessive carbon deposit; Incorrect mixture adjustment; Throttle does not open fully; Clutch slipping; Too high a gear; Ignition too far advanced or retarded; Tyres under-inflated; Brakes binding.

Miscellaneous Causes of Trouble.

(1) *Engine will not stop.* If, when switched off, the engine continues to fire, the cause may be: (*a*) Switch not working; (*b*) Pre-ignition due to excessive carbon deposit, the carbon becoming incandescent or to wrong type of plug.

(2) *Back-Firing in Carburettor.* This is caused by too weak a mixture. Shortage of petrol to the carburettor and water or dirt in the jet will cause this. Instances have come to the author's notice of a sparking plug with faulty insulation, i.e. blistered or with an oxide coating, operating satisfactorily at low and medium speeds, but causing pre-ignition or delayed combustion effects resulting in back-firing through the carburettor, with consequent loss of power, when the throttle has been opened fully.

(3) *Back-Firing in Silencer. A defective plug* will cause firing in the silencer. In the former case the unexploded contents of the cylinder are delivered into the exhaust pipe and are fired by the hot gases from the other cylinders. *A sticking exhaust valve*, or one which does not close properly, will cause backfiring. If the *ignition is timed too late*, or the valve timing is incorrect, back-firing in the silencer may occur.

If the engine is switched off, while *the car coasts down a long descent* with the car in one of its gears, i.e., the engine acting as a brake, and the ignition is again switched on at the bottom of the descent, *severe back-firing in the silencer* will occur. In this connection silencers have often been fractured by these explosions.

APPENDIX

Ministry of Transport Compulsory Vehicle Tests

UNDER the provisions of the 1956 Road Traffic Act the conditions were laid down for the compulsory testing of motor vehicles of 10 years or more old. These tests were concerned primarily with the braking, steering and electrical systems for motor vehicles, cars and motor-cycles. Subsequent Amendments to the Act reduced the age of vehicles to be compulsorily tested to 5 years; there has since been legislation to reduce this down to 3 years.

Under the provisions of this and the 1960 Motor Vehicles (Tests) Regulations (S1.1960.1083)* it is necessary to obtain a Test Certificate of Vehicle fitness before a licence will be granted or renewed.

The latter Regulations go into much detail regarding such matters as the nature of the tests, official testing stations, types of vehicles, certain exemptions from tests, test certificates, notice of refusal of test certificates, appeals, fees, etc.

The following are brief summaries of the more important of these regulations, in so far as they affect the owner-driver and mechanic, for whom the present volume has been written:

(1) *Testing Stations.* The Ministry of Transport appointed Testing Stations, which in 1964 numbered over 16,000, are listed in the Automobile Association's *Members' Handbook.* Each Official Testing Station displays the sign of three connected triangles, shown below, in white upon a blue background of square shape. Most local authorities keep a list of Official Testing Stations.

(2) *Nature of the Tests.* As mentioned earlier, the principal items that are required to pass the tests are the braking,

---

* Obtainable from H.M. Stationery Office. P.O. Box No. 569, London, S.E.1, price 1s. 6d. net or through any stationer or bookseller.

Ministry of Transport Official Testing Station sign (2 ft. square).

steering and electrical systems. At the time of writing, the question of including the testing of motor tyres is under consideration, since many accidents are believed to be due to defective tyres.

(3) *Application for a Test.* In the case of motor-cars, since some Stations specialize in motor-cycle tests, it is necessary to select an Official Station which deals with motor cars. The car owner should make an appointment for the test at some specific date and time suitable to the Testing Station. When the car is taken to the Station the examiner may refuse to make the tests for one of the following reasons: (A) If evidence of the first registration of the car is not produced. (B) If the car is in a dirty condition so that testing may be difficult. (C) If there is no licence for driving the car on the highway. (D) If there is not sufficient fuel and oil in the engine to carry out road testing, and (E) If the car, on a preliminary examination, is too dangerous to carry out the braking and (or) the steering tests.

(4) *After the Tests.* If the car passes all of the Examiners' tests the latter will issue a standard form of Certificate which must be produced when a Licence or Renewal is applied for.

(5) *Failure to Pass Tests.* In the event of a failure of the car to pass any of the specified tests the owner can either undertake to rectify the fault himself or may take it to any other

garage to have this work executed. Alternately, he can ask the Testing Station to do the work and then re-submit the car for test at the same Station or any other one of his own choice.

(6) *Appeals*. If the car owner is not satisfied with the Examiner's tests, in the event of his refusal to issue a Test Certificate the owner can make an Appeal on an official form provided for the purpose, to the Ministry of Transport; but this must be done within 14 days of the Tests and a special fee must accompany the Appeal.

(7) *Fees for the Tests*. The fee for an Official Test must accompany the Application for the Test.

The fee, for a motor-car, is 15s. and motor-cycle, 10s 6d. If a Test Certificate is refused a fee of 14s. for a car and 9s. 6d. for a motor cycle is charged, i.e. is one shilling less than when a Test Certificate is issued.

When a car has failed the Tests and is left at the Official Testing Station for the faults to be remedied, and then re-tested with satisfactory results, no Refusal Certificate is required. A Test Certificate will then be issued for a further fee of one shilling; it is the same for a motor-cycle.

If the car is taken to another garage or the rectifying work is done by the car owner, within 14 days of the previous Official Test a fee of 8s. for a car and 6s. for a motor-cycle is required when it is submitted for another Official Test.

Note. If a car cannot be present for an Official Test at the appointed time and date then, provided at least twenty-four hours' previous notice is given, the fee will be returned.

INDEX